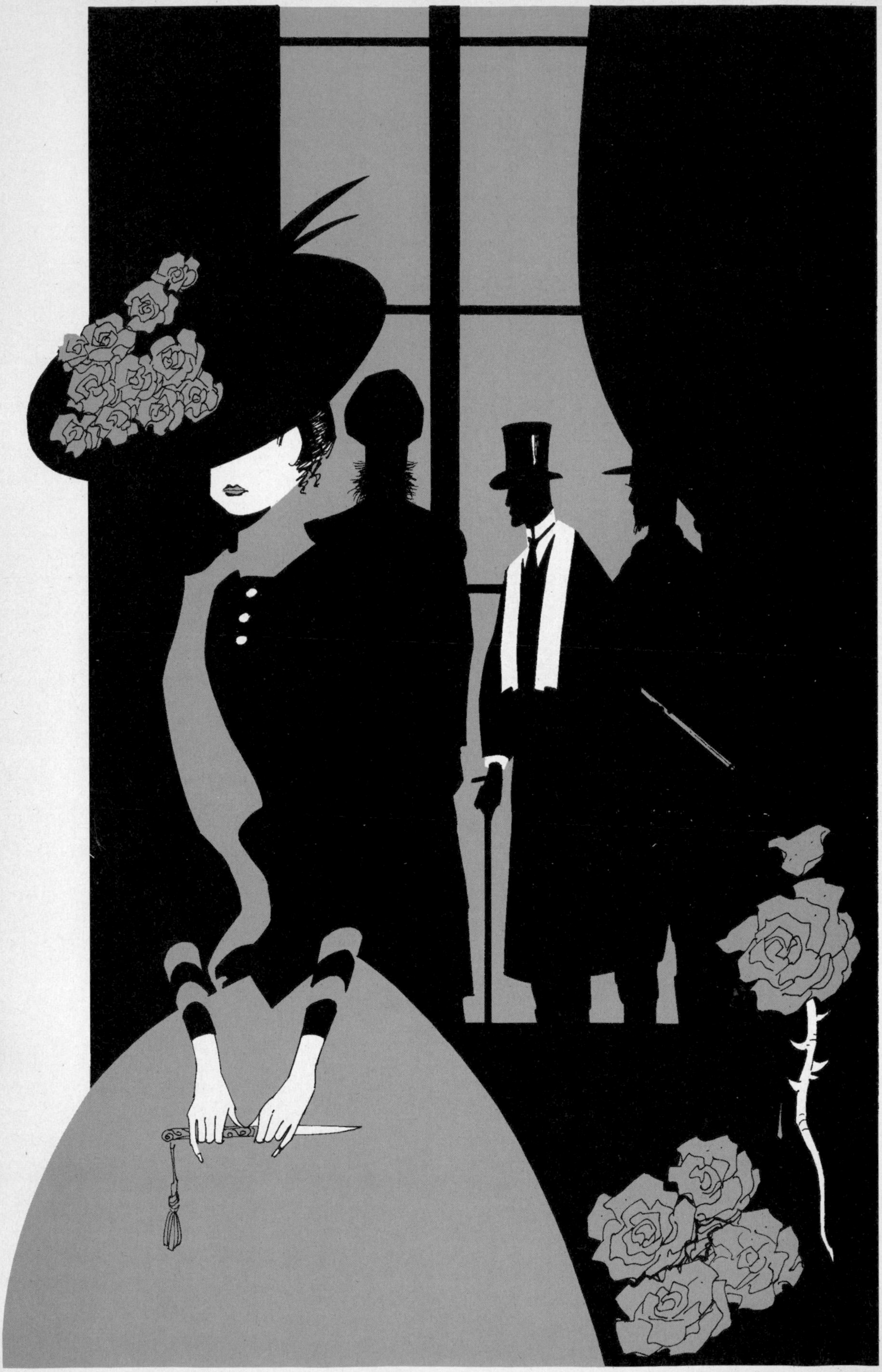

The Bloomsbury Quintet Simplicissimus—1898.

THE LEAGUE OF EXTRAORDINARY GENTLEMEN

Vol. I

1898

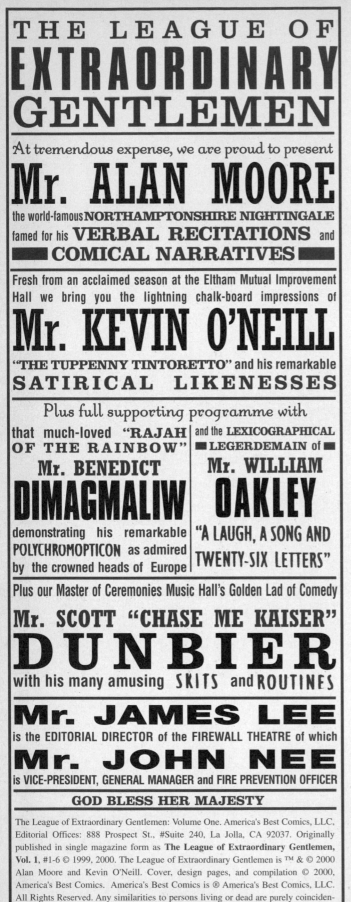

THE LEAGUE OF EXTRAORDINARY GENTLEMEN

At tremendous expense, we are proud to present

Mr. ALAN MOORE

the world-famous NORTHAMPTONSHIRE NIGHTINGALE famed for his **VERBAL RECITATIONS** and ■ **COMICAL NARRATIVES** ■

Fresh from an acclaimed season at the Eltham Mutual Improvement Hall we bring you the lightning chalk-board impressions of

Mr. KEVIN O'NEILL

"THE TUPPENNY TINTORETTO" and his remarkable **SATIRICAL LIKENESSES**

Plus full supporting programme with

that much-loved "RAJAH OF THE RAINBOW"

Mr. BENEDICT DIMAGMALIW

demonstrating his remarkable POLYCHROMOPTICON as admired by the crowned heads of Europe

and the LEXICOGRAPHICAL ■ LEGERDEMAIN of ■

Mr. WILLIAM OAKLEY

"A LAUGH, A SONG AND TWENTY-SIX LETTERS"

Plus our Master of Ceremonies Music Hall's Golden Lad of Comedy

Mr. SCOTT "CHASE ME KAISER" DUNBIER

with his many amusing *SKITS* and ROUTINES

Mr. JAMES LEE

is the EDITORIAL DIRECTOR of the FIREWALL THEATRE of which

Mr. JOHN NEE

is VICE-PRESIDENT, GENERAL MANAGER and FIRE PREVENTION OFFICER

GOD BLESS HER MAJESTY

The League of Extraordinary Gentlemen: Volume One. America's Best Comics, LLC, Editorial Offices: 888 Prospect St., #Suite 240, La Jolla, CA 92037. Originally published in single magazine form as **The League of Extraordinary Gentlemen, Vol. 1**, #1-6 © 1999, 2000. The League of Extraordinary Gentlemen is ™ & © 2000 Alan Moore and Kevin O'Neill. Cover, design pages, and compilation © 2000, America's Best Comics. America's Best Comics is ® America's Best Comics, LLC. All Rights Reserved. Any similarities to persons living or dead are purely coincidental. Printed in Canada. SEVENTH PRINTING. ISBN : 1-56389-858-6

The League of Extraordinary Gentlemen Collection Designed By
Mr. KEVIN O'NEILL
With
Mr. LAWRENCE BERRY
Additional Color By
Mr. ALEXANDER SINCLAIR
Special Thanks
French Translation Courtesy of Mr. Jean-Marc Lofficier
Arabic and Chinese Translation Provided By
Bromley Language Centre
Special Typography Sue Grant

MY MESSAGE TO OUR READERS

by Mr. Scotty Smiles

Greetings, children of vanquished and colonised nations the world o'er. Welcome to this Christmas compendium edition of our exciting picture-periodical for boys and girls. And let us bid a special welcome to those poorer children who, in four or five years time, will be gratefully reading these words in a creased and dog-eared copy of this very publication, its dust jacket torn and several pages in the second chapter stuck together, that has been donated to their orphanage or borstal by local Rotarians. To all such urchins of the future, and to our presumably more well-off, possibly Eton-educated audience of the present day, we wish you many happy fireside hours in the perusal of the thrills and chuckles here contained, though let us not forget the many serious, morally instructive points there are within this narrative: firstly, women are always going on and making a fuss. Secondly, the Chinese are brilliant, but evil. Lastly, laudanum, taken in moderation is good for the eyesight and prevents kidney-stones. With these dictums in mind, allow us to wish both many hours of pictorial reading pleasure, and also the jolliest of Christmas-times to those of you who are not bowed with rickets, currently incarcerated, or Mohammedans. With the Season's Best Regards, I remain,

A friend and confidant to boys everywhere.

S. Smiles (Editor)

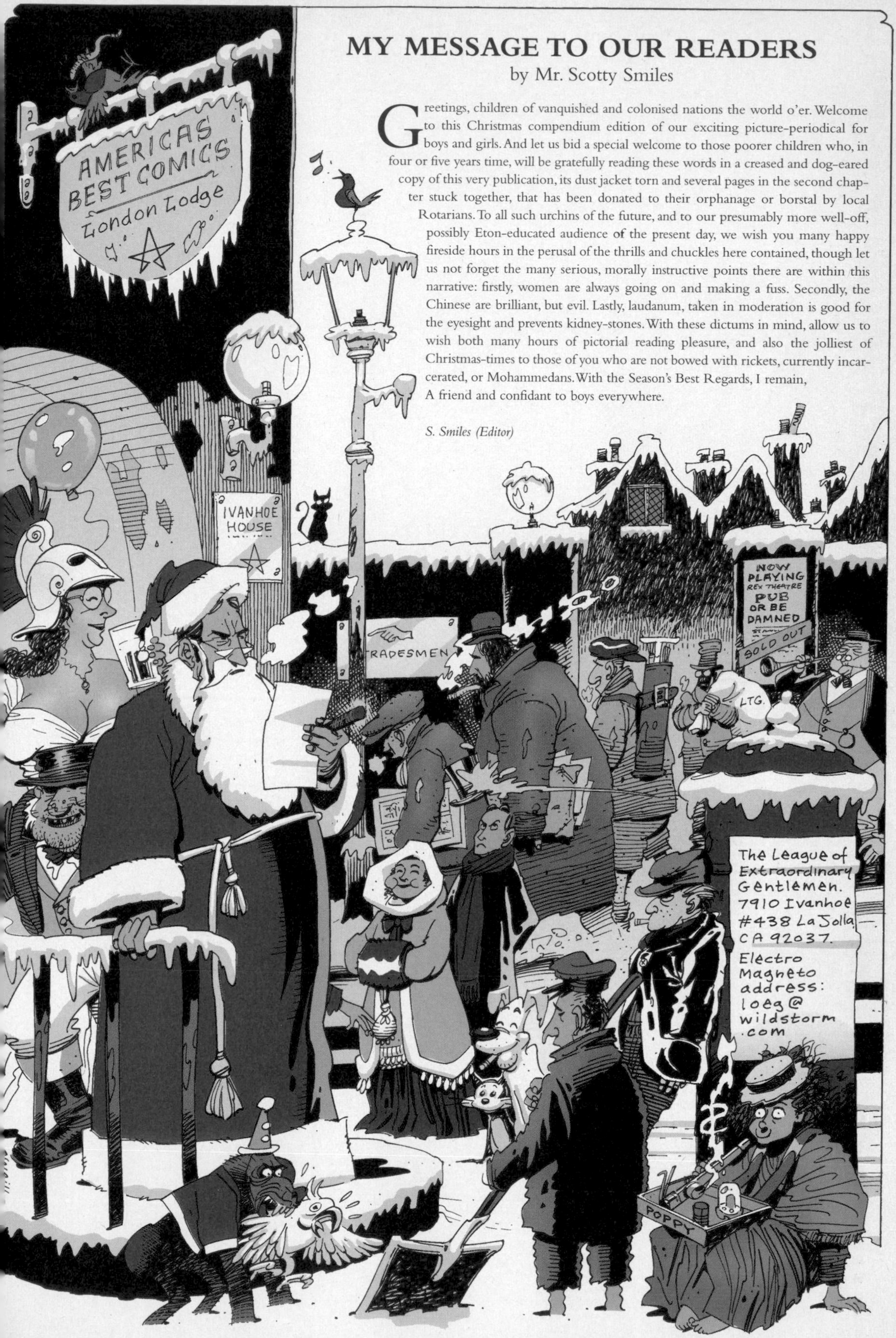
AMERICAS BEST COMICS
London Lodge
IVANHOE HOUSE
TRADESMEN
NOW PLAYING
REX THEATRE
PUB OR BE DAMNED
SOLD OUT
LTG.
The League of Extraordinary Gentlemen. 7910 Ivanhoe #438 La Jolla CA 92037.
Electro Magneto address: loeg@wildstorm.com
POPPY

"The British Empire
has always encoun-
tered difficulty in
distinguishing
between its heroes
and its monsters."

– Campion Bond
from *Memoirs of an
English Intelligencer.*
(Meeson's; 1908)

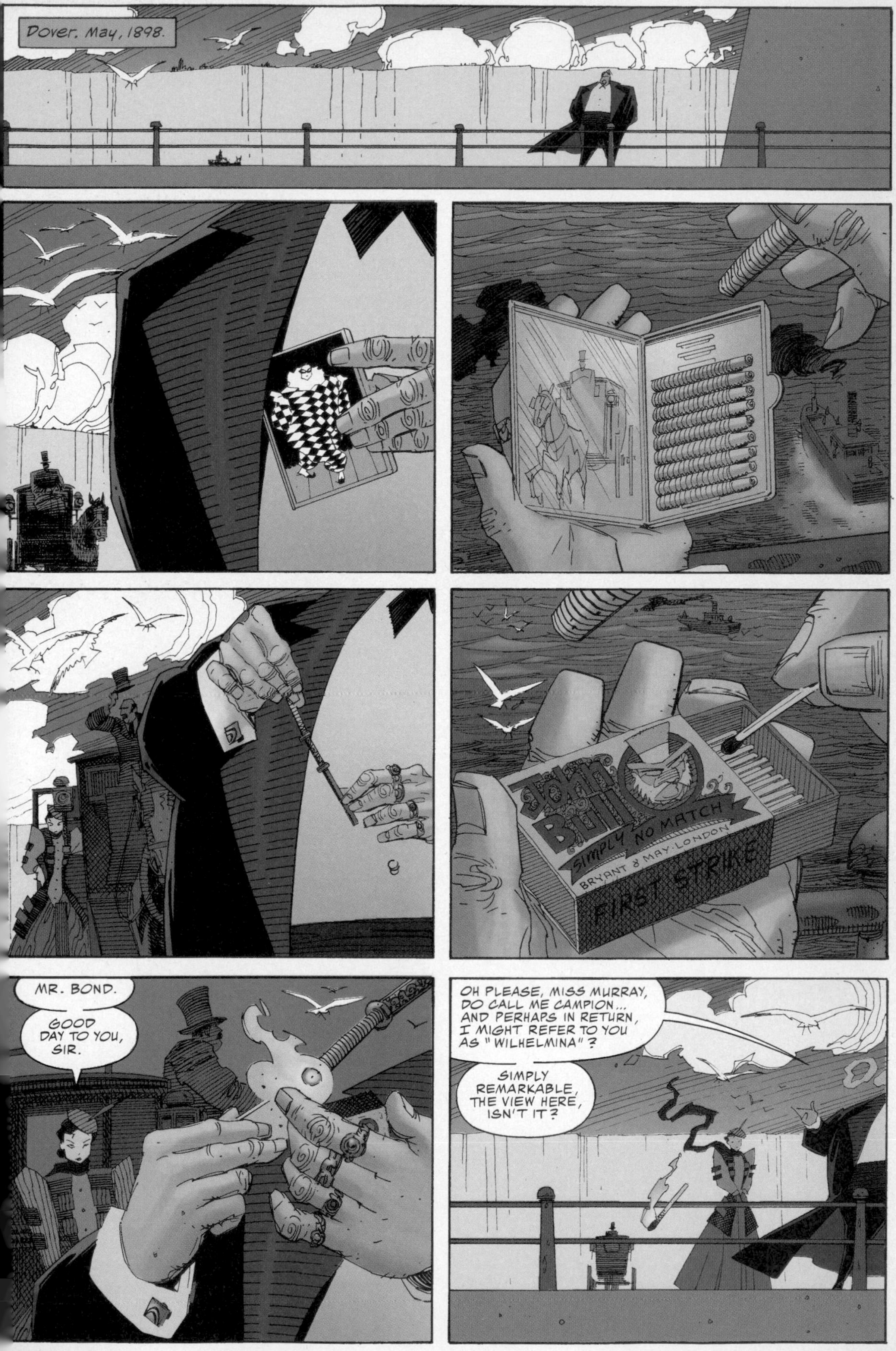
Dover. May, 1898.
John Bull
SIMPLY NO MATCH
BRYANT & MAY. LONDON
FIRST STRIKE
MR. BOND.
GOOD DAY TO YOU, SIR.
OH PLEASE, MISS MURRAY, DO CALL ME CAMPION... AND PERHAPS IN RETURN, I MIGHT REFER TO YOU AS "WILHELMINA"?
SIMPLY REMARKABLE, THE VIEW HERE, ISN'T IT?

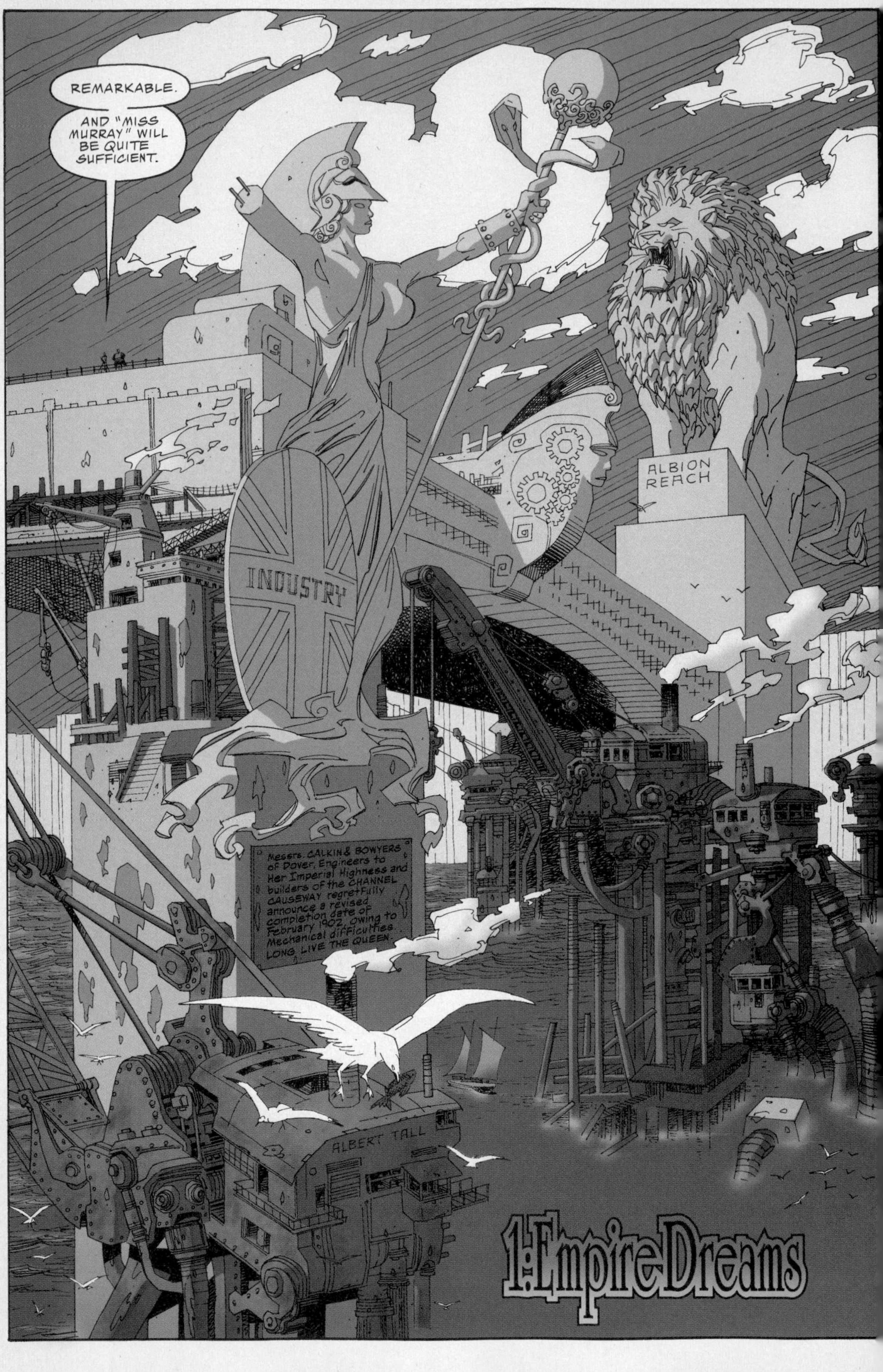
REMARKABLE.
AND "MISS MURRAY" WILL BE QUITE SUFFICIENT.
INDUSTRY
ALBION REACH
Messrs. CALKIN & BOWYERS of Dover, Engineers to Her Imperial Highness and builders of the CHANNEL CAUSEWAY regretfully announce a revised completion date of February 1902, owing to Mechanical difficulties. LONG LIVE THE QUEEN.
ALBERT TALL
1: Empire Dreams

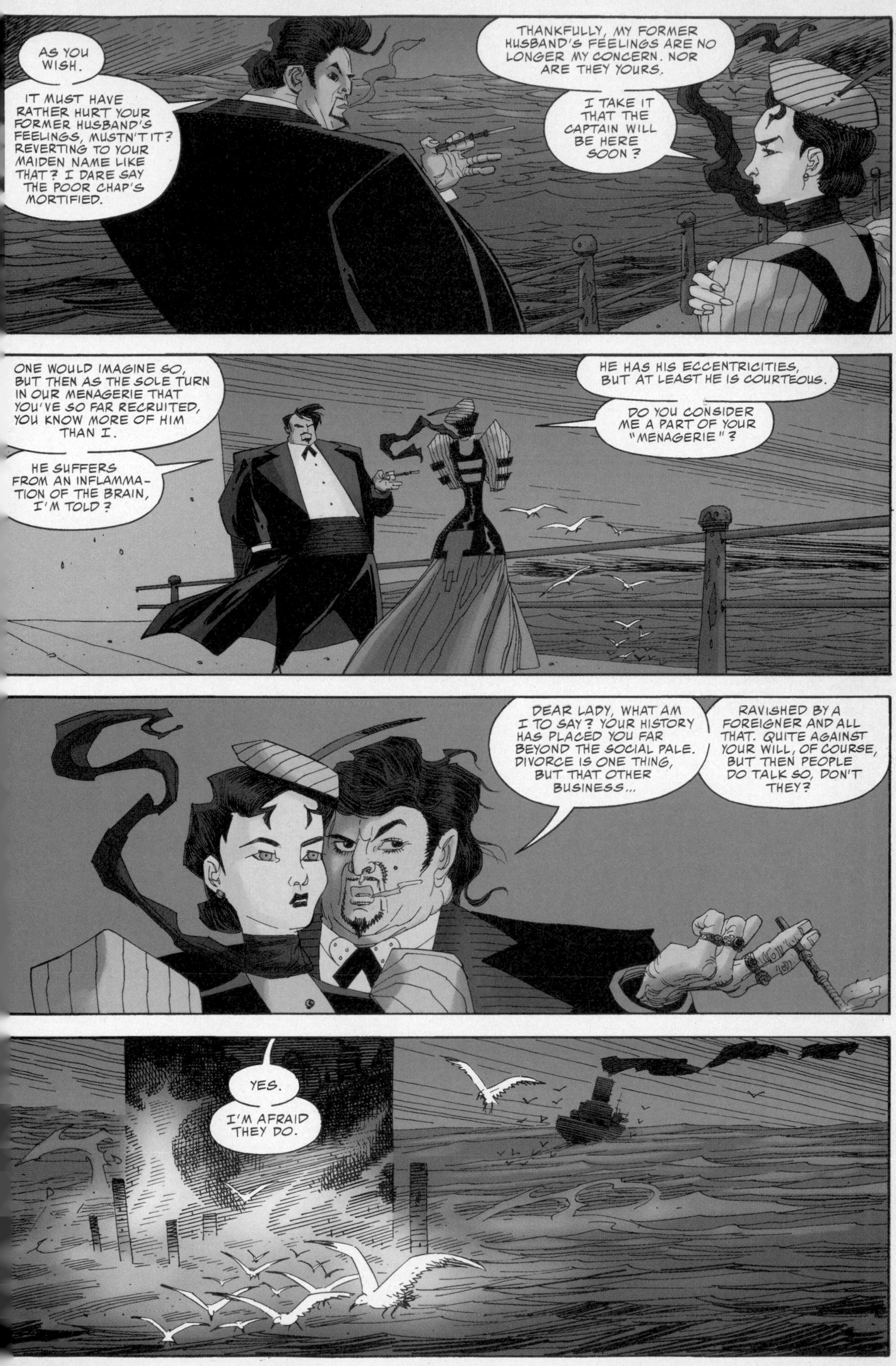

AS YOU WISH.
IT MUST HAVE RATHER HURT YOUR FORMER HUSBAND'S FEELINGS, MUSTN'T IT? REVERTING TO YOUR MAIDEN NAME LIKE THAT? I DARE SAY THE POOR CHAP'S MORTIFIED.
THANKFULLY, MY FORMER HUSBAND'S FEELINGS ARE NO LONGER MY CONCERN. NOR ARE THEY YOURS.
I TAKE IT THAT THE CAPTAIN WILL BE HERE SOON?
ONE WOULD IMAGINE SO, BUT THEN AS THE SOLE TURN IN OUR MENAGERIE THAT YOU'VE SO FAR RECRUITED, YOU KNOW MORE OF HIM THAN I.
HE SUFFERS FROM AN INFLAMMA-TION OF THE BRAIN, I'M TOLD?
HE HAS HIS ECCENTRICITIES, BUT AT LEAST HE IS COURTEOUS.
DO YOU CONSIDER ME A PART OF YOUR "MENAGERIE"?
DEAR LADY, WHAT AM I TO SAY? YOUR HISTORY HAS PLACED YOU FAR BEYOND THE SOCIAL PALE. DIVORCE IS ONE THING, BUT THAT OTHER BUSINESS...
RAVISHED BY A FOREIGNER AND ALL THAT. QUITE AGAINST YOUR WILL, OF COURSE, BUT THEN PEOPLE DO TALK SO, DON'T THEY?
YES.
I'M AFRAID THEY DO.

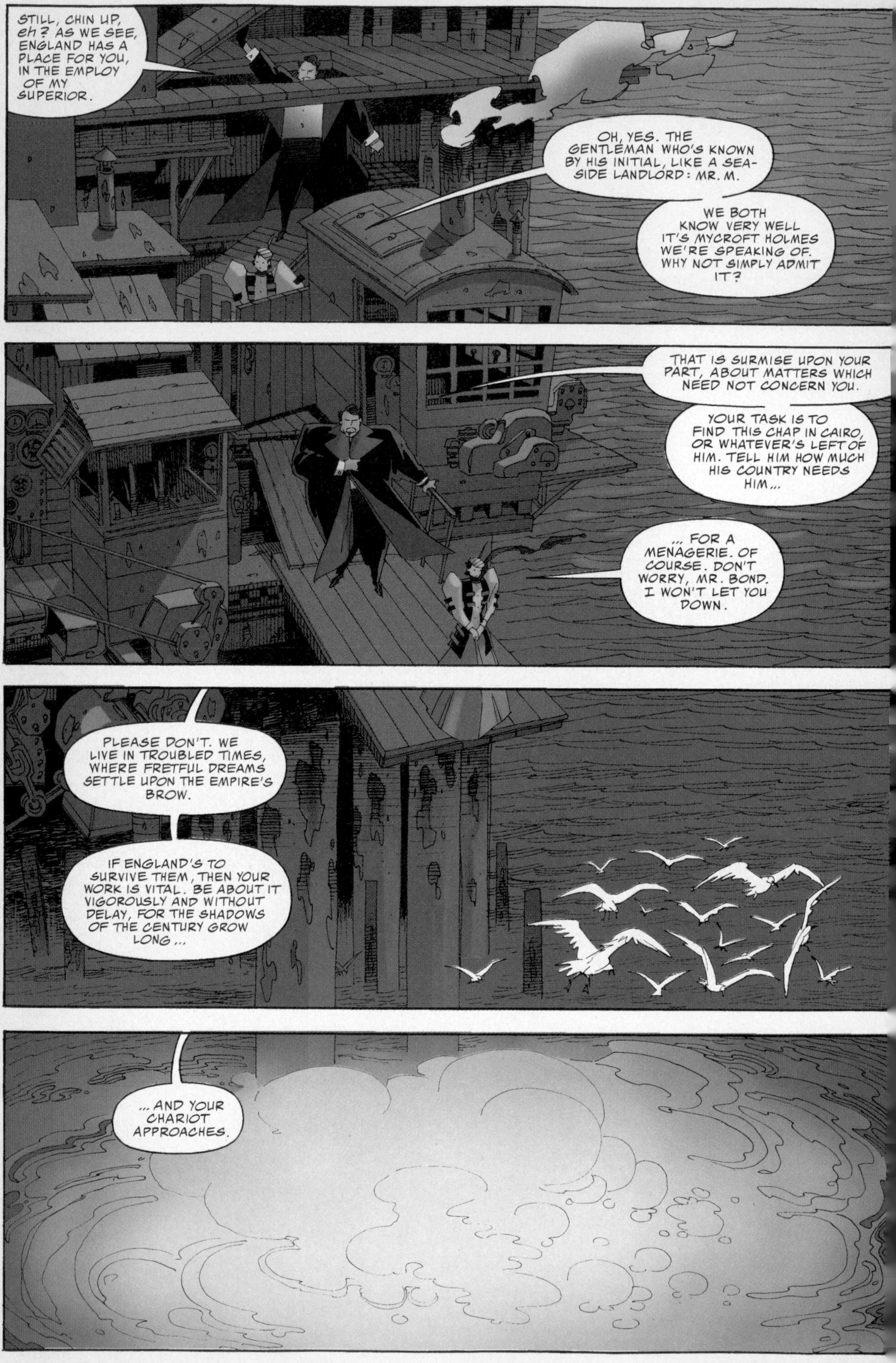
STILL, CHIN UP, *eh*? AS WE SEE, ENGLAND HAS A PLACE FOR YOU, IN THE EMPLOY OF MY SUPERIOR.
OH, YES. THE GENTLEMAN WHO'S KNOWN BY HIS INITIAL, LIKE A SEA-SIDE LANDLORD: MR. M.
WE BOTH KNOW VERY WELL IT'S MYCROFT HOLMES WE'RE SPEAKING OF. WHY NOT SIMPLY ADMIT IT?
THAT IS SURMISE UPON YOUR PART, ABOUT MATTERS WHICH NEED NOT CONCERN YOU.
YOUR TASK IS TO FIND THIS CHAP IN CAIRO, OR WHATEVER'S LEFT OF HIM. TELL HIM HOW MUCH HIS COUNTRY NEEDS HIM...
... FOR A MENAGERIE. OF COURSE. DON'T WORRY, MR. BOND. I WON'T LET YOU DOWN.
PLEASE DON'T. WE LIVE IN TROUBLED TIMES, WHERE FRETFUL DREAMS SETTLE UPON THE EMPIRE'S BROW.
IF ENGLAND'S TO SURVIVE THEM, THEN YOUR WORK IS VITAL. BE ABOUT IT VIGOROUSLY AND WITHOUT DELAY, FOR THE SHADOWS OF THE CENTURY GROW LONG ...
... AND YOUR CHARIOT APPROACHES.

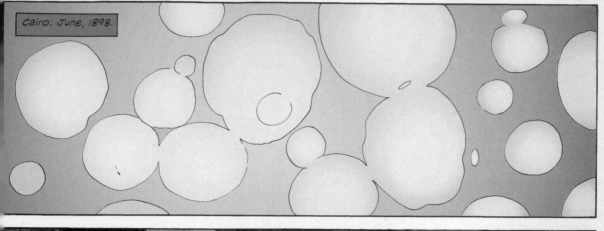

Cairo. June, 1898.

من هنا يا آنسة

اللى بتضورى عليه من هنا

متشكرة على مساعدتك الكبيرة ليه

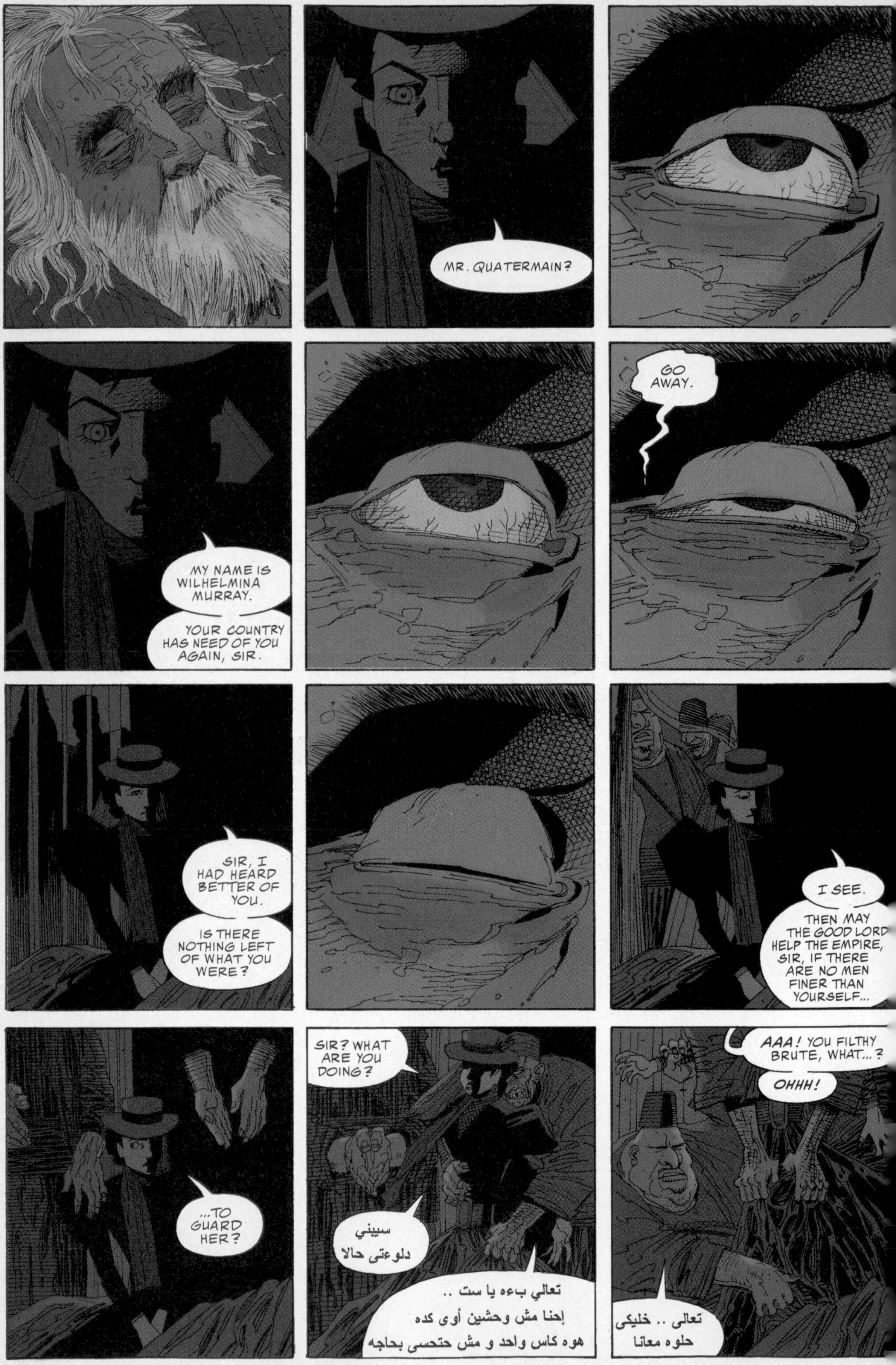
MR. QUATERMAIN?
MY NAME IS WILHELMINA MURRAY.
YOUR COUNTRY HAS NEED OF YOU AGAIN, SIR.
GO AWAY.
SIR, I HAD HEARD BETTER OF YOU.
IS THERE NOTHING LEFT OF WHAT YOU WERE?
I SEE.
THEN MAY THE GOOD LORD HELP THE EMPIRE, SIR, IF THERE ARE NO MEN FINER THAN YOURSELF...
...TO GUARD HER?
SIR? WHAT ARE YOU DOING?
سيبني دلوءتى حالا
تعالي بءه يا ست .. إحنا مش وحشين أوى كده هوه كاس واحد و مش حتحسى بحاجه
AAA! YOU FILTHY BRUTE, WHAT...?
OHHH!
تعالى .. خليكى حلوه معانا

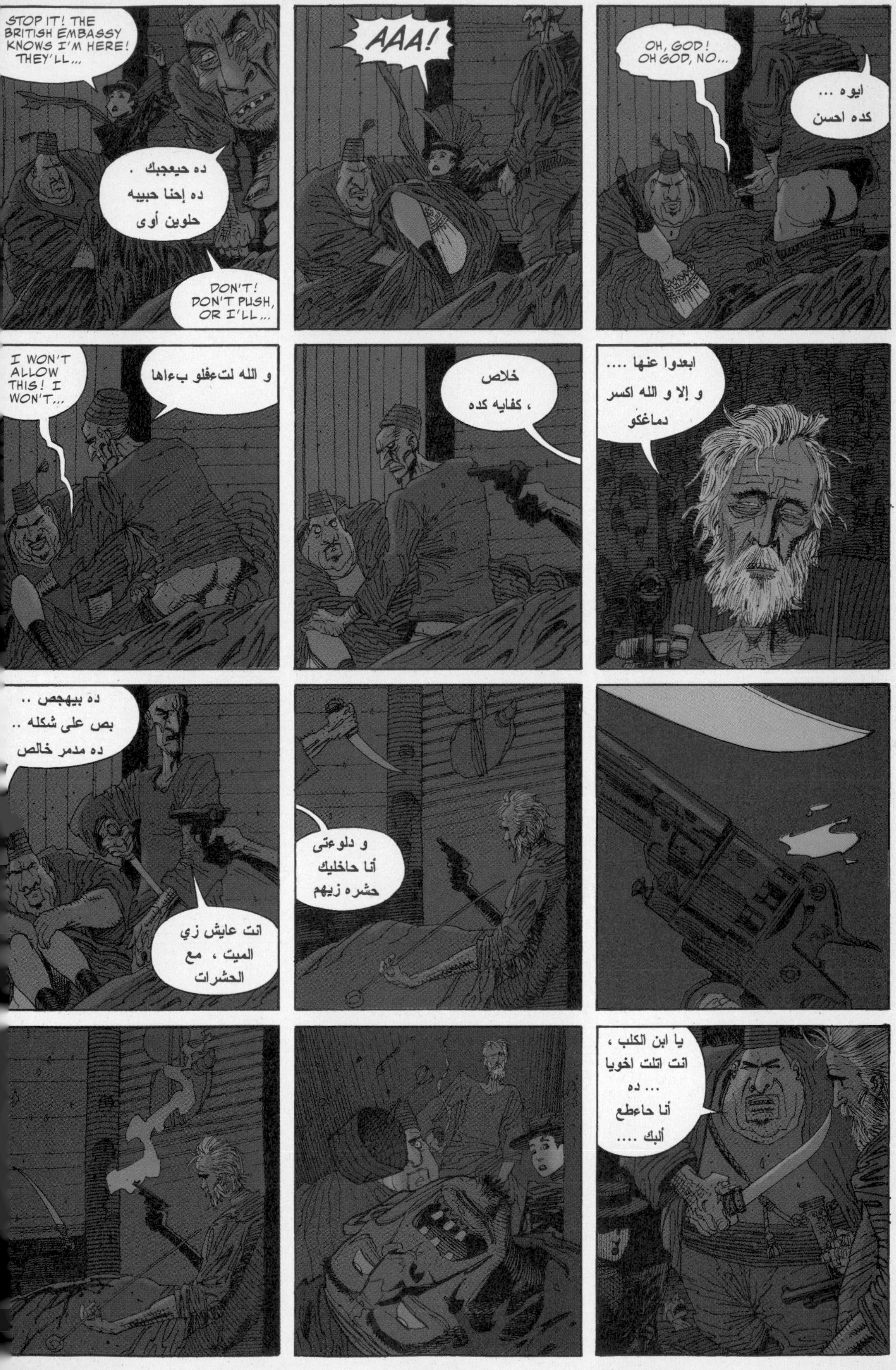
STOP IT! THE BRITISH EMBASSY KNOWS I'M HERE! THEY'LL...
ده حيعجبك . ده إحنا حبيبه حلوين أوى
DON'T! DON'T PUSH, OR I'LL...
AAA!
OH, GOD! OH GOD, NO...
ايوه ... كده احسن
I WON'T ALLOW THIS! I WON'T...
و الله لتءفلو بءاها
خلاص ، كفايه كده
ابعدوا عنها .... و إلا و الله اكسر دماغكو
ده بيهجص .. بص على شكله .. ده مدمر خالص
انت عايش زي الميت ، مع الحشرات
و دلوءتى أنا حاخليك حشره زيهم
يا ابن الكلب ، انت اتلت اخويا ... ده أنا حاعطع ألبك ....

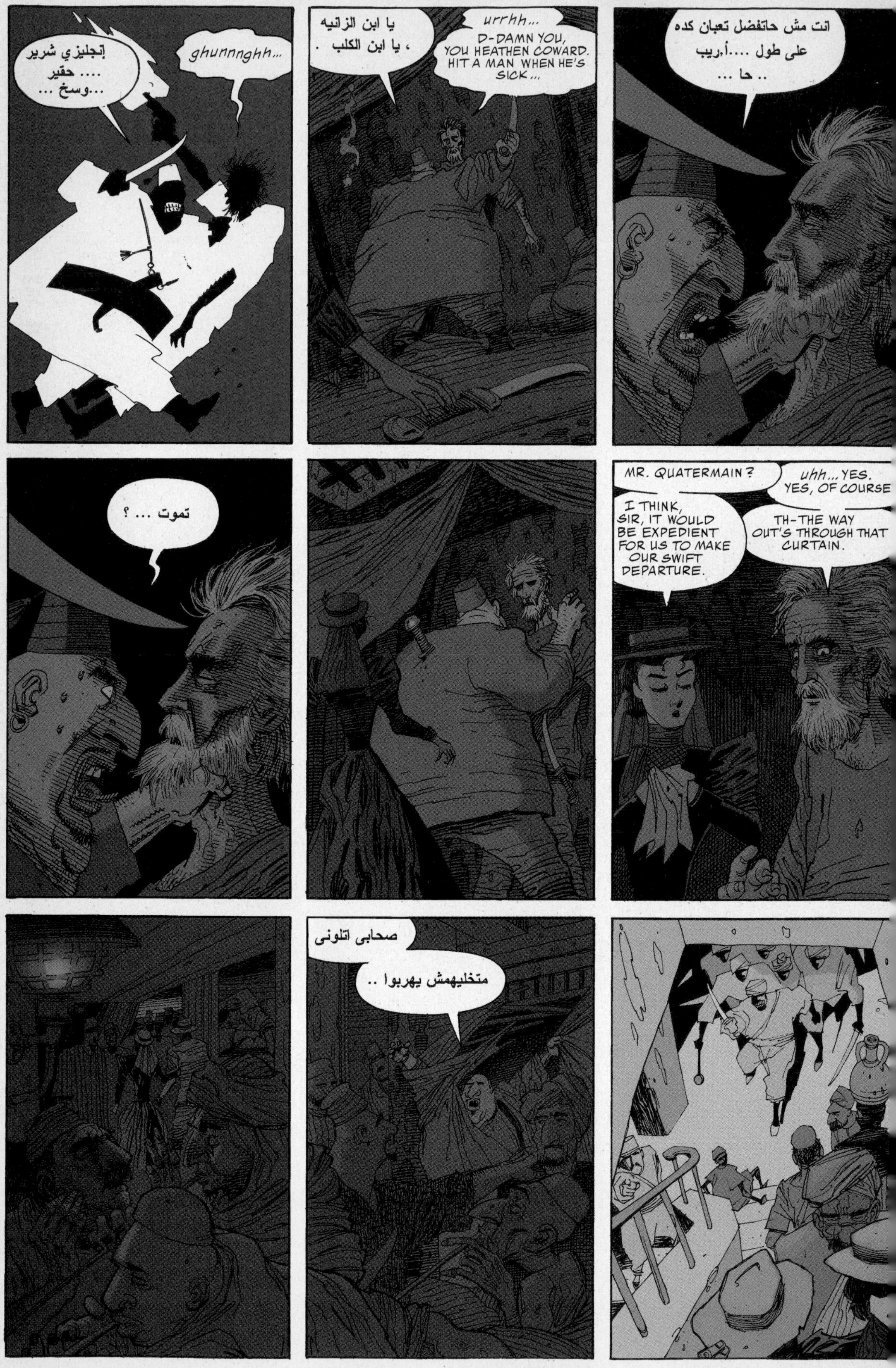
إنجليزي شرير
.... حقير
...وسخ ...
ghunnnghh...
يا ابن الزانيه
، يا ابن الكلب .
urrhh...
D-DAMN YOU, YOU HEATHEN COWARD. HIT A MAN WHEN HE'S SICK...
انت مش حاتفضل تعبان كده
على طول ....أ,ريب
.. حا ...
تموت ... ؟
MR. QUATERMAIN?
uhh... YES. YES, OF COURSE
I THINK, SIR, IT WOULD BE EXPEDIENT FOR US TO MAKE OUR SWIFT DEPARTURE.
TH-THE WAY OUT'S THROUGH THAT CURTAIN.
صحابى اتلونى
متخليهمش يهربوا ..

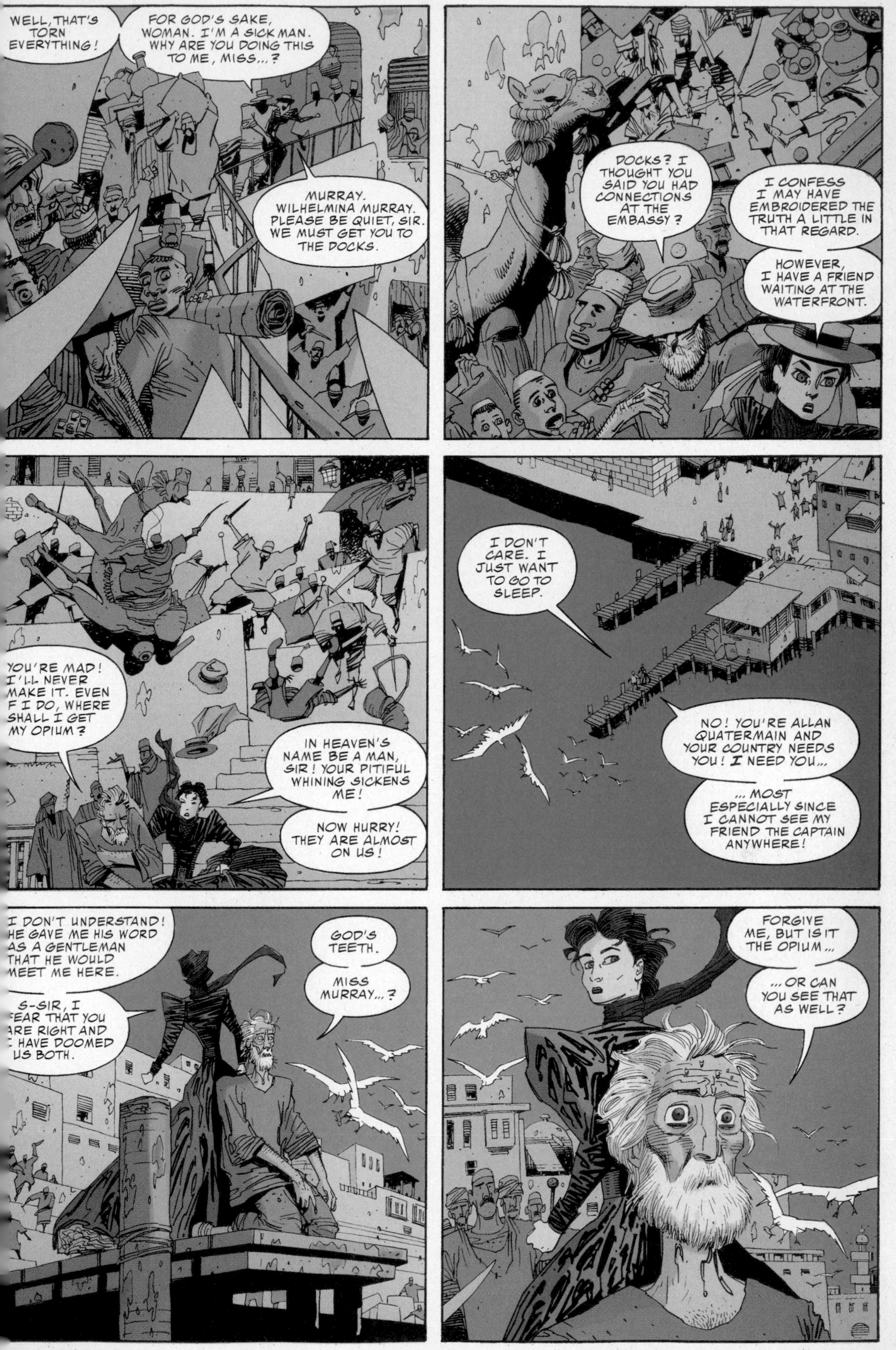
WELL, THAT'S TORN EVERYTHING!
FOR GOD'S SAKE, WOMAN. I'M A SICK MAN. WHY ARE YOU DOING THIS TO ME, MISS...?
MURRAY. WILHELMINA MURRAY. PLEASE BE QUIET, SIR. WE MUST GET YOU TO THE DOCKS.
DOCKS? I THOUGHT YOU SAID YOU HAD CONNECTIONS AT THE EMBASSY?
I CONFESS I MAY HAVE EMBROIDERED THE TRUTH A LITTLE IN THAT REGARD.
HOWEVER, I HAVE A FRIEND WAITING AT THE WATERFRONT.
YOU'RE MAD! I'LL NEVER MAKE IT. EVEN IF I DO, WHERE SHALL I GET MY OPIUM?
IN HEAVEN'S NAME BE A MAN, SIR! YOUR PITIFUL WHINING SICKENS ME!
NOW HURRY! THEY ARE ALMOST ON US!
I DON'T CARE. I JUST WANT TO GO TO SLEEP.
NO! YOU'RE ALLAN QUATERMAIN AND YOUR COUNTRY NEEDS YOU! I NEED YOU...
... MOST ESPECIALLY SINCE I CANNOT SEE MY FRIEND THE CAPTAIN ANYWHERE!
I DON'T UNDERSTAND! HE GAVE ME HIS WORD AS A GENTLEMAN THAT HE WOULD MEET ME HERE.
GOD'S TEETH.
MISS MURRAY...?
S-SIR, I FEAR THAT YOU ARE RIGHT AND I HAVE DOOMED US BOTH.
FORGIVE ME, BUT IS IT THE OPIUM...
...OR CAN YOU SEE THAT AS WELL?

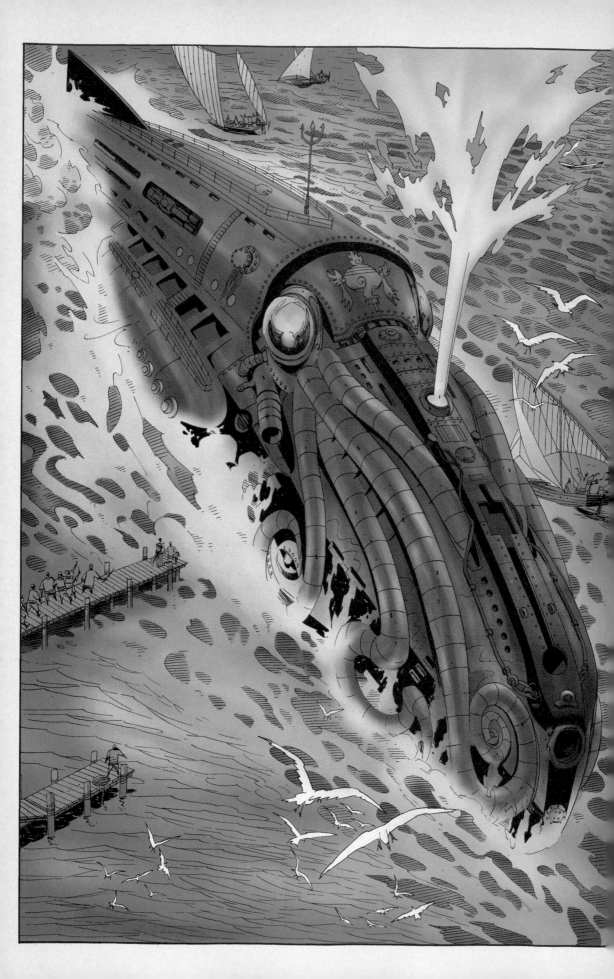

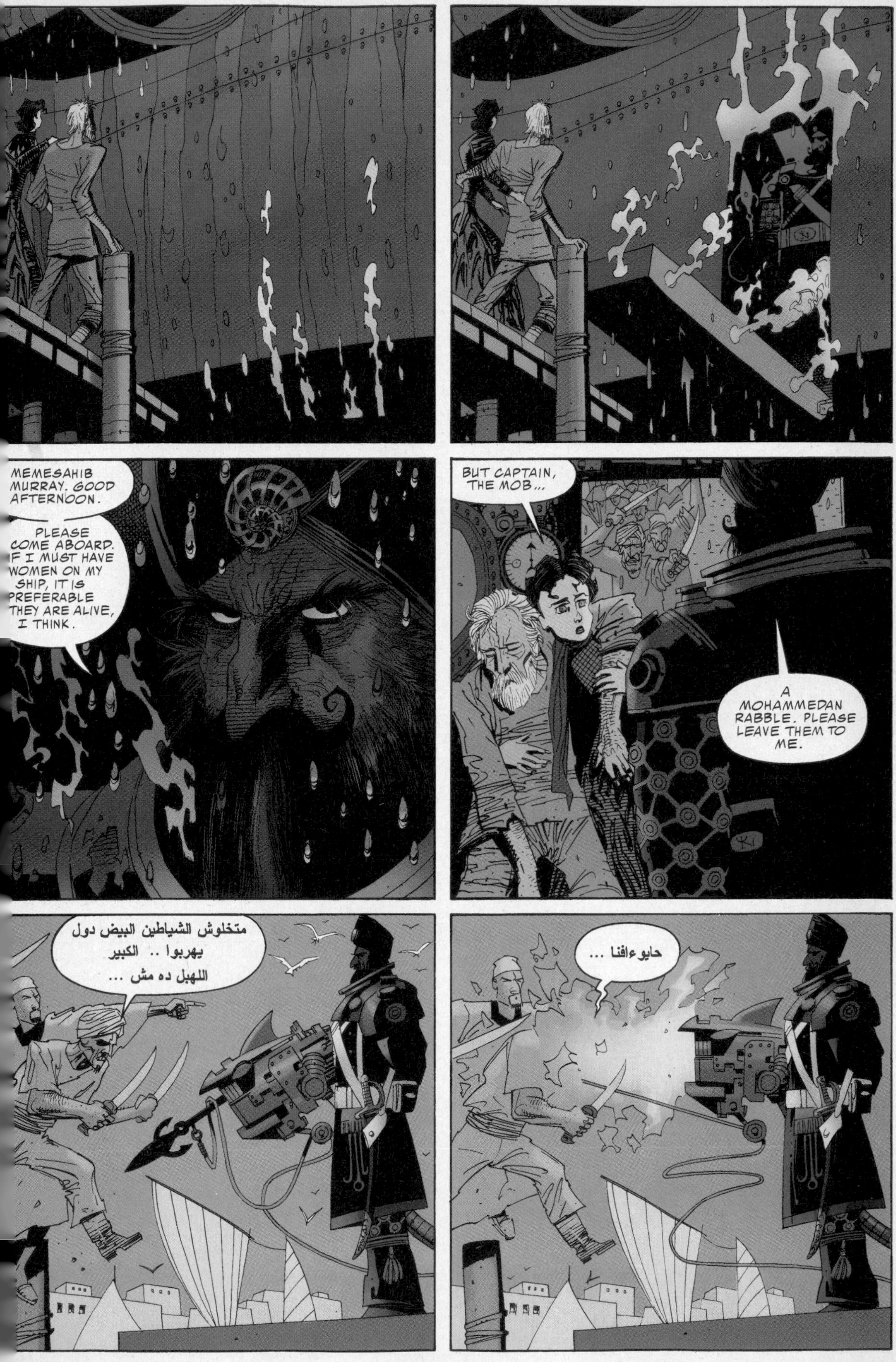
MEMESAHIB MURRAY. GOOD AFTERNOON.
PLEASE COME ABOARD. IF I MUST HAVE WOMEN ON MY SHIP, IT IS PREFERABLE THEY ARE ALIVE, I THINK.
BUT CAPTAIN, THE MOB...
A MOHAMMEDAN RABBLE. PLEASE LEAVE THEM TO ME.
متخلوش الشياطين البيض دول يهربوا .. الكبير اللهبل ده مش ...
حايوءافنا ...

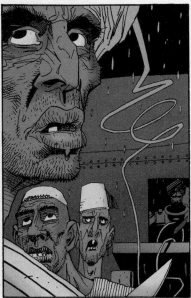

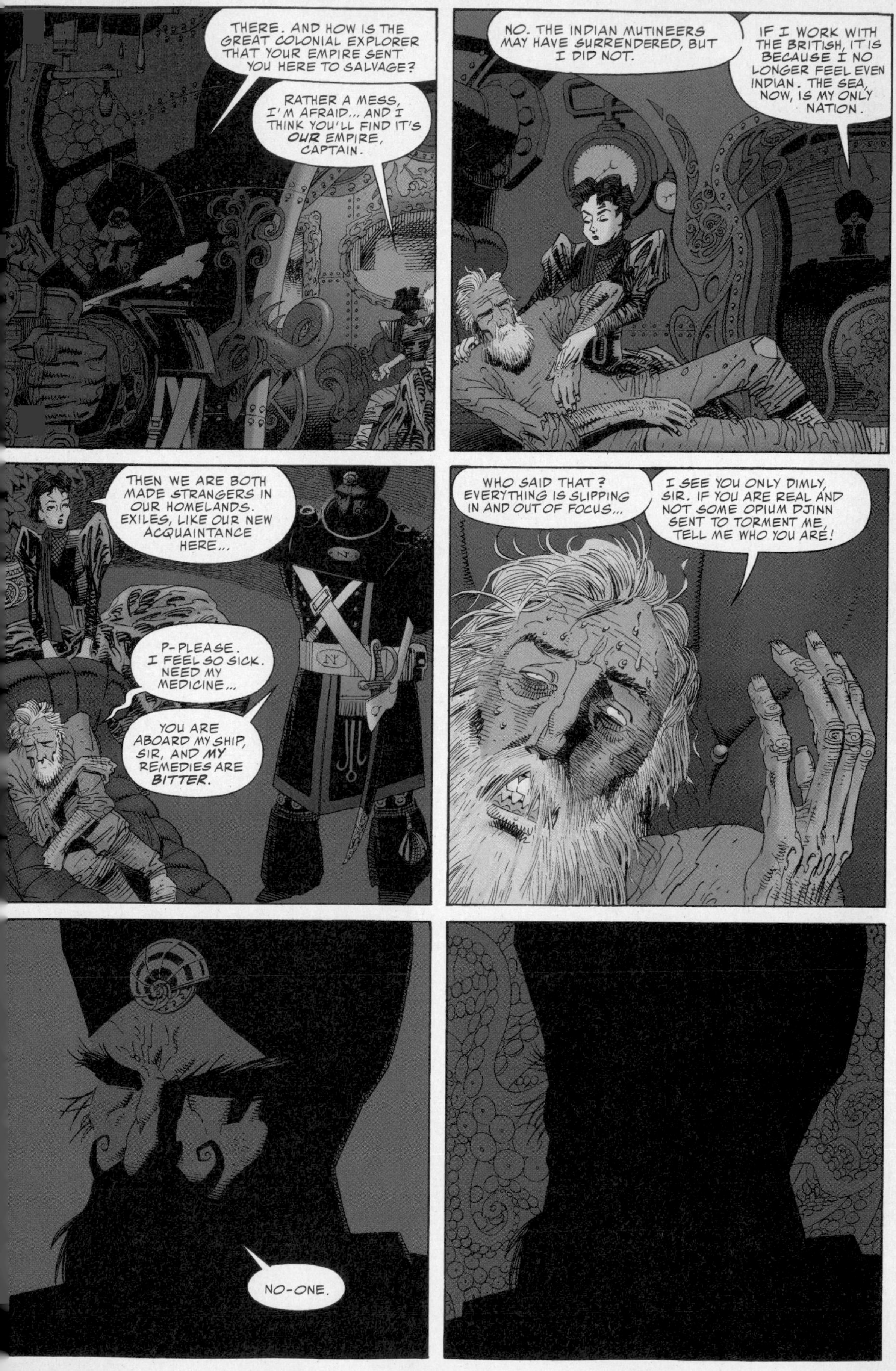
THERE. AND HOW IS THE GREAT COLONIAL EXPLORER THAT YOUR EMPIRE SENT YOU HERE TO SALVAGE?
RATHER A MESS, I'M AFRAID... AND I THINK YOU'LL FIND IT'S *OUR* EMPIRE, CAPTAIN.
NO. THE INDIAN MUTINEERS MAY HAVE SURRENDERED, BUT I DID NOT.
IF I WORK WITH THE BRITISH, IT IS BECAUSE I NO LONGER FEEL EVEN INDIAN. THE SEA, NOW, IS MY ONLY NATION.
THEN WE ARE BOTH MADE STRANGERS IN OUR HOMELANDS. EXILES, LIKE OUR NEW ACQUAINTANCE HERE...
P-PLEASE. I FEEL SO SICK. NEED MY MEDICINE...
YOU ARE ABOARD MY SHIP, SIR, AND *MY* REMEDIES ARE *BITTER*.
WHO SAID THAT? EVERYTHING IS SLIPPING IN AND OUT OF FOCUS...
I SEE YOU ONLY DIMLY, SIR. IF YOU ARE REAL AND NOT SOME OPIUM DJINN SENT TO TORMENT ME, TELL ME WHO YOU ARE!
NO-ONE.

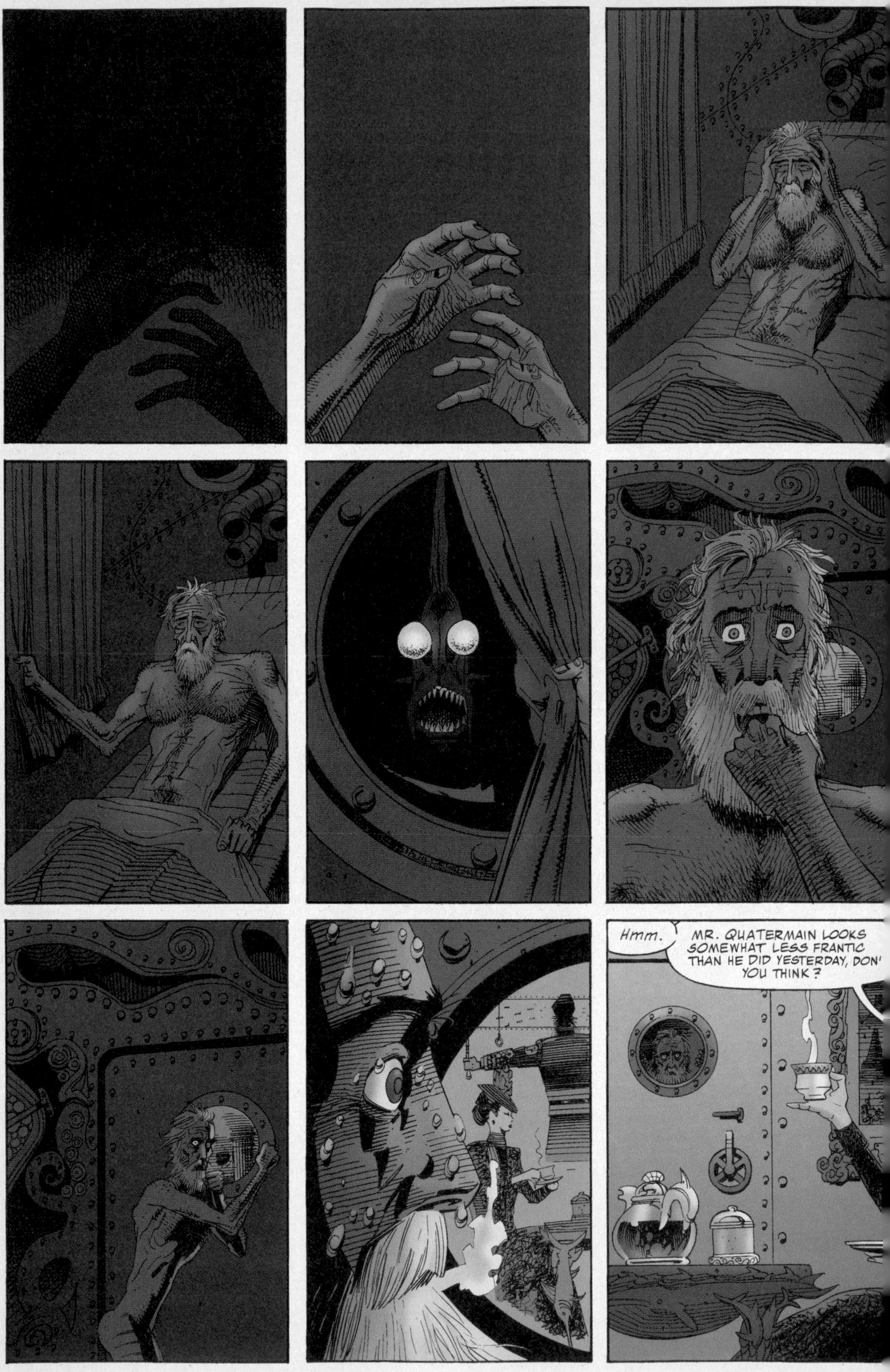
Hmm.
MR. QUATERMAIN LOOKS SOMEWHAT LESS FRANTIC THAN HE DID YESTERDAY, DON'
YOU THINK?

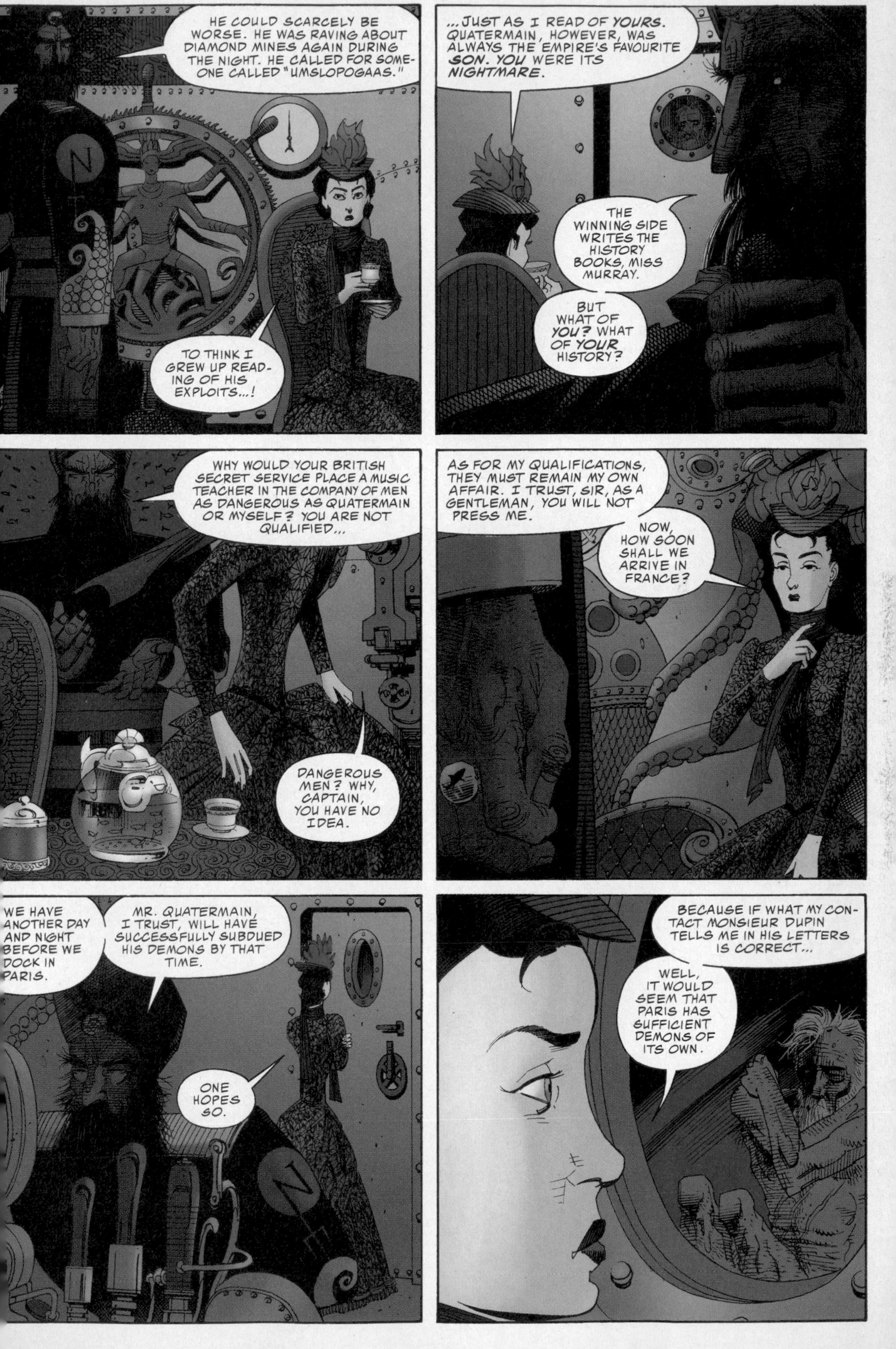
HE COULD SCARCELY BE WORSE. HE WAS RAVING ABOUT DIAMOND MINES AGAIN DURING THE NIGHT. HE CALLED FOR SOMEONE CALLED "UMSLOPOGAAS."
TO THINK I GREW UP READING OF HIS EXPLOITS...!
...JUST AS I READ OF *YOURS*. QUATERMAIN, HOWEVER, WAS ALWAYS THE EMPIRE'S FAVOURITE **SON**. *YOU* WERE ITS *NIGHTMARE*.
THE WINNING SIDE WRITES THE HISTORY BOOKS, MISS MURRAY.
BUT WHAT OF *YOU?* WHAT OF *YOUR* HISTORY?
WHY WOULD YOUR BRITISH SECRET SERVICE PLACE A MUSIC TEACHER IN THE COMPANY OF MEN AS DANGEROUS AS QUATERMAIN OR MYSELF? YOU ARE NOT QUALIFIED...
DANGEROUS MEN? WHY, CAPTAIN, YOU HAVE NO IDEA.
AS FOR MY QUALIFICATIONS, THEY MUST REMAIN MY OWN AFFAIR. I TRUST, SIR, AS A GENTLEMAN, YOU WILL NOT PRESS ME.
NOW, HOW SOON SHALL WE ARRIVE IN FRANCE?
WE HAVE ANOTHER DAY AND NIGHT BEFORE WE DOCK IN PARIS.
MR. QUATERMAIN, I TRUST, WILL HAVE SUCCESSFULLY SUBDUED HIS DEMONS BY THAT TIME.
ONE HOPES SO.
BECAUSE IF WHAT MY CONTACT MONSIEUR DUPIN TELLS ME IN HIS LETTERS IS CORRECT...
WELL, IT WOULD SEEM THAT PARIS HAS SUFFICIENT DEMONS OF ITS OWN.

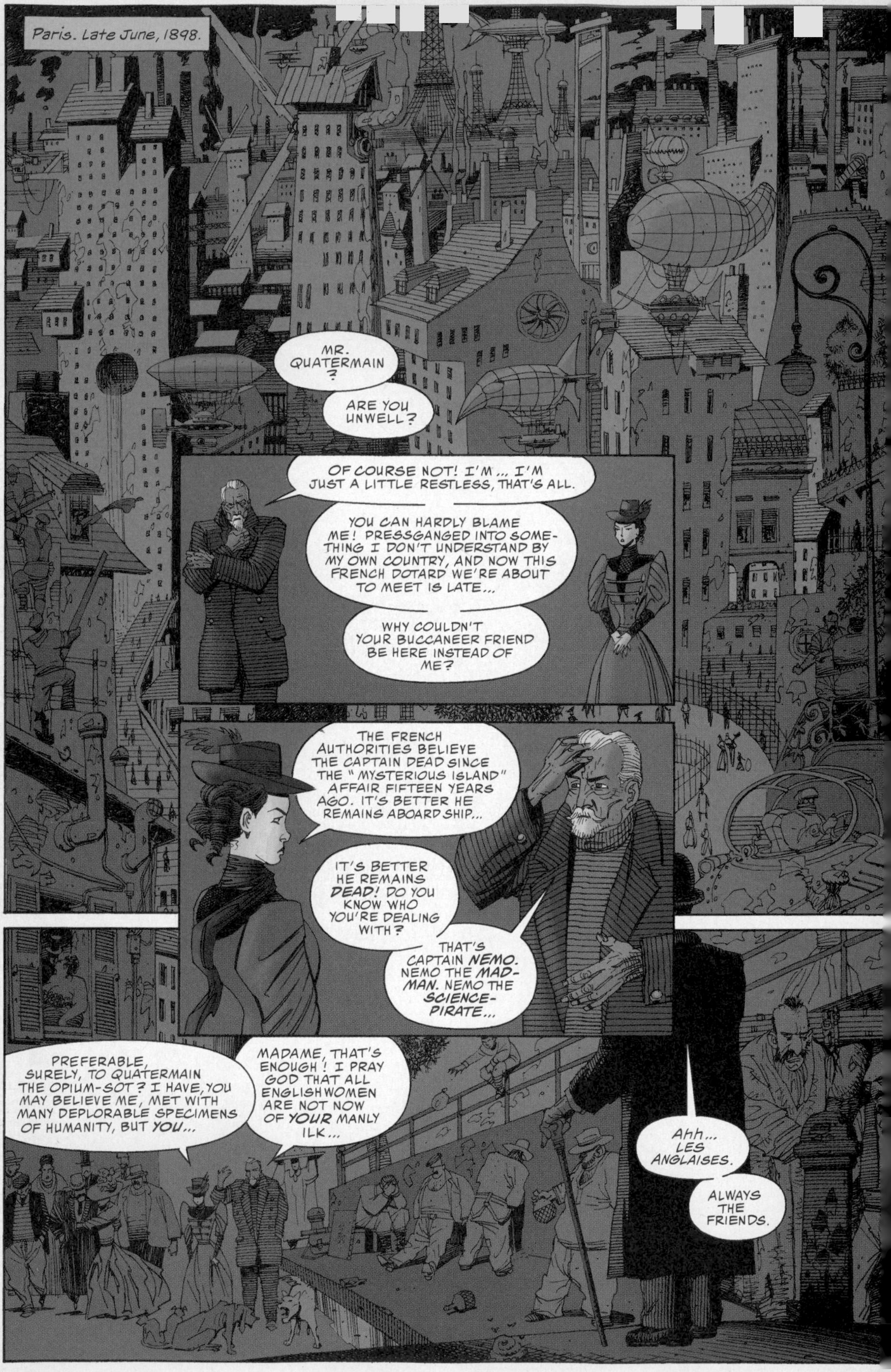
Paris. Late June, 1898.
MR. QUATERMAIN?
ARE YOU UNWELL?
OF COURSE NOT! I'M... I'M JUST A LITTLE RESTLESS, THAT'S ALL.
YOU CAN HARDLY BLAME ME! PRESSGANGED INTO SOMETHING I DON'T UNDERSTAND BY MY OWN COUNTRY, AND NOW THIS FRENCH DOTARD WE'RE ABOUT TO MEET IS LATE...
WHY COULDN'T YOUR BUCCANEER FRIEND BE HERE INSTEAD OF ME?
THE FRENCH AUTHORITIES BELIEVE THE CAPTAIN DEAD SINCE THE "MYSTERIOUS ISLAND" AFFAIR FIFTEEN YEARS AGO. IT'S BETTER HE REMAINS ABOARD SHIP...
IT'S BETTER HE REMAINS DEAD! DO YOU KNOW WHO YOU'RE DEALING WITH?
THAT'S CAPTAIN NEMO. NEMO THE MADMAN. NEMO THE SCIENCE-PIRATE...
PREFERABLE, SURELY, TO QUATERMAIN THE OPIUM-SOT? I HAVE, YOU MAY BELIEVE ME, MET WITH MANY DEPLORABLE SPECIMENS OF HUMANITY, BUT YOU...
MADAME, THAT'S ENOUGH! I PRAY GOD THAT ALL ENGLISHWOMEN ARE NOT NOW OF YOUR MANLY ILK...
Ahh... LES ANGLAISES.
ALWAYS THE FRIENDS.

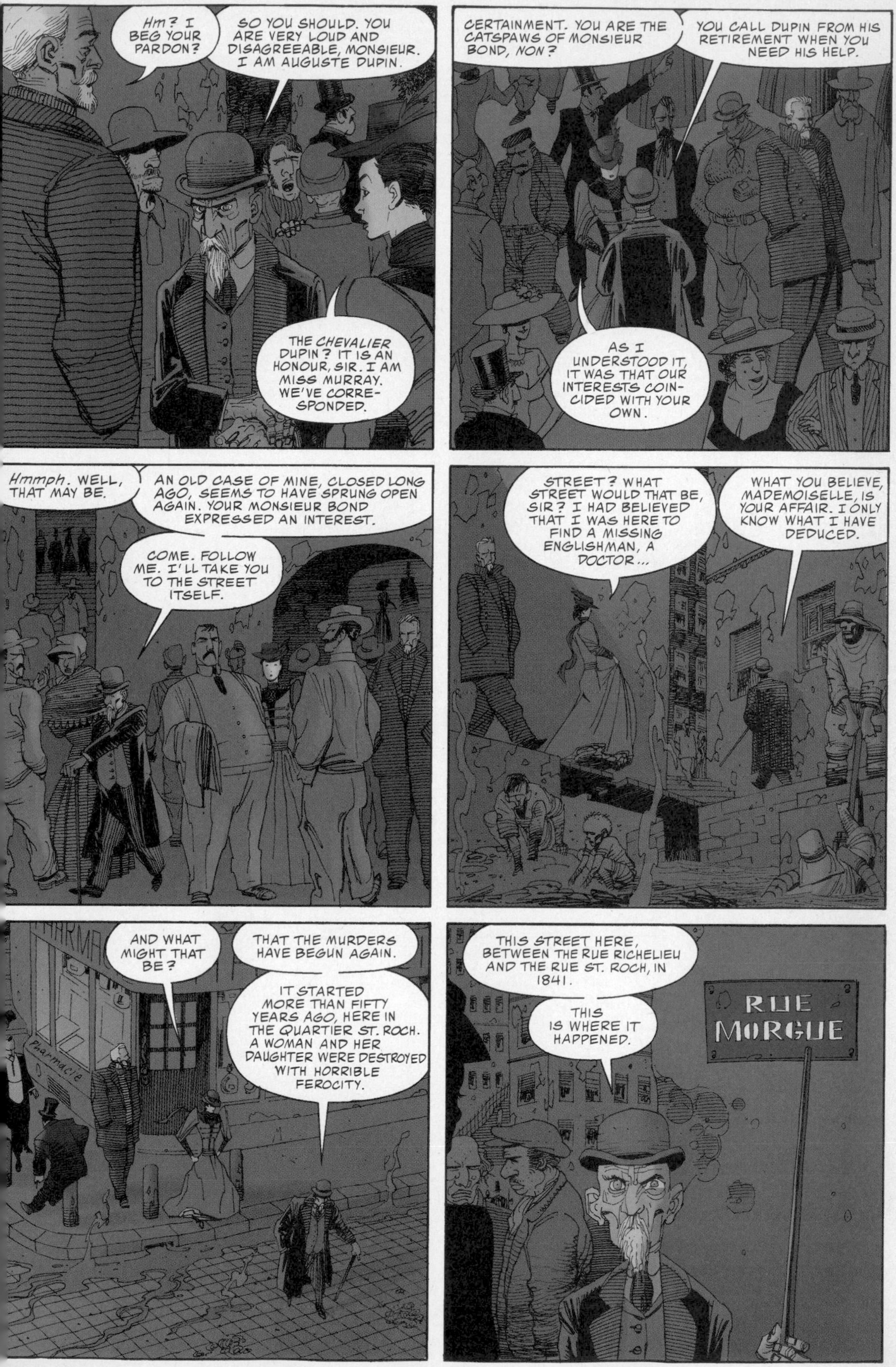

Hm? I BEG YOUR PARDON?
SO YOU SHOULD. YOU ARE VERY LOUD AND DISAGREEABLE, MONSIEUR. I AM AUGUSTE DUPIN.
THE CHEVALIER DUPIN? IT IS AN HONOUR, SIR. I AM MISS MURRAY. WE'VE CORRE-SPONDED.
CERTAINMENT. YOU ARE THE CATSPAWS OF MONSIEUR BOND, NON?
YOU CALL DUPIN FROM HIS RETIREMENT WHEN YOU NEED HIS HELP.
AS I UNDERSTOOD IT, IT WAS THAT OUR INTERESTS COIN-CIDED WITH YOUR OWN.
Hmmph. WELL, THAT MAY BE.
AN OLD CASE OF MINE, CLOSED LONG AGO, SEEMS TO HAVE SPRUNG OPEN AGAIN. YOUR MONSIEUR BOND EXPRESSED AN INTEREST.
COME. FOLLOW ME. I'LL TAKE YOU TO THE STREET ITSELF.
STREET? WHAT STREET WOULD THAT BE, SIR? I HAD BELIEVED THAT I WAS HERE TO FIND A MISSING ENGLISHMAN, A DOCTOR...
WHAT YOU BELIEVE, MADEMOISELLE, IS YOUR AFFAIR. I ONLY KNOW WHAT I HAVE DEDUCED.
Pharmacie
AND WHAT MIGHT THAT BE?
THAT THE MURDERS HAVE BEGUN AGAIN.
IT STARTED MORE THAN FIFTY YEARS AGO, HERE IN THE QUARTIER ST. ROCH. A WOMAN AND HER DAUGHTER WERE DESTROYED WITH HORRIBLE FEROCITY.
THIS STREET HERE, BETWEEN THE RUE RICHELIEU AND THE RUE ST. ROCH, IN 1841.
THIS IS WHERE IT HAPPENED.
RUE MORGUE

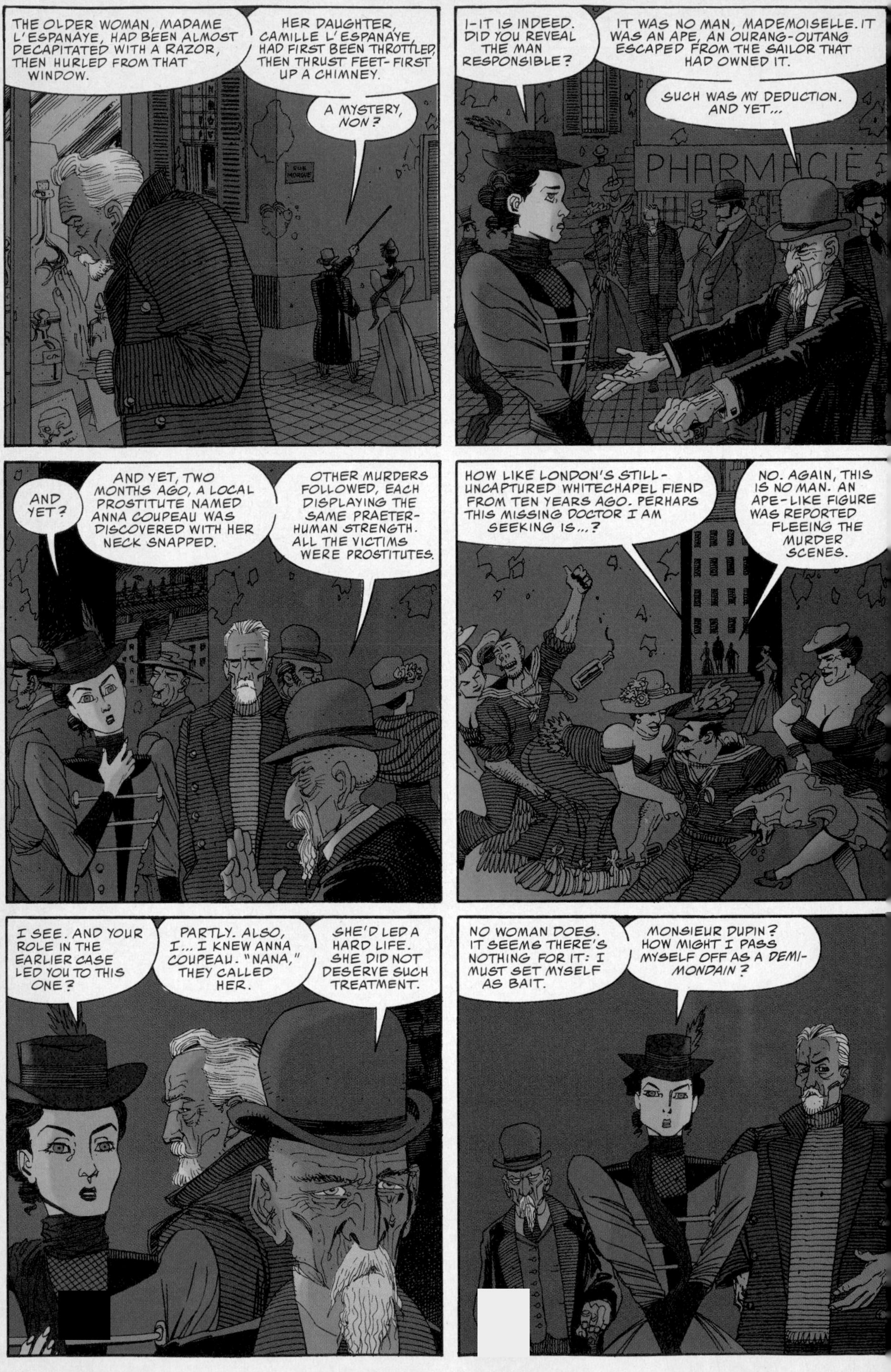
THE OLDER WOMAN, MADAME L'ESPANAYE, HAD BEEN ALMOST DECAPITATED WITH A RAZOR, THEN HURLED FROM THAT WINDOW.
HER DAUGHTER, CAMILLE L'ESPANAYE, HAD FIRST BEEN THROTTLED, THEN THRUST FEET-FIRST UP A CHIMNEY.
A MYSTERY, *NON?*
I-IT IS INDEED. DID YOU REVEAL THE MAN RESPONSIBLE?
IT WAS NO MAN, MADEMOISELLE. IT WAS AN APE, AN OURANG-OUTANG ESCAPED FROM THE SAILOR THAT HAD OWNED IT.
SUCH WAS MY DEDUCTION. AND YET...
PHARMACIE
AND YET?
AND YET, TWO MONTHS AGO, A LOCAL PROSTITUTE NAMED ANNA COUPEAU WAS DISCOVERED WITH HER NECK SNAPPED.
OTHER MURDERS FOLLOWED, EACH DISPLAYING THE SAME PRAETER-HUMAN STRENGTH. ALL THE VICTIMS WERE PROSTITUTES.
HOW LIKE LONDON'S STILL-UNCAPTURED WHITECHAPEL FIEND FROM TEN YEARS AGO. PERHAPS THIS MISSING DOCTOR I AM SEEKING IS...?
NO. AGAIN, THIS IS NO MAN. AN APE-LIKE FIGURE WAS REPORTED FLEEING THE MURDER SCENES.
I SEE. AND YOUR ROLE IN THE EARLIER CASE LED YOU TO THIS ONE?
PARTLY. ALSO, I... I KNEW ANNA COUPEAU. "NANA," THEY CALLED HER.
SHE'D LED A HARD LIFE. SHE DID NOT DESERVE SUCH TREATMENT.
NO WOMAN DOES. IT SEEMS THERE'S NOTHING FOR IT: I MUST SET MYSELF AS BAIT.
MONSIEUR DUPIN? HOW MIGHT I PASS MYSELF OFF AS A *DEMI-MONDAIN?*

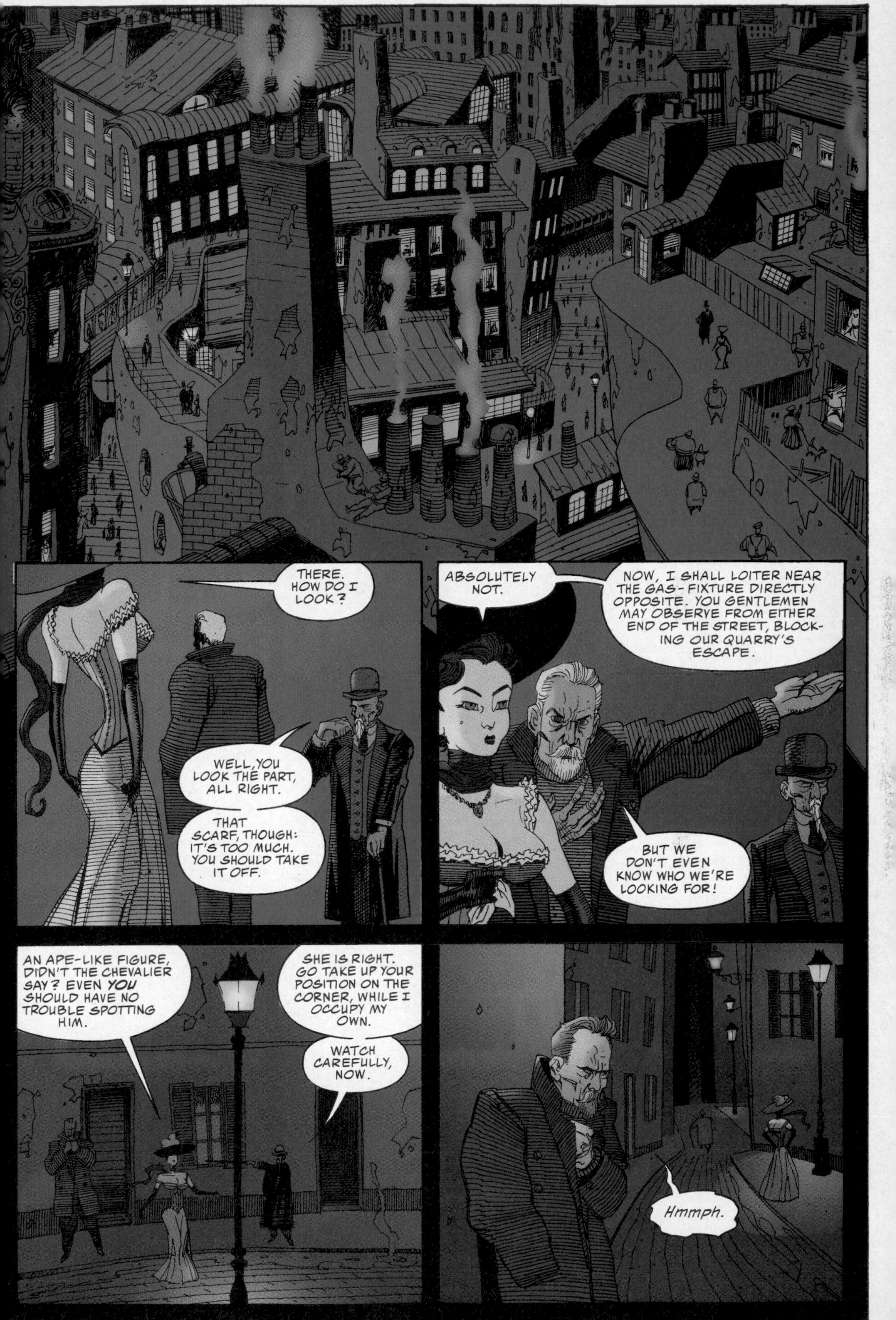

THERE. HOW DO I LOOK?
WELL, YOU LOOK THE PART, ALL RIGHT.
THAT SCARF, THOUGH: IT'S TOO MUCH. YOU SHOULD TAKE IT OFF.
ABSOLUTELY NOT.
NOW, I SHALL LOITER NEAR THE GAS-FIXTURE DIRECTLY OPPOSITE. YOU GENTLEMEN MAY OBSERVE FROM EITHER END OF THE STREET, BLOCKING OUR QUARRY'S ESCAPE.
BUT WE DON'T EVEN KNOW WHO WE'RE LOOKING FOR!
AN APE-LIKE FIGURE, DIDN'T THE CHEVALIER SAY? EVEN *YOU* SHOULD HAVE NO TROUBLE SPOTTING HIM.
SHE IS RIGHT. GO TAKE UP YOUR POSITION ON THE CORNER, WHILE I OCCUPY MY OWN.
WATCH CAREFULLY, NOW.
Hmmph.

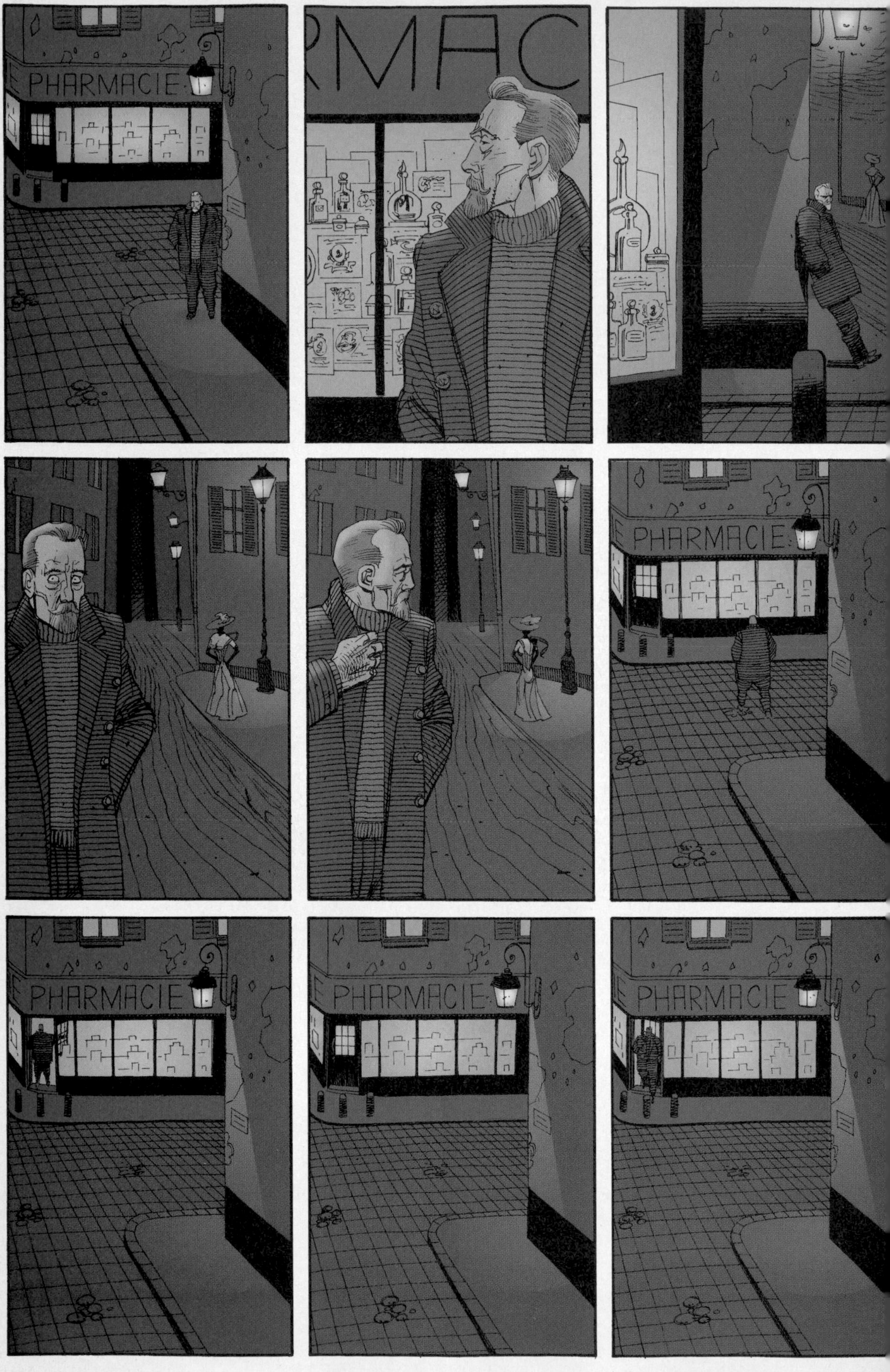
PHARMACIE
RMAC
PHARMACIE
PHARMACIE
PHARMACIE
PHARMACIE

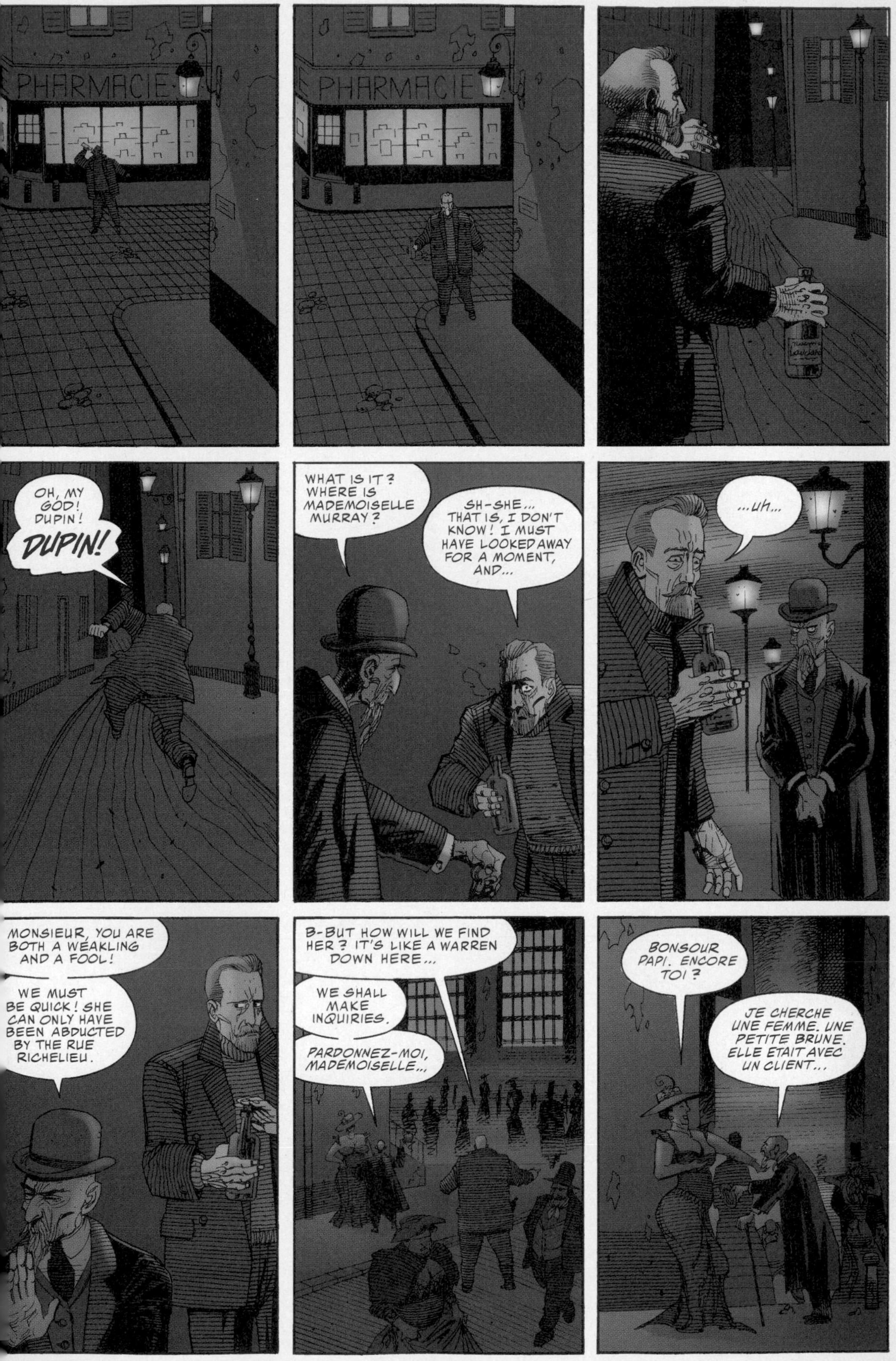
PHARMACIE
PHARMACIE
OH, MY GOD! DUPIN! DUPIN!
WHAT IS IT? WHERE IS MADEMOISELLE MURRAY?
SH-SHE... THAT IS, I DON'T KNOW! I MUST HAVE LOOKED AWAY FOR A MOMENT, AND...
...uh...
MONSIEUR, YOU ARE BOTH A WEAKLING AND A FOOL!
WE MUST BE QUICK! SHE CAN ONLY HAVE BEEN ABDUCTED BY THE RUE RICHELIEU.
B-BUT HOW WILL WE FIND HER? IT'S LIKE A WARREN DOWN HERE...
WE SHALL MAKE INQUIRIES.
PARDONNEZ-MOI, MADEMOISELLE...
BONSOUR PAPI. ENCORE TOI?
JE CHERCHE UNE FEMME. UNE PETITE BRUNE. ELLE ETAIT AVEC UN CLIENT...

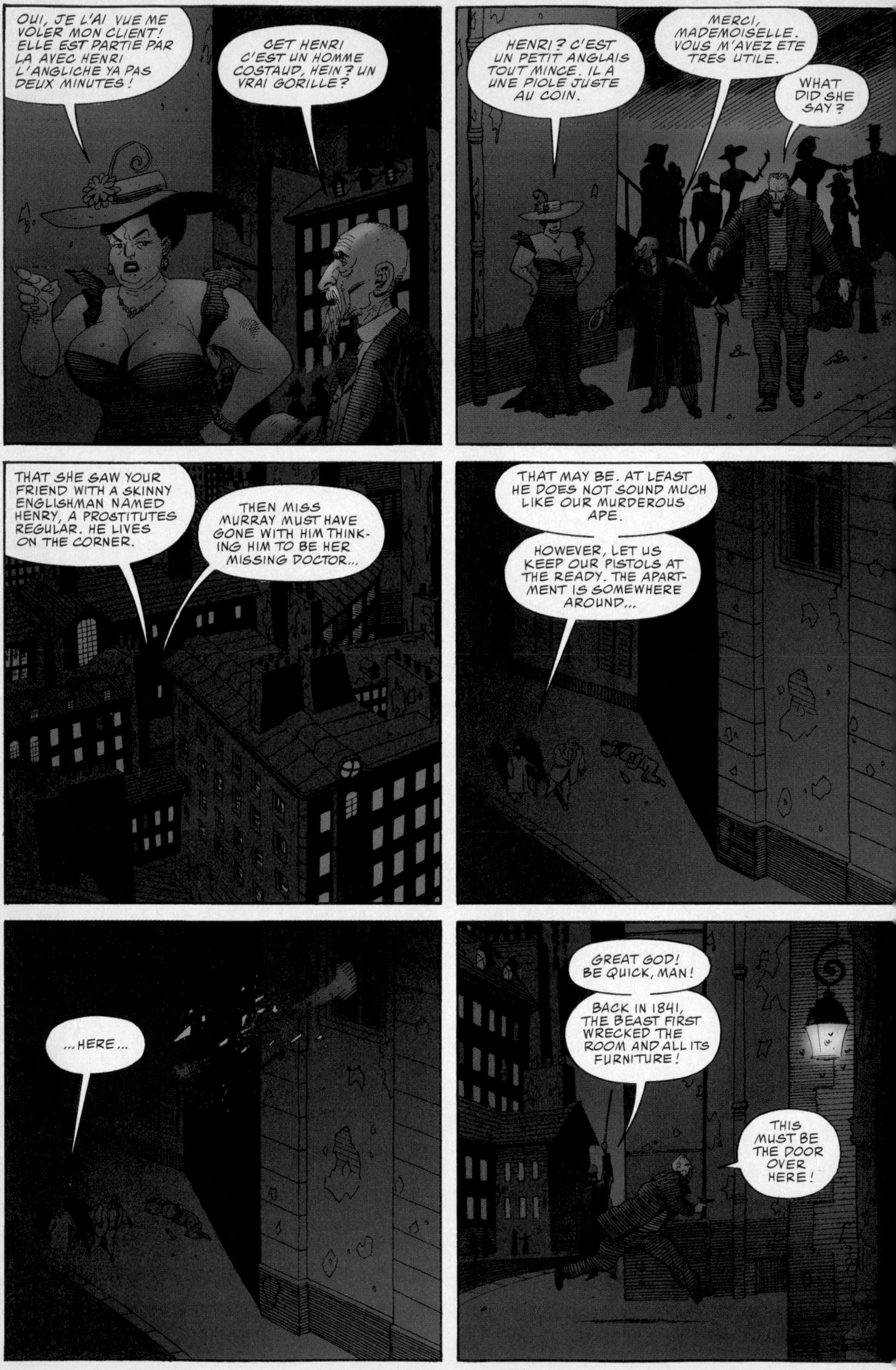
OUI, JE L'AI VUE ME VOLER MON CLIENT! ELLE EST PARTIE PAR LA AVEC HENRI L'ANGLICHE YA PAS DEUX MINUTES!
CET HENRI C'EST UN HOMME COSTAUD, HEIN? UN VRAI GORILLE?
HENRI? C'EST UN PETIT ANGLAIS TOUT MINCE. IL A UNE PIOLE JUSTE AU COIN.
MERCI, MADEMOISELLE. VOUS M'AVEZ ETE TRES UTILE.
WHAT DID SHE SAY?
THAT SHE SAW YOUR FRIEND WITH A SKINNY ENGLISHMAN NAMED HENRY, A PROSTITUTES REGULAR. HE LIVES ON THE CORNER.
THEN MISS MURRAY MUST HAVE GONE WITH HIM THINKING HIM TO BE HER MISSING DOCTOR...
THAT MAY BE. AT LEAST HE DOES NOT SOUND MUCH LIKE OUR MURDEROUS APE.
HOWEVER, LET US KEEP OUR PISTOLS AT THE READY. THE APARTMENT IS SOMEWHERE AROUND...
...HERE...
GREAT GOD! BE QUICK, MAN!
BACK IN 1841, THE BEAST FIRST WRECKED THE ROOM AND ALL ITS FURNITURE!
THIS MUST BE THE DOOR OVER HERE!

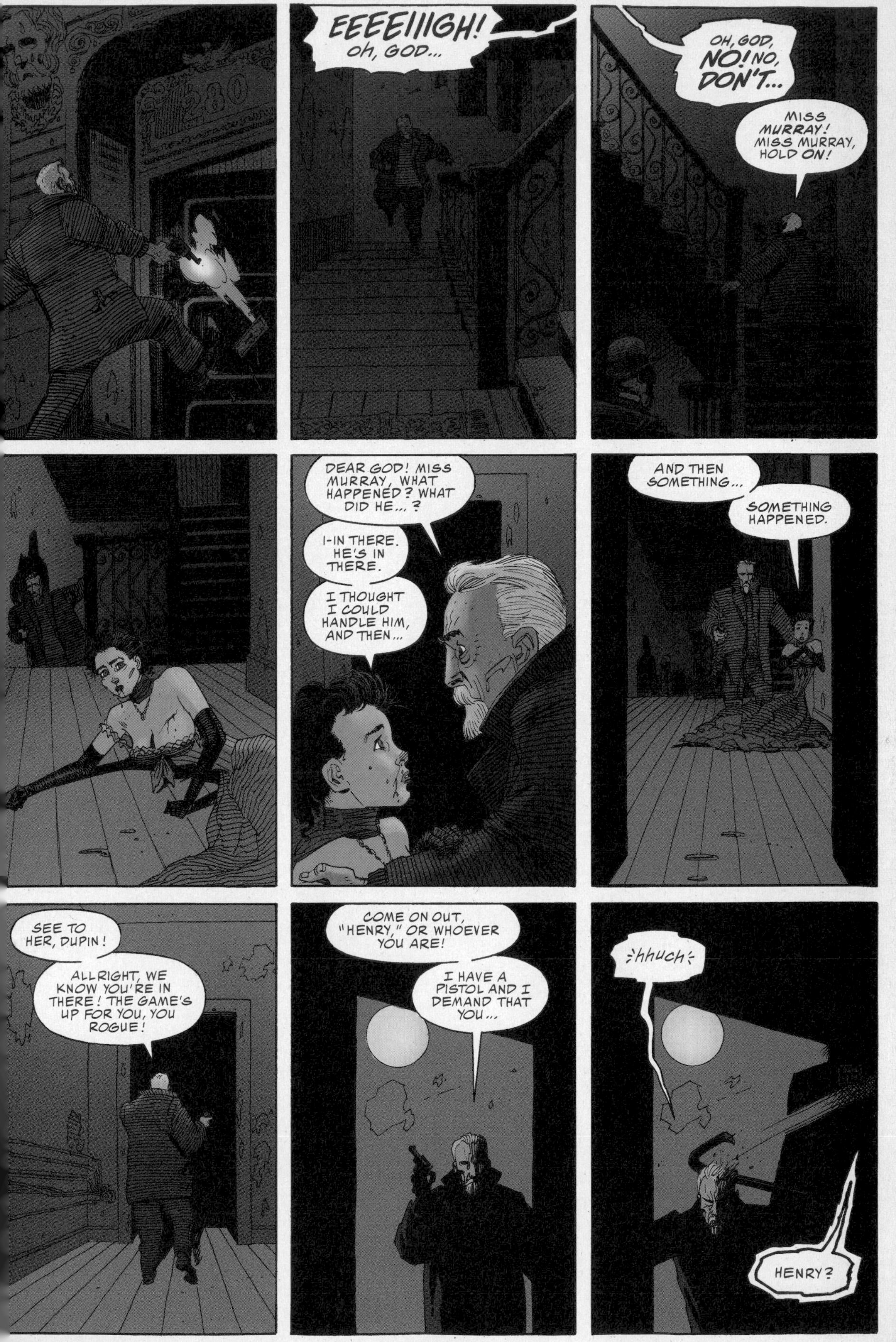
EEEEIIIGH! oh, GOD...
OH, GOD, NO! NO, DON'T...
MISS MURRAY! MISS MURRAY, HOLD ON!
DEAR GOD! MISS MURRAY, WHAT HAPPENED? WHAT DID HE...?
I-IN THERE. HE'S IN THERE.
I THOUGHT I COULD HANDLE HIM, AND THEN...
AND THEN SOMETHING...
SOMETHING HAPPENED.
SEE TO HER, DUPIN!
ALLRIGHT, WE KNOW YOU'RE IN THERE! THE GAME'S UP FOR YOU, YOU ROGUE!
COME ON OUT, "HENRY," OR WHOEVER YOU ARE!
I HAVE A PISTOL AND I DEMAND THAT YOU...
hhuch
HENRY?

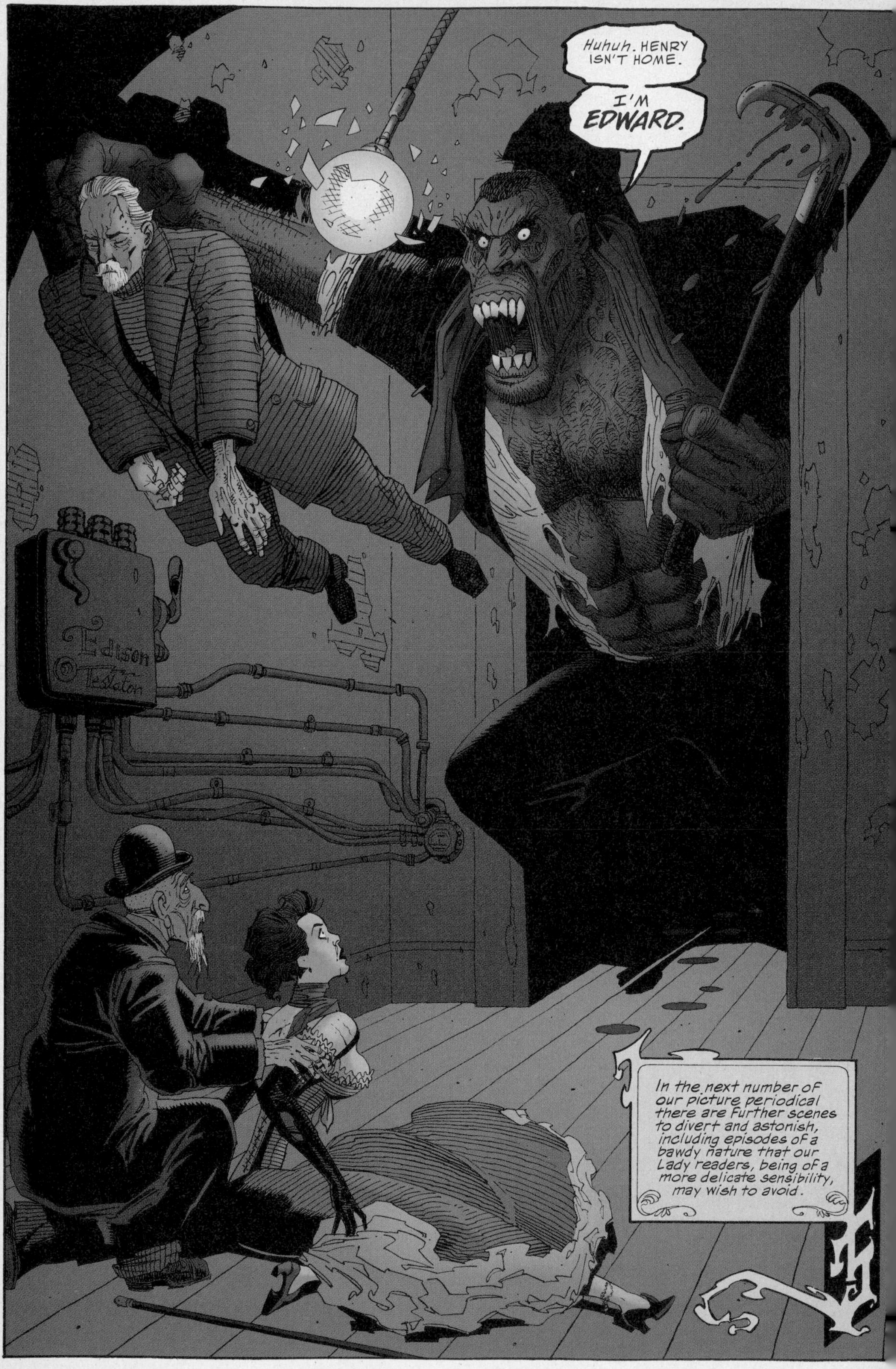
Huhuh. HENRY ISN'T HOME.
I'M EDWARD.
Edison Teslaton
In the next number of our picture periodical there are further scenes to divert and astonish, including episodes of a bawdy nature that our Lady readers, being of a more delicate sensibility, may wish to avoid.

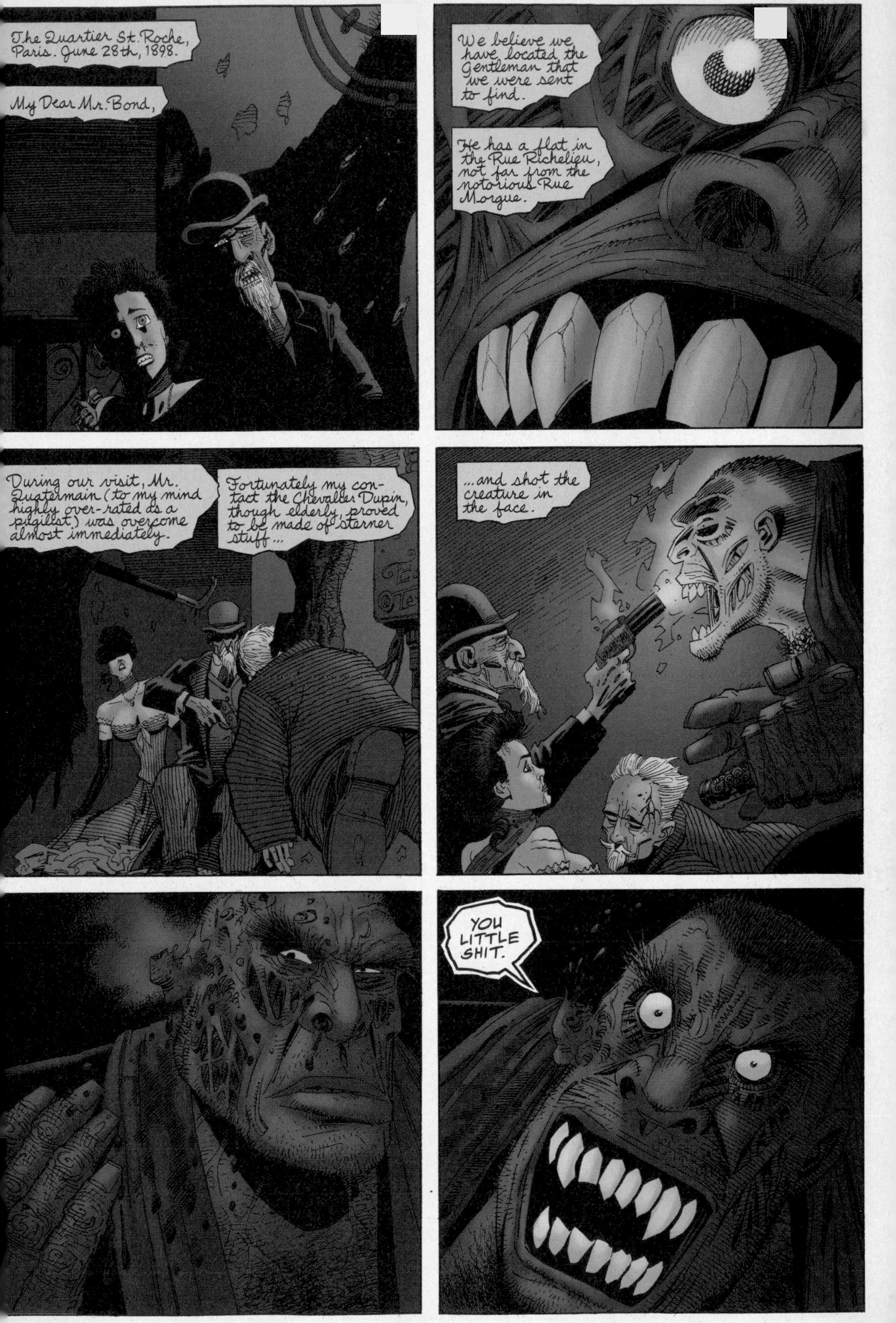
The Quartier St. Roche, Paris. June 28th, 1898.
My Dear Mr. Bond,
We believe we have located the Gentleman that we were sent to find.
He has a flat in the Rue Richelieu, not far from the notorious Rue Morgue.
During our visit, Mr. Quatermain (to my mind highly over-rated as a pugilist) was overcome almost immediately.
Fortunately my contact the Chevalier Dupin, though elderly, proved to be made of sterner stuff...
...and shot the creature in the face.
YOU LITTLE SHIT.

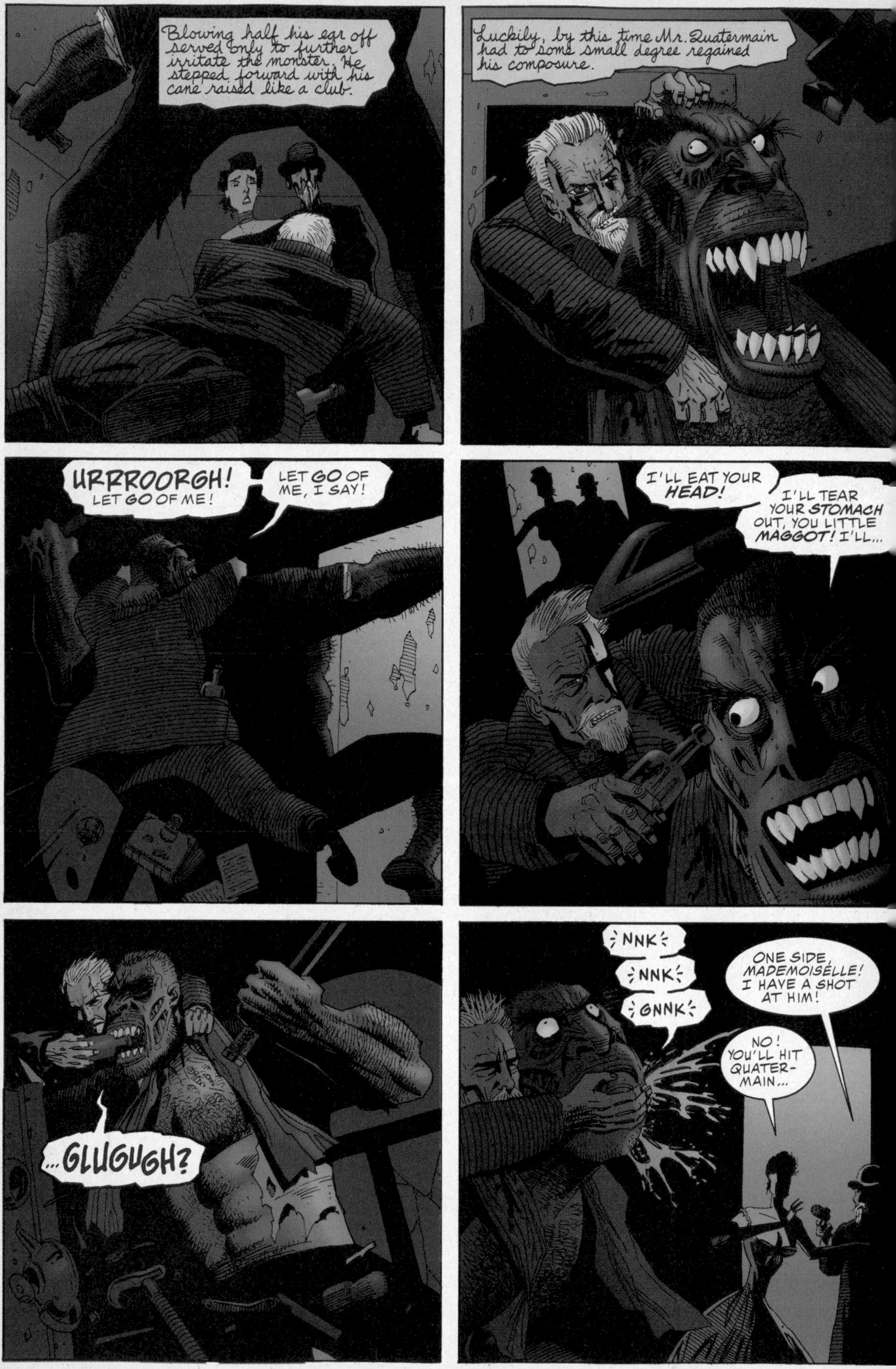
Blowing half his ear off served only to further irritate the monster. He stepped forward with his cane raised like a club.
Luckily, by this time Mr. Quatermain had to some small degree regained his composure.
URRROORGH! LET GO OF ME!
LET GO OF ME, I SAY!
I'LL EAT YOUR HEAD!
I'LL TEAR YOUR STOMACH OUT, YOU LITTLE MAGGOT! I'LL...
...GLUGUGH?
NNK
NNK
GNNK
ONE SIDE, MADEMOISELLE! I HAVE A SHOT AT HIM!
NO! YOU'LL HIT QUATER-MAIN...

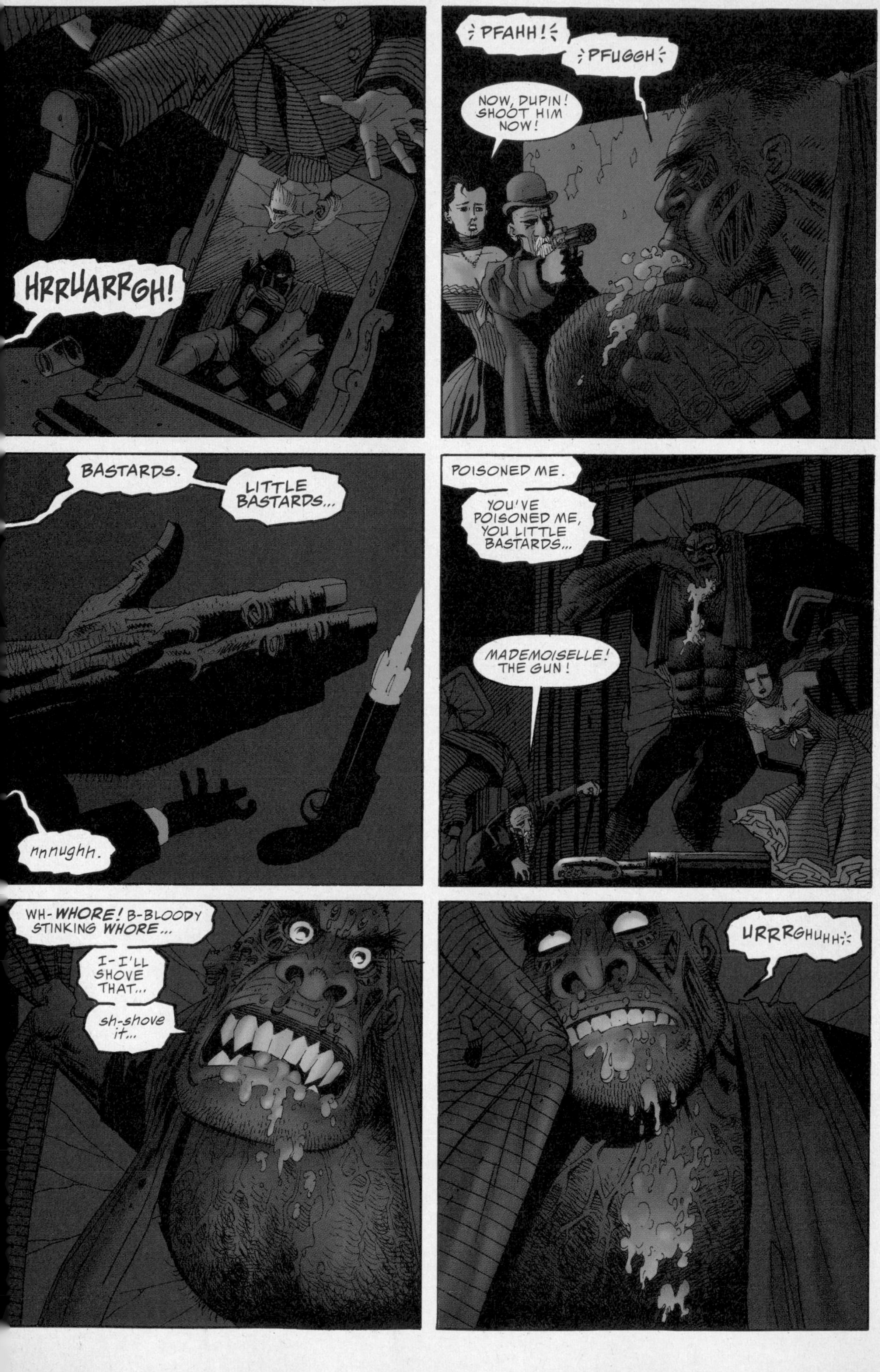
HRRUARRGH!
PFAHH!
PFUGGH
NOW, DUPIN! SHOOT HIM NOW!
BASTARDS.
LITTLE BASTARDS...
nnnughh.
POISONED ME.
YOU'VE POISONED ME, YOU LITTLE BASTARDS...
MADEMOISELLE! THE GUN!
WH-WHORE! B-BLOODY STINKING WHORE...
I-I'LL SHOVE THAT...
sh-shove it...
URRRGHUHH

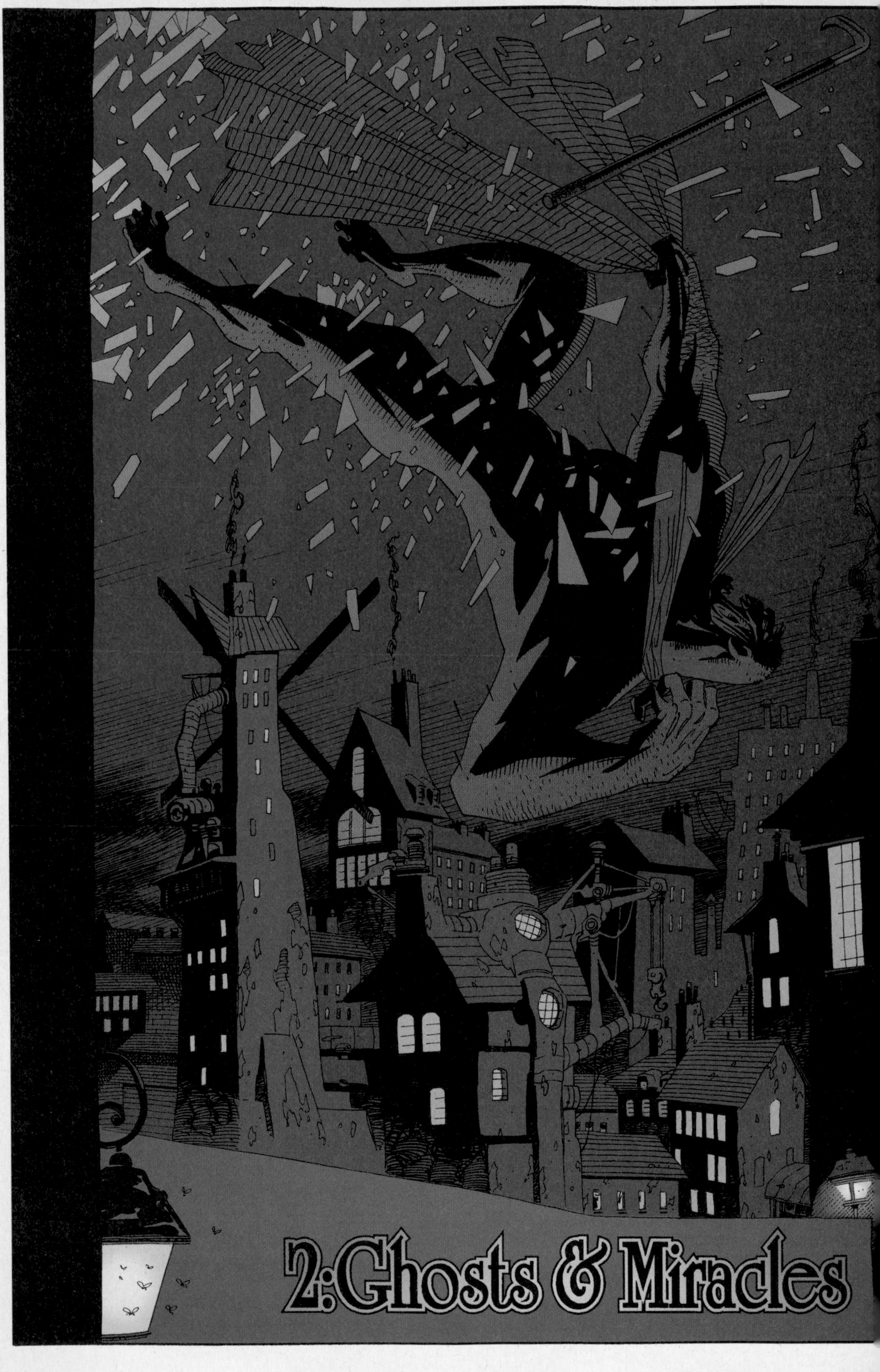
2:Ghosts & Miracles

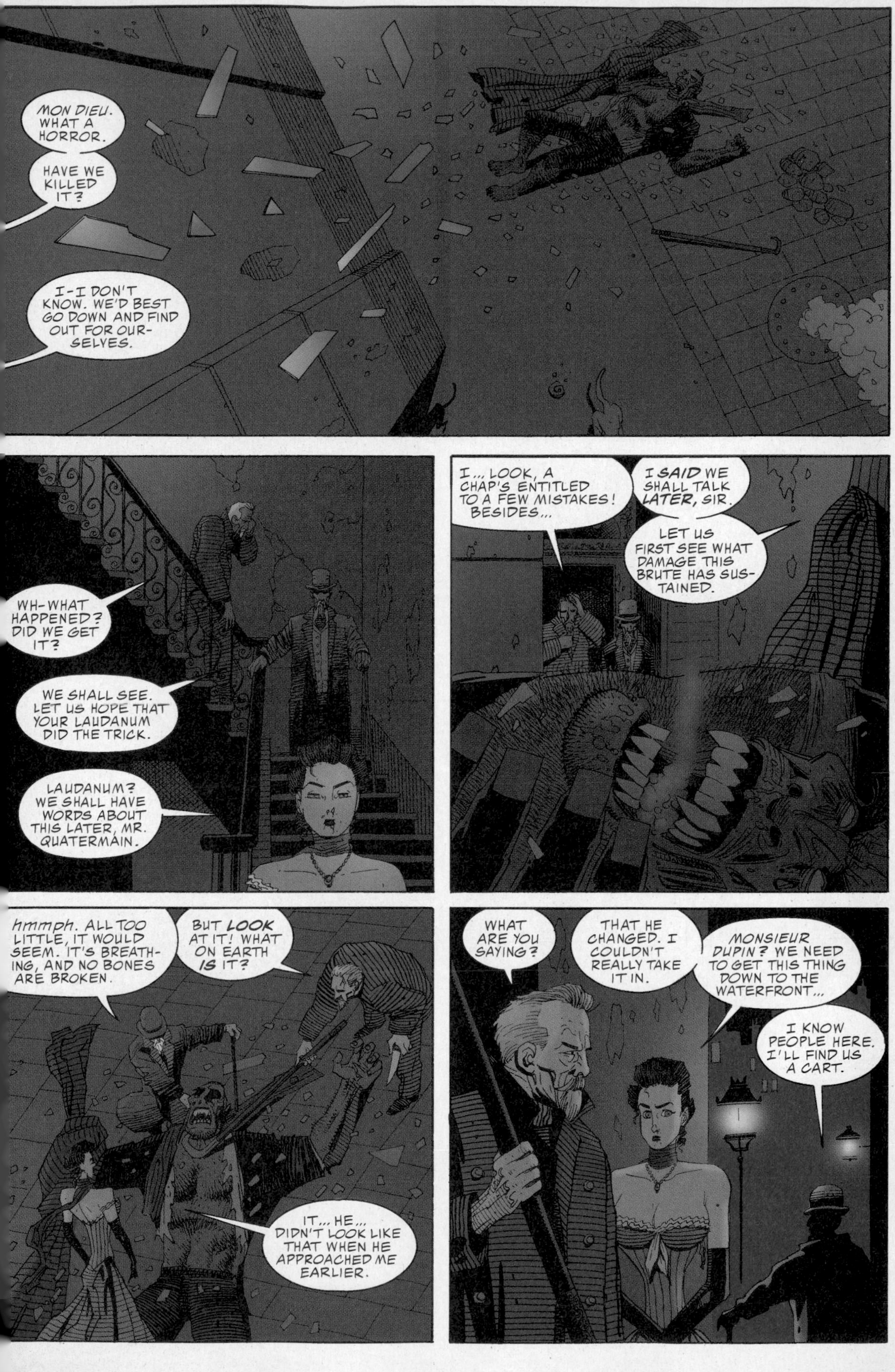
MON DIEU. WHAT A HORROR.
HAVE WE KILLED IT?
I-I DON'T KNOW. WE'D BEST GO DOWN AND FIND OUT FOR OURSELVES.
WH-WHAT HAPPENED? DID WE GET IT?
WE SHALL SEE. LET US HOPE THAT YOUR LAUDANUM DID THE TRICK.
LAUDANUM? WE SHALL HAVE WORDS ABOUT THIS LATER, MR. QUATERMAIN.
I... LOOK, A CHAP'S ENTITLED TO A FEW MISTAKES! BESIDES...
I *SAID* WE SHALL TALK *LATER*, SIR.
LET US FIRST SEE WHAT DAMAGE THIS BRUTE HAS SUSTAINED.
hmmph. ALL TOO LITTLE, IT WOULD SEEM. IT'S BREATHING, AND NO BONES ARE BROKEN.
BUT *LOOK* AT IT! WHAT ON EARTH *IS* IT?
IT... HE... DIDN'T LOOK LIKE THAT WHEN HE APPROACHED ME EARLIER.
WHAT ARE YOU SAYING?
THAT HE CHANGED. I COULDN'T REALLY TAKE IT IN.
MONSIEUR DUPIN? WE NEED TO GET THIS THING DOWN TO THE WATERFRONT...
I KNOW PEOPLE HERE. I'LL FIND US A CART.

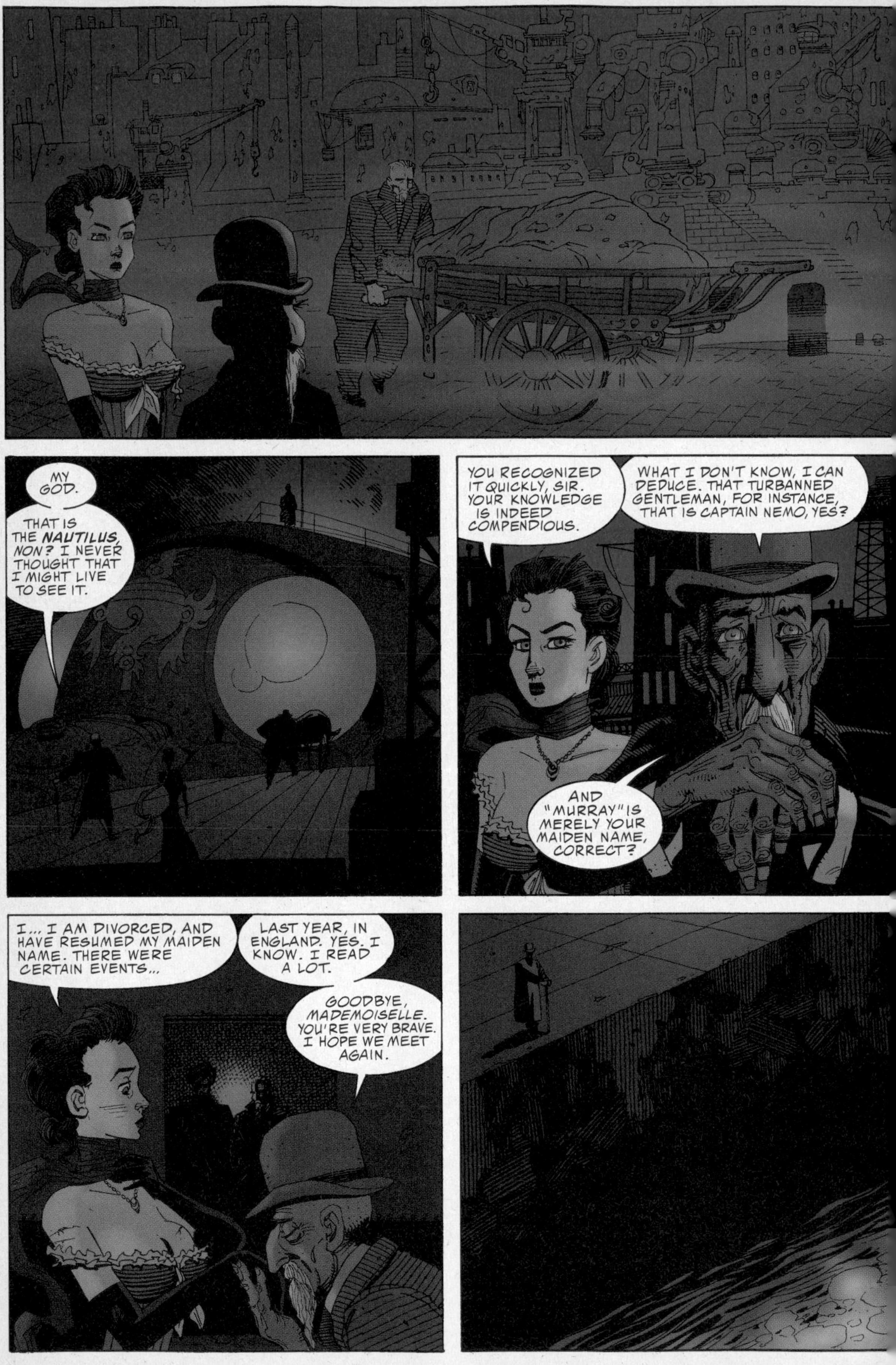
MY GOD.
THAT IS THE NAUTILUS, NON? I NEVER THOUGHT THAT I MIGHT LIVE TO SEE IT.
YOU RECOGNIZED IT QUICKLY, SIR. YOUR KNOWLEDGE IS INDEED COMPENDIOUS.
WHAT I DON'T KNOW, I CAN DEDUCE. THAT TURBANNED GENTLEMAN, FOR INSTANCE, THAT IS CAPTAIN NEMO, YES?
AND "MURRAY" IS MERELY YOUR MAIDEN NAME, CORRECT?
I... I AM DIVORCED, AND HAVE RESUMED MY MAIDEN NAME. THERE WERE CERTAIN EVENTS...
LAST YEAR, IN ENGLAND. YES. I KNOW. I READ A LOT.
GOODBYE, MADEMOISELLE. YOU'RE VERY BRAVE. I HOPE WE MEET AGAIN.

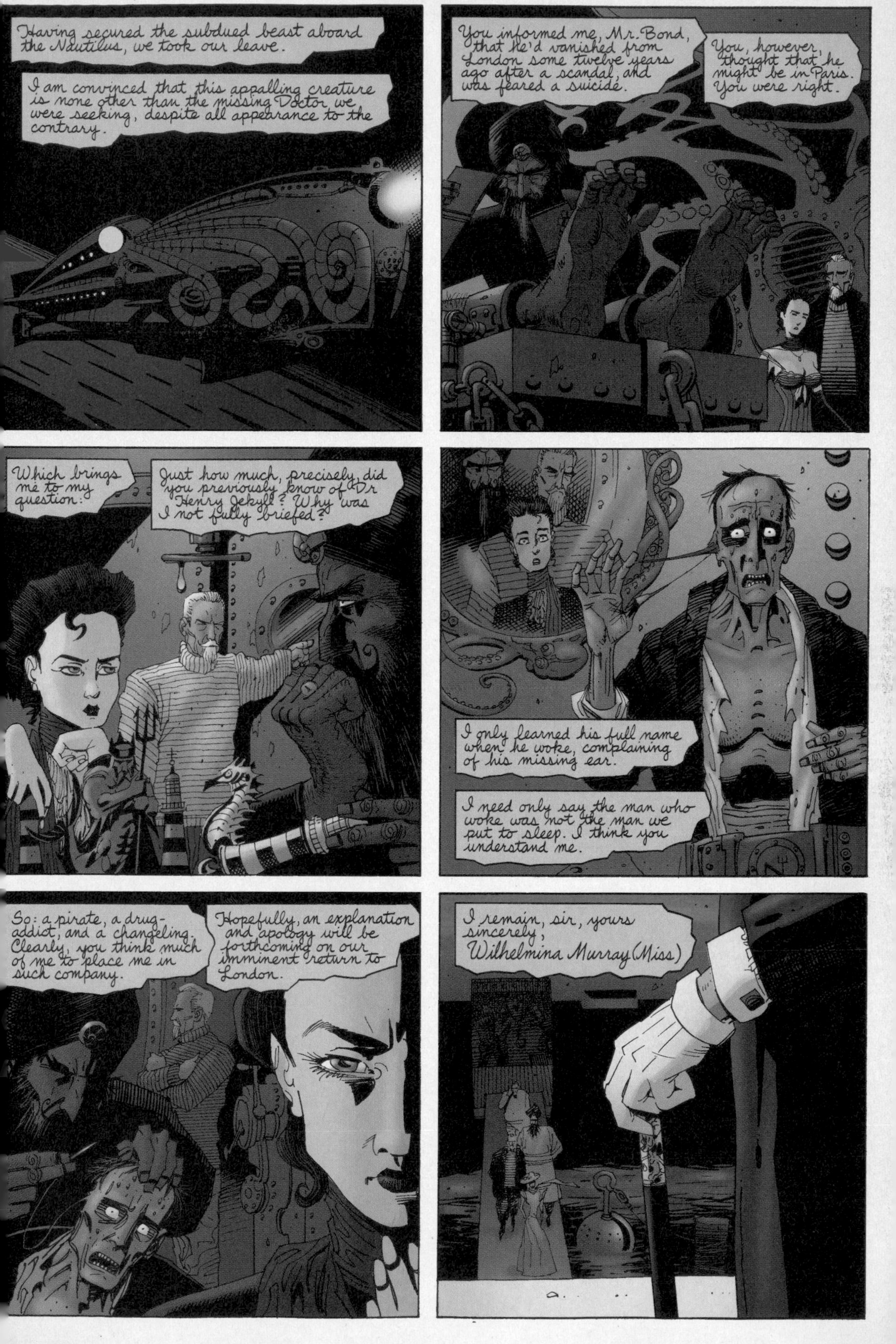
Having secured the subdued beast aboard the Nautilus, we took our leave.
I am convinced that this appalling creature is none other than the missing Doctor we were seeking, despite all appearance to the contrary.
You informed me, Mr. Bond, that he'd vanished from London some twelve years ago after a scandal, and was feared a suicide.
You, however, thought that he might be in Paris. You were right.
Which brings me to my question:
Just how much, precisely, did you previously know of Dr Henry Jekyll? Why was I not fully briefed?
I only learned his full name when he woke, complaining of his missing ear.
I need only say the man who woke was not the man we put to sleep. I think you understand me.
So: a pirate, a drug-addict, and a changeling. Clearly, you think much of me to place me in such company.
Hopefully, an explanation and apology will be forthcoming on our imminent return to London.
I remain, sir, yours sincerely,
Wilhelmina Murray (Miss)

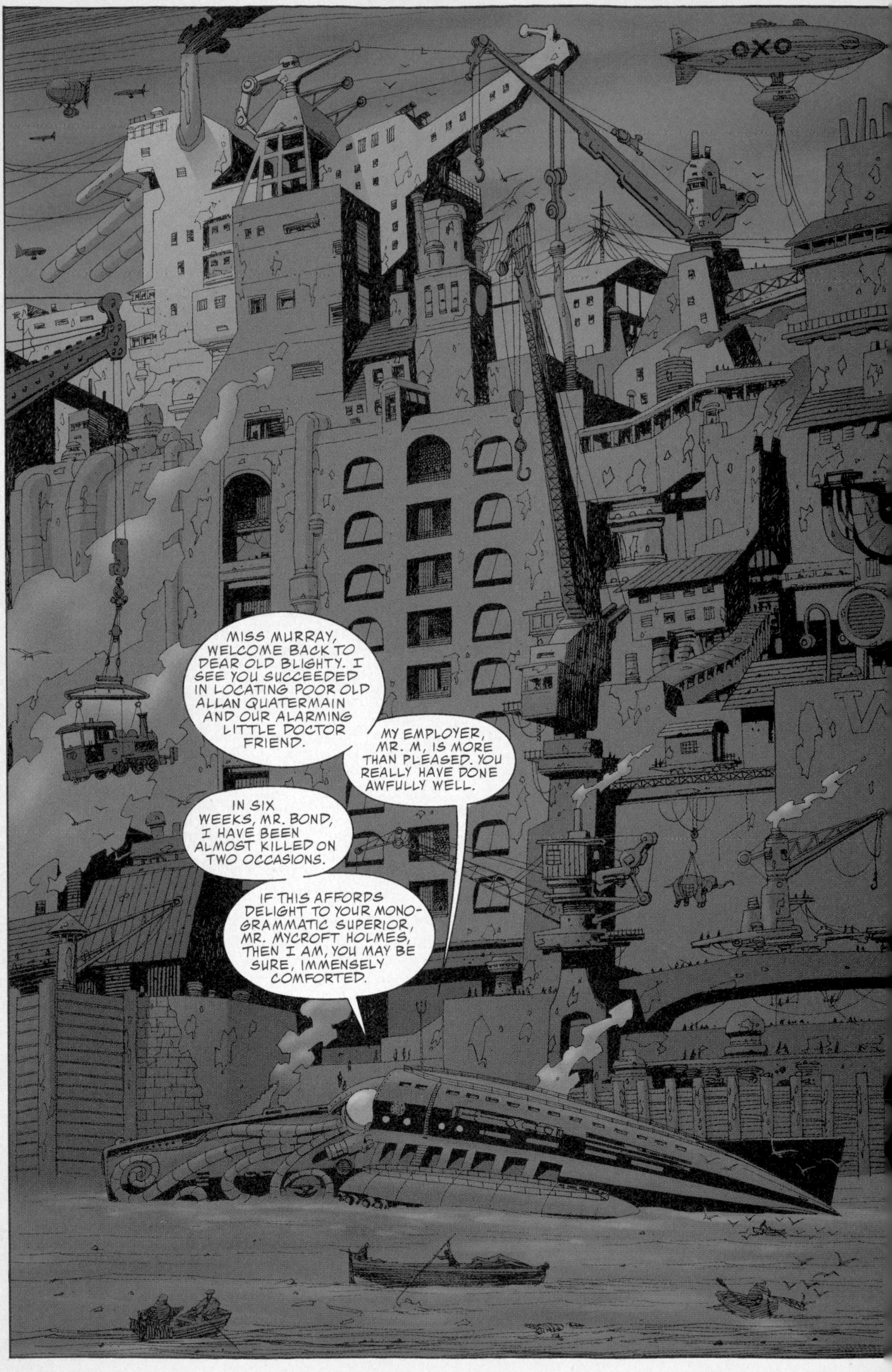
OXO
MISS MURRAY, WELCOME BACK TO DEAR OLD BLIGHTY. I SEE YOU SUCCEEDED IN LOCATING POOR OLD ALLAN QUATERMAIN AND OUR ALARMING LITTLE DOCTOR FRIEND.
MY EMPLOYER, MR. M, IS MORE THAN PLEASED. YOU REALLY HAVE DONE AWFULLY WELL.
IN SIX WEEKS, MR. BOND, I HAVE BEEN ALMOST KILLED ON TWO OCCASIONS.
IF THIS AFFORDS DELIGHT TO YOUR MONO-GRAMMATIC SUPERIOR, MR. MYCROFT HOLMES, THEN I AM, YOU MAY BE SURE, IMMENSELY COMFORTED.

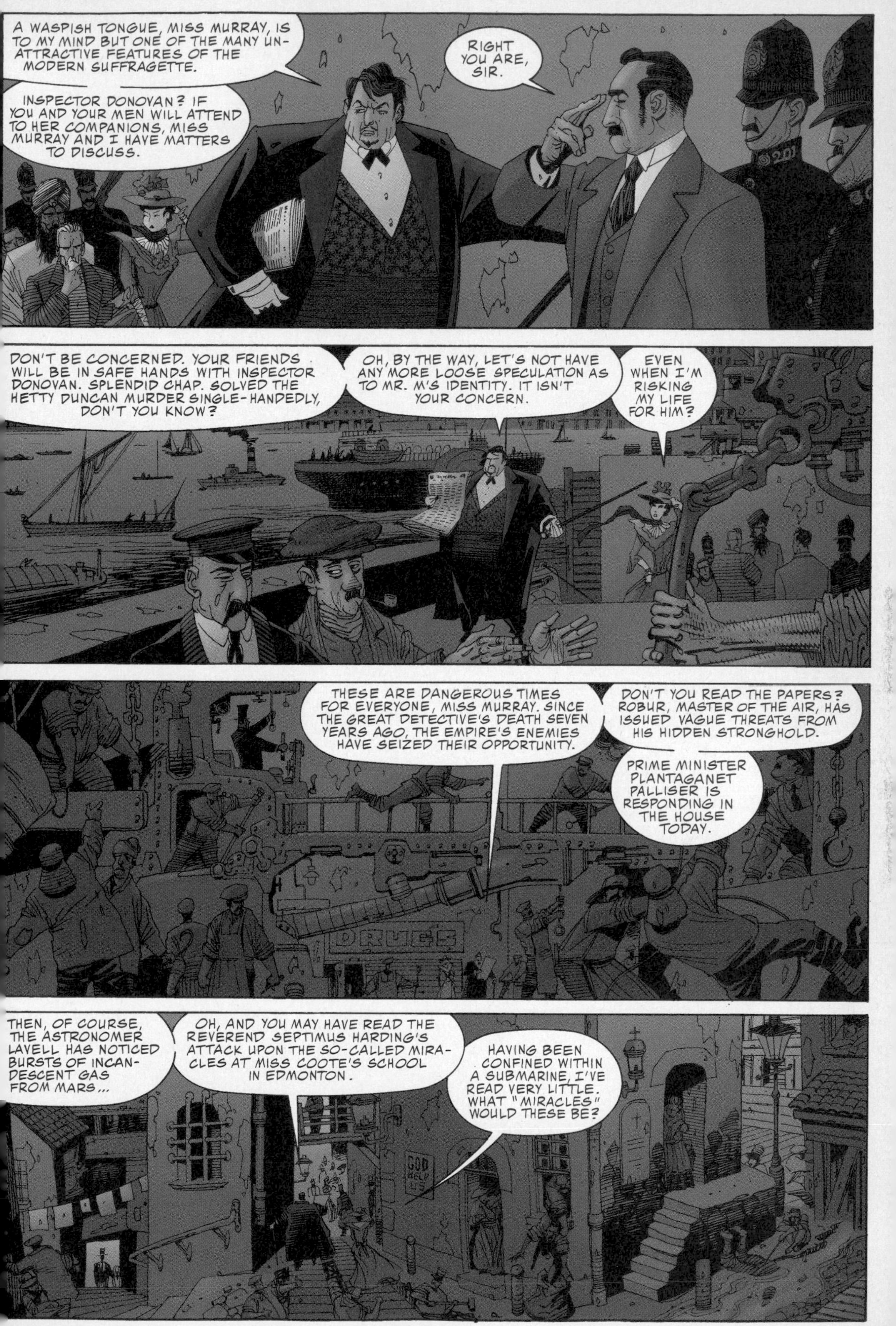
A WASPISH TONGUE, MISS MURRAY, IS TO MY MIND BUT ONE OF THE MANY UN-ATTRACTIVE FEATURES OF THE MODERN SUFFRAGETTE.
INSPECTOR DONOVAN? IF YOU AND YOUR MEN WILL ATTEND TO HER COMPANIONS, MISS MURRAY AND I HAVE MATTERS TO DISCUSS.
RIGHT YOU ARE, SIR.
DON'T BE CONCERNED. YOUR FRIENDS WILL BE IN SAFE HANDS WITH INSPECTOR DONOVAN. SPLENDID CHAP. SOLVED THE HETTY DUNCAN MURDER SINGLE-HANDEDLY, DON'T YOU KNOW?
OH, BY THE WAY, LET'S NOT HAVE ANY MORE LOOSE SPECULATION AS TO MR. M'S IDENTITY. IT ISN'T YOUR CONCERN.
EVEN WHEN I'M RISKING MY LIFE FOR HIM?
THESE ARE DANGEROUS TIMES FOR EVERYONE, MISS MURRAY. SINCE THE GREAT DETECTIVE'S DEATH SEVEN YEARS AGO, THE EMPIRE'S ENEMIES HAVE SEIZED THEIR OPPORTUNITY.
DON'T YOU READ THE PAPERS? ROBUR, MASTER OF THE AIR, HAS ISSUED VAGUE THREATS FROM HIS HIDDEN STRONGHOLD.
PRIME MINISTER PLANTAGANET PALLISER IS RESPONDING IN THE HOUSE TODAY.
DRUGS
THEN, OF COURSE, THE ASTRONOMER LAVELL HAS NOTICED BURSTS OF INCAN-DESCENT GAS FROM MARS...
OH, AND YOU MAY HAVE READ THE REVEREND SEPTIMUS HARDING'S ATTACK UPON THE SO-CALLED MIRA-CLES AT MISS COOTE'S SCHOOL IN EDMONTON.
HAVING BEEN CONFINED WITHIN A SUBMARINE, I'VE READ VERY LITTLE. WHAT "MIRACLES" WOULD THESE BE?
GOD HELP US

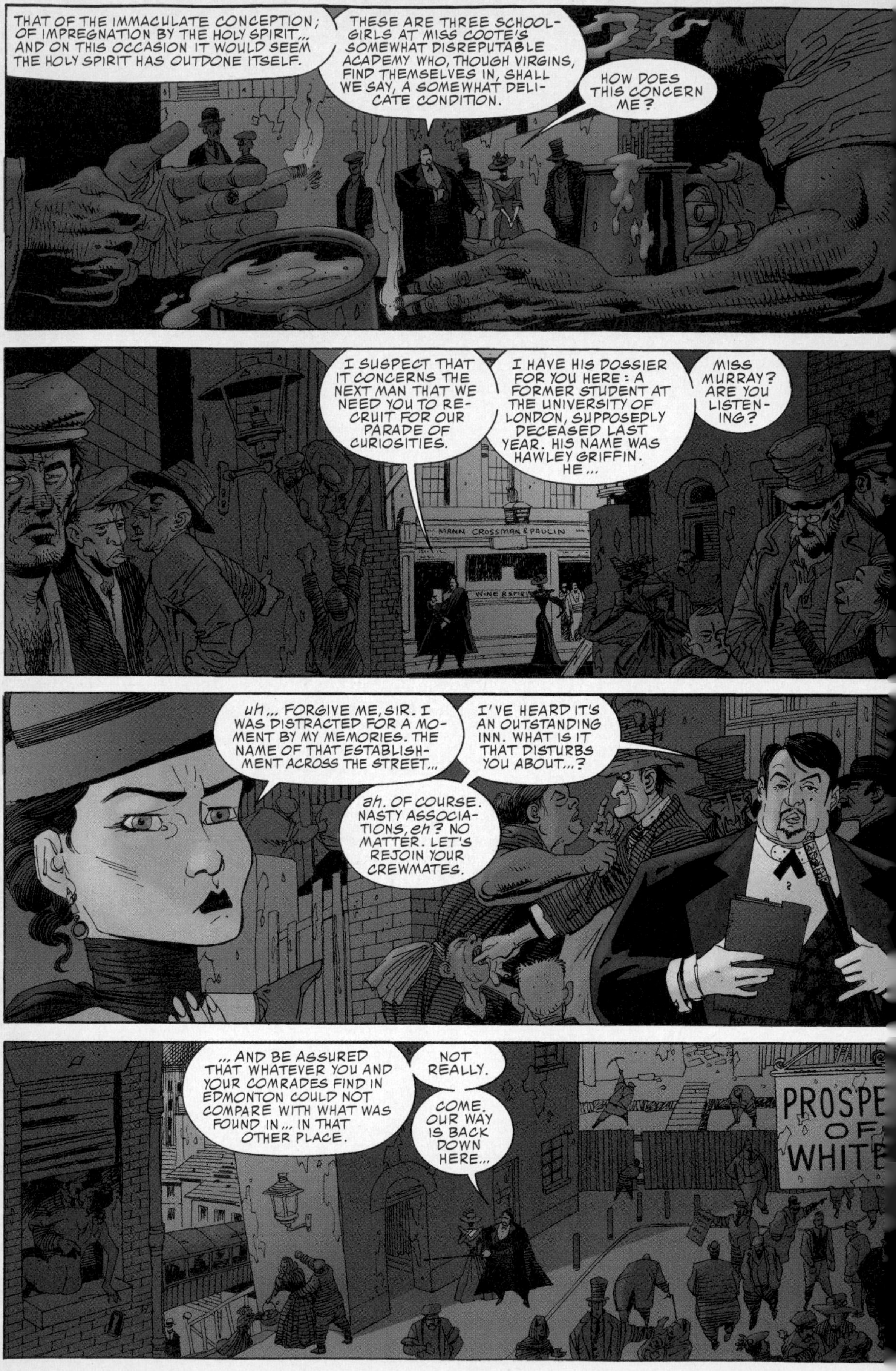
THAT OF THE IMMACULATE CONCEPTION; OF IMPREGNATION BY THE HOLY SPIRIT... AND ON THIS OCCASION IT WOULD SEEM THE HOLY SPIRIT HAS OUTDONE ITSELF.
THESE ARE THREE SCHOOL-GIRLS AT MISS COOTE'S SOMEWHAT DISREPUTABLE ACADEMY WHO, THOUGH VIRGINS, FIND THEMSELVES IN, SHALL WE SAY, A SOMEWHAT DELI-CATE CONDITION.
HOW DOES THIS CONCERN ME?
I SUSPECT THAT IT CONCERNS THE NEXT MAN THAT WE NEED YOU TO RE-CRUIT FOR OUR PARADE OF CURIOSITIES.
I HAVE HIS DOSSIER FOR YOU HERE: A FORMER STUDENT AT THE UNIVERSITY OF LONDON, SUPPOSEDLY DECEASED LAST YEAR. HIS NAME WAS HAWLEY GRIFFIN. HE...
MISS MURRAY? ARE YOU LISTEN-ING?
MANN CROSSMAN & PAULIN
WINE & SPIRITS
uh... FORGIVE ME, SIR. I WAS DISTRACTED FOR A MO-MENT BY MY MEMORIES. THE NAME OF THAT ESTABLISH-MENT ACROSS THE STREET...
I'VE HEARD IT'S AN OUTSTANDING INN. WHAT IS IT THAT DISTURBS YOU ABOUT...?
ah. OF COURSE. NASTY ASSOCIA-TIONS, eh? NO MATTER. LET'S REJOIN YOUR CREWMATES.
...AND BE ASSURED THAT WHATEVER YOU AND YOUR COMRADES FIND IN EDMONTON COULD NOT COMPARE WITH WHAT WAS FOUND IN... IN THAT OTHER PLACE.
NOT REALLY.
COME. OUR WAY IS BACK DOWN HERE...
PROSPE OF WHITE

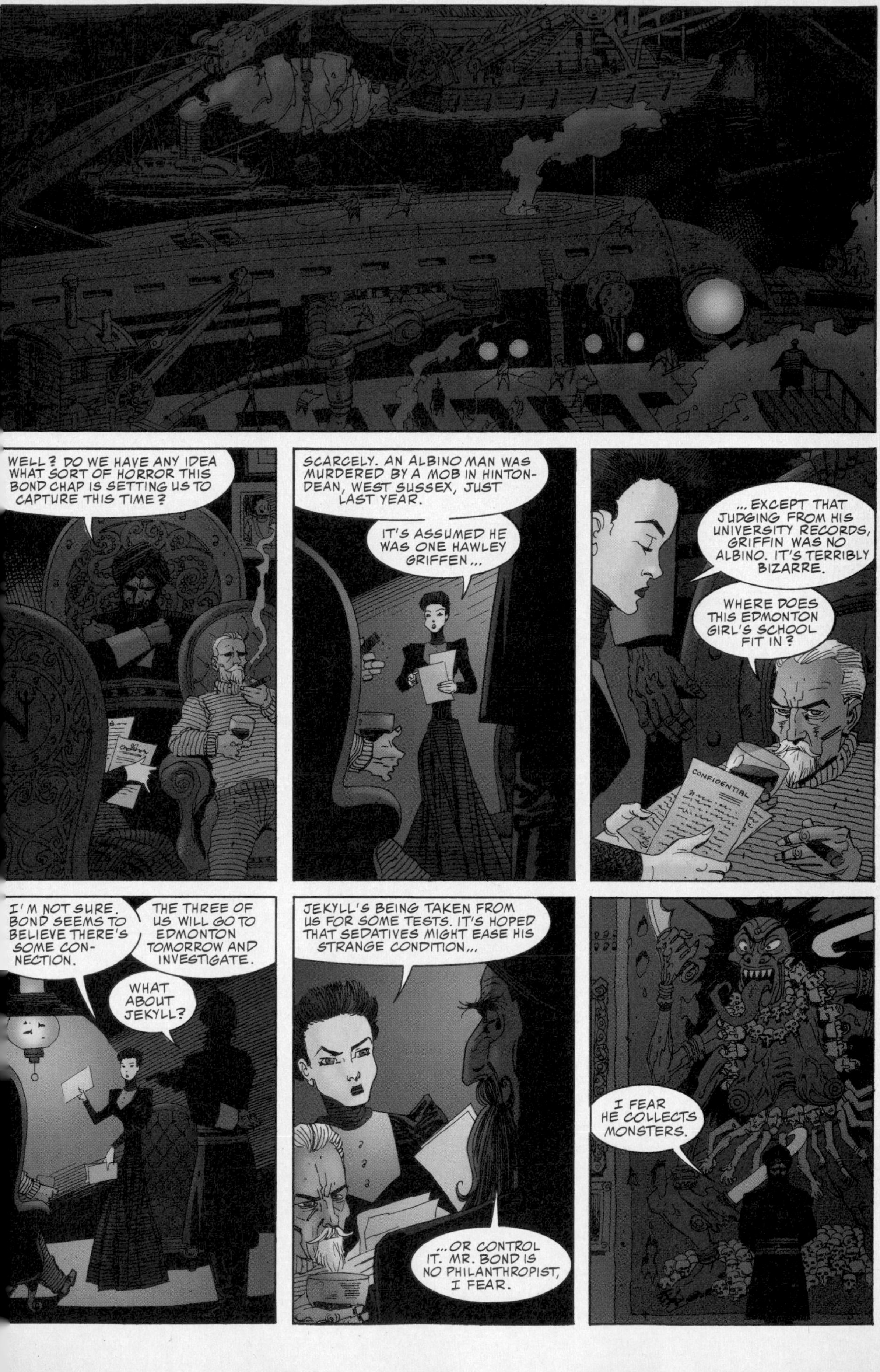
WELL? DO WE HAVE ANY IDEA WHAT SORT OF HORROR THIS BOND CHAP IS SETTING US TO CAPTURE THIS TIME?
SCARCELY. AN ALBINO MAN WAS MURDERED BY A MOB IN HINTON-DEAN, WEST SUSSEX, JUST LAST YEAR.
IT'S ASSUMED HE WAS ONE HAWLEY GRIFFEN...
...EXCEPT THAT JUDGING FROM HIS UNIVERSITY RECORDS, GRIFFIN WAS NO ALBINO. IT'S TERRIBLY BIZARRE.
WHERE DOES THIS EDMONTON GIRL'S SCHOOL FIT IN?
CONFIDENTIAL
I'M NOT SURE. BOND SEEMS TO BELIEVE THERE'S SOME CON-NECTION.
THE THREE OF US WILL GO TO EDMONTON TOMORROW AND INVESTIGATE.
WHAT ABOUT JEKYLL?
JEKYLL'S BEING TAKEN FROM US FOR SOME TESTS. IT'S HOPED THAT SEDATIVES MIGHT EASE HIS STRANGE CONDITION...
...OR CONTROL IT. MR. BOND IS NO PHILANTHROPIST, I FEAR.
I FEAR HE COLLECTS MONSTERS.

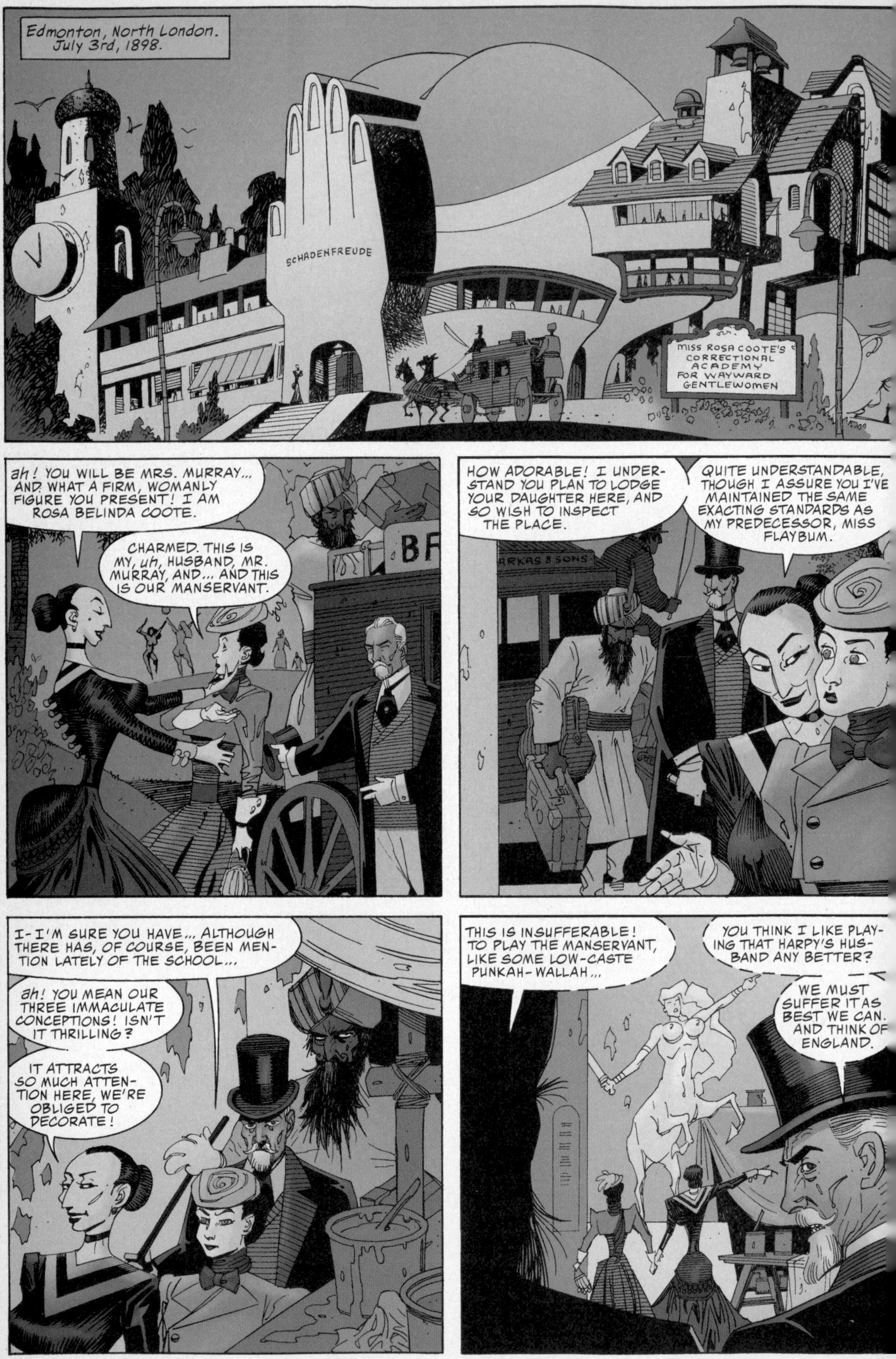
Edmonton, North London. July 3rd, 1898.
SCHADENFREUDE
MISS ROSA COOTE'S CORRECTIONAL ACADEMY FOR WAYWARD GENTLEWOMEN
ah! YOU WILL BE MRS. MURRAY... AND WHAT A FIRM, WOMANLY FIGURE YOU PRESENT! I AM ROSA BELINDA COOTE.
CHARMED. THIS IS MY, uh, HUSBAND, MR. MURRAY, AND... AND THIS IS OUR MANSERVANT.
HOW ADORABLE! I UNDERSTAND YOU PLAN TO LODGE YOUR DAUGHTER HERE, AND SO WISH TO INSPECT THE PLACE.
QUITE UNDERSTANDABLE, THOUGH I ASSURE YOU I'VE MAINTAINED THE SAME EXACTING STANDARDS AS MY PREDECESSOR, MISS FLAYBUM.
I- I'M SURE YOU HAVE... ALTHOUGH THERE HAS, OF COURSE, BEEN MENTION LATELY OF THE SCHOOL...
ah! YOU MEAN OUR THREE IMMACULATE CONCEPTIONS! ISN'T IT THRILLING?
IT ATTRACTS SO MUCH ATTENTION HERE, WE'RE OBLIGED TO DECORATE!
THIS IS INSUFFERABLE! TO PLAY THE MANSERVANT, LIKE SOME LOW-CASTE PUNKAH-WALLAH...
YOU THINK I LIKE PLAYING THAT HARPY'S HUSBAND ANY BETTER?
WE MUST SUFFER IT AS BEST WE CAN. AND THINK OF ENGLAND.

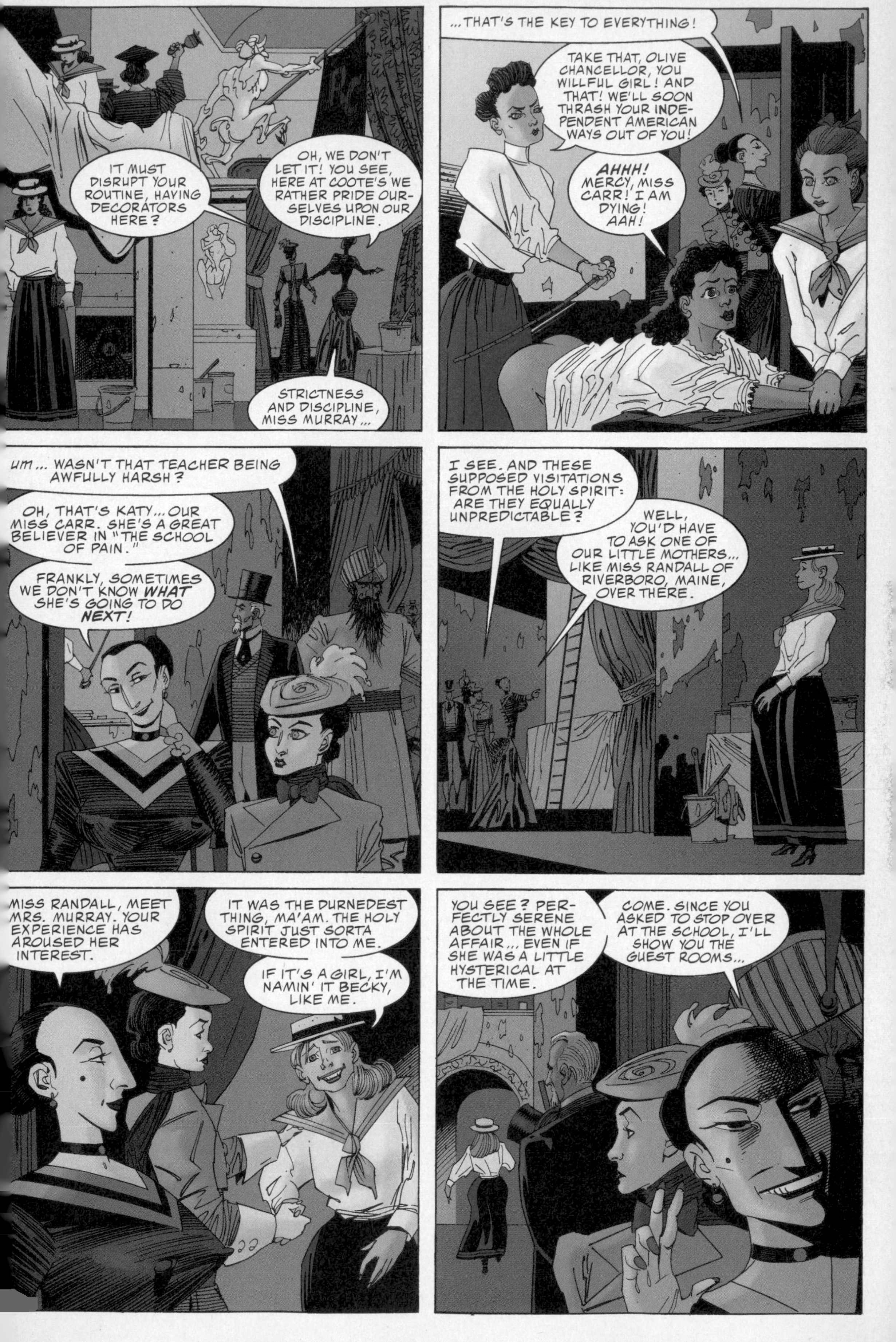
IT MUST DISRUPT YOUR ROUTINE, HAVING DECORATORS HERE?
OH, WE DON'T LET IT! YOU SEE, HERE AT COOTE'S WE RATHER PRIDE OURSELVES UPON OUR DISCIPLINE.
STRICTNESS AND DISCIPLINE, MISS MURRAY...
...THAT'S THE KEY TO EVERYTHING!
TAKE THAT, OLIVE CHANCELLOR, YOU WILLFUL GIRL! AND THAT! WE'LL SOON THRASH YOUR INDEPENDENT AMERICAN WAYS OUT OF YOU!
AHHH! MERCY, MISS CARR! I AM DYING! AAH!
UM... WASN'T THAT TEACHER BEING AWFULLY HARSH?
OH, THAT'S KATY... OUR MISS CARR. SHE'S A GREAT BELIEVER IN "THE SCHOOL OF PAIN."
FRANKLY, SOMETIMES WE DON'T KNOW WHAT SHE'S GOING TO DO NEXT!
I SEE. AND THESE SUPPOSED VISITATIONS FROM THE HOLY SPIRIT: ARE THEY EQUALLY UNPREDICTABLE?
WELL, YOU'D HAVE TO ASK ONE OF OUR LITTLE MOTHERS... LIKE MISS RANDALL OF RIVERBORO, MAINE, OVER THERE.
MISS RANDALL, MEET MRS. MURRAY. YOUR EXPERIENCE HAS AROUSED HER INTEREST.
IT WAS THE DURNEDEST THING, MA'AM. THE HOLY SPIRIT JUST SORTA ENTERED INTO ME.
IF IT'S A GIRL, I'M NAMIN' IT BECKY, LIKE ME.
YOU SEE? PERFECTLY SERENE ABOUT THE WHOLE AFFAIR... EVEN IF SHE WAS A LITTLE HYSTERICAL AT THE TIME.
COME. SINCE YOU ASKED TO STOP OVER AT THE SCHOOL, I'LL SHOW YOU THE GUEST ROOMS...

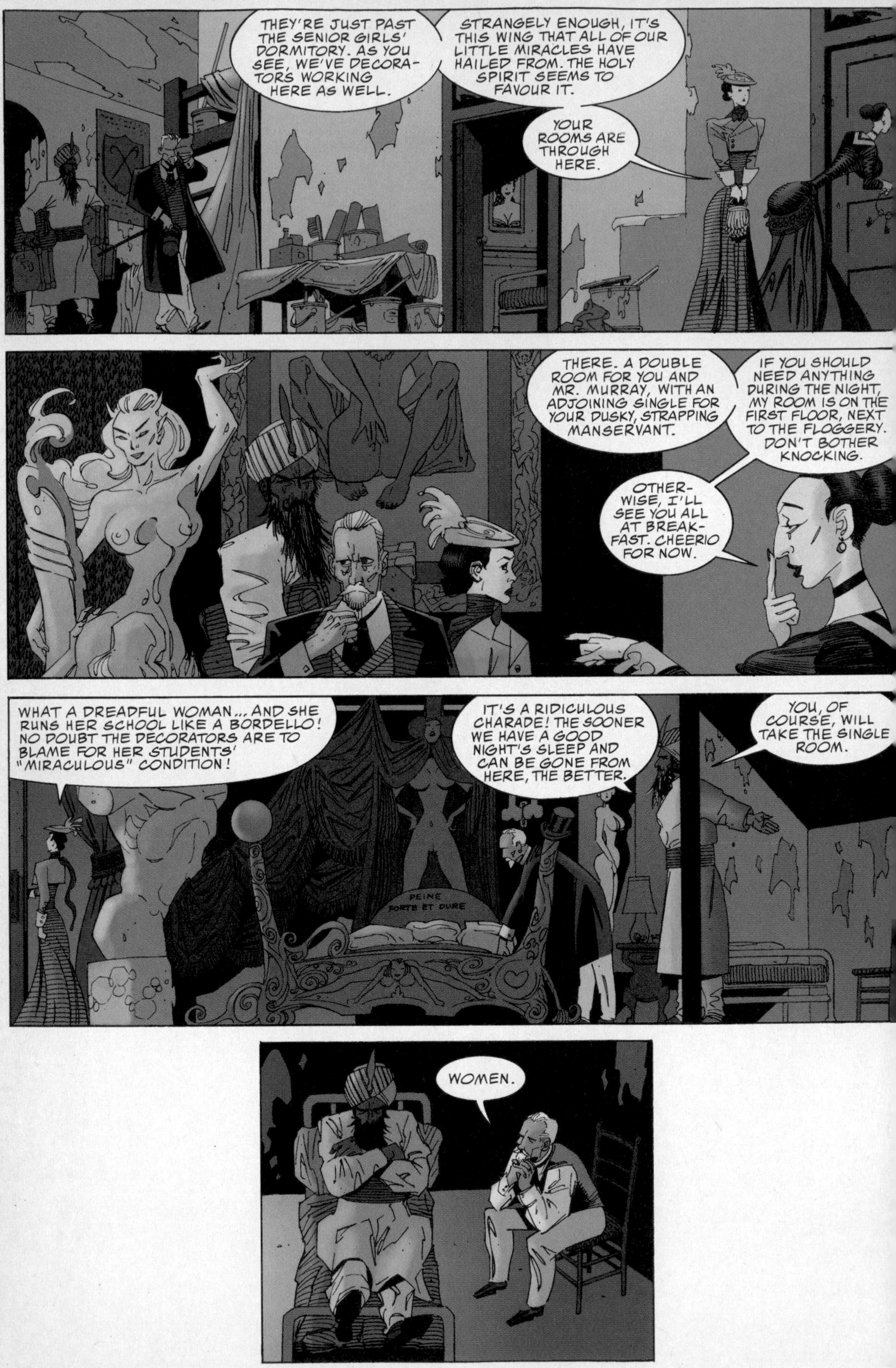
THEY'RE JUST PAST THE SENIOR GIRLS' DORMITORY. AS YOU SEE, WE'VE DECORATORS WORKING HERE AS WELL.
STRANGELY ENOUGH, IT'S THIS WING THAT ALL OF OUR LITTLE MIRACLES HAVE HAILED FROM. THE HOLY SPIRIT SEEMS TO FAVOUR IT.
YOUR ROOMS ARE THROUGH HERE.
THERE. A DOUBLE ROOM FOR YOU AND MR. MURRAY, WITH AN ADJOINING SINGLE FOR YOUR DUSKY, STRAPPING MANSERVANT.
IF YOU SHOULD NEED ANYTHING DURING THE NIGHT, MY ROOM IS ON THE FIRST FLOOR, NEXT TO THE FLOGGERY. DON'T BOTHER KNOCKING.
OTHERWISE, I'LL SEE YOU ALL AT BREAKFAST. CHEERIO FOR NOW.
WHAT A DREADFUL WOMAN... AND SHE RUNS HER SCHOOL LIKE A BORDELLO! NO DOUBT THE DECORATORS ARE TO BLAME FOR HER STUDENTS' "MIRACULOUS" CONDITION!
IT'S A RIDICULOUS CHARADE! THE SOONER WE HAVE A GOOD NIGHT'S SLEEP AND CAN BE GONE FROM HERE, THE BETTER.
YOU, OF COURSE, WILL TAKE THE SINGLE ROOM.
PEINE FORTE ET DURE
WOMEN.

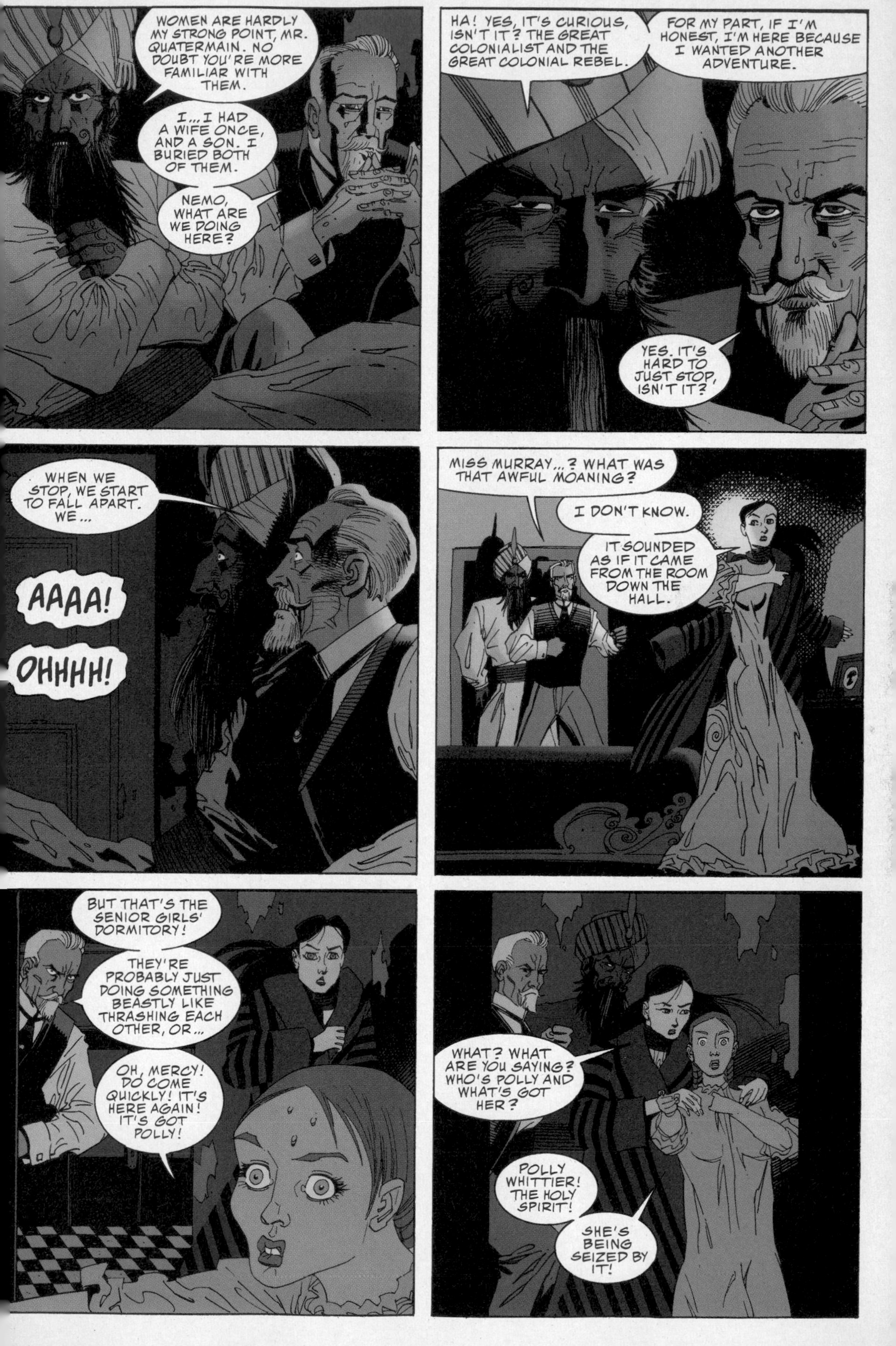
WOMEN ARE HARDLY MY STRONG POINT, MR. QUATERMAIN. NO DOUBT YOU'RE MORE FAMILIAR WITH THEM.
I... I HAD A WIFE ONCE, AND A SON. I BURIED BOTH OF THEM.
NEMO, WHAT ARE WE DOING HERE?
HA! YES, IT'S CURIOUS, ISN'T IT? THE GREAT COLONIALIST AND THE GREAT COLONIAL REBEL.
FOR MY PART, IF I'M HONEST, I'M HERE BECAUSE I WANTED ANOTHER ADVENTURE.
YES. IT'S HARD TO JUST STOP, ISN'T IT?
WHEN WE STOP, WE START TO FALL APART. WE...
AAAA!
OHHHH!
MISS MURRAY...? WHAT WAS THAT AWFUL MOANING?
I DON'T KNOW.
IT SOUNDED AS IF IT CAME FROM THE ROOM DOWN THE HALL.
BUT THAT'S THE SENIOR GIRLS' DORMITORY!
THEY'RE PROBABLY JUST DOING SOMETHING BEASTLY LIKE THRASHING EACH OTHER, OR...
OH, MERCY! DO COME QUICKLY! IT'S HERE AGAIN! IT'S GOT POLLY!
WHAT? WHAT ARE YOU SAYING? WHO'S POLLY AND WHAT'S GOT HER?
POLLY WHITTIER! THE HOLY SPIRIT!
SHE'S BEING SEIZED BY IT!

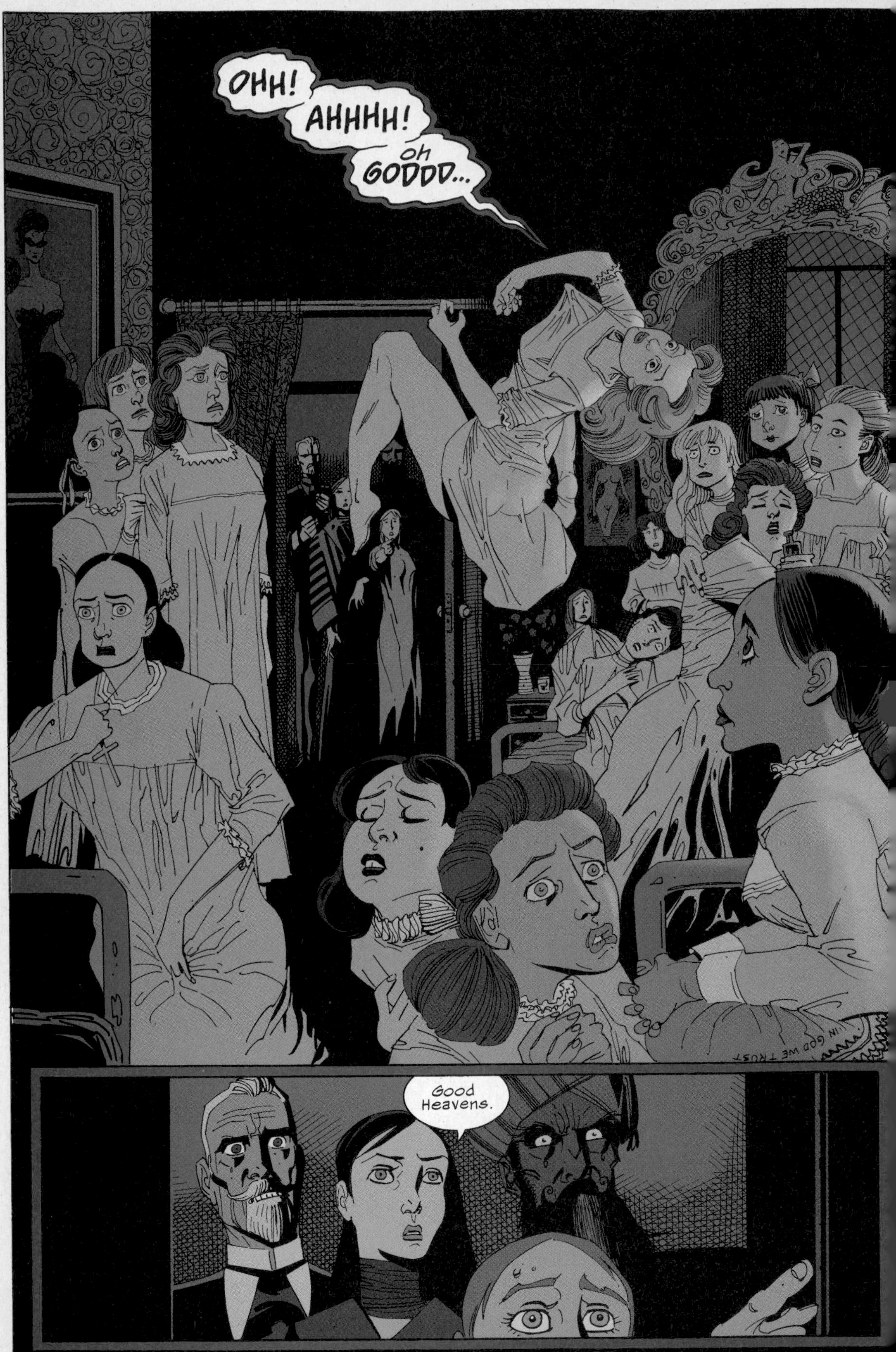
OHH!
AHHHH!
oh GODDD...
IN GOD WE TRUST
Good Heavens.

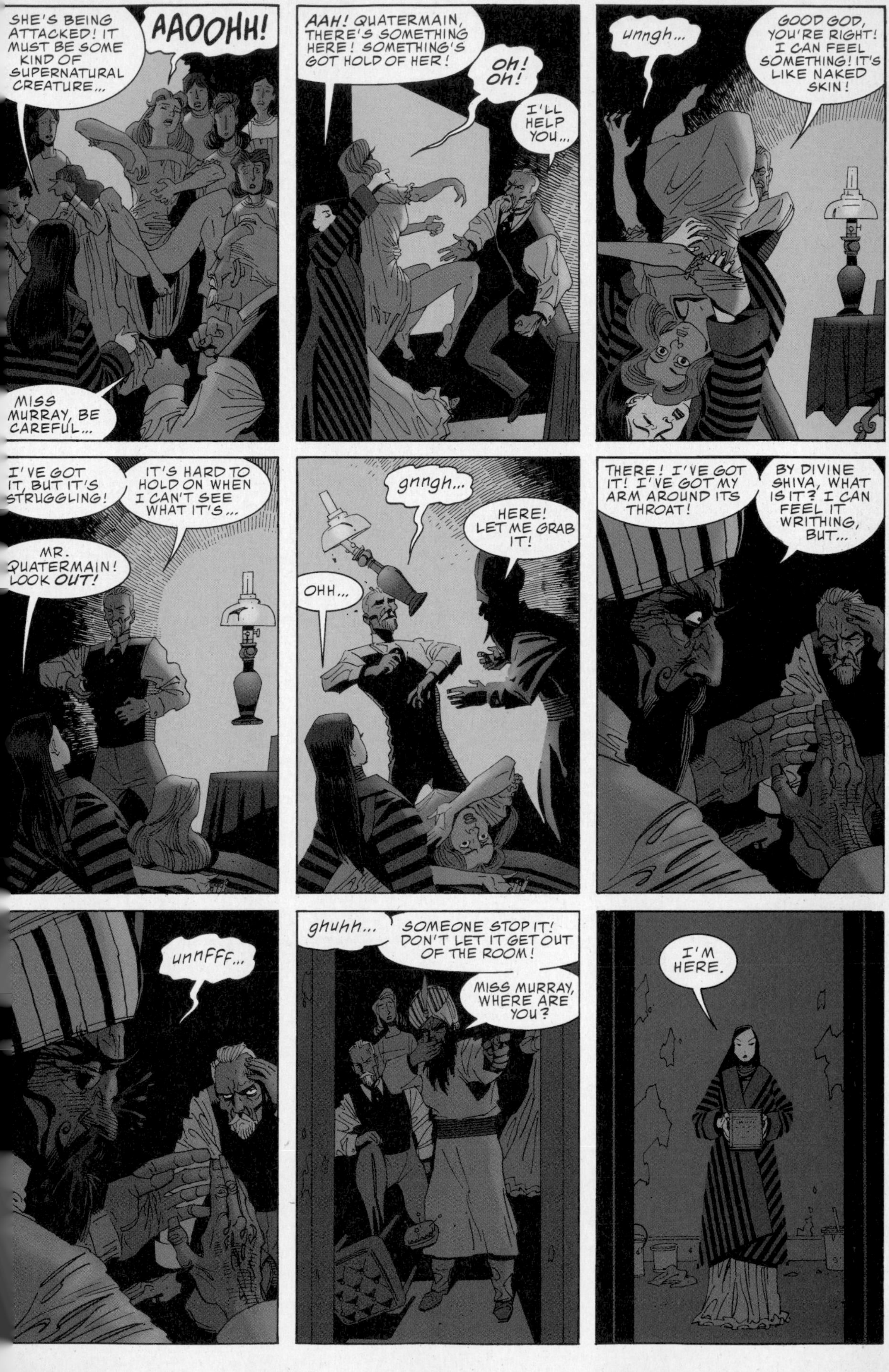
SHE'S BEING ATTACKED! IT MUST BE SOME KIND OF SUPERNATURAL CREATURE...
AAOOHH!
MISS MURRAY, BE CAREFUL...
AAH! QUATERMAIN, THERE'S SOMETHING HERE! SOMETHING'S GOT HOLD OF HER!
oh! oh!
I'LL HELP YOU...
unngh...
GOOD GOD, YOU'RE RIGHT! I CAN FEEL SOMETHING! IT'S LIKE NAKED SKIN!
I'VE GOT IT, BUT IT'S STRUGGLING!
IT'S HARD TO HOLD ON WHEN I CAN'T SEE WHAT IT'S...
MR. QUATERMAIN! LOOK OUT!
gnngh...
HERE! LET ME GRAB IT!
OHH...
THERE! I'VE GOT IT! I'VE GOT MY ARM AROUND ITS THROAT!
BY DIVINE SHIVA, WHAT IS IT? I CAN FEEL IT WRITHING, BUT...
unnFFF...
ghuhh...
SOMEONE STOP IT! DON'T LET IT GET OUT OF THE ROOM!
MISS MURRAY, WHERE ARE YOU?
I'M HERE.

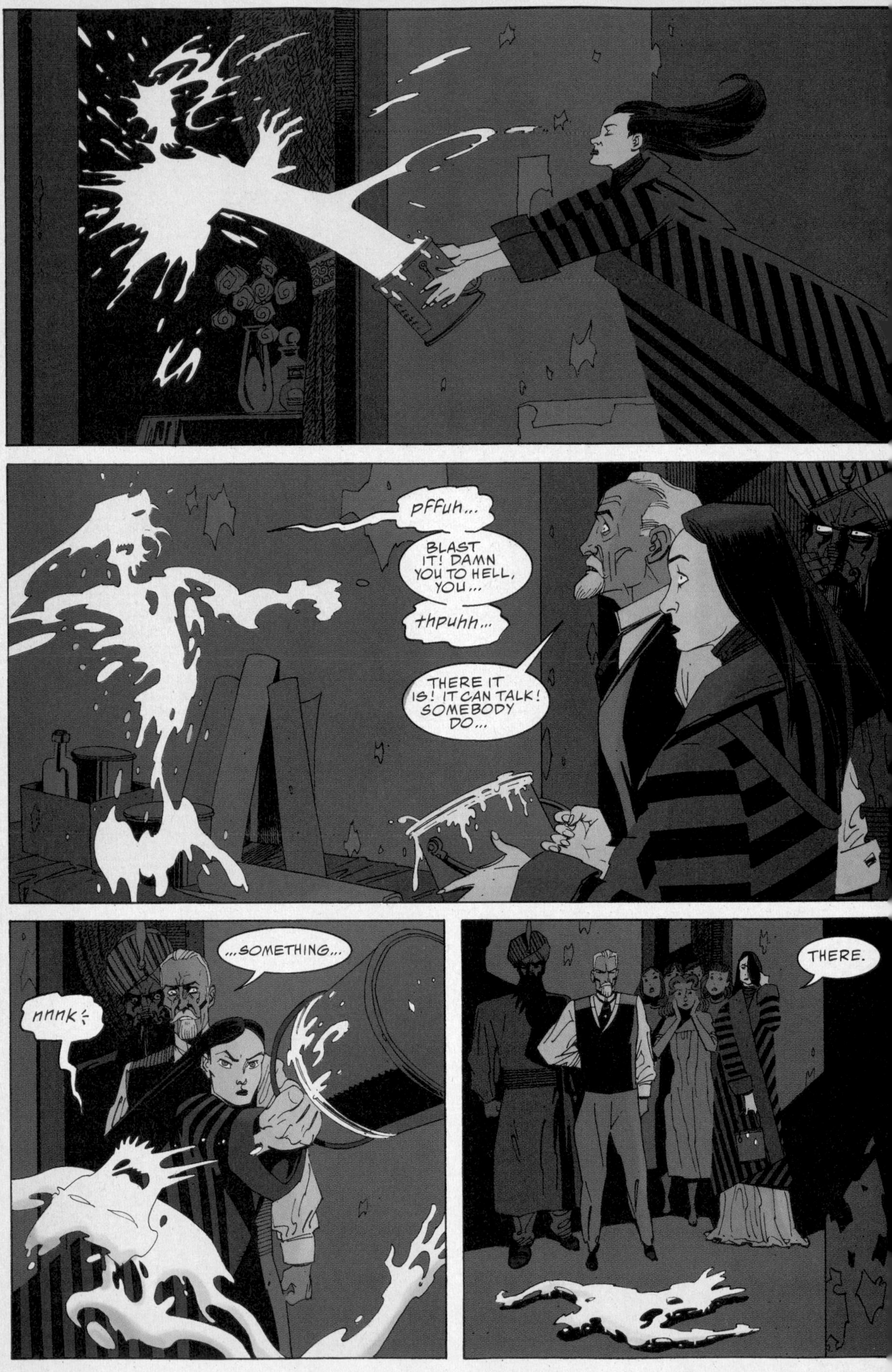
pffuh...
BLAST IT! DAMN YOU TO HELL, YOU...
thpuhh...
THERE IT IS! IT CAN TALK! SOMEBODY DO...
...SOMETHING...
nnnk
THERE.

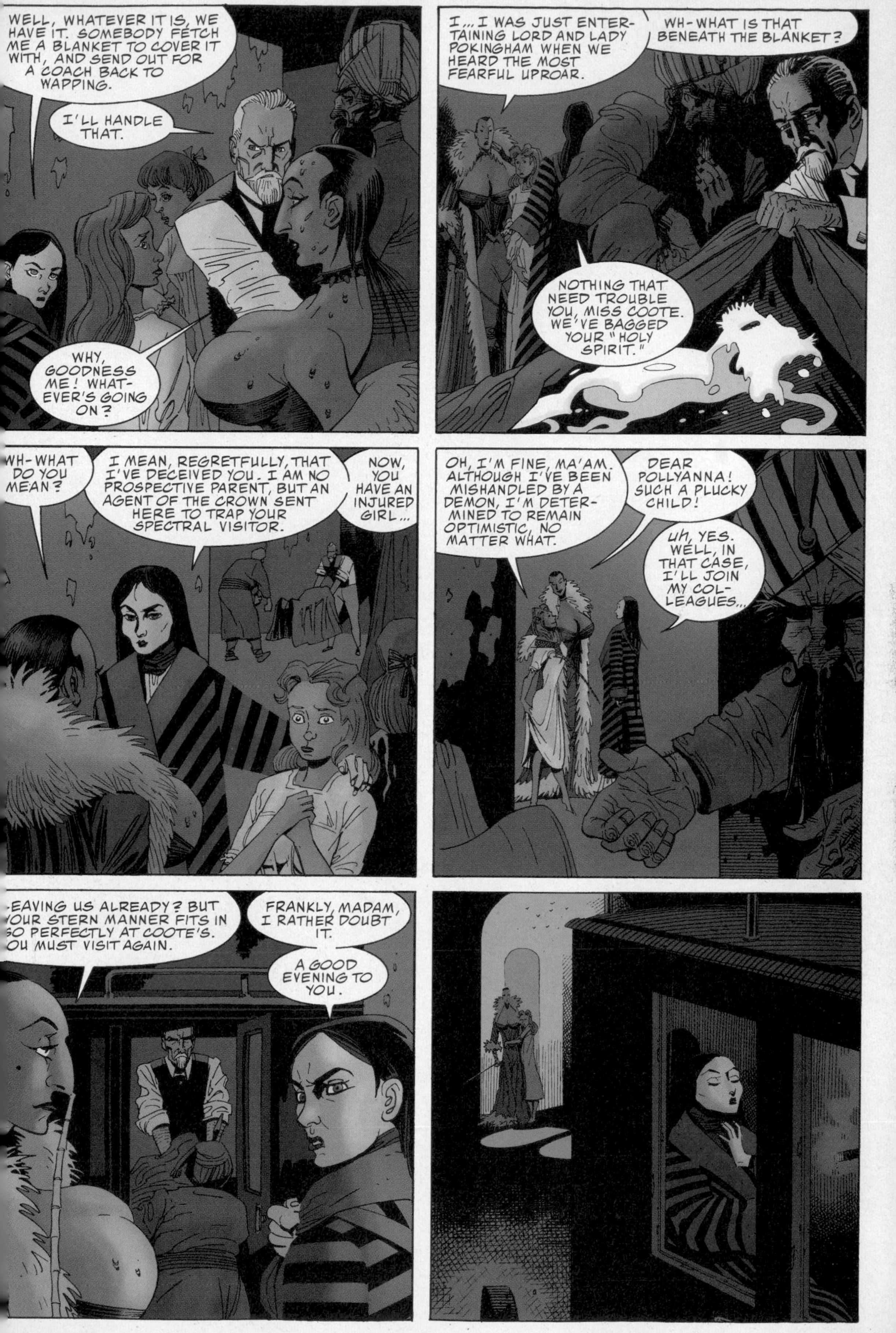
WELL, WHATEVER IT IS, WE HAVE IT. SOMEBODY FETCH ME A BLANKET TO COVER IT WITH, AND SEND OUT FOR A COACH BACK TO WAPPING.
I'LL HANDLE THAT.
WHY, GOODNESS ME! WHAT-EVER'S GOING ON?
I... I WAS JUST ENTER-TAINING LORD AND LADY POKINGHAM WHEN WE HEARD THE MOST FEARFUL UPROAR.
WH-WHAT IS THAT BENEATH THE BLANKET?
NOTHING THAT NEED TROUBLE YOU, MISS COOTE. WE'VE BAGGED YOUR "HOLY SPIRIT."
WH-WHAT DO YOU MEAN?
I MEAN, REGRETFULLY, THAT I'VE DECEIVED YOU. I AM NO PROSPECTIVE PARENT, BUT AN AGENT OF THE CROWN SENT HERE TO TRAP YOUR SPECTRAL VISITOR.
NOW, YOU HAVE AN INJURED GIRL...
OH, I'M FINE, MA'AM. ALTHOUGH I'VE BEEN MISHANDLED BY A DEMON, I'M DETER-MINED TO REMAIN OPTIMISTIC, NO MATTER WHAT.
DEAR POLLYANNA! SUCH A PLUCKY CHILD!
UH, YES. WELL, IN THAT CASE, I'LL JOIN MY COL-LEAGUES...
-EAVING US ALREADY? BUT YOUR STERN MANNER FITS IN SO PERFECTLY AT COOTE'S. YOU MUST VISIT AGAIN.
FRANKLY, MADAM, I RATHER DOUBT IT.
A GOOD EVENING TO YOU.

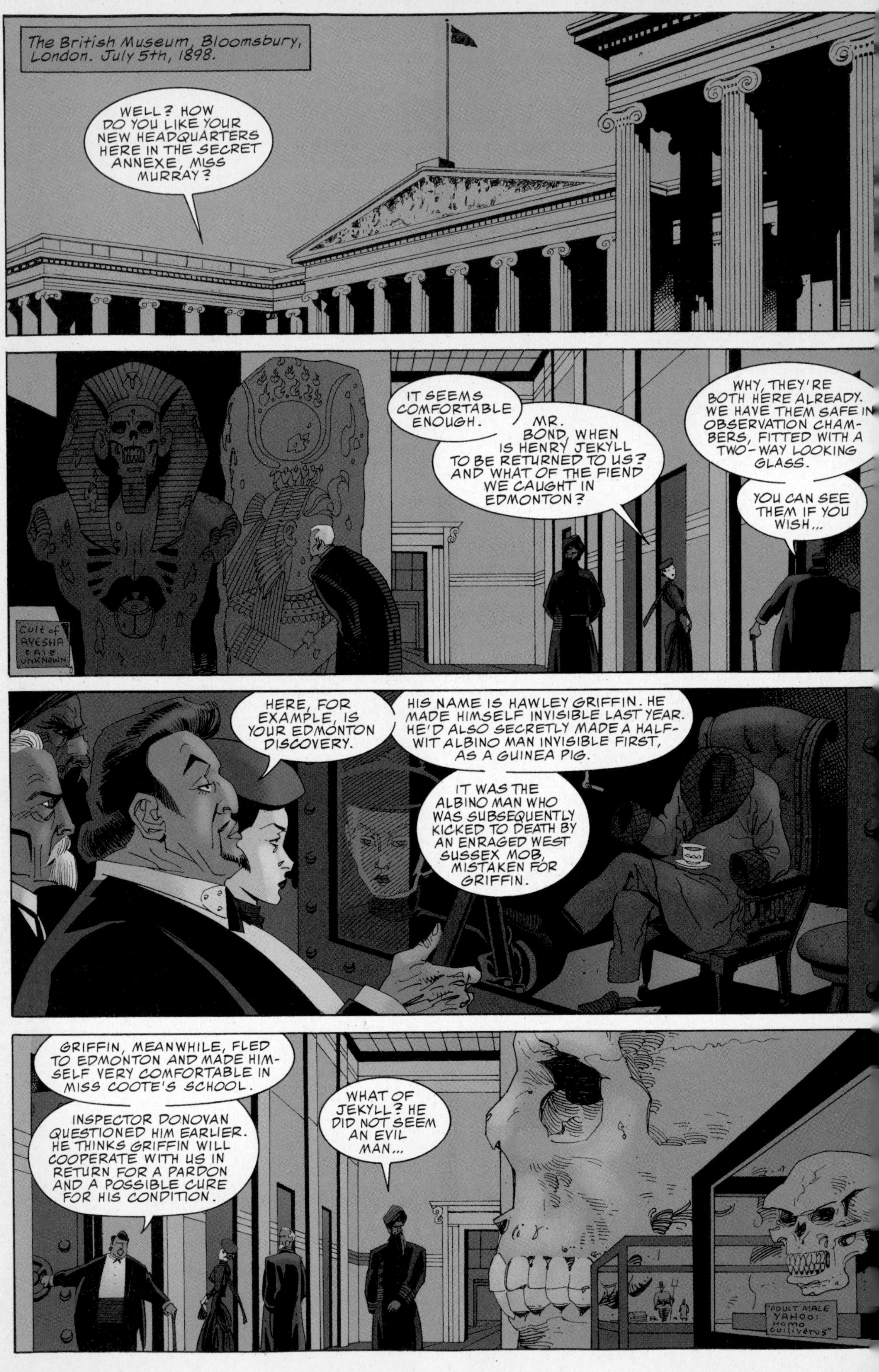
The British Museum, Bloomsbury, London. July 5th, 1898.
WELL? HOW DO YOU LIKE YOUR NEW HEADQUARTERS HERE IN THE SECRET ANNEXE, MISS MURRAY?
CULT of AYESHA DATE UNKNOWN
IT SEEMS COMFORTABLE ENOUGH.
MR. BOND, WHEN IS HENRY JEKYLL TO BE RETURNED TO US? AND WHAT OF THE FIEND WE CAUGHT IN EDMONTON?
WHY, THEY'RE BOTH HERE ALREADY. WE HAVE THEM SAFE IN OBSERVATION CHAMBERS, FITTED WITH A TWO-WAY LOOKING GLASS.
YOU CAN SEE THEM IF YOU WISH...
HERE, FOR EXAMPLE, IS YOUR EDMONTON DISCOVERY.
HIS NAME IS HAWLEY GRIFFIN. HE MADE HIMSELF INVISIBLE LAST YEAR. HE'D ALSO SECRETLY MADE A HALF-WIT ALBINO MAN INVISIBLE FIRST, AS A GUINEA PIG.
IT WAS THE ALBINO MAN WHO WAS SUBSEQUENTLY KICKED TO DEATH BY AN ENRAGED WEST SUSSEX MOB, MISTAKEN FOR GRIFFIN.
GRIFFIN, MEANWHILE, FLED TO EDMONTON AND MADE HIMSELF VERY COMFORTABLE IN MISS COOTE'S SCHOOL.
INSPECTOR DONOVAN QUESTIONED HIM EARLIER. HE THINKS GRIFFIN WILL COOPERATE WITH US IN RETURN FOR A PARDON AND A POSSIBLE CURE FOR HIS CONDITION.
WHAT OF JEKYLL? HE DID NOT SEEM AN EVIL MAN...
"ADULT MALE YAHOO: Homo Gulliverus"

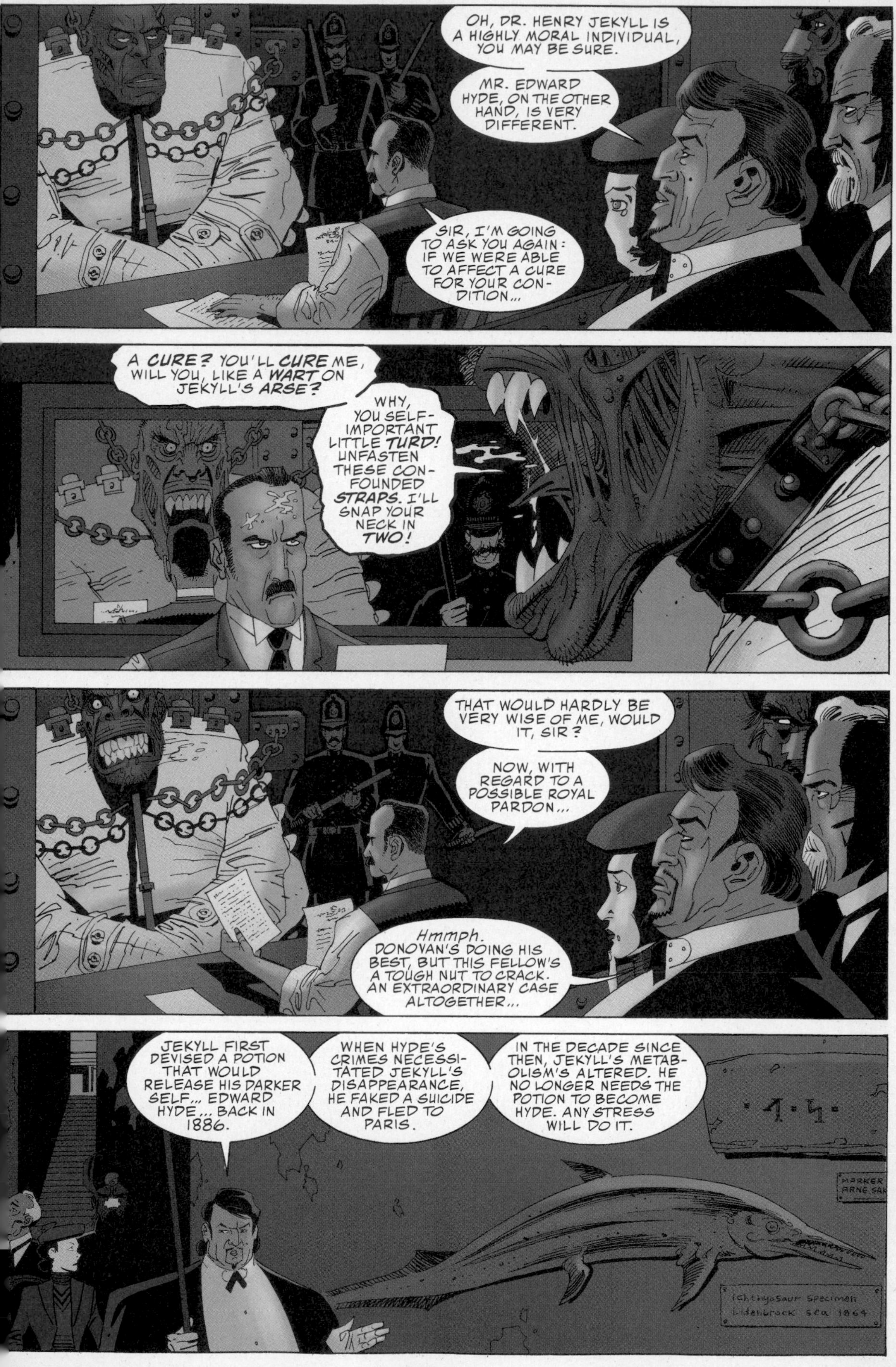
OH, DR. HENRY JEKYLL IS A HIGHLY MORAL INDIVIDUAL, YOU MAY BE SURE.
MR. EDWARD HYDE, ON THE OTHER HAND, IS VERY DIFFERENT.
SIR, I'M GOING TO ASK YOU AGAIN: IF WE WERE ABLE TO AFFECT A CURE FOR YOUR CON-DITION...
A CURE? YOU'LL CURE ME, WILL YOU, LIKE A WART ON JEKYLL'S ARSE?
WHY, YOU SELF-IMPORTANT LITTLE TURD! UNFASTEN THESE CON-FOUNDED STRAPS. I'LL SNAP YOUR NECK IN TWO!
THAT WOULD HARDLY BE VERY WISE OF ME, WOULD IT, SIR?
NOW, WITH REGARD TO A POSSIBLE ROYAL PARDON...
Hmmph. DONOVAN'S DOING HIS BEST, BUT THIS FELLOW'S A TOUGH NUT TO CRACK. AN EXTRAORDINARY CASE ALTOGETHER...
JEKYLL FIRST DEVISED A POTION THAT WOULD RELEASE HIS DARKER SELF... EDWARD HYDE... BACK IN 1886.
WHEN HYDE'S CRIMES NECESSI-TATED JEKYLL'S DISAPPEARANCE, HE FAKED A SUICIDE AND FLED TO PARIS.
IN THE DECADE SINCE THEN, JEKYLL'S METAB-OLISM'S ALTERED. HE NO LONGER NEEDS THE POTION TO BECOME HYDE. ANY STRESS WILL DO IT.
Ichthyosaur Specimen
Lidenbrock Sea 1864

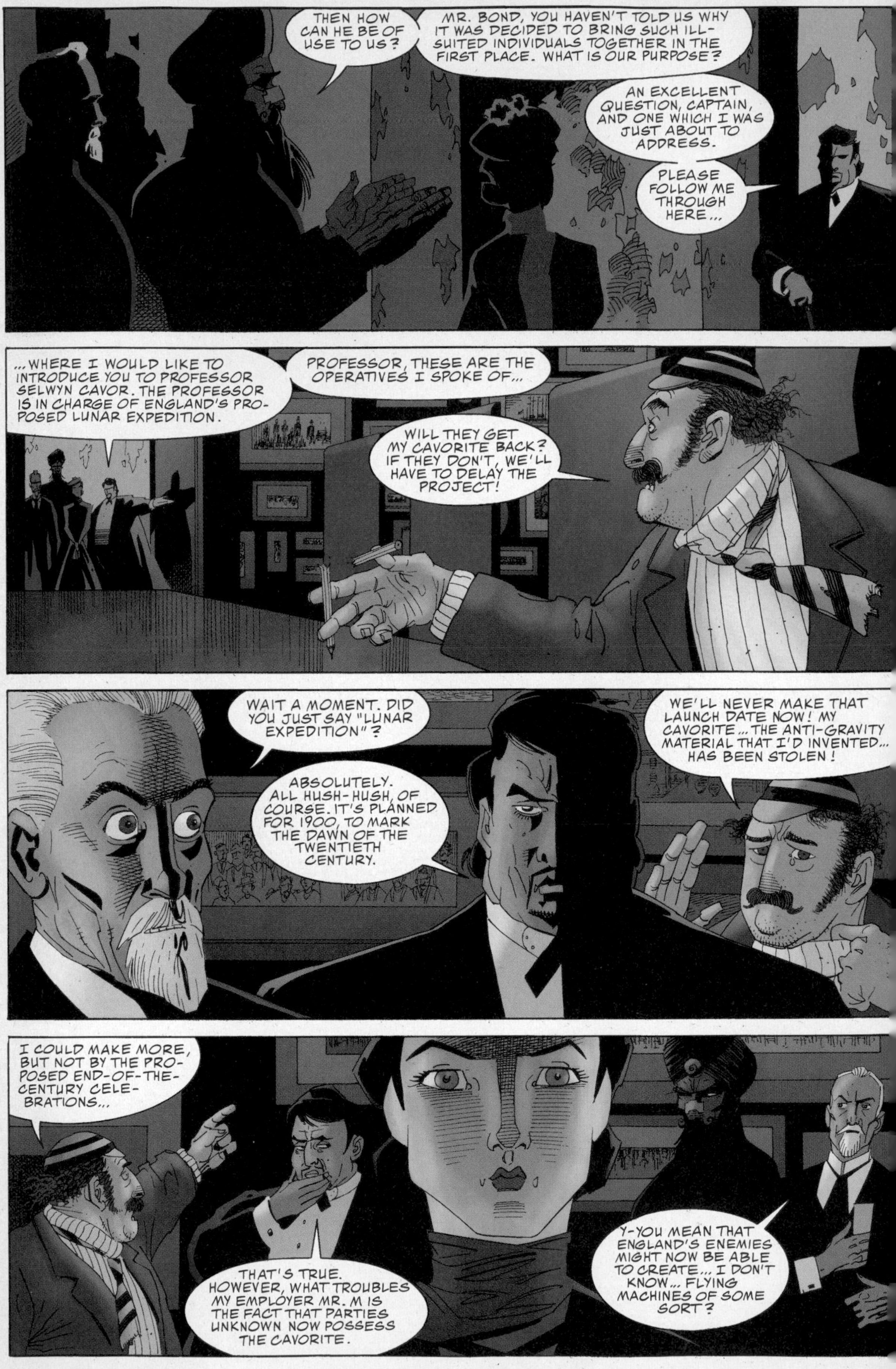
THEN HOW CAN HE BE OF USE TO US?
MR. BOND, YOU HAVEN'T TOLD US WHY IT WAS DECIDED TO BRING SUCH ILL-SUITED INDIVIDUALS TOGETHER IN THE FIRST PLACE. WHAT IS OUR PURPOSE?
AN EXCELLENT QUESTION, CAPTAIN, AND ONE WHICH I WAS JUST ABOUT TO ADDRESS.
PLEASE FOLLOW ME THROUGH HERE...
...WHERE I WOULD LIKE TO INTRODUCE YOU TO PROFESSOR SELWYN CAVOR. THE PROFESSOR IS IN CHARGE OF ENGLAND'S PROPOSED LUNAR EXPEDITION.
PROFESSOR, THESE ARE THE OPERATIVES I SPOKE OF...
WILL THEY GET MY CAVORITE BACK? IF THEY DON'T, WE'LL HAVE TO DELAY THE PROJECT!
WAIT A MOMENT. DID YOU JUST SAY "LUNAR EXPEDITION"?
ABSOLUTELY. ALL HUSH-HUSH, OF COURSE. IT'S PLANNED FOR 1900, TO MARK THE DAWN OF THE TWENTIETH CENTURY.
WE'LL NEVER MAKE THAT LAUNCH DATE NOW! MY CAVORITE... THE ANTI-GRAVITY MATERIAL THAT I'D INVENTED... HAS BEEN STOLEN!
I COULD MAKE MORE, BUT NOT BY THE PROPOSED END-OF-THE-CENTURY CELEBRATIONS...
THAT'S TRUE. HOWEVER, WHAT TROUBLES MY EMPLOYER MR. M IS THE FACT THAT PARTIES UNKNOWN NOW POSSESS THE CAVORITE.
Y-YOU MEAN THAT ENGLAND'S ENEMIES MIGHT NOW BE ABLE TO CREATE... I DON'T KNOW... FLYING MACHINES OF SOME SORT?

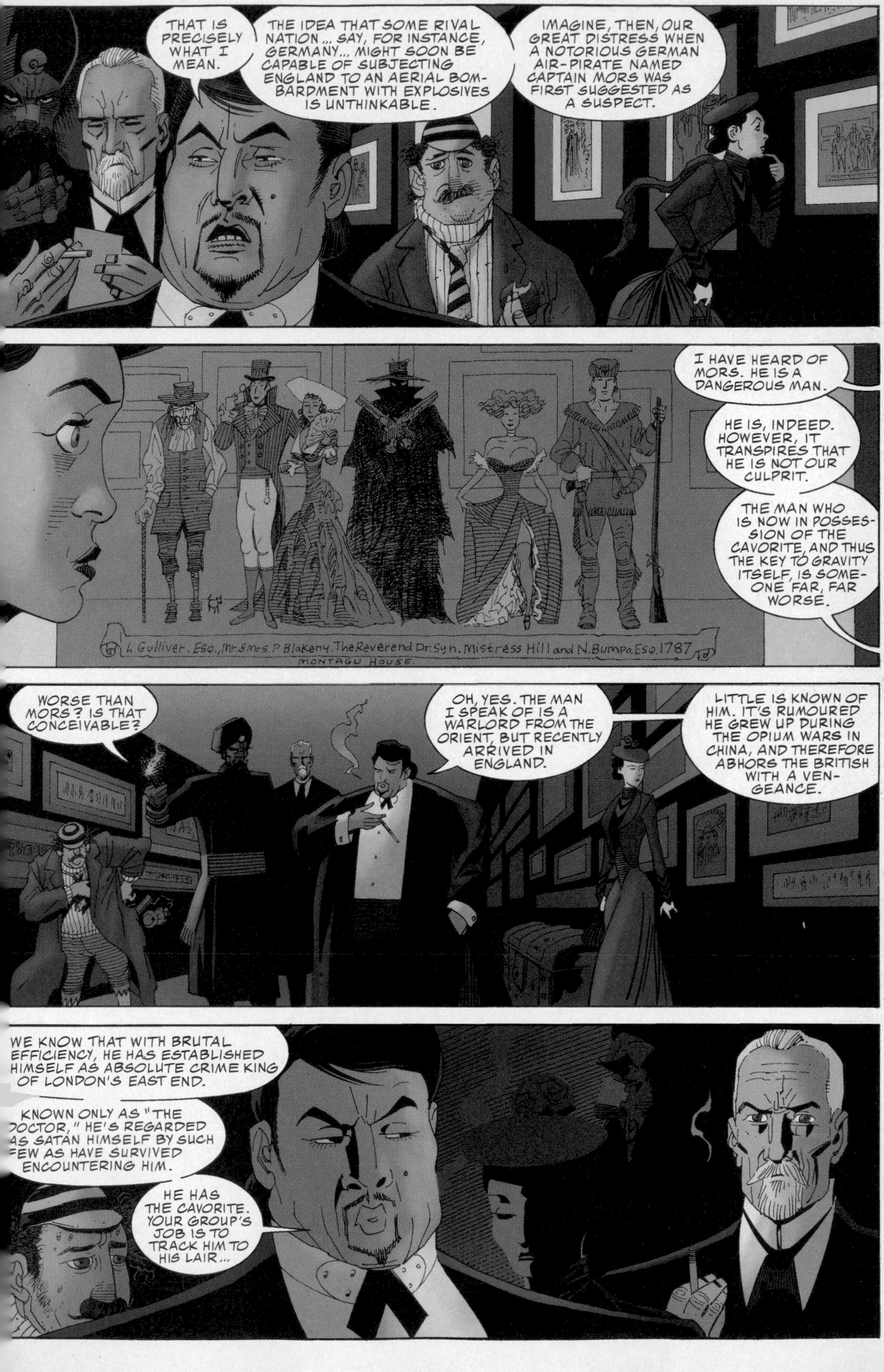
THAT IS PRECISELY WHAT I MEAN.
THE IDEA THAT SOME RIVAL NATION... SAY, FOR INSTANCE, GERMANY... MIGHT SOON BE CAPABLE OF SUBJECTING ENGLAND TO AN AERIAL BOMBARDMENT WITH EXPLOSIVES IS UNTHINKABLE.
IMAGINE, THEN, OUR GREAT DISTRESS WHEN A NOTORIOUS GERMAN AIR-PIRATE NAMED CAPTAIN MORS WAS FIRST SUGGESTED AS A SUSPECT.
I HAVE HEARD OF MORS. HE IS A DANGEROUS MAN.
HE IS, INDEED. HOWEVER, IT TRANSPIRES THAT HE IS NOT OUR CULPRIT.
THE MAN WHO IS NOW IN POSSESSION OF THE CAVORITE, AND THUS THE KEY TO GRAVITY ITSELF, IS SOMEONE FAR, FAR WORSE.
L. Gulliver. Esq., Mr. & Mrs. P. Blakeny. The Reverend Dr. Syn. Mistress Hill and N. Bumpo. Esq. 1787
MONTAGU HOUSE.
WORSE THAN MORS? IS THAT CONCEIVABLE?
OH, YES. THE MAN I SPEAK OF IS A WARLORD FROM THE ORIENT, BUT RECENTLY ARRIVED IN ENGLAND.
LITTLE IS KNOWN OF HIM. IT'S RUMOURED HE GREW UP DURING THE OPIUM WARS IN CHINA, AND THEREFORE ABHORS THE BRITISH WITH A VENGEANCE.
WE KNOW THAT WITH BRUTAL EFFICIENCY, HE HAS ESTABLISHED HIMSELF AS ABSOLUTE CRIME KING OF LONDON'S EAST END.
KNOWN ONLY AS "THE DOCTOR," HE'S REGARDED AS SATAN HIMSELF BY SUCH FEW AS HAVE SURVIVED ENCOUNTERING HIM.
HE HAS THE CAVORITE. YOUR GROUP'S JOB IS TO TRACK HIM TO HIS LAIR...

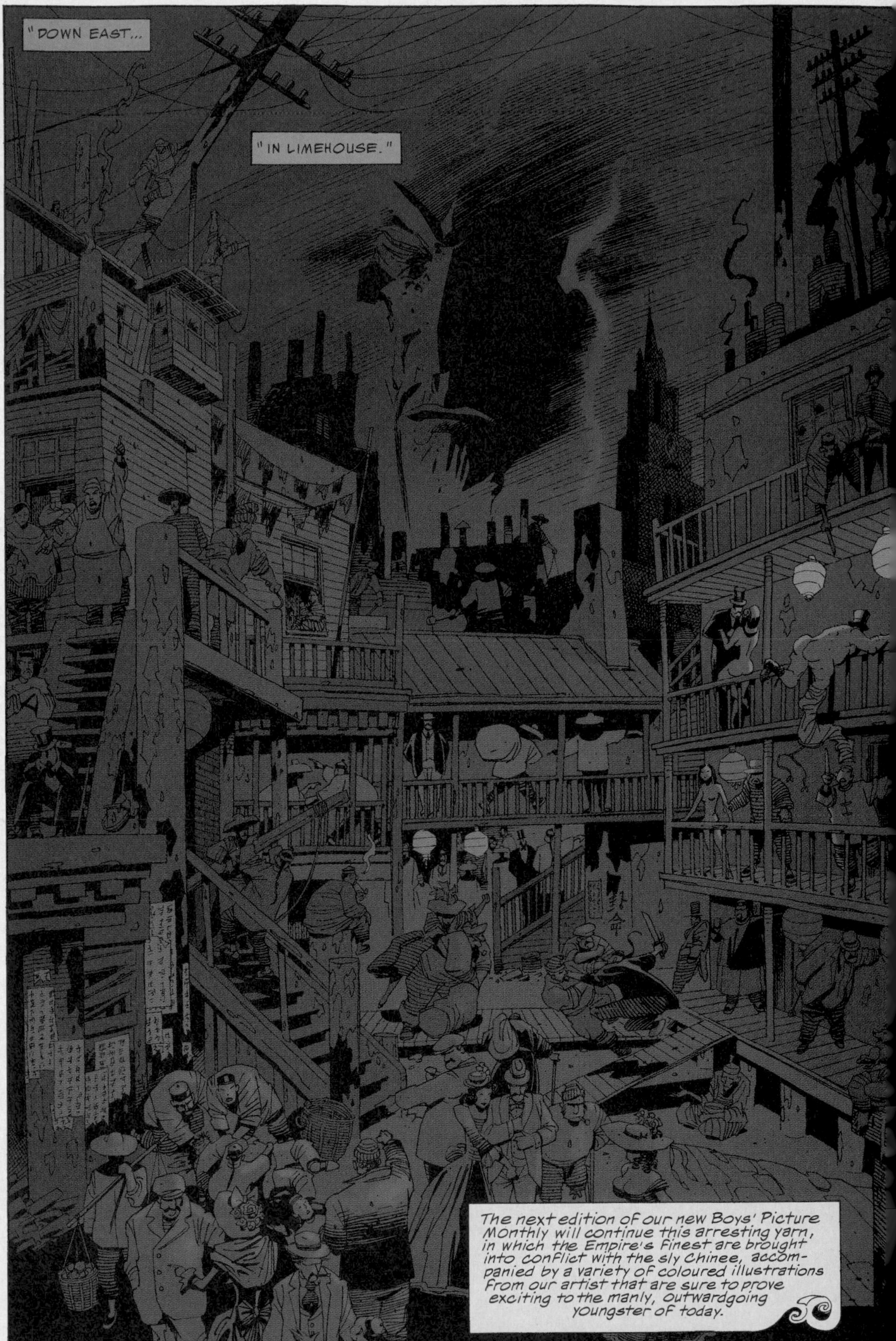
"DOWN EAST...
"IN LIMEHOUSE."
The next edition of our new Boys' Picture Monthly will continue this arresting yarn, in which the Empire's Finest are brought into conflict with the sly Chinee, accompanied by a variety of coloured illustrations from our artist that are sure to prove exciting to the manly, outwardgoing youngster of today.

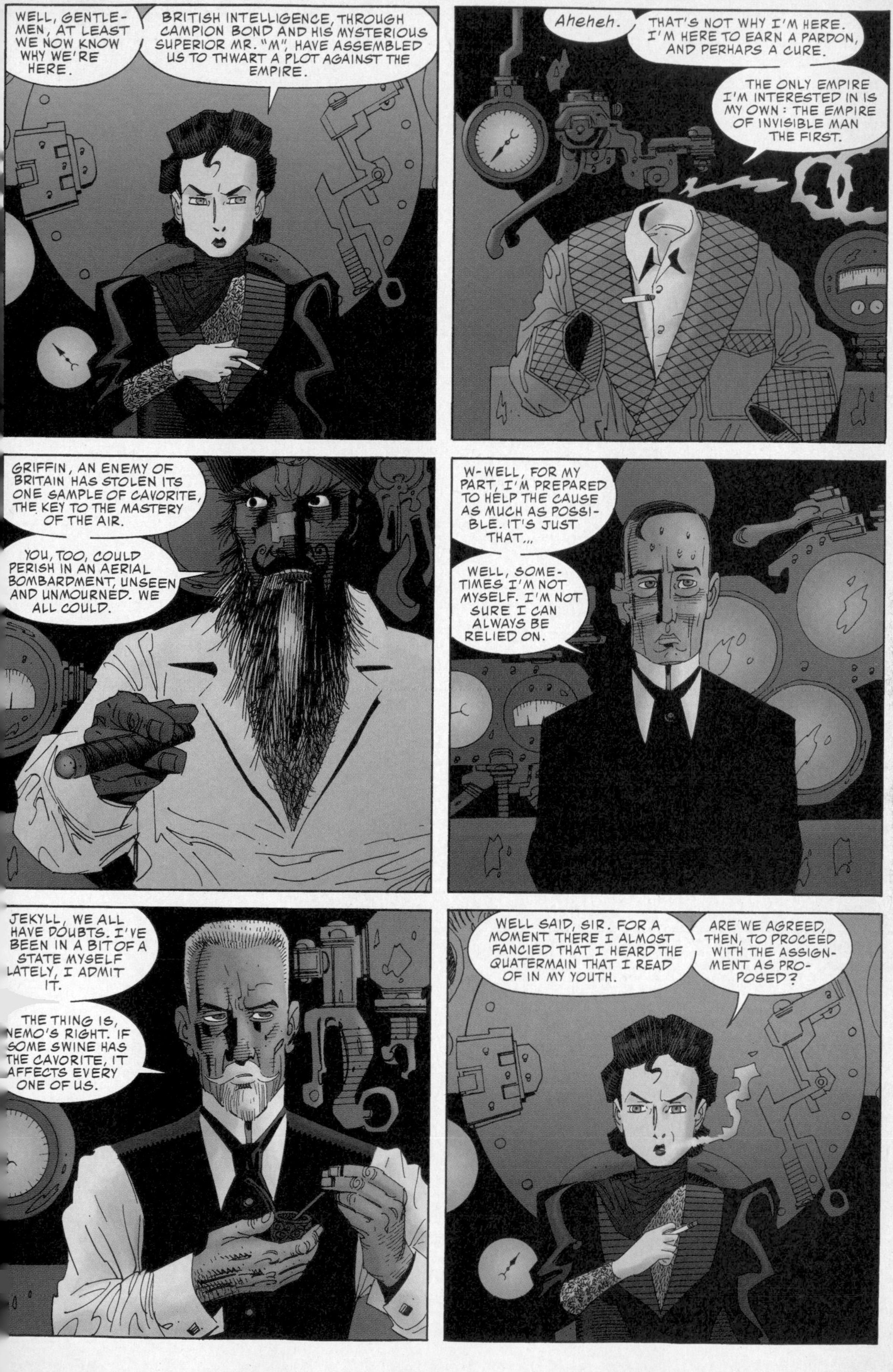
WELL, GENTLEMEN, AT LEAST WE NOW KNOW WHY WE'RE HERE.
BRITISH INTELLIGENCE, THROUGH CAMPION BOND AND HIS MYSTERIOUS SUPERIOR MR. "M", HAVE ASSEMBLED US TO THWART A PLOT AGAINST THE EMPIRE.
Aheheh.
THAT'S NOT WHY I'M HERE. I'M HERE TO EARN A PARDON, AND PERHAPS A CURE.
THE ONLY EMPIRE I'M INTERESTED IN IS MY OWN : THE EMPIRE OF INVISIBLE MAN THE FIRST.
GRIFFIN, AN ENEMY OF BRITAIN HAS STOLEN ITS ONE SAMPLE OF CAVORITE, THE KEY TO THE MASTERY OF THE AIR.
YOU, TOO, COULD PERISH IN AN AERIAL BOMBARDMENT, UNSEEN AND UNMOURNED. WE ALL COULD.
W-WELL, FOR MY PART, I'M PREPARED TO HELP THE CAUSE AS MUCH AS POSSIBLE. IT'S JUST THAT...
WELL, SOMETIMES I'M NOT MYSELF. I'M NOT SURE I CAN ALWAYS BE RELIED ON.
JEKYLL, WE ALL HAVE DOUBTS. I'VE BEEN IN A BIT OF A STATE MYSELF LATELY, I ADMIT IT.
THE THING IS, NEMO'S RIGHT. IF SOME SWINE HAS THE CAVORITE, IT AFFECTS EVERY ONE OF US.
WELL SAID, SIR. FOR A MOMENT THERE I ALMOST FANCIED THAT I HEARD THE QUATERMAIN THAT I READ OF IN MY YOUTH.
ARE WE AGREED, THEN, TO PROCEED WITH THE ASSIGNMENT AS PROPOSED?

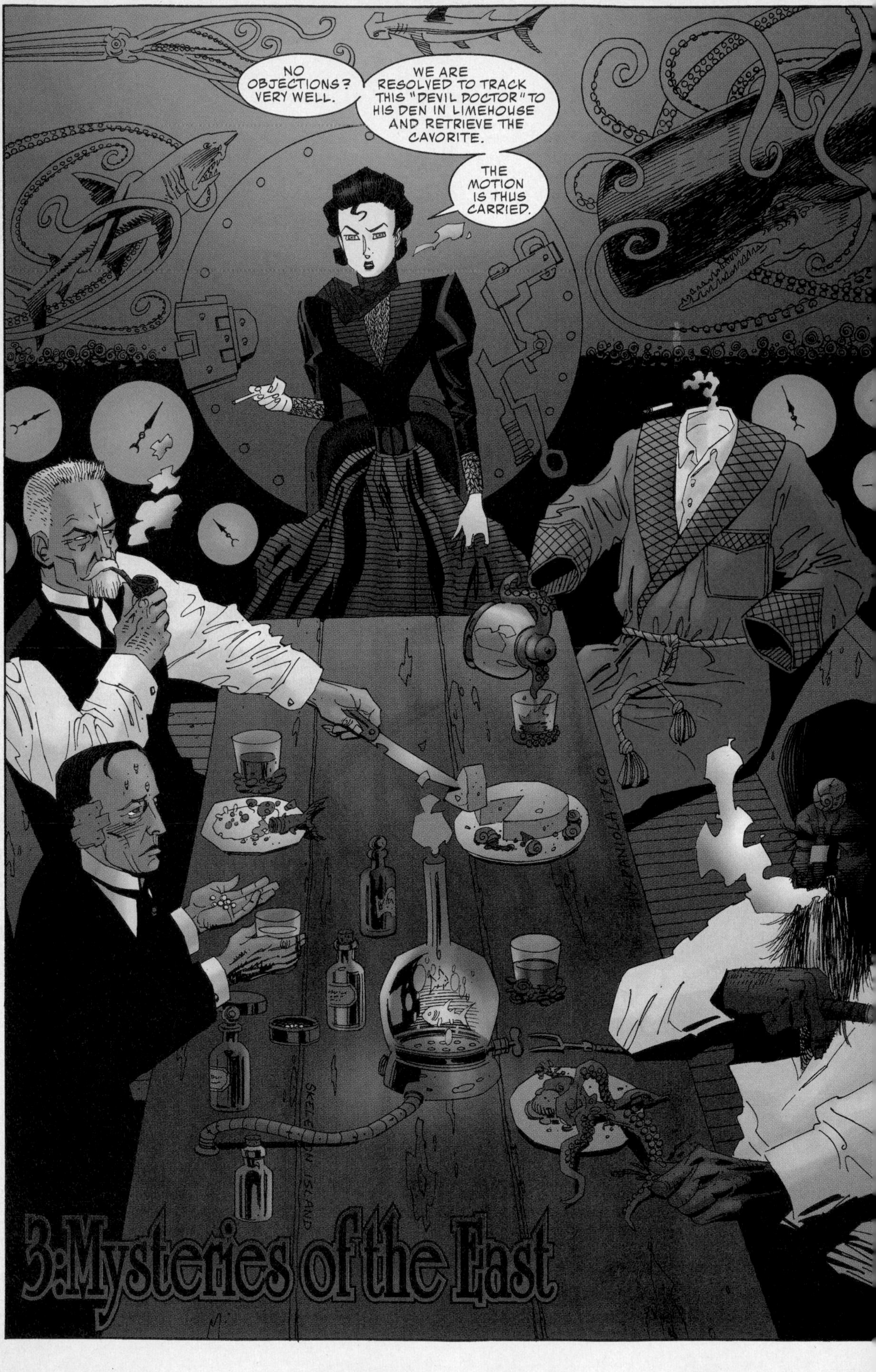
NO OBJECTIONS? VERY WELL.
WE ARE RESOLVED TO TRACK THIS "DEVIL DOCTOR" TO HIS DEN IN LIMEHOUSE AND RETRIEVE THE CAVORITE.
THE MOTION IS THUS CARRIED.
3: Mysteries of the East

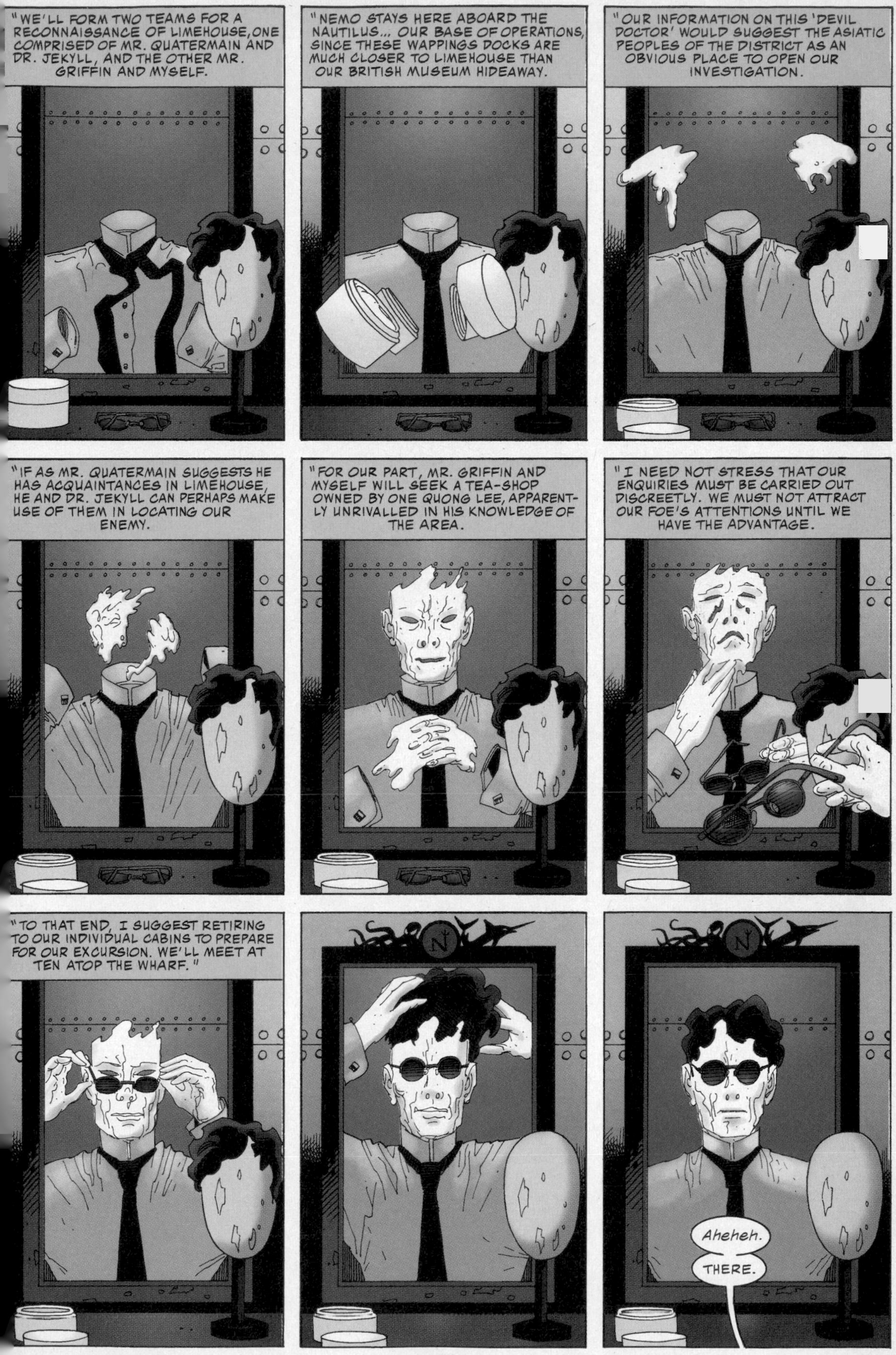
"WE'LL FORM TWO TEAMS FOR A RECONNAISSANCE OF LIMEHOUSE, ONE COMPRISED OF MR. QUATERMAIN AND DR. JEKYLL, AND THE OTHER MR. GRIFFIN AND MYSELF.
"NEMO STAYS HERE ABOARD THE NAUTILUS... OUR BASE OF OPERATIONS, SINCE THESE WAPPINGS DOCKS ARE MUCH CLOSER TO LIMEHOUSE THAN OUR BRITISH MUSEUM HIDEAWAY.
"OUR INFORMATION ON THIS 'DEVIL DOCTOR' WOULD SUGGEST THE ASIATIC PEOPLES OF THE DISTRICT AS AN OBVIOUS PLACE TO OPEN OUR INVESTIGATION.
"IF AS MR. QUATERMAIN SUGGESTS HE HAS ACQUAINTANCES IN LIMEHOUSE, HE AND DR. JEKYLL CAN PERHAPS MAKE USE OF THEM IN LOCATING OUR ENEMY.
"FOR OUR PART, MR. GRIFFIN AND MYSELF WILL SEEK A TEA-SHOP OWNED BY ONE QUONG LEE, APPARENTLY UNRIVALLED IN HIS KNOWLEDGE OF THE AREA.
"I NEED NOT STRESS THAT OUR ENQUIRIES MUST BE CARRIED OUT DISCREETLY. WE MUST NOT ATTRACT OUR FOE'S ATTENTIONS UNTIL WE HAVE THE ADVANTAGE.
"TO THAT END, I SUGGEST RETIRING TO OUR INDIVIDUAL CABINS TO PREPARE FOR OUR EXCURSION. WE'LL MEET AT TEN ATOP THE WHARF."
Aheheh.
THERE.

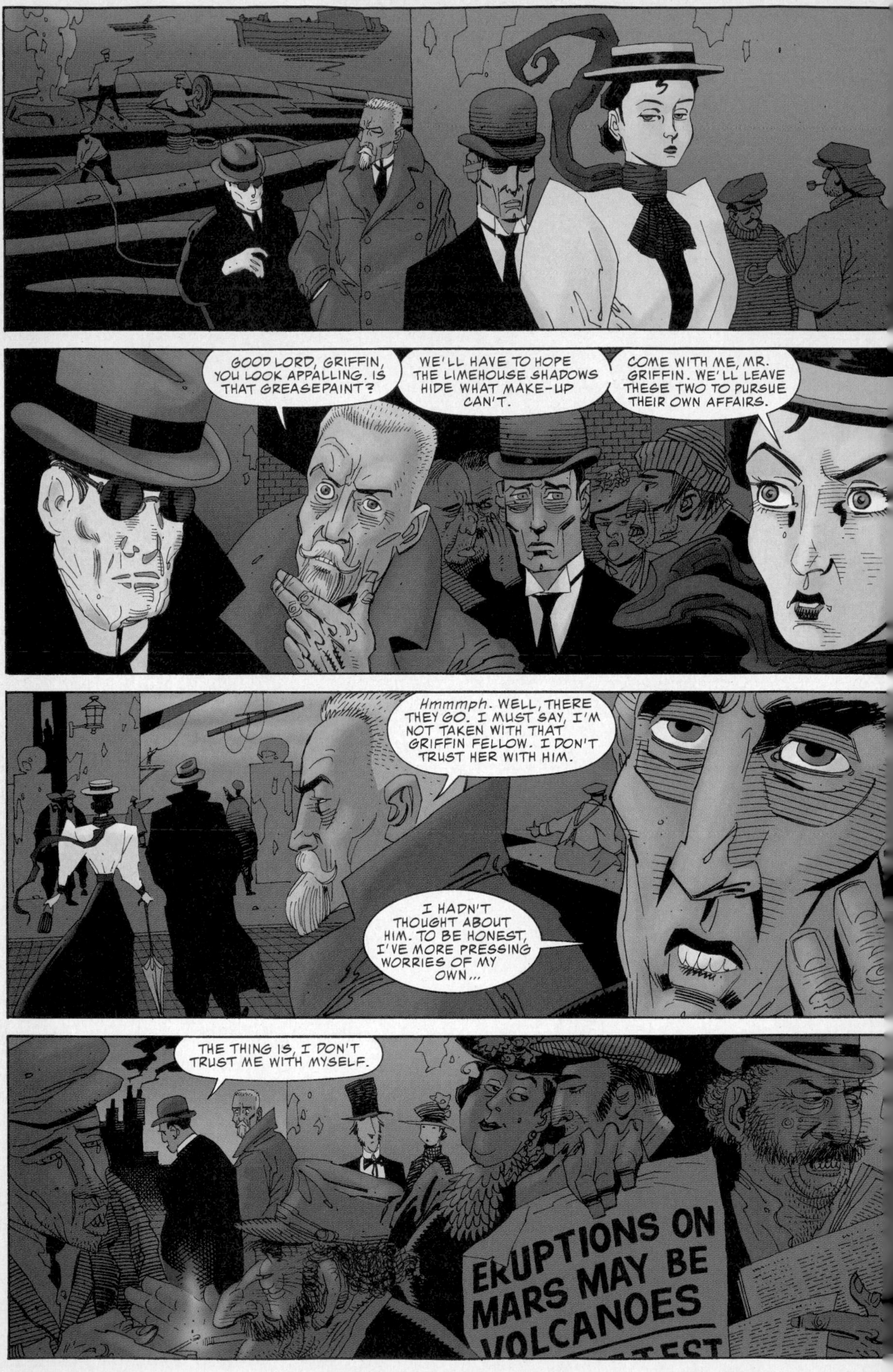
GOOD LORD, GRIFFIN, YOU LOOK APPALLING. IS THAT GREASEPAINT?
WE'LL HAVE TO HOPE THE LIMEHOUSE SHADOWS HIDE WHAT MAKE-UP CAN'T.
COME WITH ME, MR. GRIFFIN. WE'LL LEAVE THESE TWO TO PURSUE THEIR OWN AFFAIRS.
Hmmmph. WELL, THERE THEY GO. I MUST SAY, I'M NOT TAKEN WITH THAT GRIFFIN FELLOW. I DON'T TRUST HER WITH HIM.
I HADN'T THOUGHT ABOUT HIM. TO BE HONEST, I'VE MORE PRESSING WORRIES OF MY OWN...
THE THING IS, I DON'T TRUST ME WITH MYSELF.
ERUPTIONS ON MARS MAY BE VOLCANOES

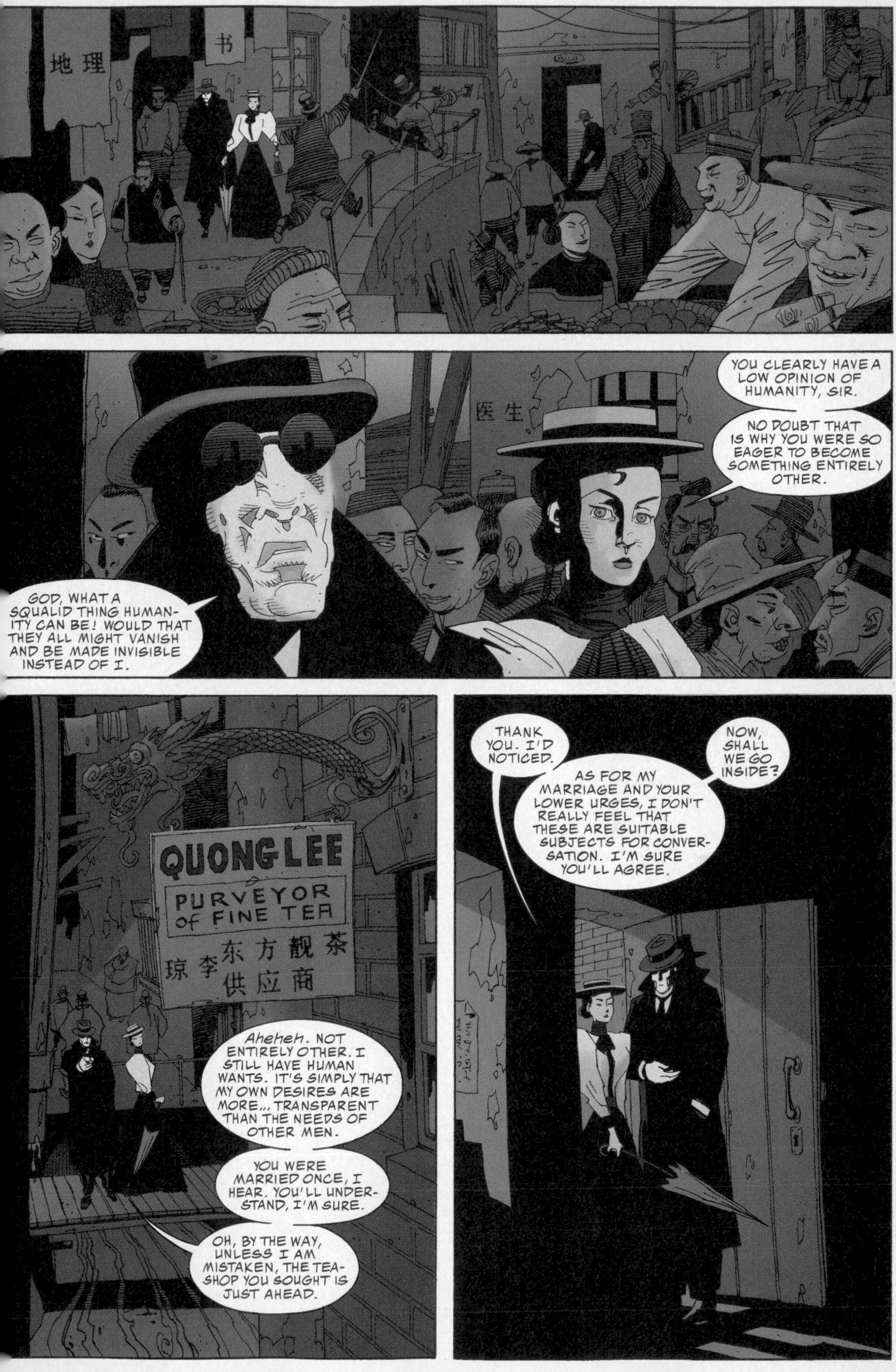
地理
书
医生
YOU CLEARLY HAVE A LOW OPINION OF HUMANITY, SIR.
NO DOUBT THAT IS WHY YOU WERE SO EAGER TO BECOME SOMETHING ENTIRELY OTHER.
GOD, WHAT A SQUALID THING HUMANITY CAN BE! WOULD THAT THEY ALL MIGHT VANISH AND BE MADE INVISIBLE INSTEAD OF I.
QUONG LEE
PURVEYOR of FINE TEA
琼李 东方靓茶 供应商
Aheheh. NOT ENTIRELY OTHER. I STILL HAVE HUMAN WANTS. IT'S SIMPLY THAT MY OWN DESIRES ARE MORE... TRANSPARENT THAN THE NEEDS OF OTHER MEN.
YOU WERE MARRIED ONCE, I HEAR. YOU'LL UNDERSTAND, I'M SURE.
OH, BY THE WAY, UNLESS I AM MISTAKEN, THE TEA-SHOP YOU SOUGHT IS JUST AHEAD.
THANK YOU. I'D NOTICED.
AS FOR MY MARRIAGE AND YOUR LOWER URGES, I DON'T REALLY FEEL THAT THESE ARE SUITABLE SUBJECTS FOR CONVERSATION. I'M SURE YOU'LL AGREE.
NOW, SHALL WE GO INSIDE?

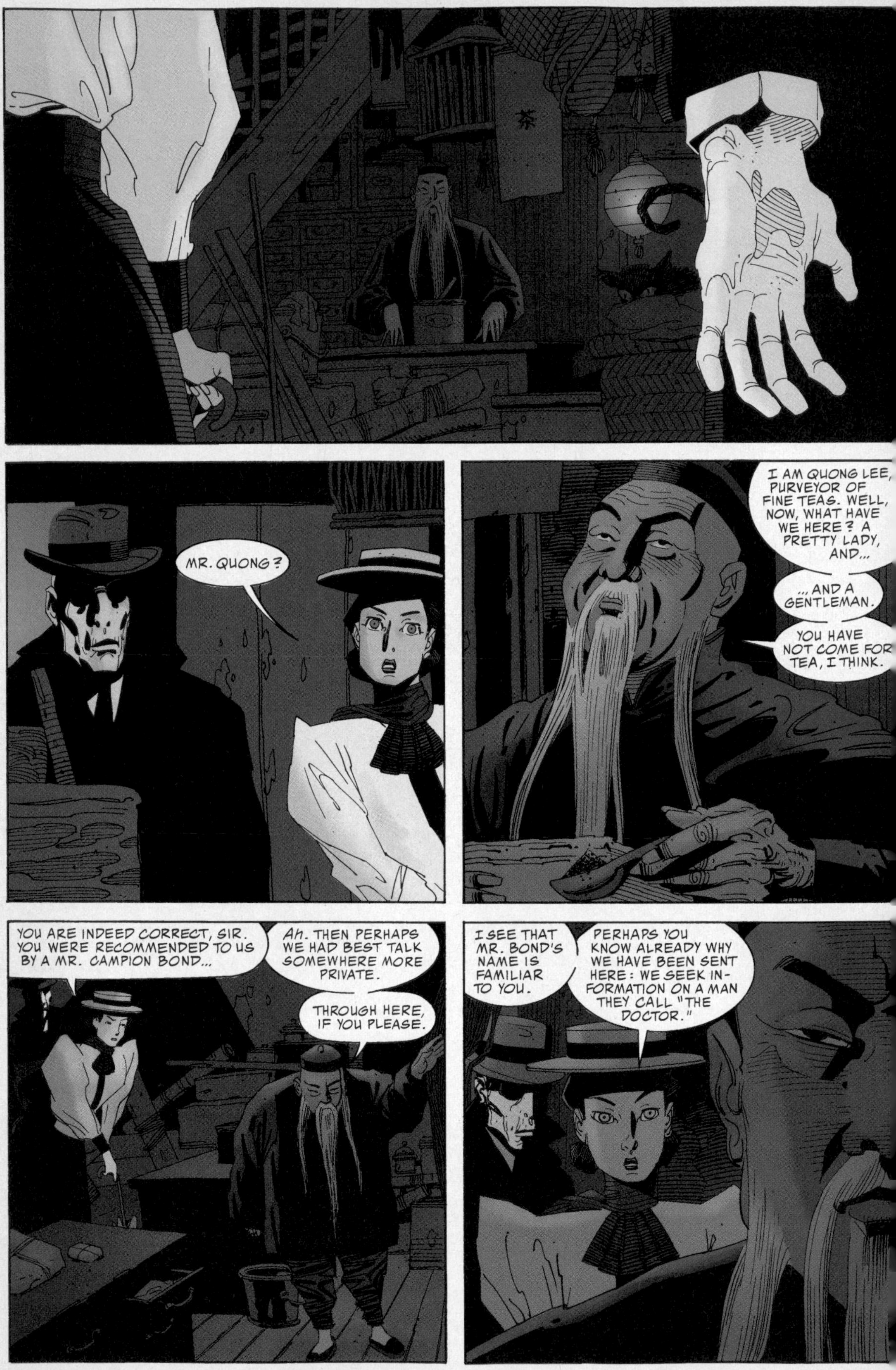
MR. QUONG?
I AM QUONG LEE, PURVEYOR OF FINE TEAS. WELL, NOW, WHAT HAVE WE HERE? A PRETTY LADY, AND...
...AND A GENTLEMAN.
YOU HAVE NOT COME FOR TEA, I THINK.
YOU ARE INDEED CORRECT, SIR. YOU WERE RECOMMENDED TO US BY A MR. CAMPION BOND...
Ah. THEN PERHAPS WE HAD BEST TALK SOMEWHERE MORE PRIVATE.
THROUGH HERE, IF YOU PLEASE.
I SEE THAT MR. BOND'S NAME IS FAMILIAR TO YOU.
PERHAPS YOU KNOW ALREADY WHY WE HAVE BEEN SENT HERE: WE SEEK INFORMATION ON A MAN THEY CALL "THE DOCTOR."

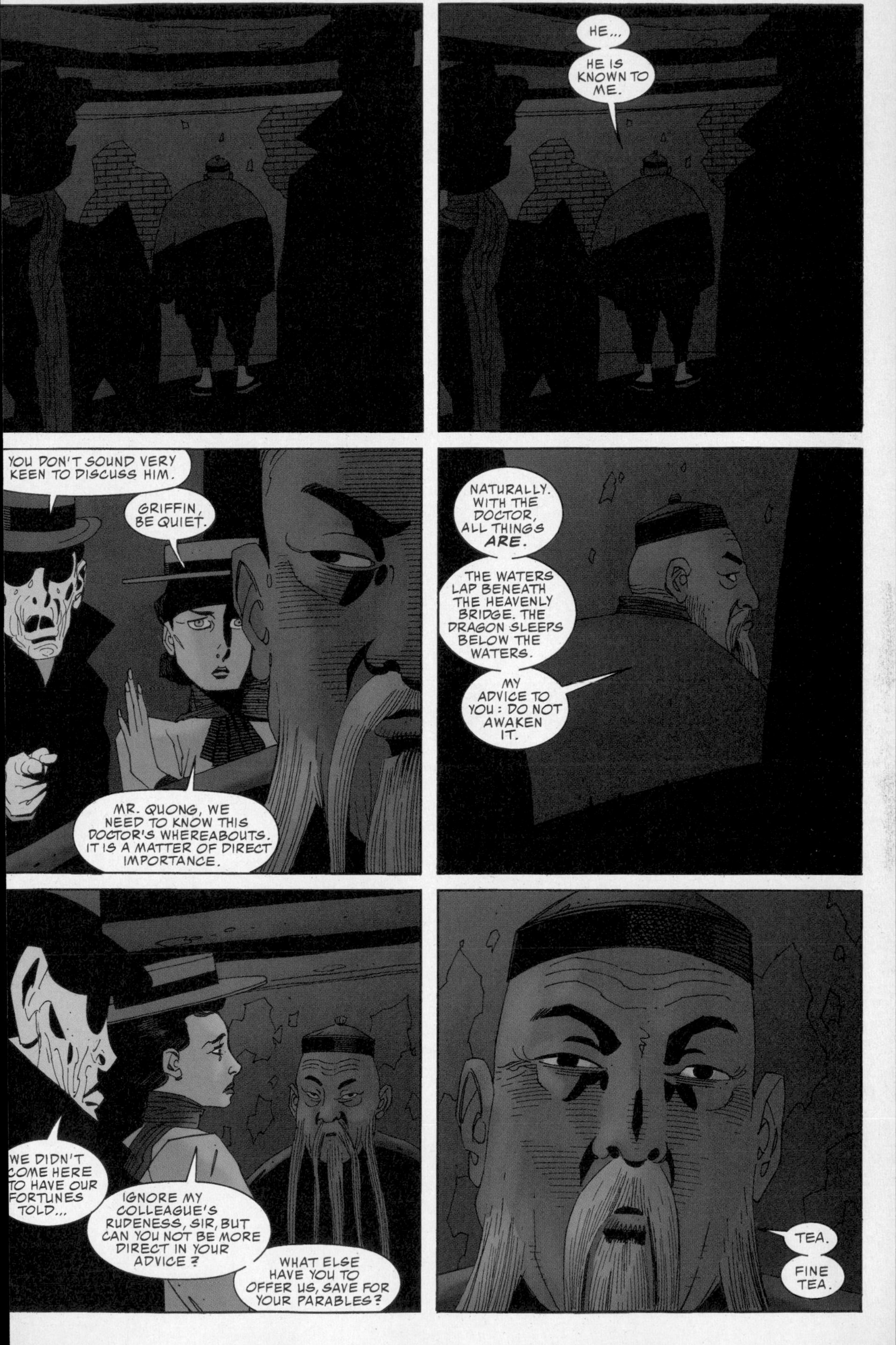
HE...
HE IS KNOWN TO ME.
YOU DON'T SOUND VERY KEEN TO DISCUSS HIM.
GRIFFIN, BE QUIET.
MR. QUONG, WE NEED TO KNOW THIS DOCTOR'S WHEREABOUTS. IT IS A MATTER OF DIRECT IMPORTANCE.
NATURALLY. WITH THE DOCTOR, ALL THINGS ARE.
THE WATERS LAP BENEATH THE HEAVENLY BRIDGE. THE DRAGON SLEEPS BELOW THE WATERS.
MY ADVICE TO YOU : DO NOT AWAKEN IT.
WE DIDN'T COME HERE TO HAVE OUR FORTUNES TOLD...
IGNORE MY COLLEAGUE'S RUDENESS, SIR, BUT CAN YOU NOT BE MORE DIRECT IN YOUR ADVICE ?
WHAT ELSE HAVE YOU TO OFFER US, SAVE FOR YOUR PARABLES?
TEA.
FINE TEA.

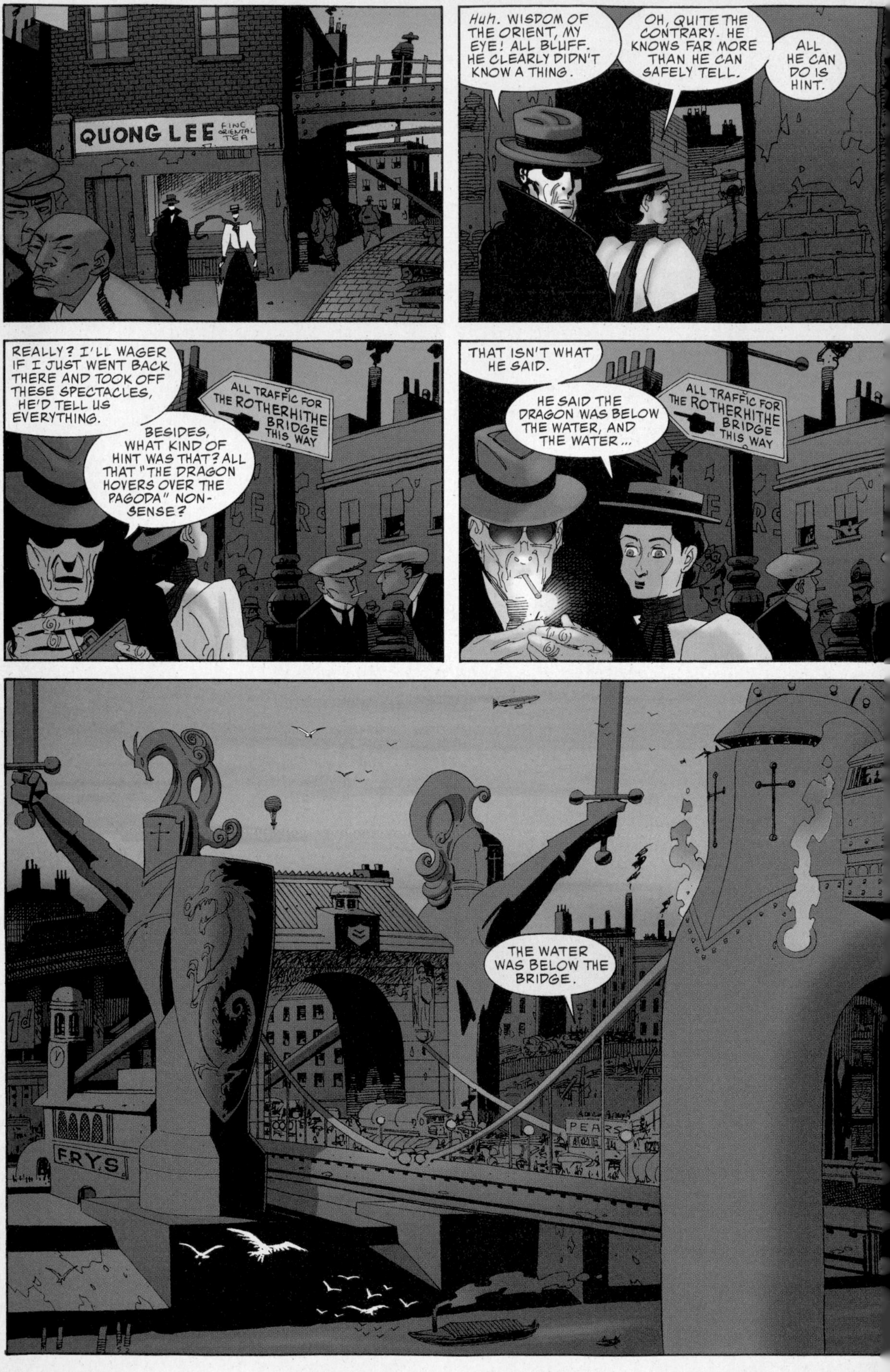
QUONG LEE
FINE ORIENTAL TEA
Huh. WISDOM OF THE ORIENT, MY EYE! ALL BLUFF. HE CLEARLY DIDN'T KNOW A THING.
OH, QUITE THE CONTRARY. HE KNOWS FAR MORE THAN HE CAN SAFELY TELL.
ALL HE CAN DO IS HINT.
REALLY? I'LL WAGER IF I JUST WENT BACK THERE AND TOOK OFF THESE SPECTACLES, HE'D TELL US EVERYTHING.
ALL TRAFFIC FOR THE ROTHERHITHE BRIDGE THIS WAY
BESIDES, WHAT KIND OF HINT WAS THAT? ALL THAT "THE DRAGON HOVERS OVER THE PAGODA" NON-SENSE?
THAT ISN'T WHAT HE SAID.
HE SAID THE DRAGON WAS BELOW THE WATER, AND THE WATER...
ALL TRAFFIC FOR THE ROTHERHITHE BRIDGE THIS WAY
THE WATER WAS BELOW THE BRIDGE.
FRY'S
PEARS

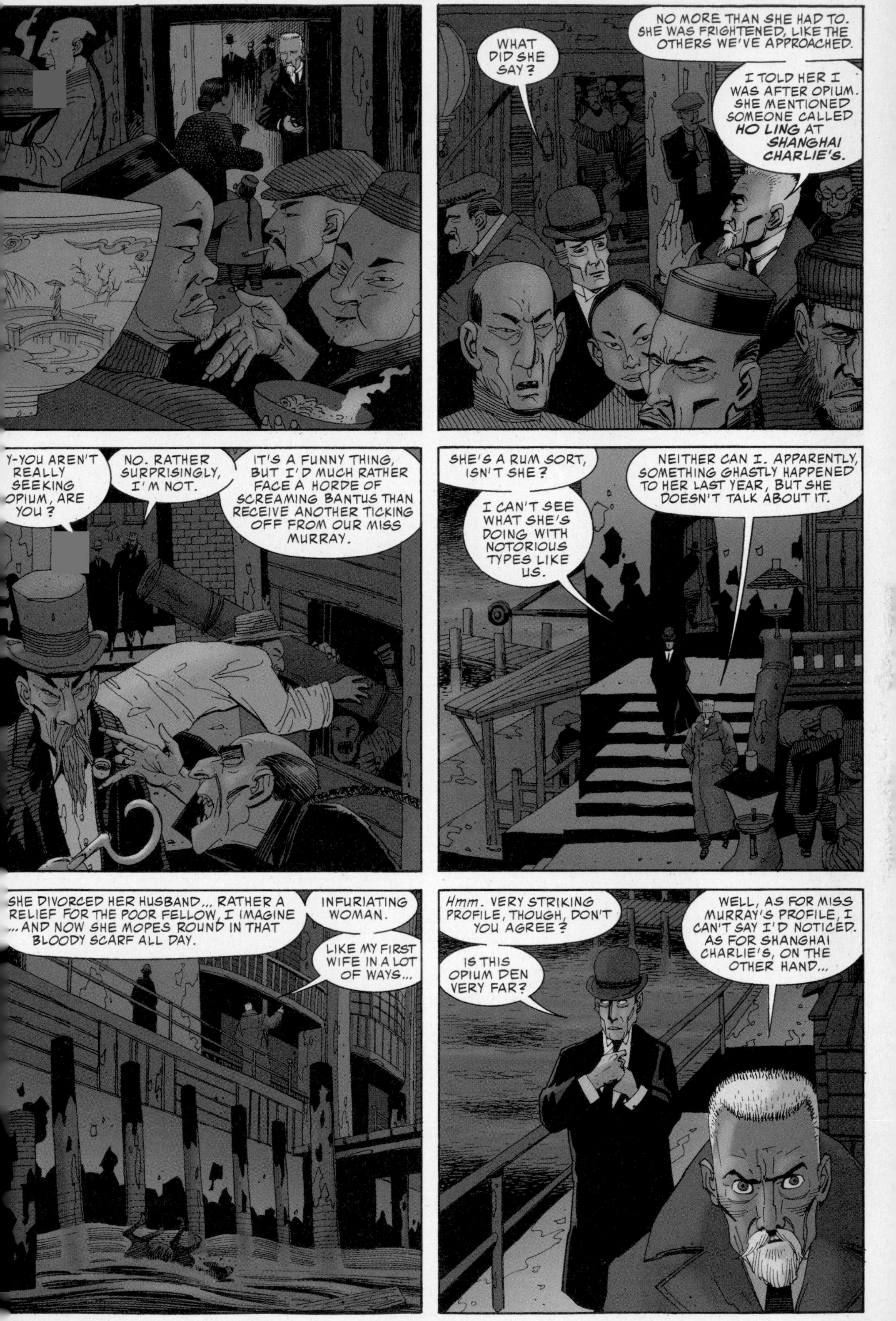
WHAT DID SHE SAY?
NO MORE THAN SHE HAD TO. SHE WAS FRIGHTENED, LIKE THE OTHERS WE'VE APPROACHED.
I TOLD HER I WAS AFTER OPIUM. SHE MENTIONED SOMEONE CALLED HO LING AT SHANGHAI CHARLIE'S.
Y-YOU AREN'T REALLY SEEKING OPIUM, ARE YOU?
NO. RATHER SURPRISINGLY, I'M NOT.
IT'S A FUNNY THING, BUT I'D MUCH RATHER FACE A HORDE OF SCREAMING BANTUS THAN RECEIVE ANOTHER TICKING OFF FROM OUR MISS MURRAY.
SHE'S A RUM SORT, ISN'T SHE?
I CAN'T SEE WHAT SHE'S DOING WITH NOTORIOUS TYPES LIKE US.
NEITHER CAN I. APPARENTLY, SOMETHING GHASTLY HAPPENED TO HER LAST YEAR, BUT SHE DOESN'T TALK ABOUT IT.
SHE DIVORCED HER HUSBAND... RATHER A RELIEF FOR THE POOR FELLOW, I IMAGINE ...AND NOW SHE MOPES ROUND IN THAT BLOODY SCARF ALL DAY.
INFURIATING WOMAN.
LIKE MY FIRST WIFE IN A LOT OF WAYS...
Hmm. VERY STRIKING PROFILE, THOUGH, DON'T YOU AGREE?
IS THIS OPIUM DEN VERY FAR?
WELL, AS FOR MISS MURRAY'S PROFILE, I CAN'T SAY I'D NOTICED. AS FOR SHANGHAI CHARLIE'S, ON THE OTHER HAND...

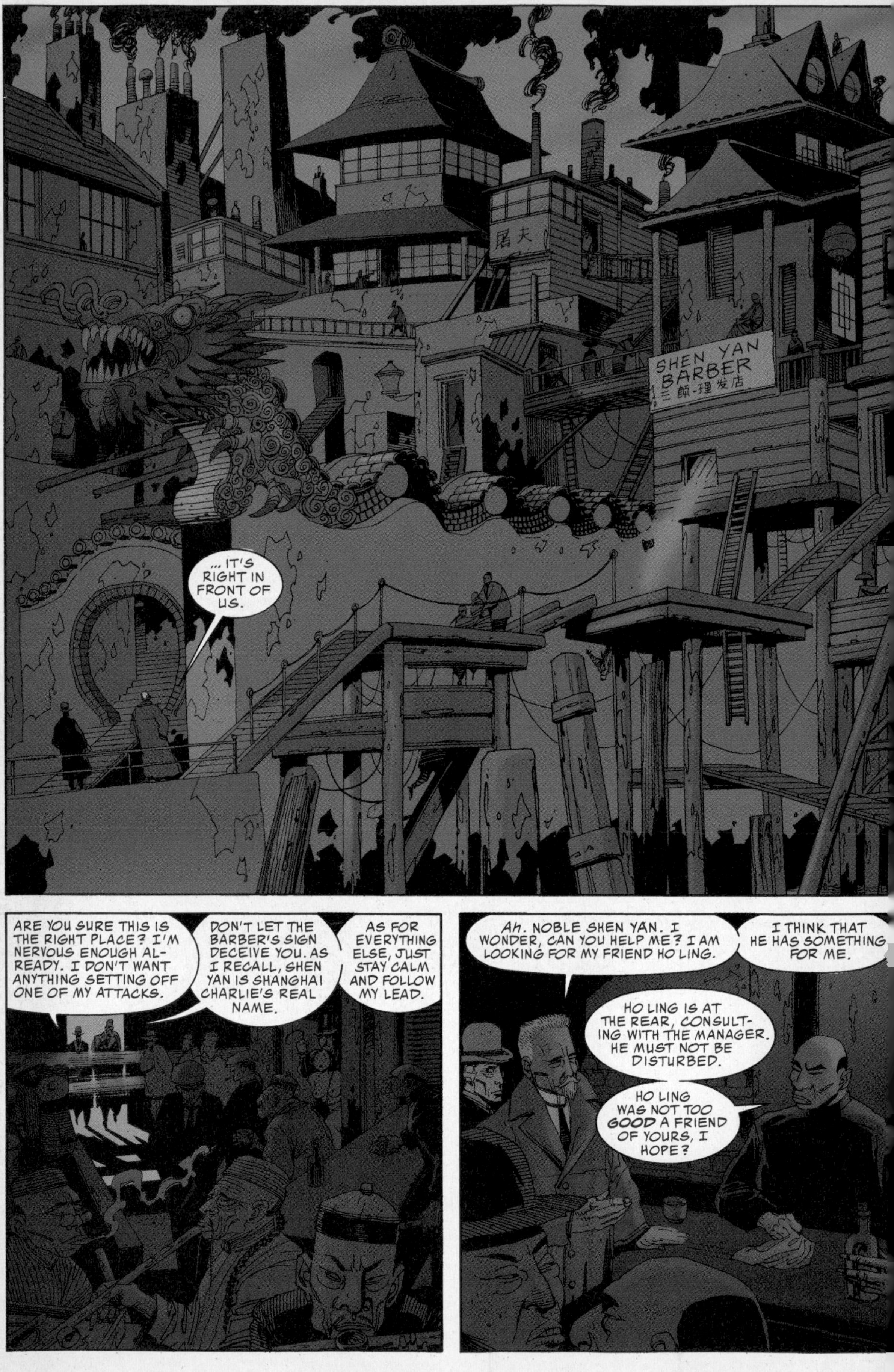
SHEN YAN BARBER
... IT'S RIGHT IN FRONT OF US.
ARE YOU SURE THIS IS THE RIGHT PLACE? I'M NERVOUS ENOUGH ALREADY. I DON'T WANT ANYTHING SETTING OFF ONE OF MY ATTACKS.
DON'T LET THE BARBER'S SIGN DECEIVE YOU. AS I RECALL, SHEN YAN IS SHANGHAI CHARLIE'S REAL NAME.
AS FOR EVERYTHING ELSE, JUST STAY CALM AND FOLLOW MY LEAD.
Ah. NOBLE SHEN YAN. I WONDER, CAN YOU HELP ME? I AM LOOKING FOR MY FRIEND HO LING.
I THINK THAT HE HAS SOMETHING FOR ME.
HO LING IS AT THE REAR, CONSULTING WITH THE MANAGER. HE MUST NOT BE DISTURBED.
HO LING WAS NOT TOO GOOD A FRIEND OF YOURS, I HOPE?

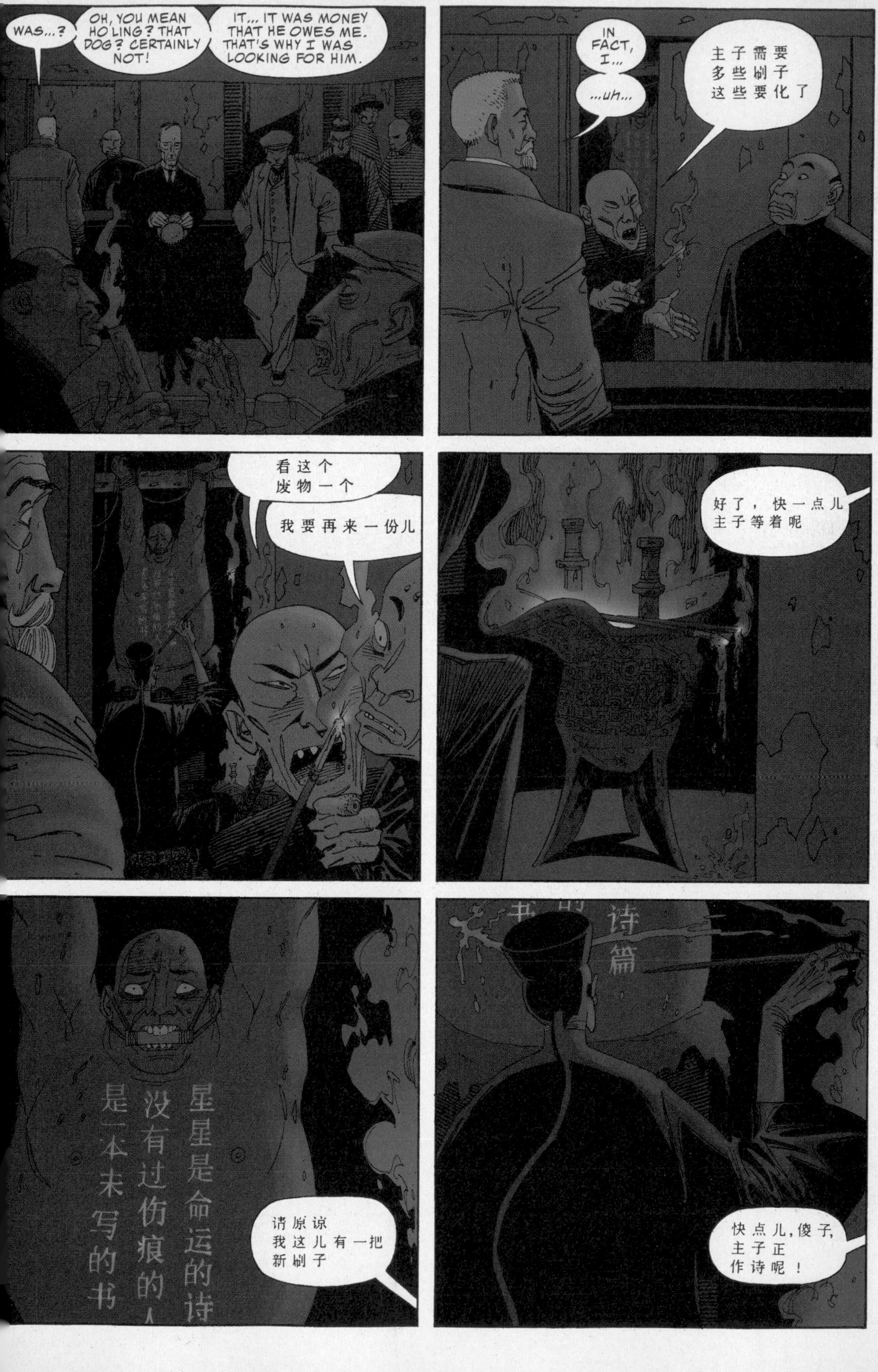
WAS...?
OH, YOU MEAN HO LING? THAT DOG? CERTAINLY NOT!
IT... IT WAS MONEY THAT HE OWES ME. THAT'S WHY I WAS LOOKING FOR HIM.
IN FACT, I...
...uh...
主子需要多些刷子这些要化了
看这个废物一个
我要再来一份儿
好了，快一点儿主子等着呢
星星是命运的诗
没有过伤痕的人
是一本未写的书
请原谅我这儿有一把新刷子
诗篇
快点儿,傻子,主子正作诗呢！

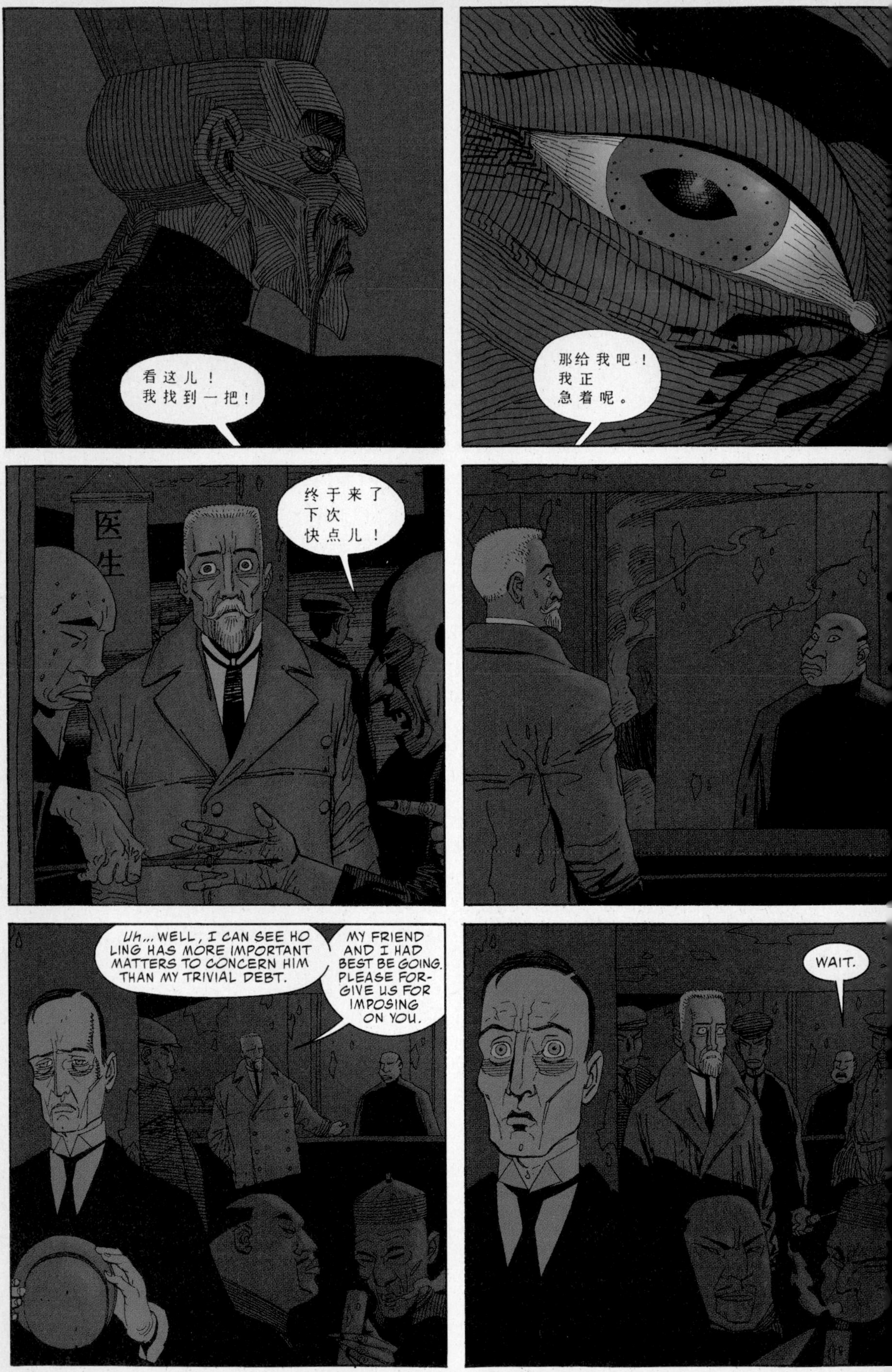

看这儿！我找到一把！
那给我吧！我正急着呢。
医生
终于来了下次快点儿！
Uh... WELL, I CAN SEE HO LING HAS MORE IMPORTANT MATTERS TO CONCERN HIM THAN MY TRIVIAL DEBT.
MY FRIEND AND I HAD BEST BE GOING. PLEASE FOR-GIVE US FOR IMPOSING ON YOU.
WAIT.

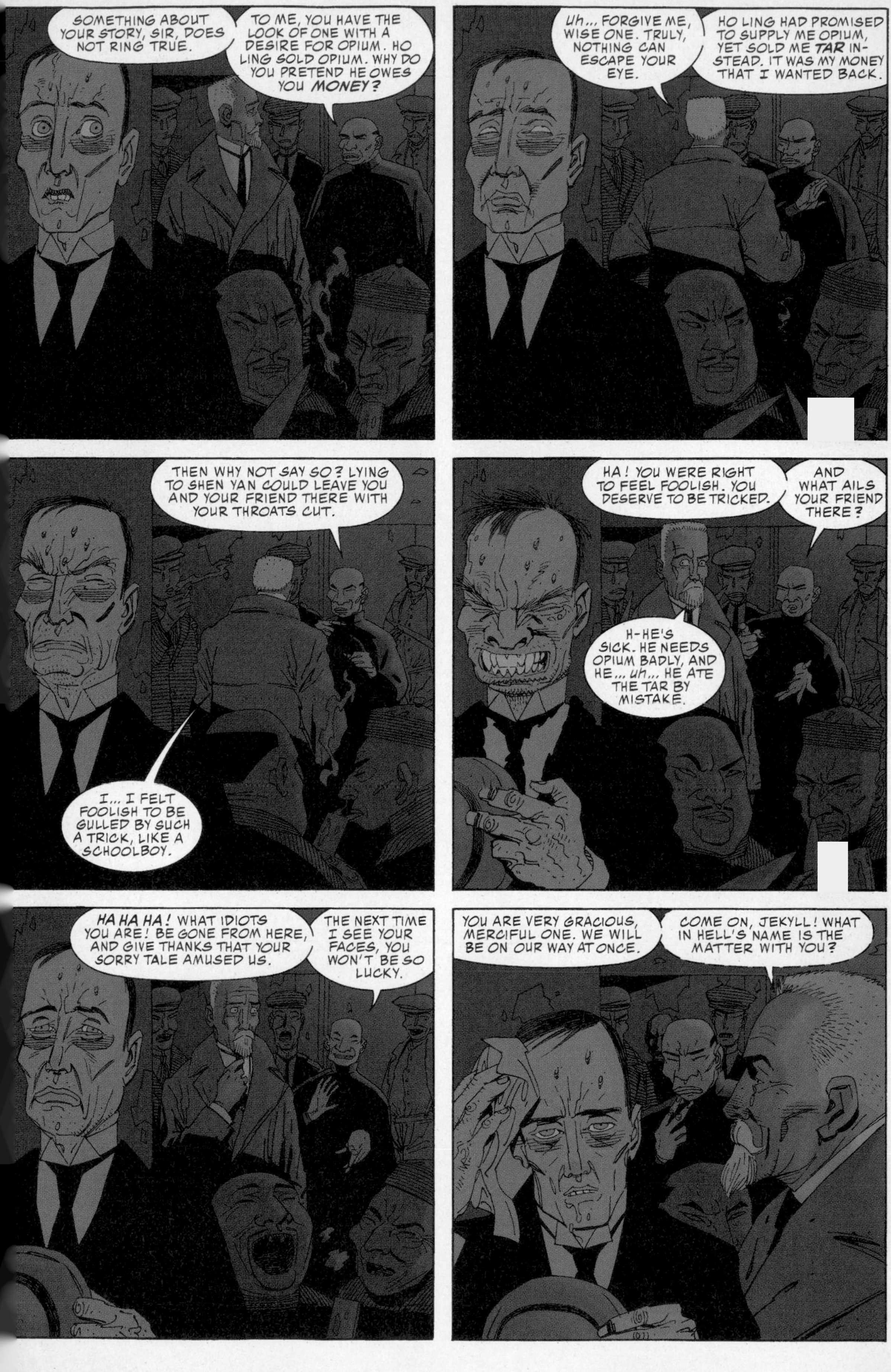
SOMETHING ABOUT YOUR STORY, SIR, DOES NOT RING TRUE.
TO ME, YOU HAVE THE LOOK OF ONE WITH A DESIRE FOR OPIUM. HO LING SOLD OPIUM. WHY DO YOU PRETEND HE OWES YOU MONEY?
Uh... FORGIVE ME, WISE ONE. TRULY, NOTHING CAN ESCAPE YOUR EYE.
HO LING HAD PROMISED TO SUPPLY ME OPIUM, YET SOLD ME TAR INSTEAD. IT WAS MY MONEY THAT I WANTED BACK.
THEN WHY NOT SAY SO? LYING TO SHEN YAN COULD LEAVE YOU AND YOUR FRIEND THERE WITH YOUR THROATS CUT.
I... I FELT FOOLISH TO BE GULLED BY SUCH A TRICK, LIKE A SCHOOLBOY.
HA! YOU WERE RIGHT TO FEEL FOOLISH. YOU DESERVE TO BE TRICKED.
AND WHAT AILS YOUR FRIEND THERE?
H-HE'S SICK. HE NEEDS OPIUM BADLY, AND HE... uh... HE ATE THE TAR BY MISTAKE.
HA HA HA! WHAT IDIOTS YOU ARE! BE GONE FROM HERE, AND GIVE THANKS THAT YOUR SORRY TALE AMUSED US.
THE NEXT TIME I SEE YOUR FACES, YOU WON'T BE SO LUCKY.
YOU ARE VERY GRACIOUS, MERCIFUL ONE. WE WILL BE ON OUR WAY AT ONCE.
COME ON, JEKYLL! WHAT IN HELL'S NAME IS THE MATTER WITH YOU?

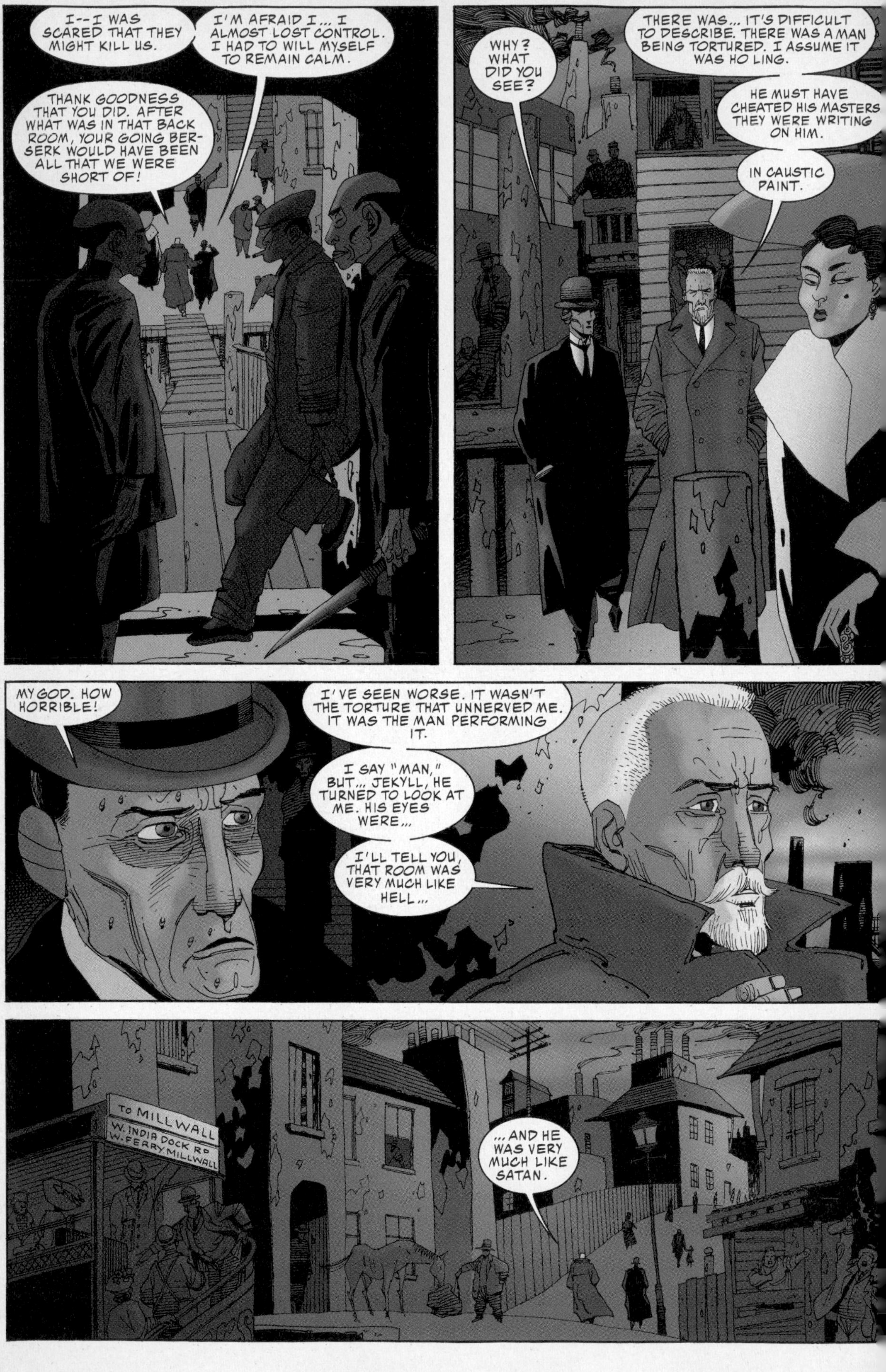
I--I WAS SCARED THAT THEY MIGHT KILL US.
I'M AFRAID I... I ALMOST LOST CONTROL. I HAD TO WILL MYSELF TO REMAIN CALM.
THANK GOODNESS THAT YOU DID. AFTER WHAT WAS IN THAT BACK ROOM, YOUR GOING BER-SERK WOULD HAVE BEEN ALL THAT WE WERE SHORT OF!
WHY? WHAT DID YOU SEE?
THERE WAS... IT'S DIFFICULT TO DESCRIBE. THERE WAS A MAN BEING TORTURED. I ASSUME IT WAS HO LING.
HE MUST HAVE CHEATED HIS MASTERS THEY WERE WRITING ON HIM.
IN CAUSTIC PAINT.
MY GOD. HOW HORRIBLE!
I'VE SEEN WORSE. IT WASN'T THE TORTURE THAT UNNERVED ME. IT WAS THE MAN PERFORMING IT.
I SAY "MAN," BUT... JEKYLL, HE TURNED TO LOOK AT ME. HIS EYES WERE...
I'LL TELL YOU, THAT ROOM WAS VERY MUCH LIKE HELL...
TO MILLWALL
W. INDIA DOCK RD
W. FERRY. MILLWALL
...AND HE WAS VERY MUCH LIKE SATAN.

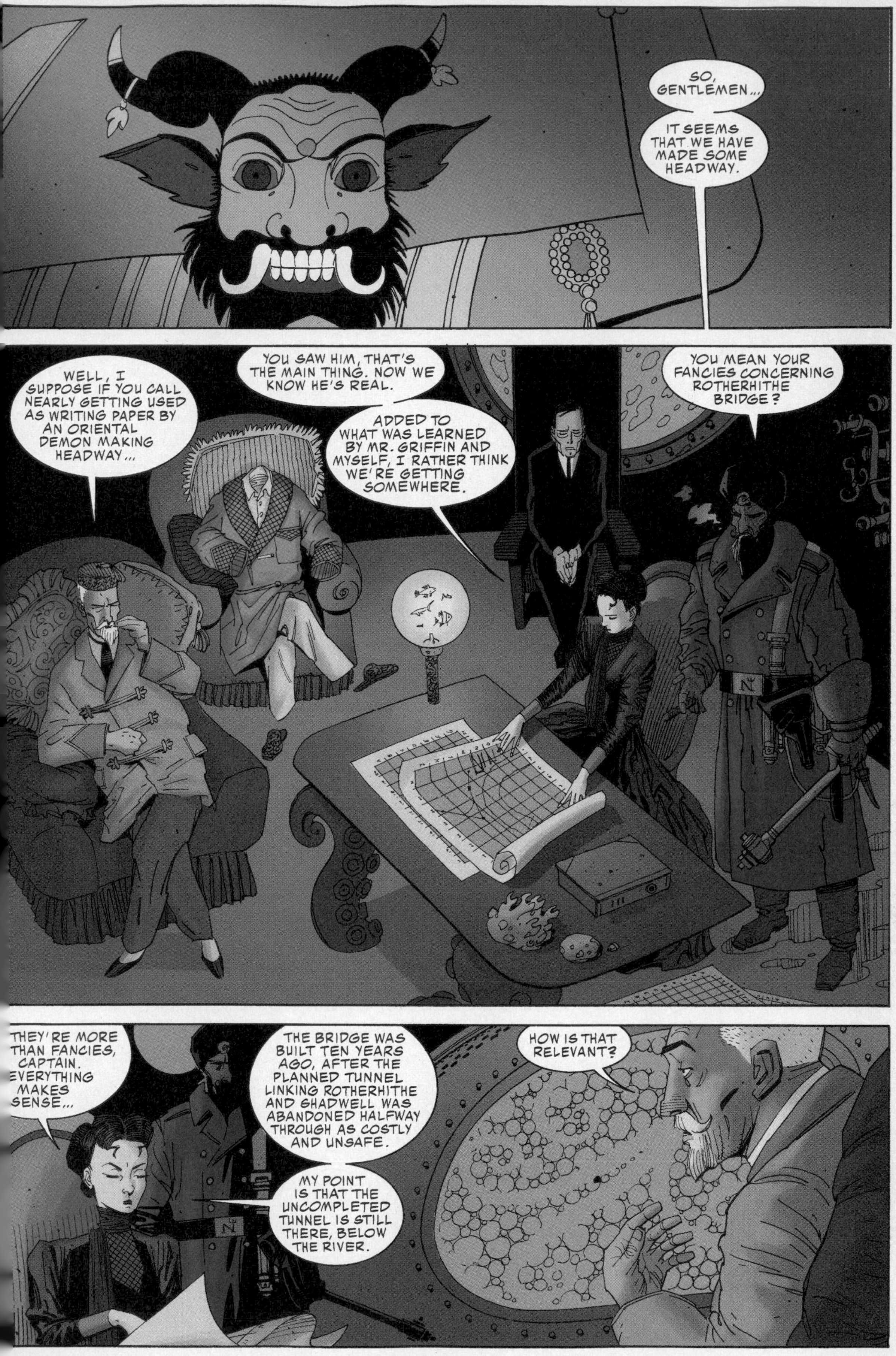
SO, GENTLEMEN...
IT SEEMS THAT WE HAVE MADE SOME HEADWAY.
WELL, I SUPPOSE IF YOU CALL NEARLY GETTING USED AS WRITING PAPER BY AN ORIENTAL DEMON MAKING HEADWAY...
YOU SAW HIM, THAT'S THE MAIN THING. NOW WE KNOW HE'S REAL.
ADDED TO WHAT WAS LEARNED BY MR. GRIFFIN AND MYSELF, I RATHER THINK WE'RE GETTING SOMEWHERE.
YOU MEAN YOUR FANCIES CONCERNING ROTHERHITHE BRIDGE?
THEY'RE MORE THAN FANCIES, CAPTAIN. EVERYTHING MAKES SENSE...
THE BRIDGE WAS BUILT TEN YEARS AGO, AFTER THE PLANNED TUNNEL LINKING ROTHERHITHE AND SHADWELL WAS ABANDONED HALFWAY THROUGH AS COSTLY AND UNSAFE.
MY POINT IS THAT THE UNCOMPLETED TUNNEL IS STILL THERE, BELOW THE RIVER.
HOW IS THAT RELEVANT?

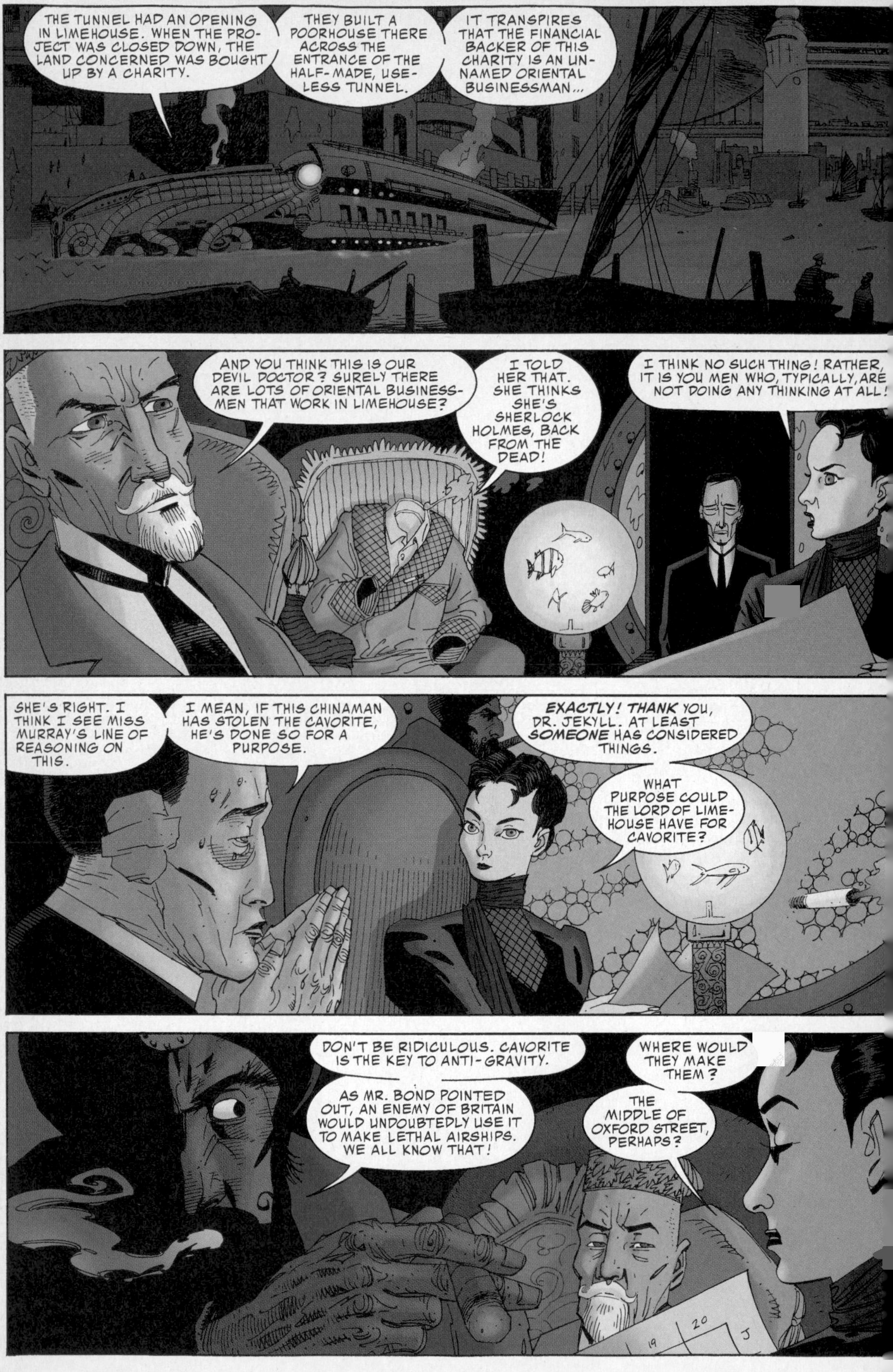
THE TUNNEL HAD AN OPENING IN LIMEHOUSE. WHEN THE PROJECT WAS CLOSED DOWN, THE LAND CONCERNED WAS BOUGHT UP BY A CHARITY.
THEY BUILT A POORHOUSE THERE ACROSS THE ENTRANCE OF THE HALF-MADE, USELESS TUNNEL.
IT TRANSPIRES THAT THE FINANCIAL BACKER OF THIS CHARITY IS AN UNNAMED ORIENTAL BUSINESSMAN...
AND YOU THINK THIS IS OUR DEVIL DOCTOR? SURELY THERE ARE LOTS OF ORIENTAL BUSINESSMEN THAT WORK IN LIMEHOUSE?
I TOLD HER THAT. SHE THINKS SHE'S SHERLOCK HOLMES, BACK FROM THE DEAD!
I THINK NO SUCH THING! RATHER, IT IS YOU MEN WHO, TYPICALLY, ARE NOT DOING ANY THINKING AT ALL!
SHE'S RIGHT. I THINK I SEE MISS MURRAY'S LINE OF REASONING ON THIS.
I MEAN, IF THIS CHINAMAN HAS STOLEN THE CAVORITE, HE'S DONE SO FOR A PURPOSE.
EXACTLY! THANK YOU, DR. JEKYLL. AT LEAST SOMEONE HAS CONSIDERED THINGS.
WHAT PURPOSE COULD THE LORD OF LIMEHOUSE HAVE FOR CAVORITE?
DON'T BE RIDICULOUS. CAVORITE IS THE KEY TO ANTI-GRAVITY.
AS MR. BOND POINTED OUT, AN ENEMY OF BRITAIN WOULD UNDOUBTEDLY USE IT TO MAKE LETHAL AIRSHIPS. WE ALL KNOW THAT!
WHERE WOULD THEY MAKE THEM?
THE MIDDLE OF OXFORD STREET, PERHAPS?

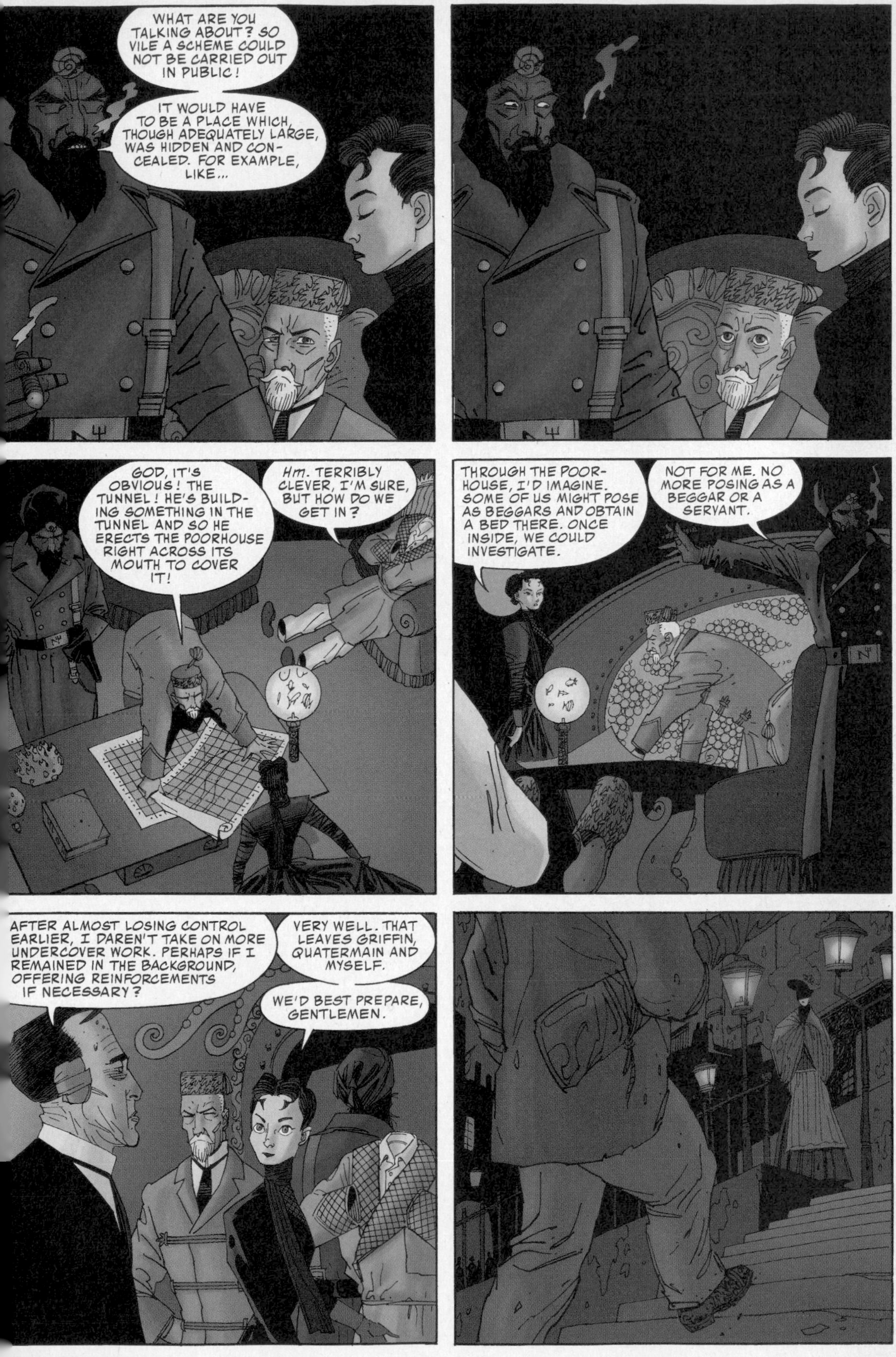
WHAT ARE YOU TALKING ABOUT? SO VILE A SCHEME COULD NOT BE CARRIED OUT IN PUBLIC!
IT WOULD HAVE TO BE A PLACE WHICH, THOUGH ADEQUATELY LARGE, WAS HIDDEN AND CONCEALED. FOR EXAMPLE, LIKE...
GOD, IT'S OBVIOUS! THE TUNNEL! HE'S BUILDING SOMETHING IN THE TUNNEL AND SO HE ERECTS THE POORHOUSE RIGHT ACROSS ITS MOUTH TO COVER IT!
Hm. TERRIBLY CLEVER, I'M SURE, BUT HOW DO WE GET IN?
THROUGH THE POORHOUSE, I'D IMAGINE. SOME OF US MIGHT POSE AS BEGGARS AND OBTAIN A BED THERE. ONCE INSIDE, WE COULD INVESTIGATE.
NOT FOR ME. NO MORE POSING AS A BEGGAR OR A SERVANT.
AFTER ALMOST LOSING CONTROL EARLIER, I DAREN'T TAKE ON MORE UNDERCOVER WORK. PERHAPS IF I REMAINED IN THE BACKGROUND, OFFERING REINFORCEMENTS IF NECESSARY?
VERY WELL. THAT LEAVES GRIFFIN, QUATERMAIN AND MYSELF.
WE'D BEST PREPARE, GENTLEMEN.

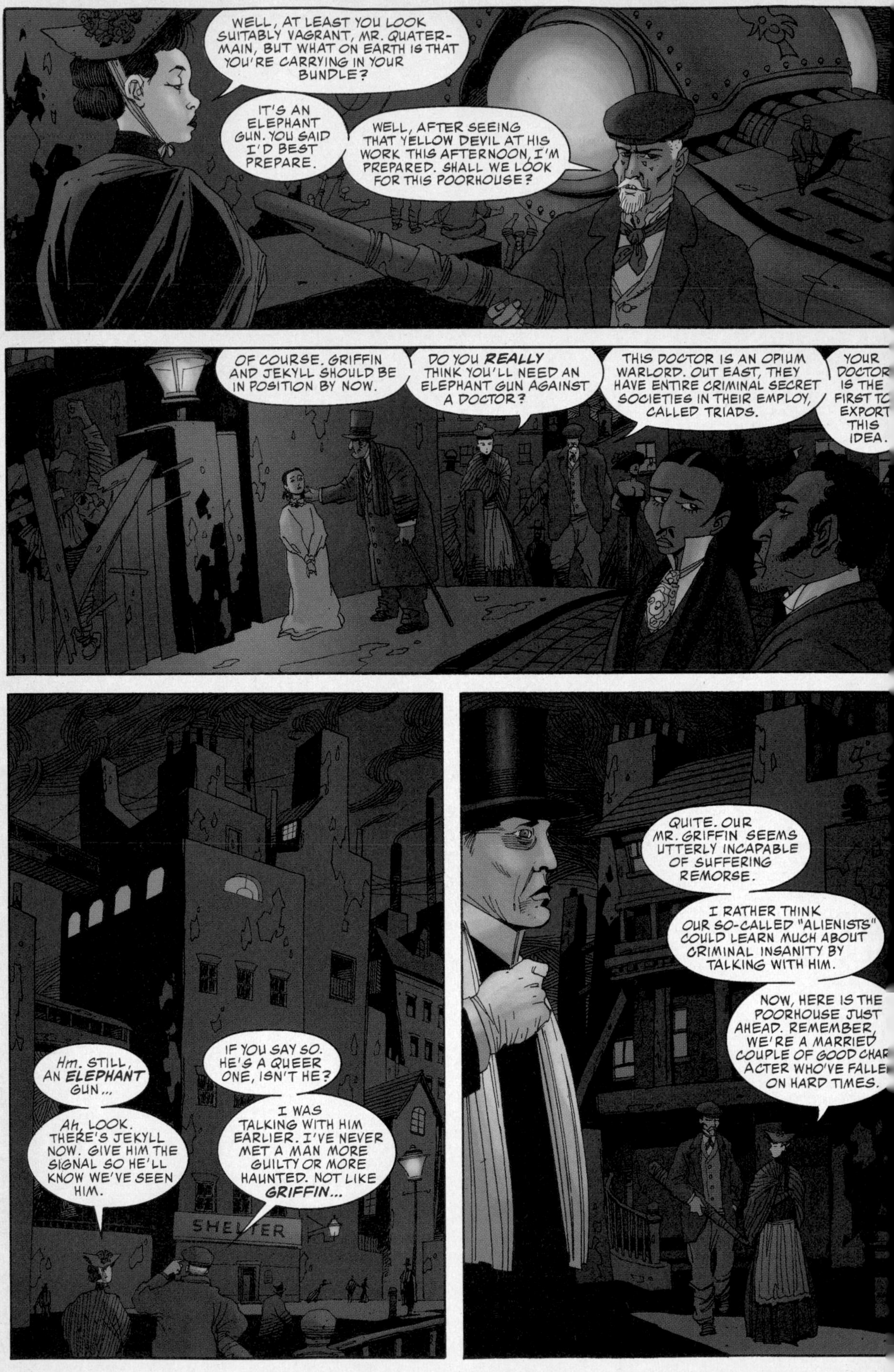
WELL, AT LEAST YOU LOOK SUITABLY VAGRANT, MR. QUATERMAIN, BUT WHAT ON EARTH IS THAT YOU'RE CARRYING IN YOUR BUNDLE?
IT'S AN ELEPHANT GUN. YOU SAID I'D BEST PREPARE.
WELL, AFTER SEEING THAT YELLOW DEVIL AT HIS WORK THIS AFTERNOON, I'M PREPARED. SHALL WE LOOK FOR THIS POORHOUSE?
OF COURSE. GRIFFIN AND JEKYLL SHOULD BE IN POSITION BY NOW.
DO YOU REALLY THINK YOU'LL NEED AN ELEPHANT GUN AGAINST A DOCTOR?
THIS DOCTOR IS AN OPIUM WARLORD. OUT EAST, THEY HAVE ENTIRE CRIMINAL SECRET SOCIETIES IN THEIR EMPLOY, CALLED TRIADS.
YOUR DOCTOR IS THE FIRST TO EXPORT THIS IDEA.
Hm. STILL, AN ELEPHANT GUN...
Ah, LOOK. THERE'S JEKYLL NOW. GIVE HIM THE SIGNAL SO HE'LL KNOW WE'VE SEEN HIM.
IF YOU SAY SO. HE'S A QUEER ONE, ISN'T HE?
I WAS TALKING WITH HIM EARLIER. I'VE NEVER MET A MAN MORE GUILTY OR MORE HAUNTED. NOT LIKE GRIFFIN...
SHELTER
QUITE. OUR MR. GRIFFIN SEEMS UTTERLY INCAPABLE OF SUFFERING REMORSE.
I RATHER THINK OUR SO-CALLED "ALIENISTS" COULD LEARN MUCH ABOUT CRIMINAL INSANITY BY TALKING WITH HIM.
NOW, HERE IS THE POORHOUSE JUST AHEAD. REMEMBER, WE'RE A MARRIED COUPLE OF GOOD CHAR ACTER WHO'VE FALLE ON HARD TIMES.

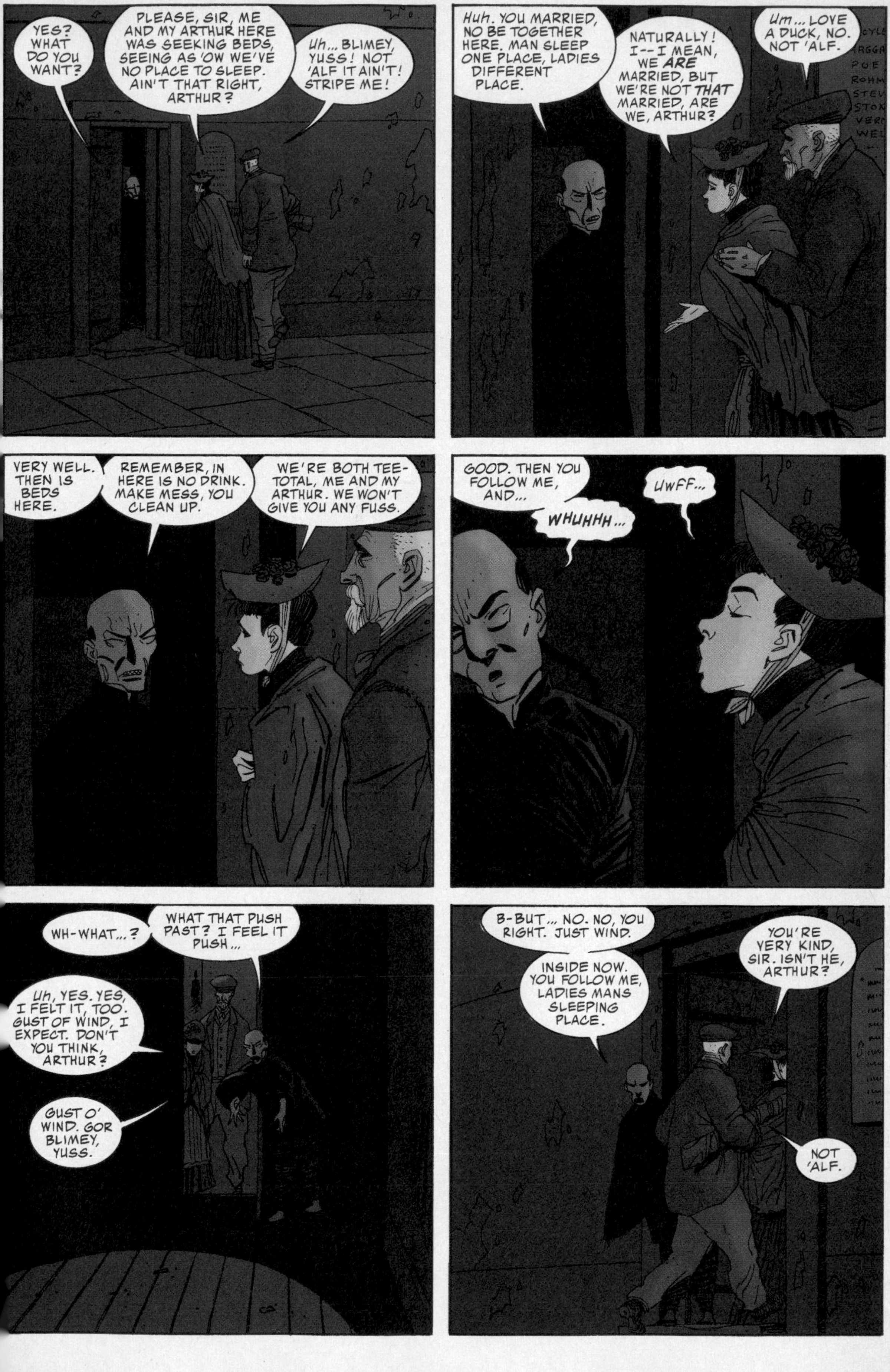

YES? WHAT DO YOU WANT?
PLEASE, SIR, ME AND MY ARTHUR HERE WAS SEEKING BEDS, SEEING AS 'OW WE'VE NO PLACE TO SLEEP. AIN'T THAT RIGHT, ARTHUR?
Uh... BLIMEY, YUSS! NOT 'ALF IT AIN'T! STRIPE ME!
Huh. YOU MARRIED, NO BE TOGETHER HERE. MAN SLEEP ONE PLACE, LADIES DIFFERENT PLACE.
NATURALLY! I-- I MEAN, WE ARE MARRIED, BUT WE'RE NOT THAT MARRIED, ARE WE, ARTHUR?
Um... LOVE A DUCK, NO. NOT 'ALF.
VERY WELL. THEN IS BEDS HERE.
REMEMBER, IN HERE IS NO DRINK. MAKE MESS, YOU CLEAN UP.
WE'RE BOTH TEE-TOTAL, ME AND MY ARTHUR. WE WON'T GIVE YOU ANY FUSS.
GOOD. THEN YOU FOLLOW ME, AND...
WHUHHH...
UWFF...
WH-WHAT...?
WHAT THAT PUSH PAST? I FEEL IT PUSH...
Uh, YES. YES, I FELT IT, TOO. GUST OF WIND, I EXPECT. DON'T YOU THINK, ARTHUR?
GUST O' WIND. GOR BLIMEY, YUSS.
B-BUT... NO. NO, YOU RIGHT. JUST WIND.
INSIDE NOW. YOU FOLLOW ME, LADIES MANS SLEEPING PLACE.
YOU'RE VERY KIND, SIR. ISN'T HE, ARTHUR?
NOT 'ALF.

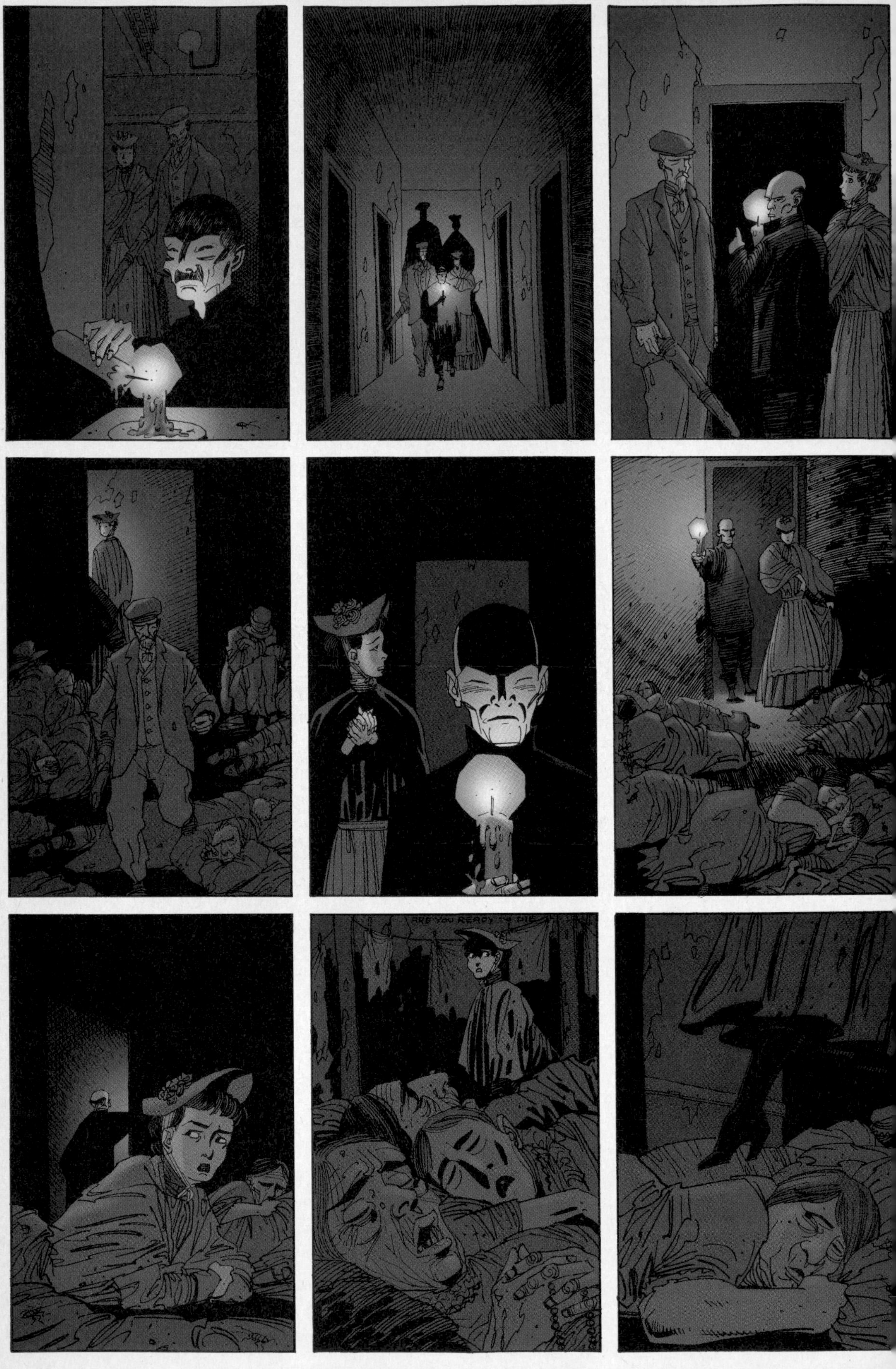
ARE YOU READY TO DIE

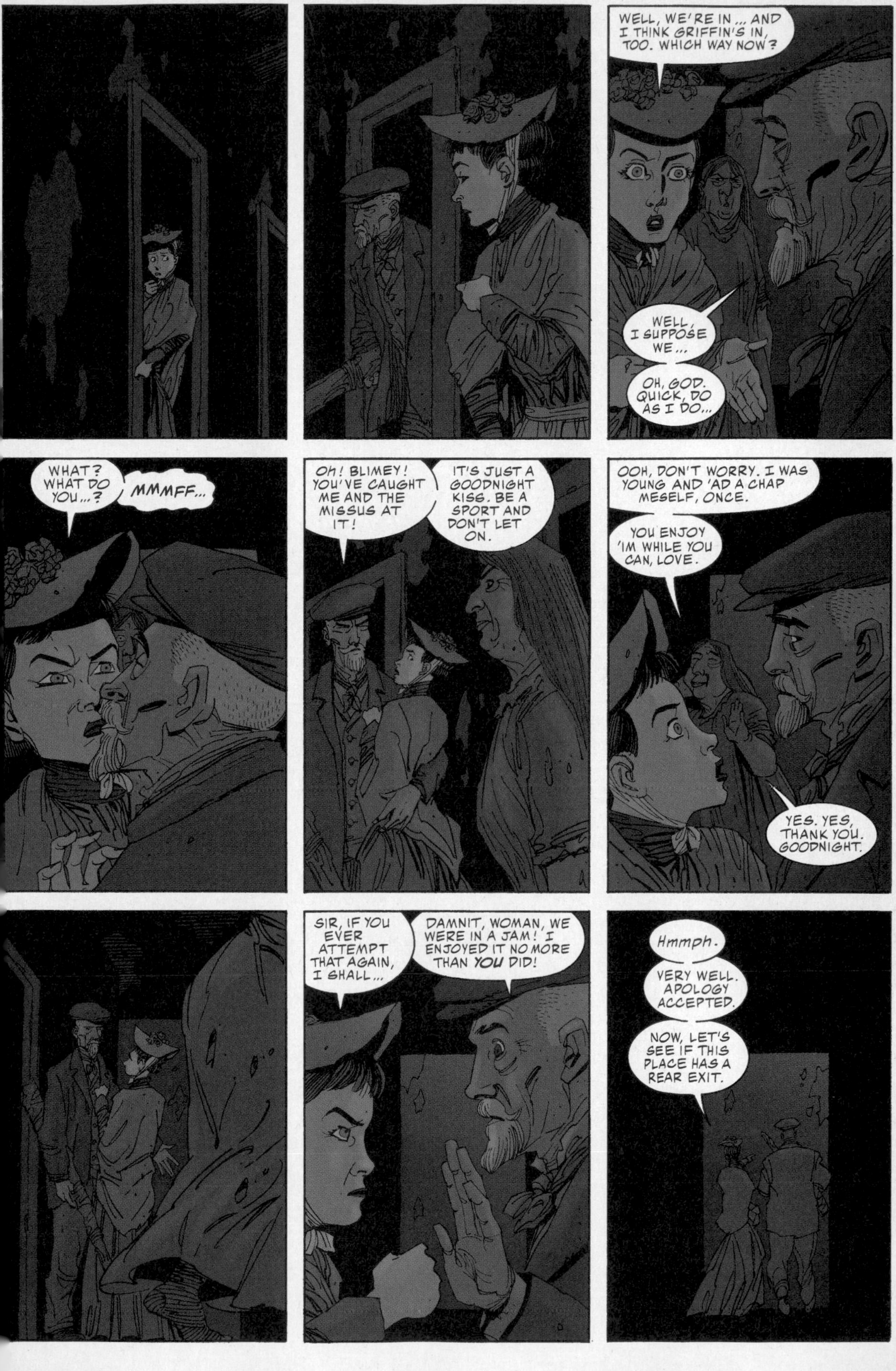
WELL, WE'RE IN... AND I THINK GRIFFIN'S IN, TOO. WHICH WAY NOW?
WELL, I SUPPOSE WE...
OH, GOD. QUICK, DO AS I DO...
WHAT? WHAT DO YOU...?
MMMFF...
Oh! BLIMEY! YOU'VE CAUGHT ME AND THE MISSUS AT IT!
IT'S JUST A GOODNIGHT KISS. BE A SPORT AND DON'T LET ON.
OOH, DON'T WORRY. I WAS YOUNG AND 'AD A CHAP MESELF, ONCE.
YOU ENJOY 'IM WHILE YOU CAN, LOVE.
YES. YES, THANK YOU. GOODNIGHT.
SIR, IF YOU EVER ATTEMPT THAT AGAIN, I SHALL...
DAMNIT, WOMAN, WE WERE IN A JAM! I ENJOYED IT NO MORE THAN YOU DID!
Hmmph.
VERY WELL. APOLOGY ACCEPTED.
NOW, LET'S SEE IF THIS PLACE HAS A REAR EXIT.

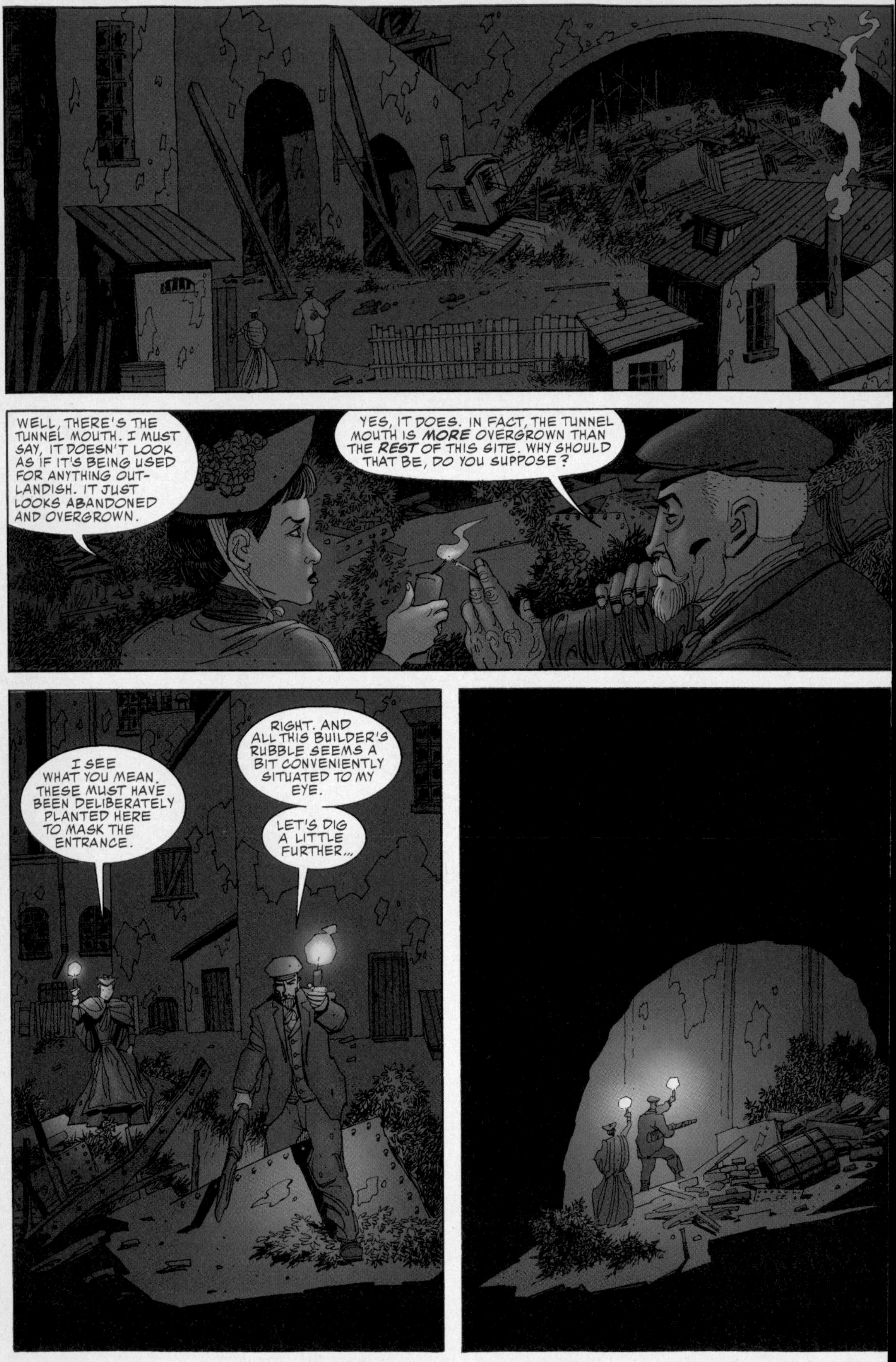
WELL, THERE'S THE TUNNEL MOUTH. I MUST SAY, IT DOESN'T LOOK AS IF IT'S BEING USED FOR ANYTHING OUT-LANDISH. IT JUST LOOKS ABANDONED AND OVERGROWN.
YES, IT DOES. IN FACT, THE TUNNEL MOUTH IS MORE OVERGROWN THAN THE REST OF THIS SITE. WHY SHOULD THAT BE, DO YOU SUPPOSE?
I SEE WHAT YOU MEAN. THESE MUST HAVE BEEN DELIBERATELY PLANTED HERE TO MASK THE ENTRANCE.
RIGHT. AND ALL THIS BUILDER'S RUBBLE SEEMS A BIT CONVENIENTLY SITUATED TO MY EYE.
LET'S DIG A LITTLE FURTHER...

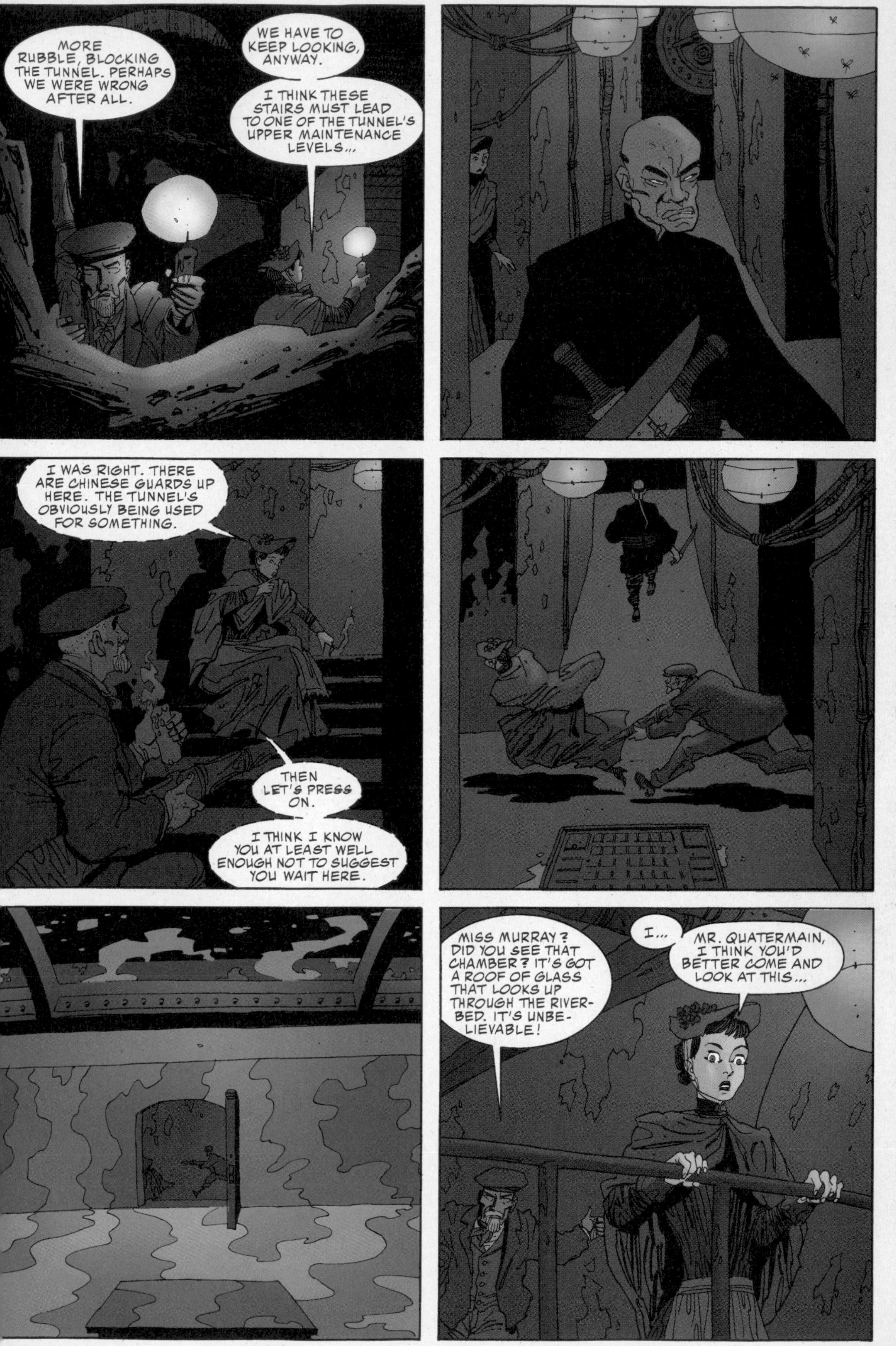
MORE RUBBLE, BLOCKING THE TUNNEL. PERHAPS WE WERE WRONG AFTER ALL.
WE HAVE TO KEEP LOOKING, ANYWAY.
I THINK THESE STAIRS MUST LEAD TO ONE OF THE TUNNEL'S UPPER MAINTENANCE LEVELS...
I WAS RIGHT. THERE ARE CHINESE GUARDS UP HERE. THE TUNNEL'S OBVIOUSLY BEING USED FOR SOMETHING.
THEN LET'S PRESS ON.
I THINK I KNOW YOU AT LEAST WELL ENOUGH NOT TO SUGGEST YOU WAIT HERE.
MISS MURRAY? DID YOU SEE THAT CHAMBER? IT'S GOT A ROOF OF GLASS THAT LOOKS UP THROUGH THE RIVER-BED. IT'S UNBE-LIEVABLE!
I...
MR. QUATERMAIN, I THINK YOU'D BETTER COME AND LOOK AT THIS...

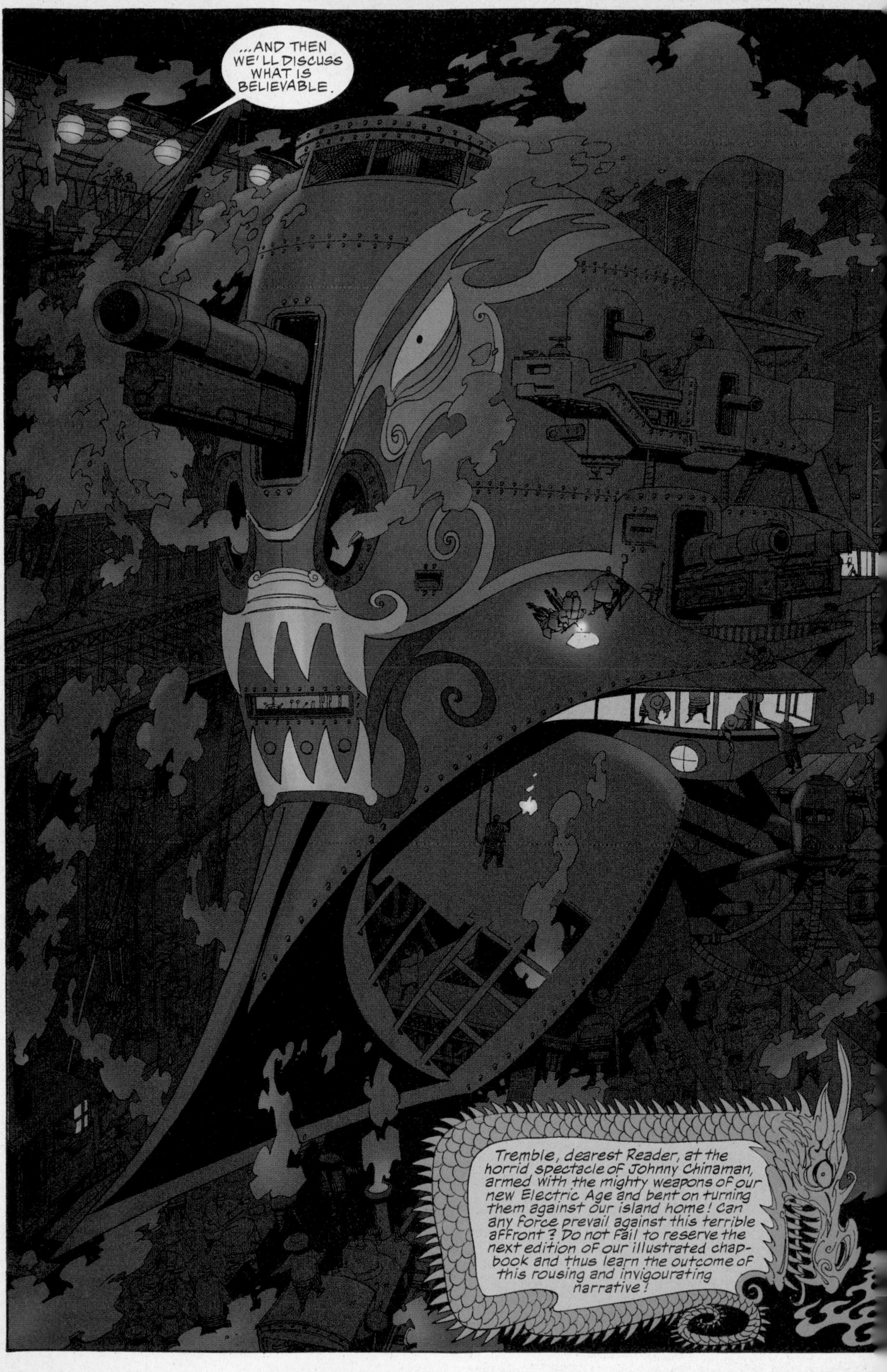
...AND THEN WE'LL DISCUSS WHAT IS BELIEVABLE.
Tremble, dearest Reader, at the horrid spectacle of Johnny Chinaman, armed with the mighty weapons of our new Electric Age and bent on turning them against our island home! Can any force prevail against this terrible affront? Do not fail to reserve the next edition of our illustrated chap-book and thus learn the outcome of this rousing and invigourating narrative!

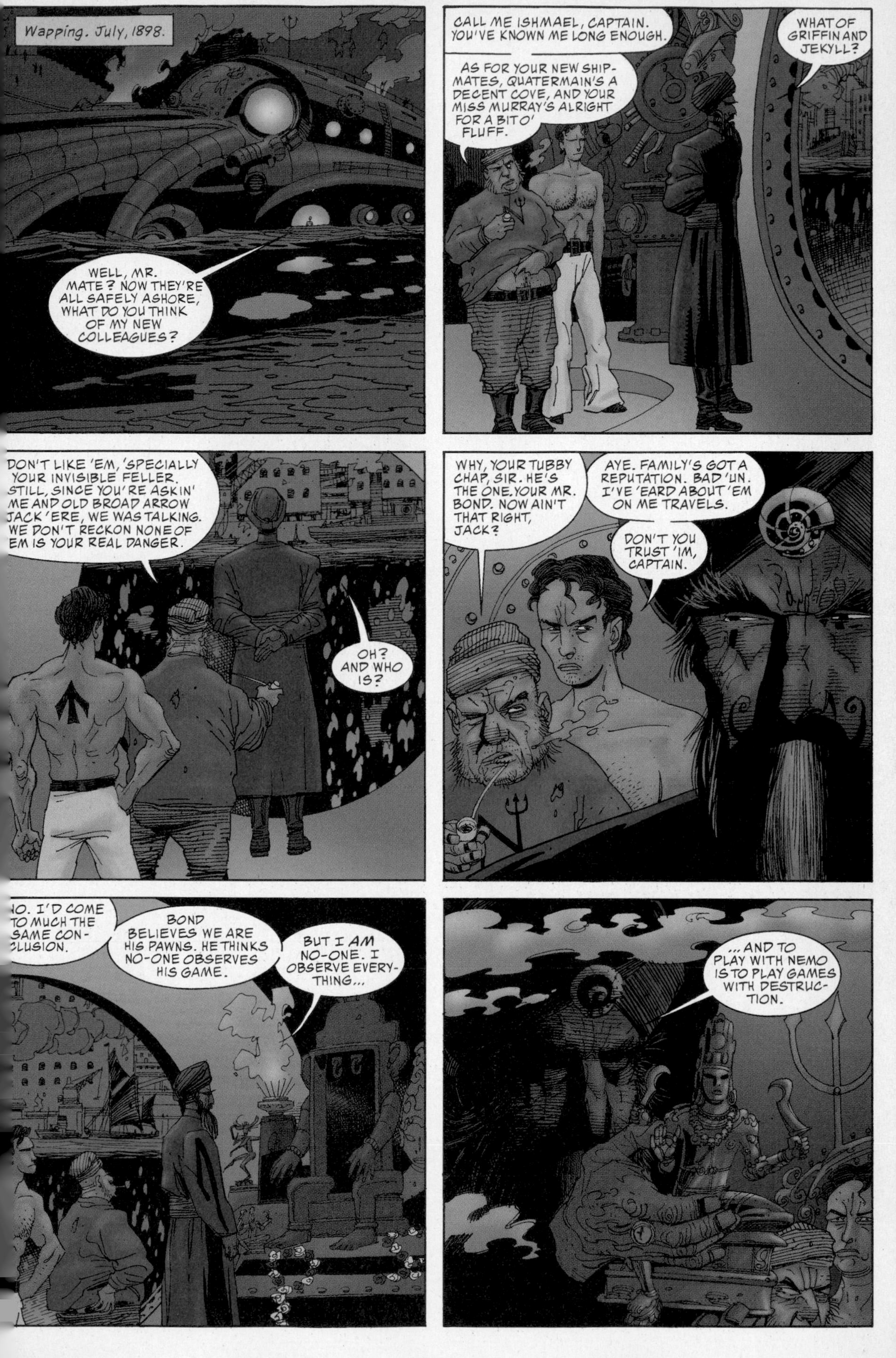

Wapping. July, 1898.
WELL, MR. MATE? NOW THEY'RE ALL SAFELY ASHORE, WHAT DO YOU THINK OF MY NEW COLLEAGUES?
CALL ME ISHMAEL, CAPTAIN. YOU'VE KNOWN ME LONG ENOUGH.
AS FOR YOUR NEW SHIPMATES, QUATERMAIN'S A DECENT COVE, AND YOUR MISS MURRAY'S ALRIGHT FOR A BIT O' FLUFF.
WHAT OF GRIFFIN AND JEKYLL?
DON'T LIKE 'EM, 'SPECIALLY YOUR INVISIBLE FELLER. STILL, SINCE YOU'RE ASKIN' ME AND OLD BROAD ARROW JACK 'ERE, WE WAS TALKING. WE DON'T RECKON NONE OF 'EM IS YOUR REAL DANGER.
OH? AND WHO IS?
WHY, YOUR TUBBY CHAP, SIR. HE'S THE ONE. YOUR MR. BOND. NOW AIN'T THAT RIGHT, JACK?
AYE. FAMILY'S GOT A REPUTATION. BAD 'UN. I'VE 'EARD ABOUT 'EM ON ME TRAVELS.
DON'T YOU TRUST 'IM, CAPTAIN.
NO. I'D COME TO MUCH THE SAME CONCLUSION.
BOND BELIEVES WE ARE HIS PAWNS. HE THINKS NO-ONE OBSERVES HIS GAME.
BUT I AM NO-ONE. I OBSERVE EVERYTHING...
...AND TO PLAY WITH NEMO IS TO PLAY GAMES WITH DESTRUCTION.

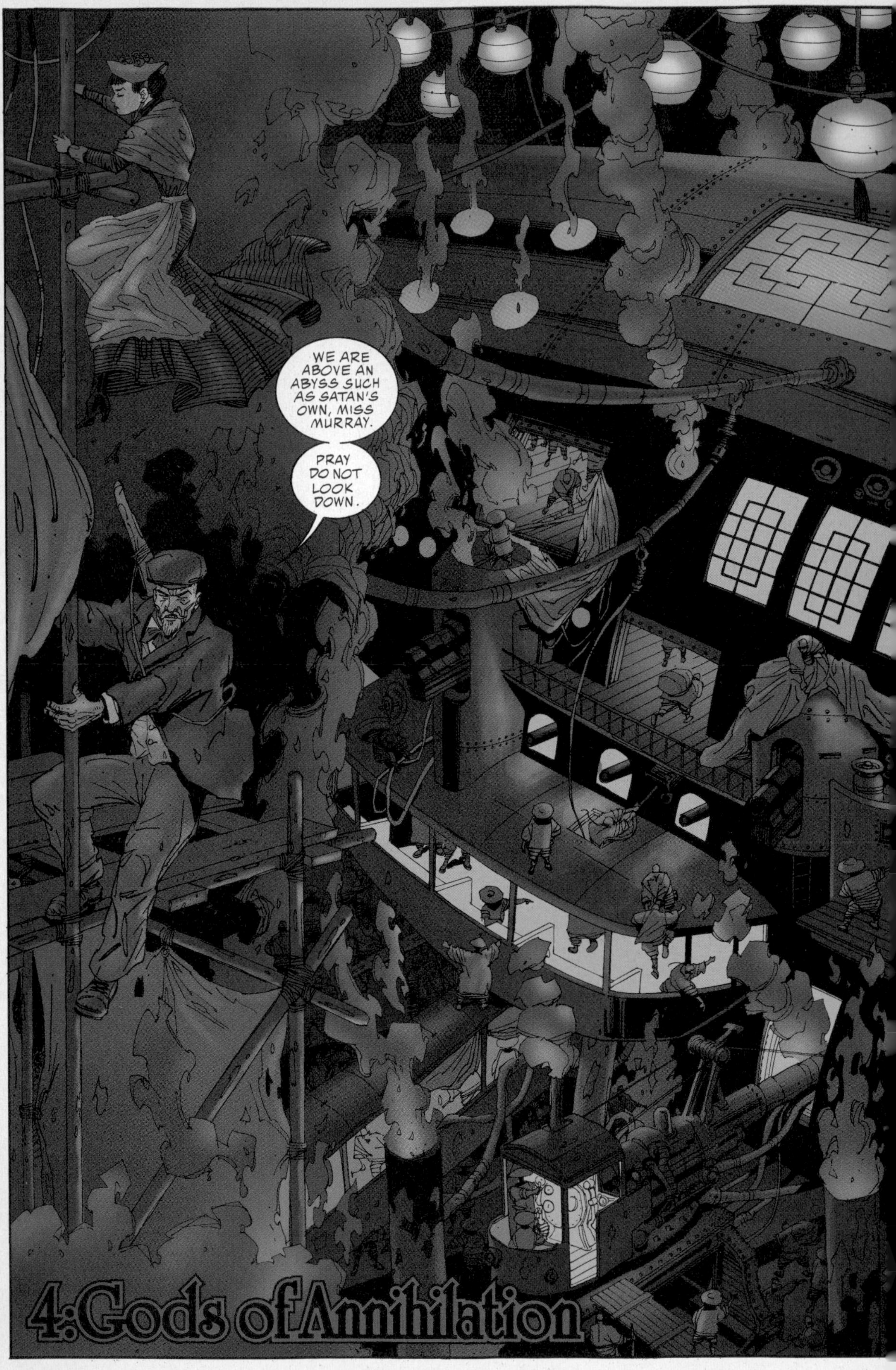
WE ARE ABOVE AN ABYSS SUCH AS SATAN'S OWN, MISS MURRAY.
PRAY DO NOT LOOK DOWN.
4:Gods of Annihilation

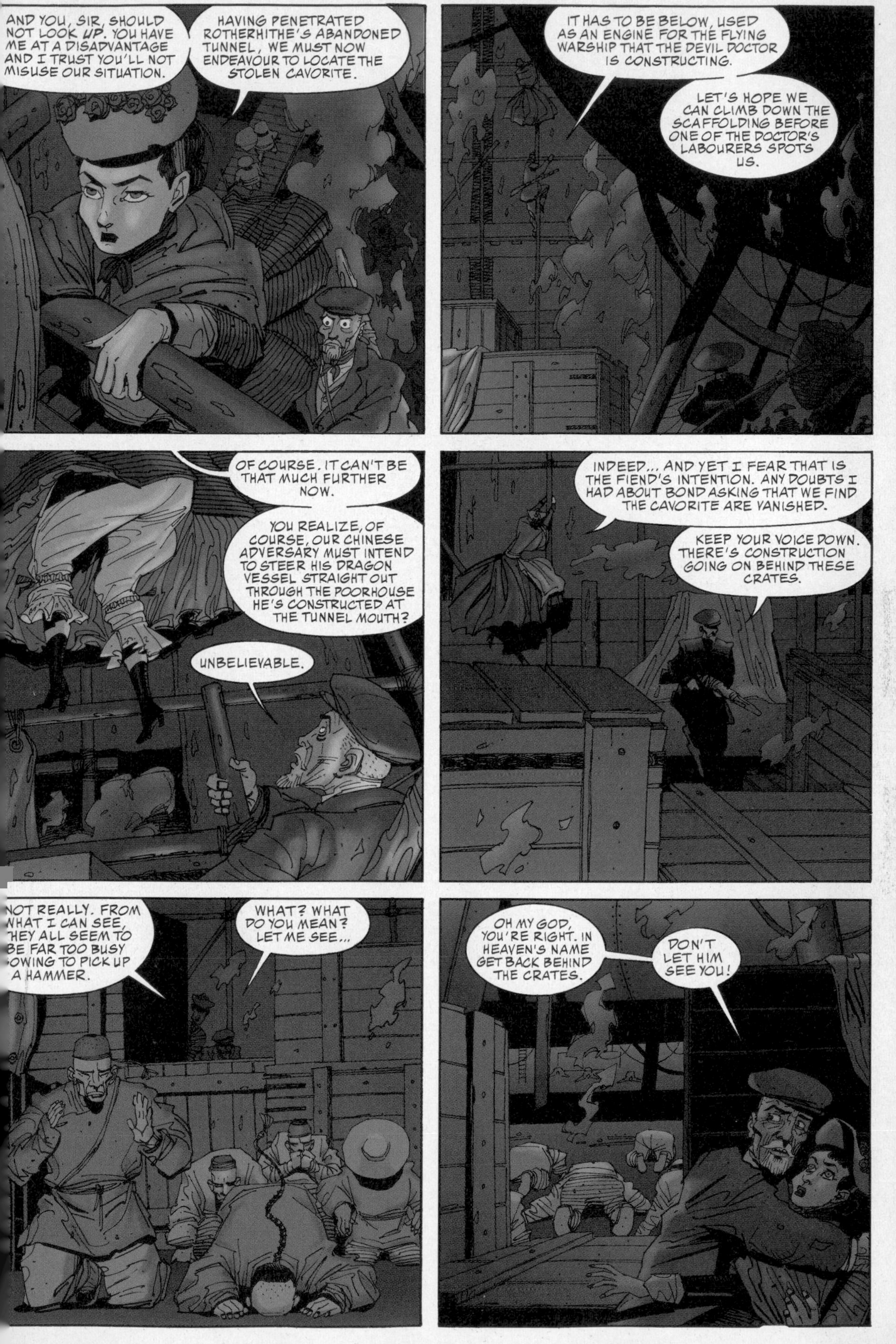
AND YOU, SIR, SHOULD NOT LOOK UP. YOU HAVE ME AT A DISADVANTAGE AND I TRUST YOU'LL NOT MISUSE OUR SITUATION.
HAVING PENETRATED ROTHERHITHE'S ABANDONED TUNNEL, WE MUST NOW ENDEAVOUR TO LOCATE THE STOLEN CAVORITE.
IT HAS TO BE BELOW, USED AS AN ENGINE FOR THE FLYING WARSHIP THAT THE DEVIL DOCTOR IS CONSTRUCTING.
LET'S HOPE WE CAN CLIMB DOWN THE SCAFFOLDING BEFORE ONE OF THE DOCTOR'S LABOURERS SPOTS US.
OF COURSE. IT CAN'T BE THAT MUCH FURTHER NOW.
YOU REALIZE, OF COURSE, OUR CHINESE ADVERSARY MUST INTEND TO STEER HIS DRAGON VESSEL STRAIGHT OUT THROUGH THE POORHOUSE HE'S CONSTRUCTED AT THE TUNNEL MOUTH?
UNBELIEVABLE.
INDEED... AND YET I FEAR THAT IS THE FIEND'S INTENTION. ANY DOUBTS I HAD ABOUT BOND ASKING THAT WE FIND THE CAVORITE ARE VANISHED.
KEEP YOUR VOICE DOWN. THERE'S CONSTRUCTION GOING ON BEHIND THESE CRATES.
NOT REALLY. FROM WHAT I CAN SEE, THEY ALL SEEM TO BE FAR TOO BUSY BOWING TO PICK UP A HAMMER.
WHAT? WHAT DO YOU MEAN? LET ME SEE...
OH MY GOD, YOU'RE RIGHT. IN HEAVEN'S NAME GET BACK BEHIND THE CRATES.
DON'T LET HIM SEE YOU!

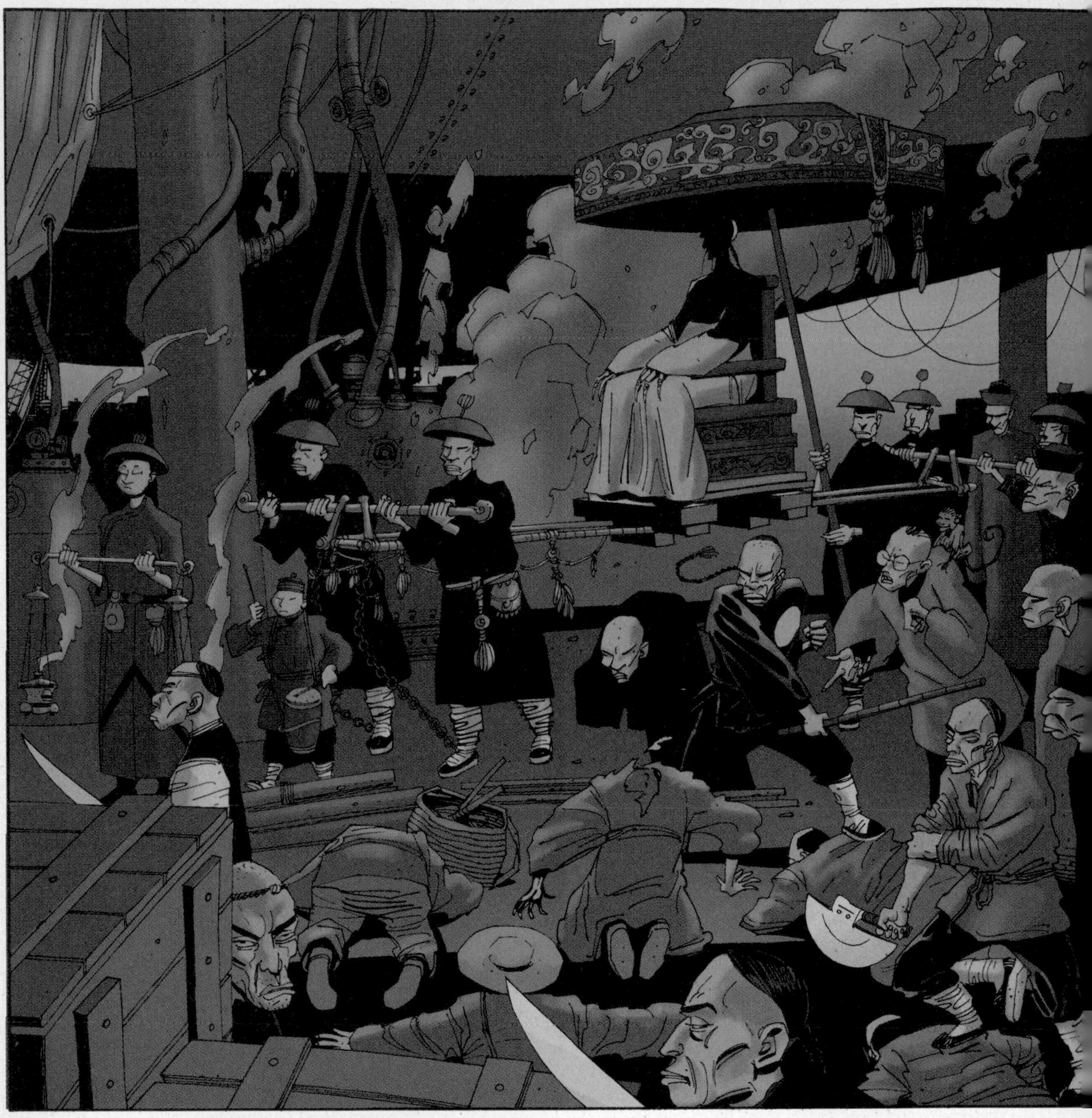

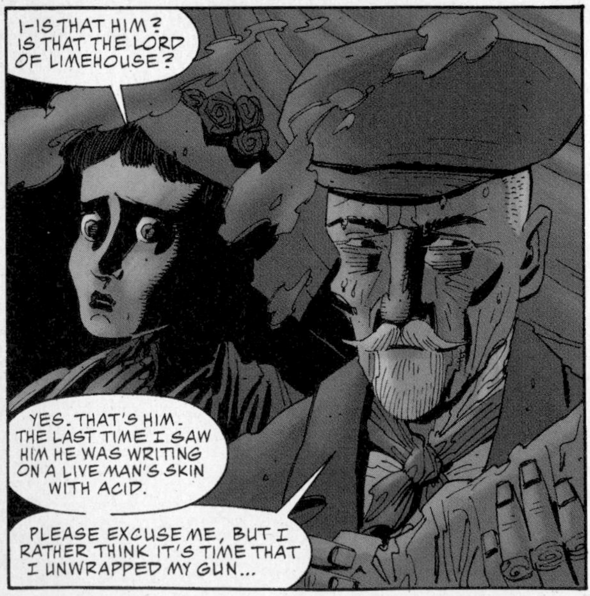
I-IS THAT HIM? IS THAT THE LORD OF LIMEHOUSE?
YES. THAT'S HIM. THE LAST TIME I SAW HIM HE WAS WRITING ON A LIVE MAN'S SKIN WITH ACID.
PLEASE EXCUSE ME, BUT I RATHER THINK IT'S TIME THAT I UNWRAPPED MY GUN...

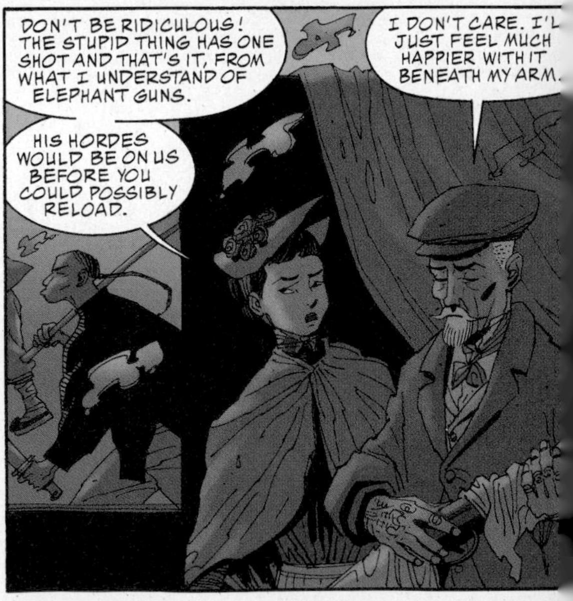
DON'T BE RIDICULOUS! THE STUPID THING HAS ONE SHOT AND THAT'S IT, FROM WHAT I UNDERSTAND OF ELEPHANT GUNS.
HIS HORDES WOULD BE ON US BEFORE YOU COULD POSSIBLY RELOAD.
I DON'T CARE. I'L JUST FEEL MUCH HAPPIER WITH IT BENEATH MY ARM.

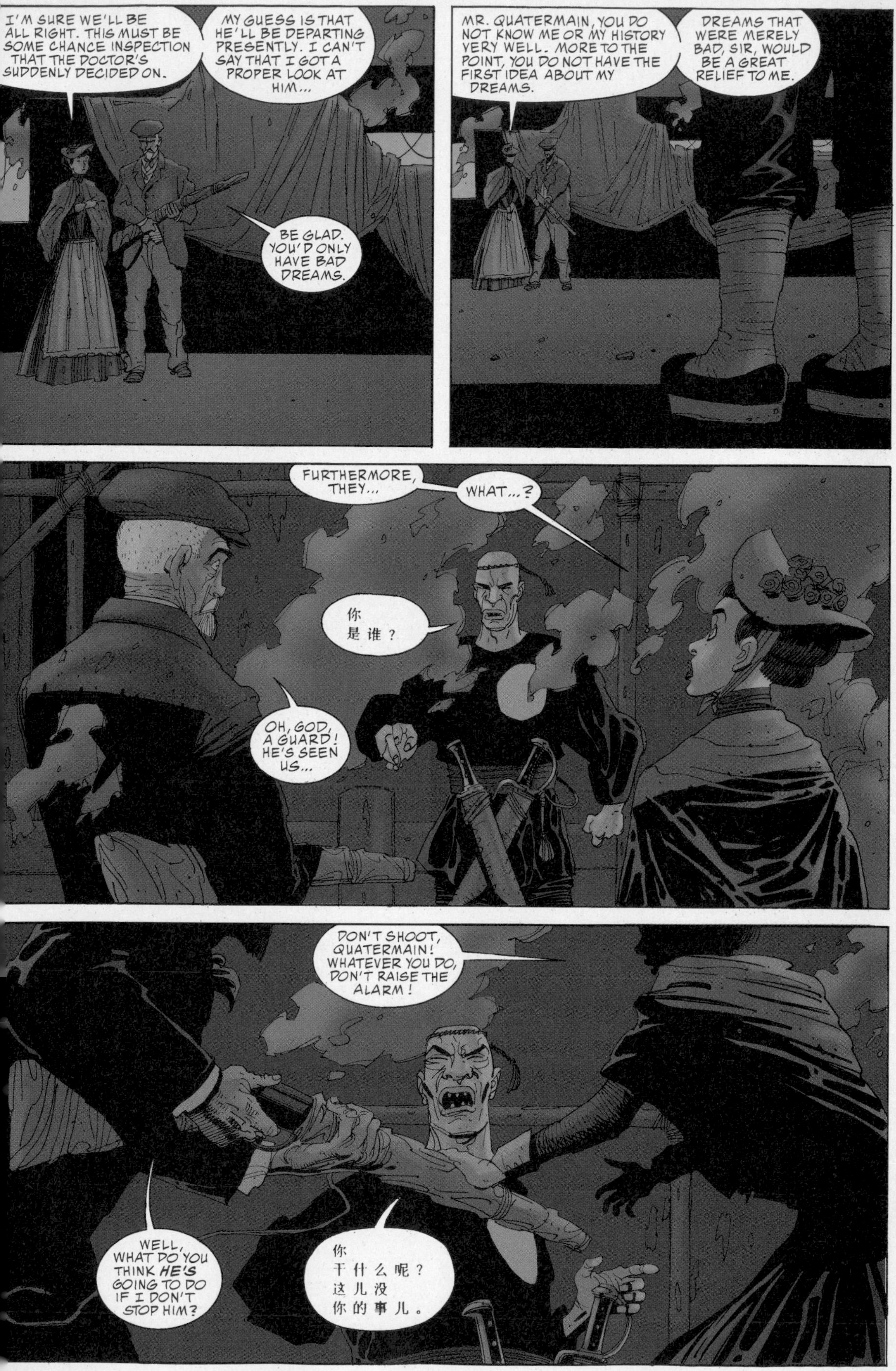
I'M SURE WE'LL BE ALL RIGHT. THIS MUST BE SOME CHANCE INSPECTION THAT THE DOCTOR'S SUDDENLY DECIDED ON.
MY GUESS IS THAT HE'LL BE DEPARTING PRESENTLY. I CAN'T SAY THAT I GOT A PROPER LOOK AT HIM...
BE GLAD. YOU'D ONLY HAVE BAD DREAMS.
MR. QUATERMAIN, YOU DO NOT KNOW ME OR MY HISTORY VERY WELL. MORE TO THE POINT, YOU DO NOT HAVE THE FIRST IDEA ABOUT MY DREAMS.
DREAMS THAT WERE MERELY BAD, SIR, WOULD BE A GREAT RELIEF TO ME.
FURTHERMORE, THEY...
WHAT...?
你是谁？
OH, GOD, A GUARD! HE'S SEEN US...
DON'T SHOOT, QUATERMAIN! WHATEVER YOU DO, DON'T RAISE THE ALARM!
WELL, WHAT DO YOU THINK HE'S GOING TO DO IF I DON'T STOP HIM?
你干什么呢？这儿没你的事儿。

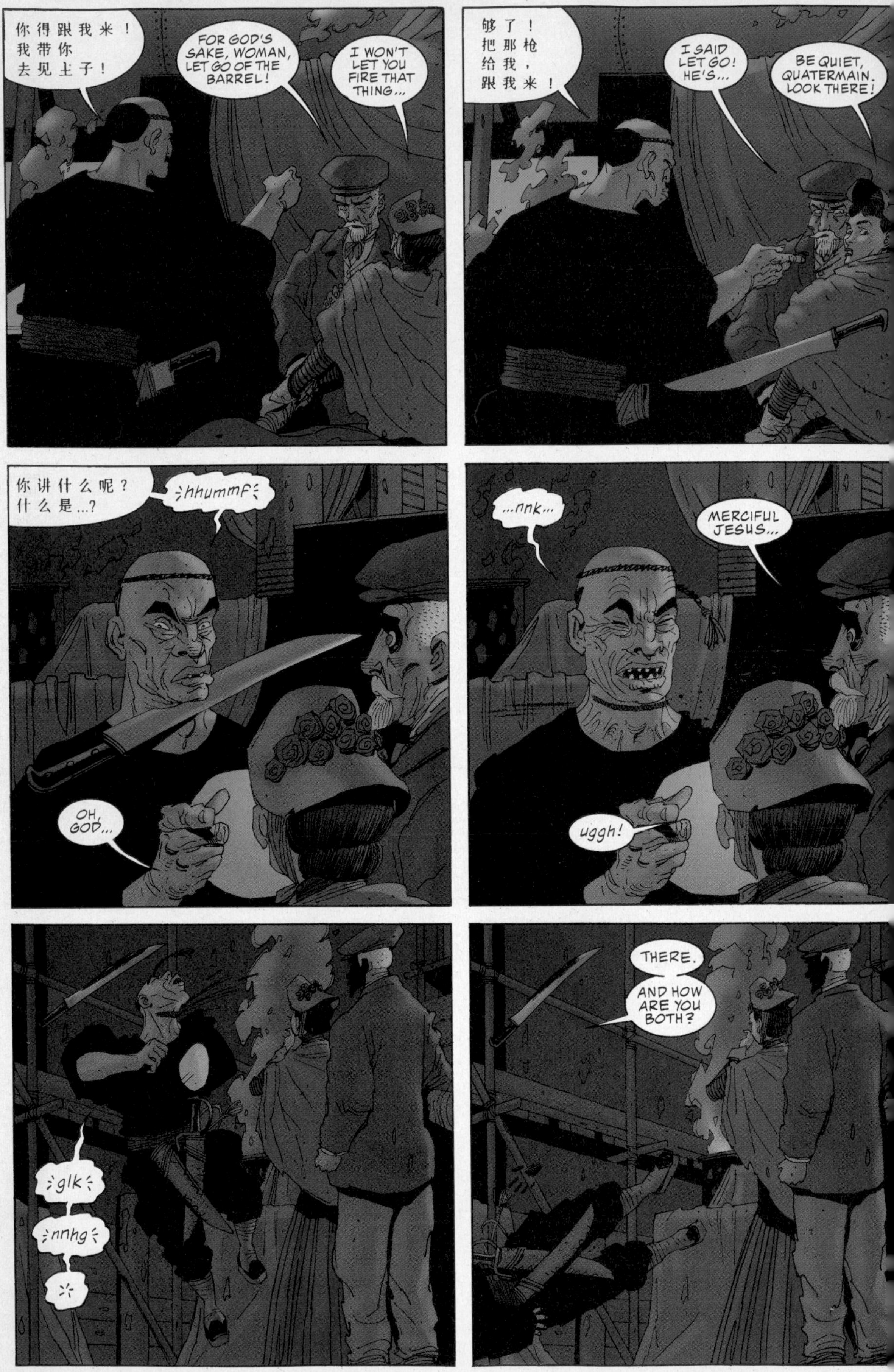
你得跟我来！我带你去见王子！
FOR GOD'S SAKE, WOMAN, LET GO OF THE BARREL!
I WON'T LET YOU FIRE THAT THING...
够了！把那枪给我，跟我来！
I SAID LET GO! HE'S...
BE QUIET, QUATERMAIN. LOOK THERE!
你讲什么呢？什么是...?
hhummf
OH, GOD...
...nnk...
MERCIFUL JESUS...
uggh!
glk
nnhg
THERE.
AND HOW ARE YOU BOTH?

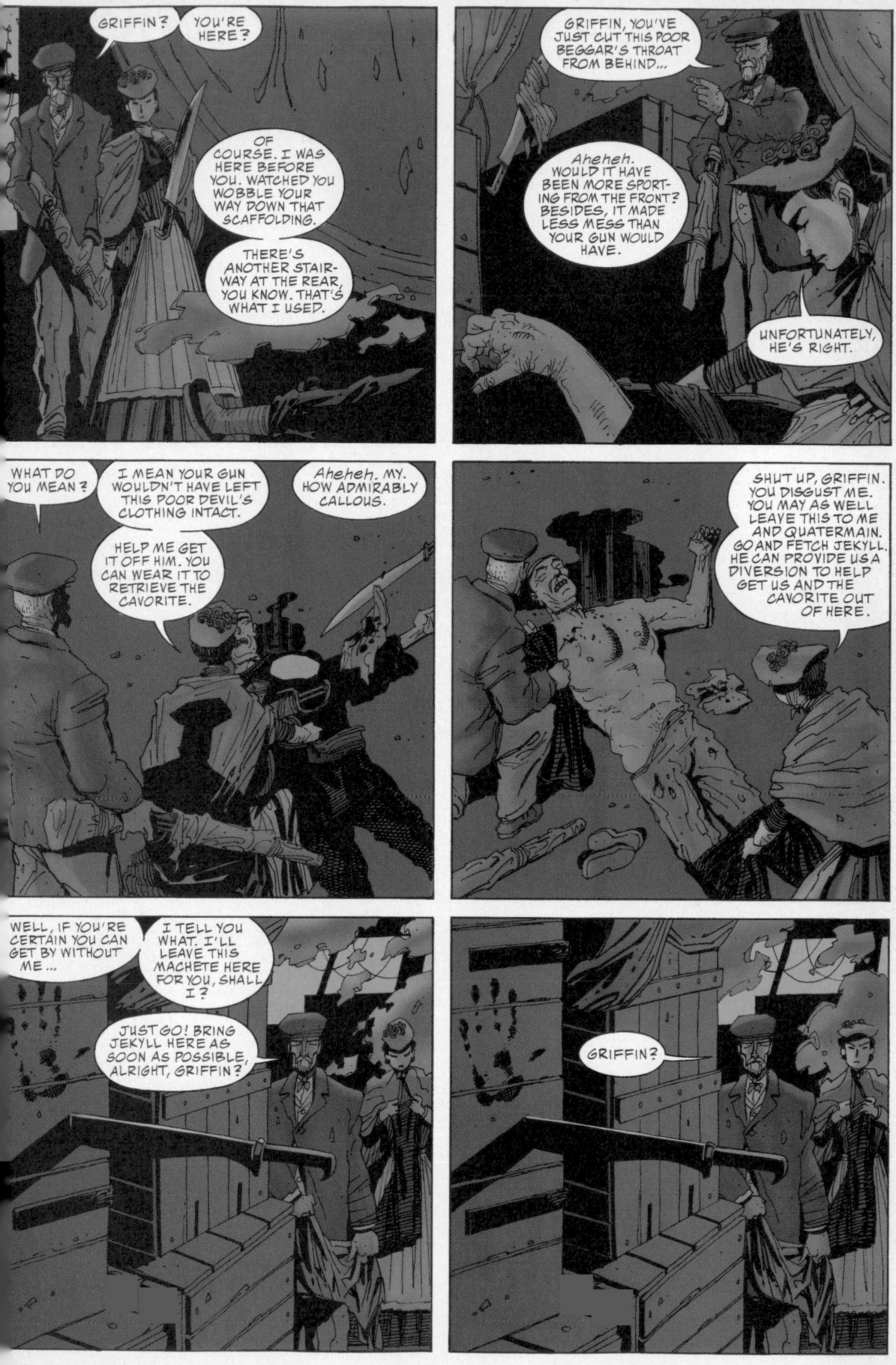
GRIFFIN?
YOU'RE HERE?
OF COURSE. I WAS HERE BEFORE YOU. WATCHED YOU WOBBLE YOUR WAY DOWN THAT SCAFFOLDING.
THERE'S ANOTHER STAIRWAY AT THE REAR, YOU KNOW. THAT'S WHAT I USED.
GRIFFIN, YOU'VE JUST CUT THIS POOR BEGGAR'S THROAT FROM BEHIND...
Aheheh. WOULD IT HAVE BEEN MORE SPORTING FROM THE FRONT? BESIDES, IT MADE LESS MESS THAN YOUR GUN WOULD HAVE.
UNFORTUNATELY, HE'S RIGHT.
WHAT DO YOU MEAN?
I MEAN YOUR GUN WOULDN'T HAVE LEFT THIS POOR DEVIL'S CLOTHING INTACT.
Aheheh. MY. HOW ADMIRABLY CALLOUS.
HELP ME GET IT OFF HIM. YOU CAN WEAR IT TO RETRIEVE THE CAVORITE.
SHUT UP, GRIFFIN. YOU DISGUST ME. YOU MAY AS WELL LEAVE THIS TO ME AND QUATERMAIN. GO AND FETCH JEKYLL. HE CAN PROVIDE US A DIVERSION TO HELP GET US AND THE CAVORITE OUT OF HERE.
WELL, IF YOU'RE CERTAIN YOU CAN GET BY WITHOUT ME...
I TELL YOU WHAT. I'LL LEAVE THIS MACHETE HERE FOR YOU, SHALL I?
JUST GO! BRING JEKYLL HERE AS SOON AS POSSIBLE, ALRIGHT, GRIFFIN?
GRIFFIN?

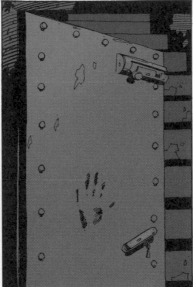

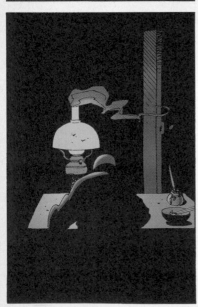

JEKYLL...

AAAA!

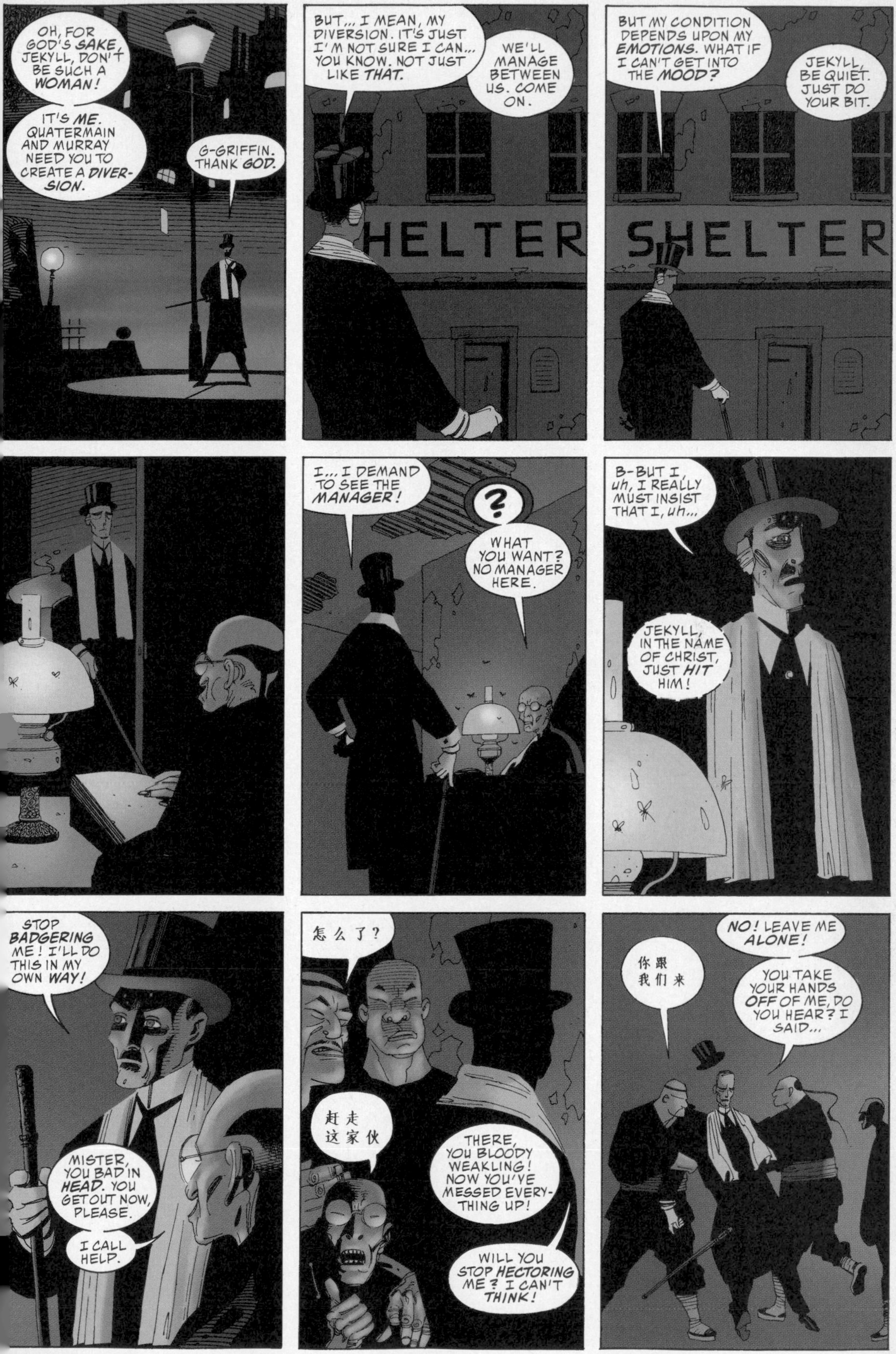
OH, FOR GOD'S SAKE, JEKYLL, DON'T BE SUCH A WOMAN!
IT'S ME. QUATERMAIN AND MURRAY NEED YOU TO CREATE A DIVERSION.
G-GRIFFIN. THANK GOD.
BUT... I MEAN, MY DIVERSION. IT'S JUST I'M NOT SURE I CAN... YOU KNOW. NOT JUST LIKE THAT.
WE'LL MANAGE BETWEEN US. COME ON.
HELTER
BUT MY CONDITION DEPENDS UPON MY EMOTIONS. WHAT IF I CAN'T GET INTO THE MOOD?
JEKYLL, BE QUIET. JUST DO YOUR BIT.
SHELTER
I... I DEMAND TO SEE THE MANAGER!
?
WHAT YOU WANT? NO MANAGER HERE.
B-BUT I, uh, I REALLY MUST INSIST THAT I, uh...
JEKYLL, IN THE NAME OF CHRIST, JUST HIT HIM!
STOP BADGERING ME! I'LL DO THIS IN MY OWN WAY!
MISTER, YOU BAD IN HEAD. YOU GET OUT NOW, PLEASE.
I CALL HELP.
怎么了？
赶走这家伙
THERE, YOU BLOODY WEAKLING! NOW YOU'VE MESSED EVERYTHING UP!
WILL YOU STOP HECTORING ME? I CAN'T THINK!
你跟我们来
NO! LEAVE ME ALONE!
YOU TAKE YOUR HANDS OFF OF ME, DO YOU HEAR? I SAID...

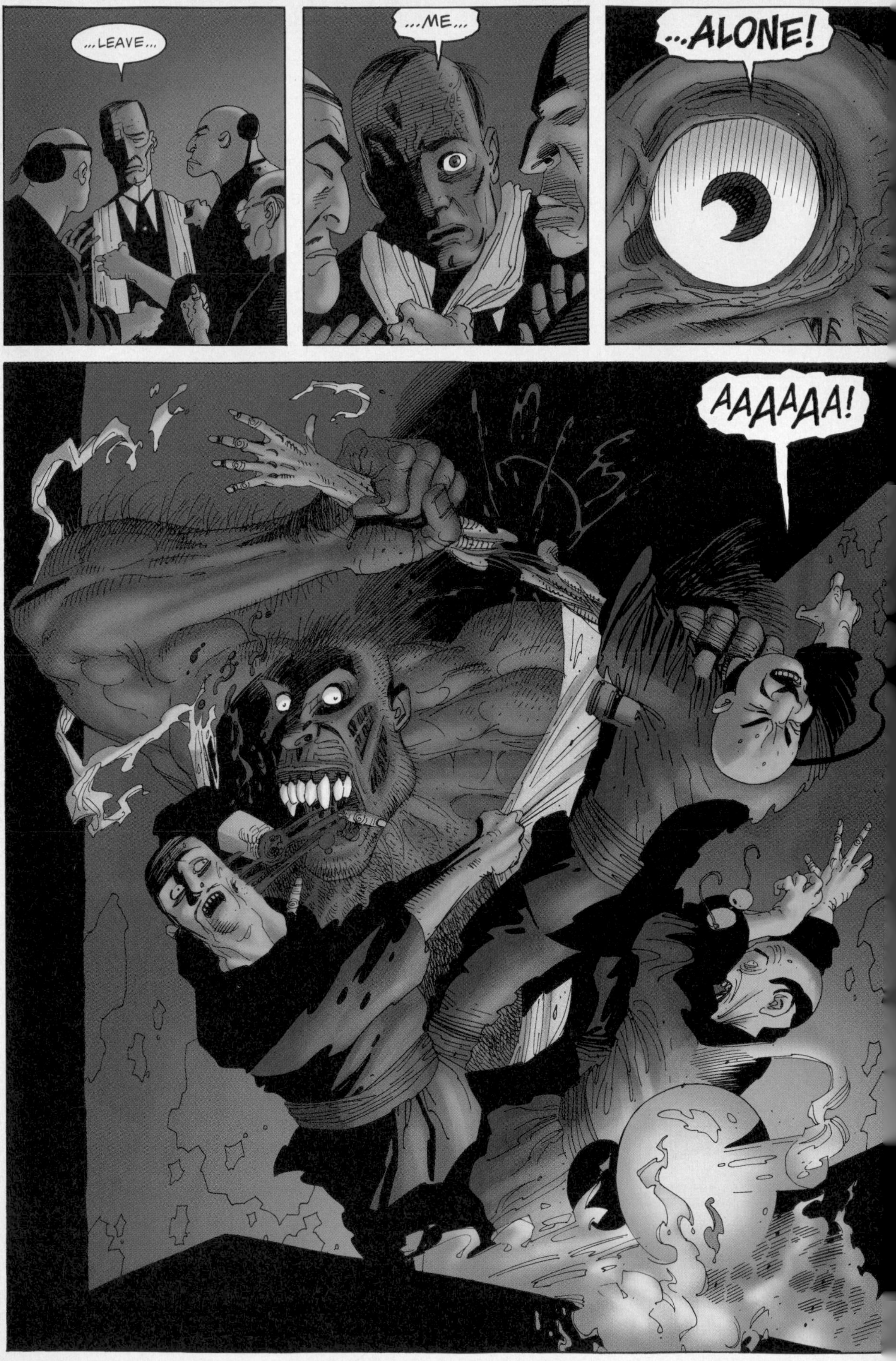
...LEAVE...
...ME...
...ALONE!
AAAAAA!

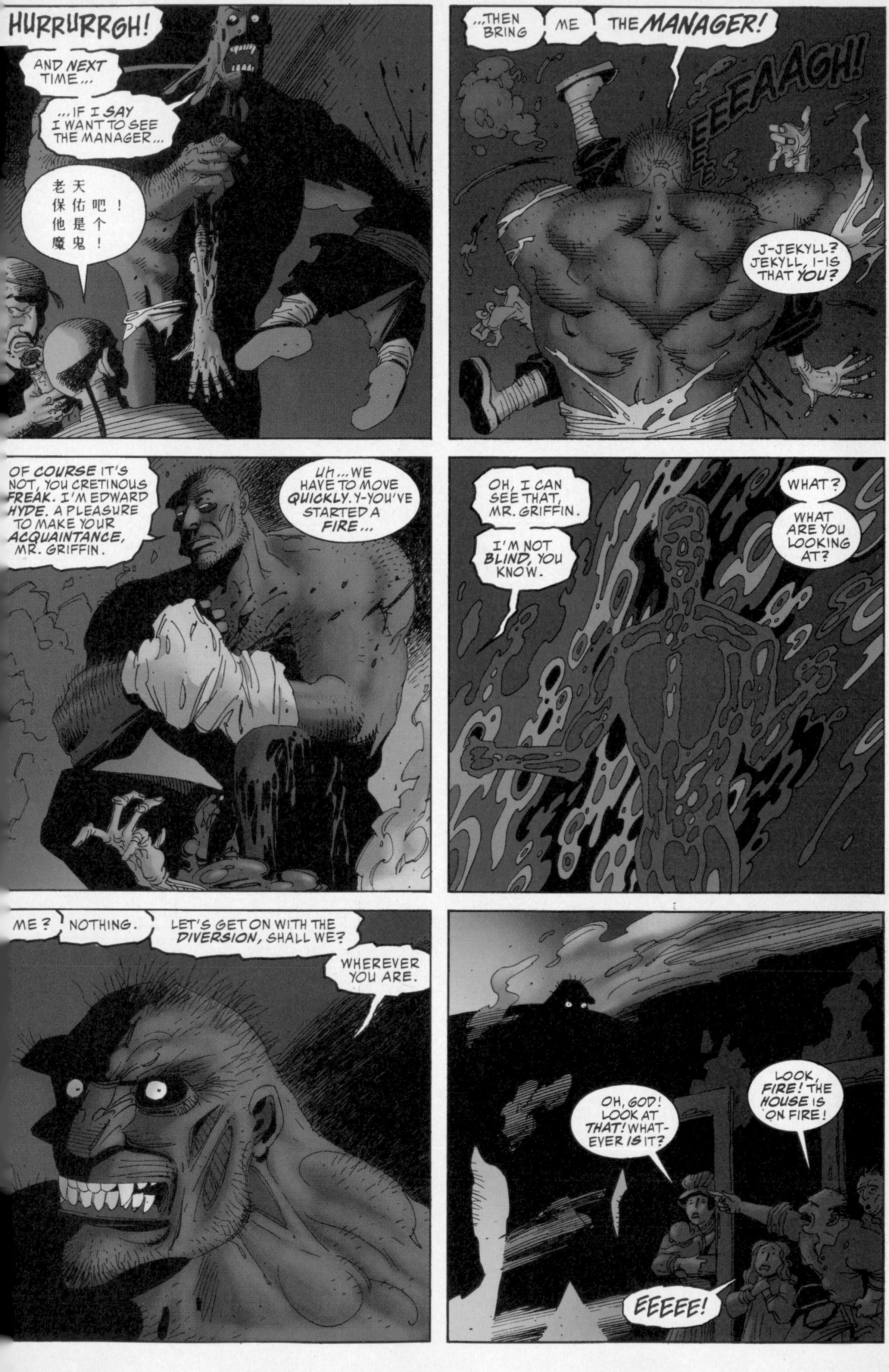
HURRURRGH!
AND NEXT TIME...
...IF I SAY I WANT TO SEE THE MANAGER...
老天保佑吧！他是个魔鬼！
...THEN BRING
ME
THE MANAGER!
EEEAAGH!
J-JEKYLL? JEKYLL, I-IS THAT YOU?
OF COURSE IT'S NOT, YOU CRETINOUS FREAK. I'M EDWARD HYDE. A PLEASURE TO MAKE YOUR ACQUAINTANCE, MR. GRIFFIN.
UH...WE HAVE TO MOVE QUICKLY. Y-YOU'VE STARTED A FIRE...
OH, I CAN SEE THAT, MR. GRIFFIN.
I'M NOT BLIND, YOU KNOW.
WHAT?
WHAT ARE YOU LOOKING AT?
ME?
NOTHING.
LET'S GET ON WITH THE DIVERSION, SHALL WE?
WHEREVER YOU ARE.
OH, GOD! LOOK AT THAT! WHATEVER IS IT?
LOOK, FIRE! THE HOUSE IS ON FIRE!
EEEEE!

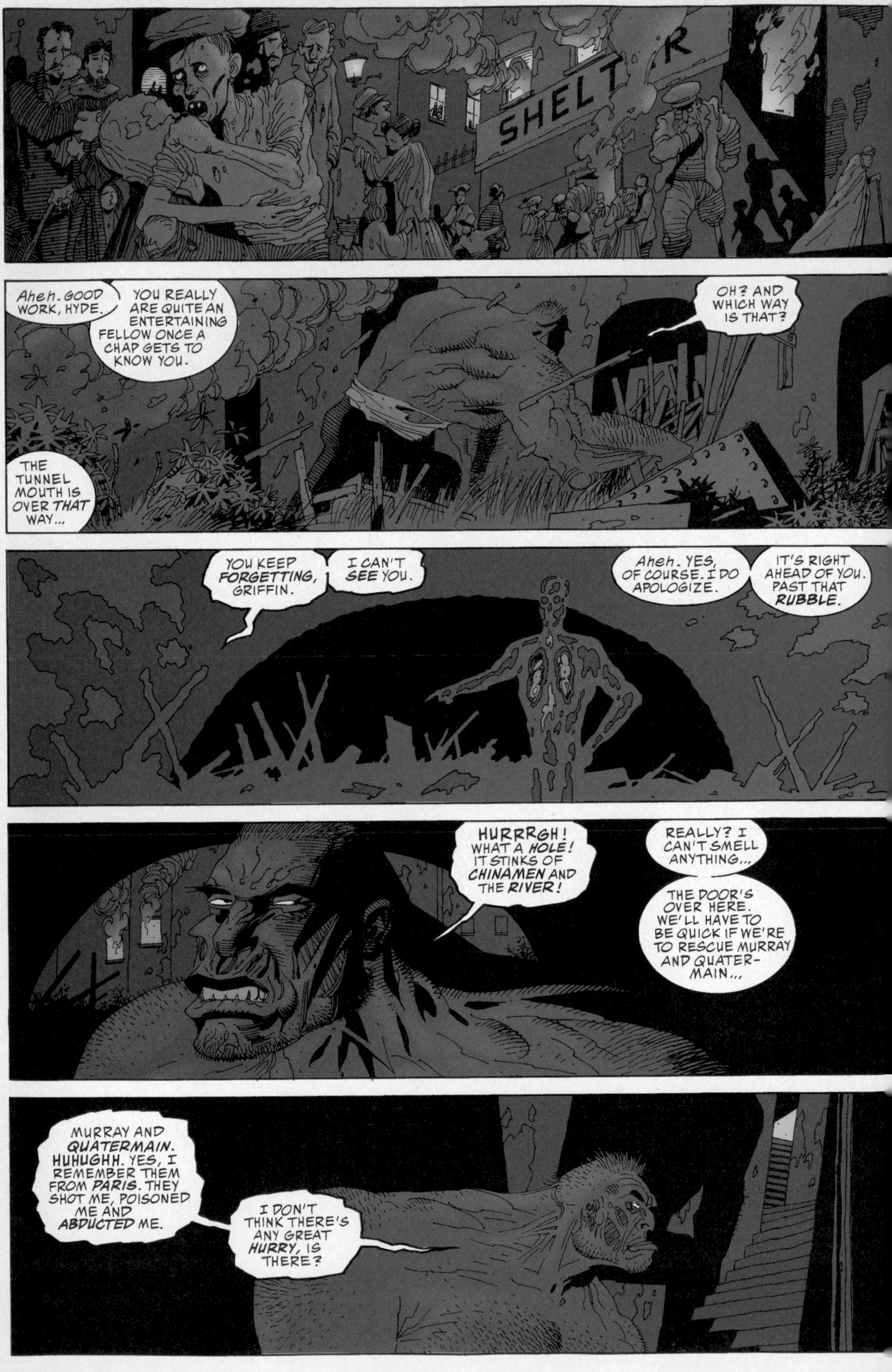
SHELT R
Aheh. GOOD WORK, HYDE.
YOU REALLY ARE QUITE AN ENTERTAINING FELLOW ONCE A CHAP GETS TO KNOW YOU.
THE TUNNEL MOUTH IS OVER THAT WAY...
OH? AND WHICH WAY IS THAT?
YOU KEEP FORGETTING, GRIFFIN.
I CAN'T SEE YOU.
Aheh. YES, OF COURSE. I DO APOLOGIZE.
IT'S RIGHT AHEAD OF YOU. PAST THAT RUBBLE.
HURRRGH! WHAT A HOLE! IT STINKS OF CHINAMEN AND THE RIVER!
REALLY? I CAN'T SMELL ANYTHING...
THE DOOR'S OVER HERE. WE'LL HAVE TO BE QUICK IF WE'RE TO RESCUE MURRAY AND QUATER-MAIN...
MURRAY AND QUATERMAIN. HUHUGHH. YES, I REMEMBER THEM FROM PARIS. THEY SHOT ME, POISONED ME AND ABDUCTED ME.
I DON'T THINK THERE'S ANY GREAT HURRY, IS THERE?

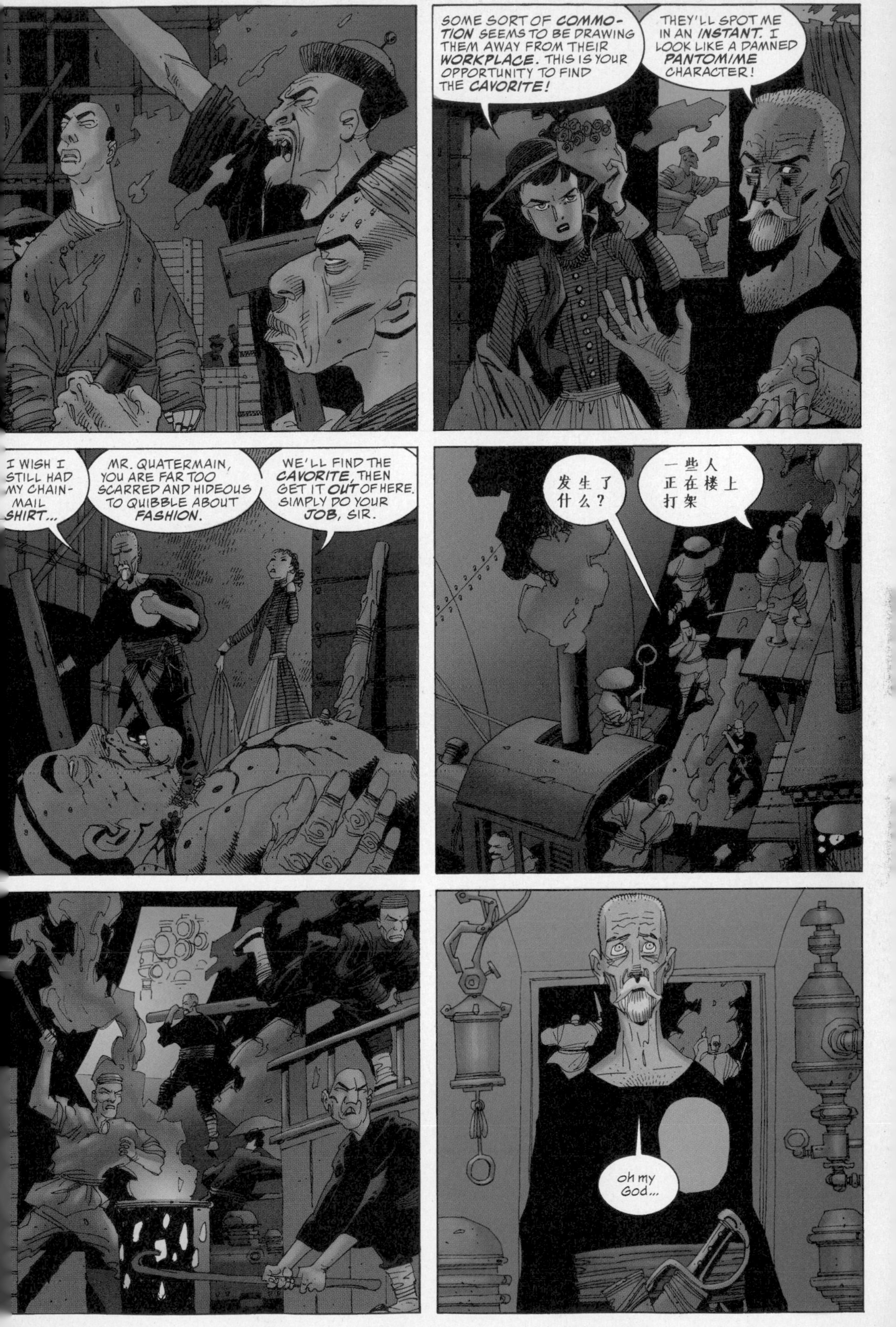
SOME SORT OF COMMOTION SEEMS TO BE DRAWING THEM AWAY FROM THEIR WORKPLACE. THIS IS YOUR OPPORTUNITY TO FIND THE CAVORITE!
THEY'LL SPOT ME IN AN INSTANT. I LOOK LIKE A DAMNED PANTOMIME CHARACTER!
I WISH I STILL HAD MY CHAIN-MAIL SHIRT...
MR. QUATERMAIN, YOU ARE FAR TOO SCARRED AND HIDEOUS TO QUIBBLE ABOUT FASHION.
WE'LL FIND THE CAVORITE, THEN GET IT OUT OF HERE. SIMPLY DO YOUR JOB, SIR.
发生了什么？
一些人正在楼上打架
oh my God...

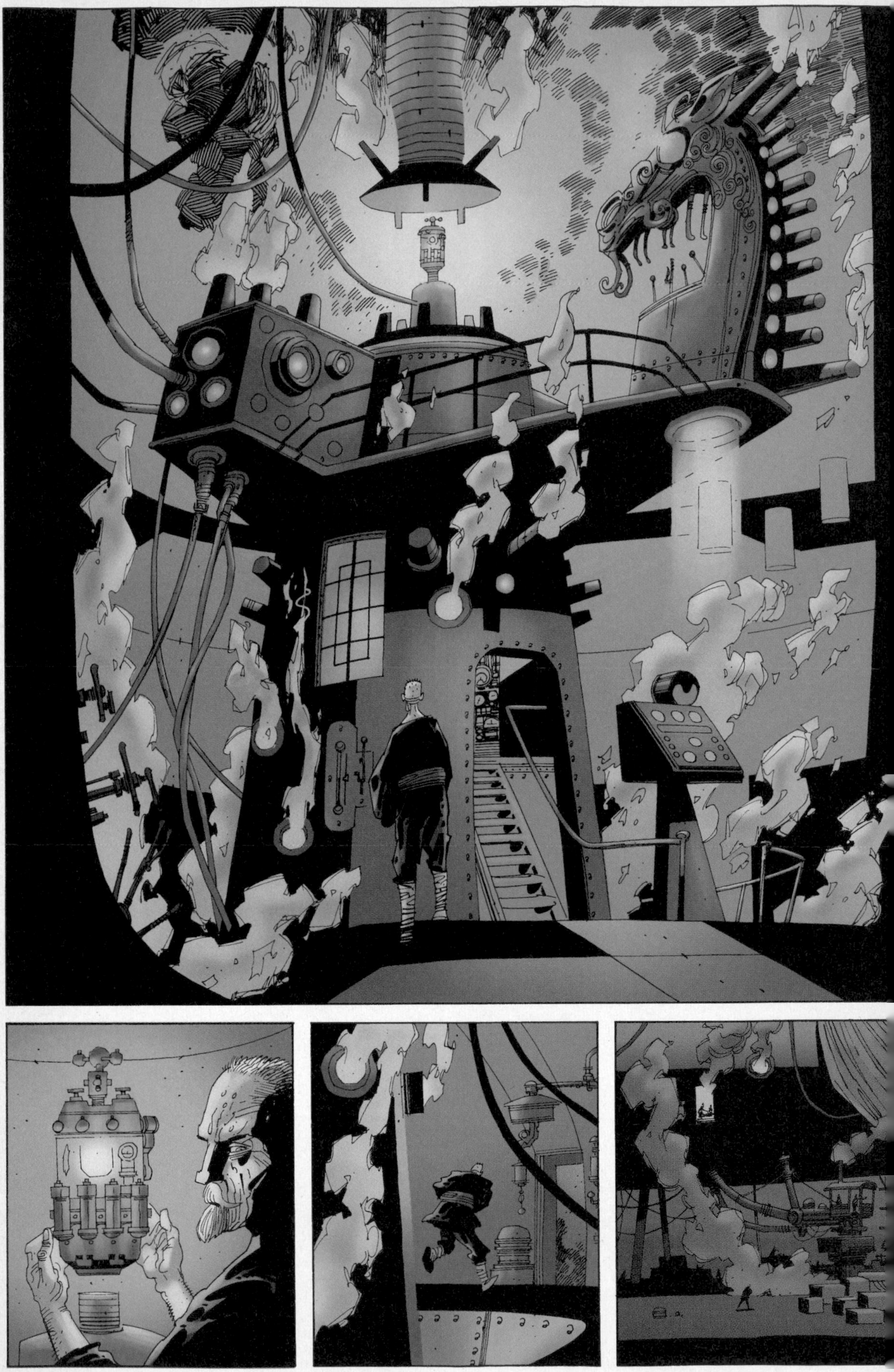

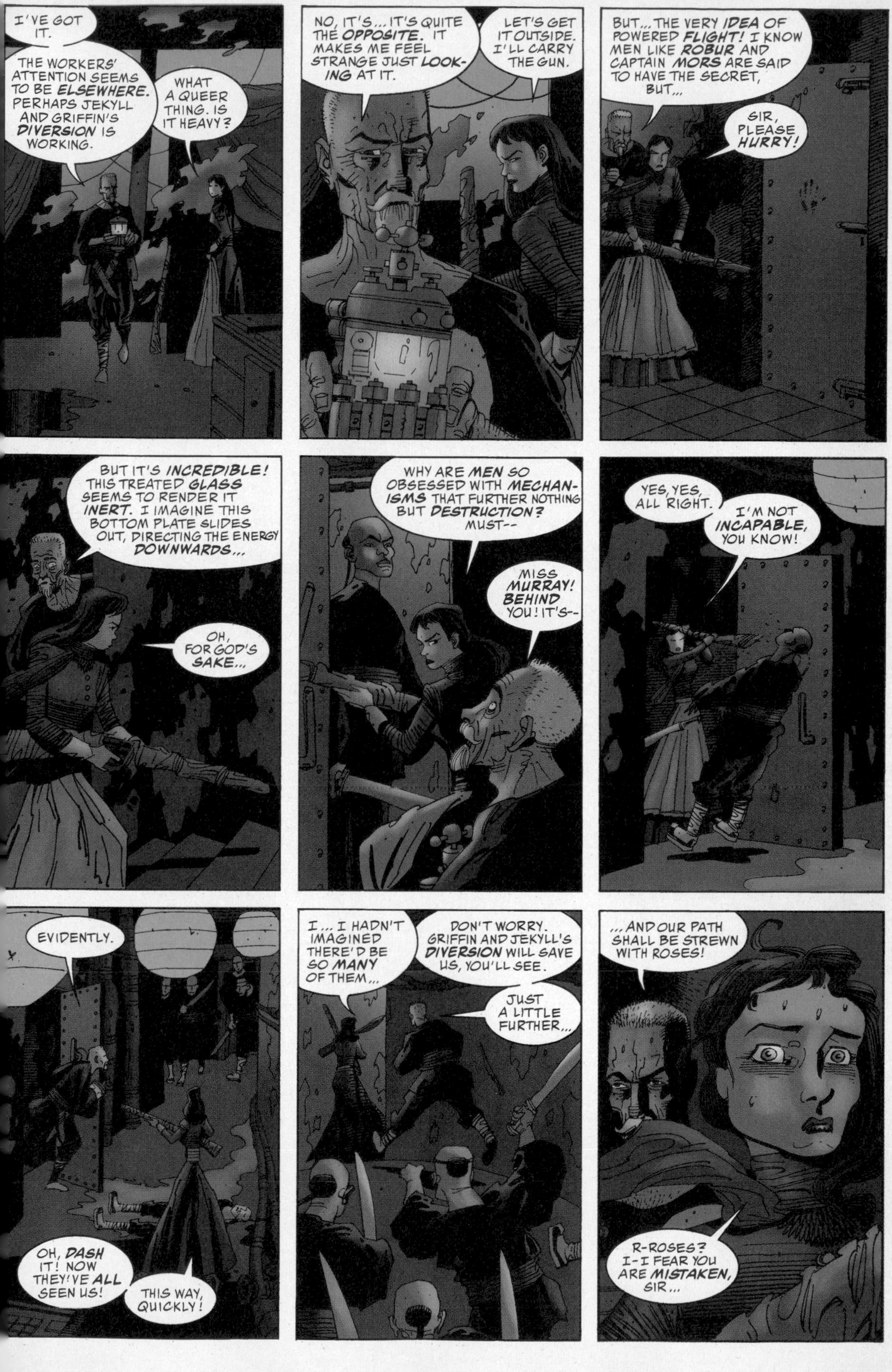
I'VE GOT IT.
THE WORKERS' ATTENTION SEEMS TO BE ELSEWHERE. PERHAPS JEKYLL AND GRIFFIN'S DIVERSION IS WORKING.
WHAT A QUEER THING. IS IT HEAVY?
NO, IT'S... IT'S QUITE THE OPPOSITE. IT MAKES ME FEEL STRANGE JUST LOOKING AT IT.
LET'S GET IT OUTSIDE. I'LL CARRY THE GUN.
BUT... THE VERY IDEA OF POWERED FLIGHT! I KNOW MEN LIKE ROBUR AND CAPTAIN MORS ARE SAID TO HAVE THE SECRET, BUT...
SIR, PLEASE HURRY!
BUT IT'S INCREDIBLE! THIS TREATED GLASS SEEMS TO RENDER IT INERT. I IMAGINE THIS BOTTOM PLATE SLIDES OUT, DIRECTING THE ENERGY DOWNWARDS...
OH, FOR GOD'S SAKE...
WHY ARE MEN SO OBSESSED WITH MECHANISMS THAT FURTHER NOTHING BUT DESTRUCTION? MUST--
MISS MURRAY! BEHIND YOU! IT'S--
YES, YES, ALL RIGHT.
I'M NOT INCAPABLE, YOU KNOW!
EVIDENTLY.
OH, DASH IT! NOW THEY'VE ALL SEEN US!
THIS WAY, QUICKLY!
I... I HADN'T IMAGINED THERE'D BE SO MANY OF THEM...
DON'T WORRY. GRIFFIN AND JEKYLL'S DIVERSION WILL SAVE US, YOU'LL SEE.
JUST A LITTLE FURTHER...
...AND OUR PATH SHALL BE STREWN WITH ROSES!
R-ROSES? I-I FEAR YOU ARE MISTAKEN, SIR...

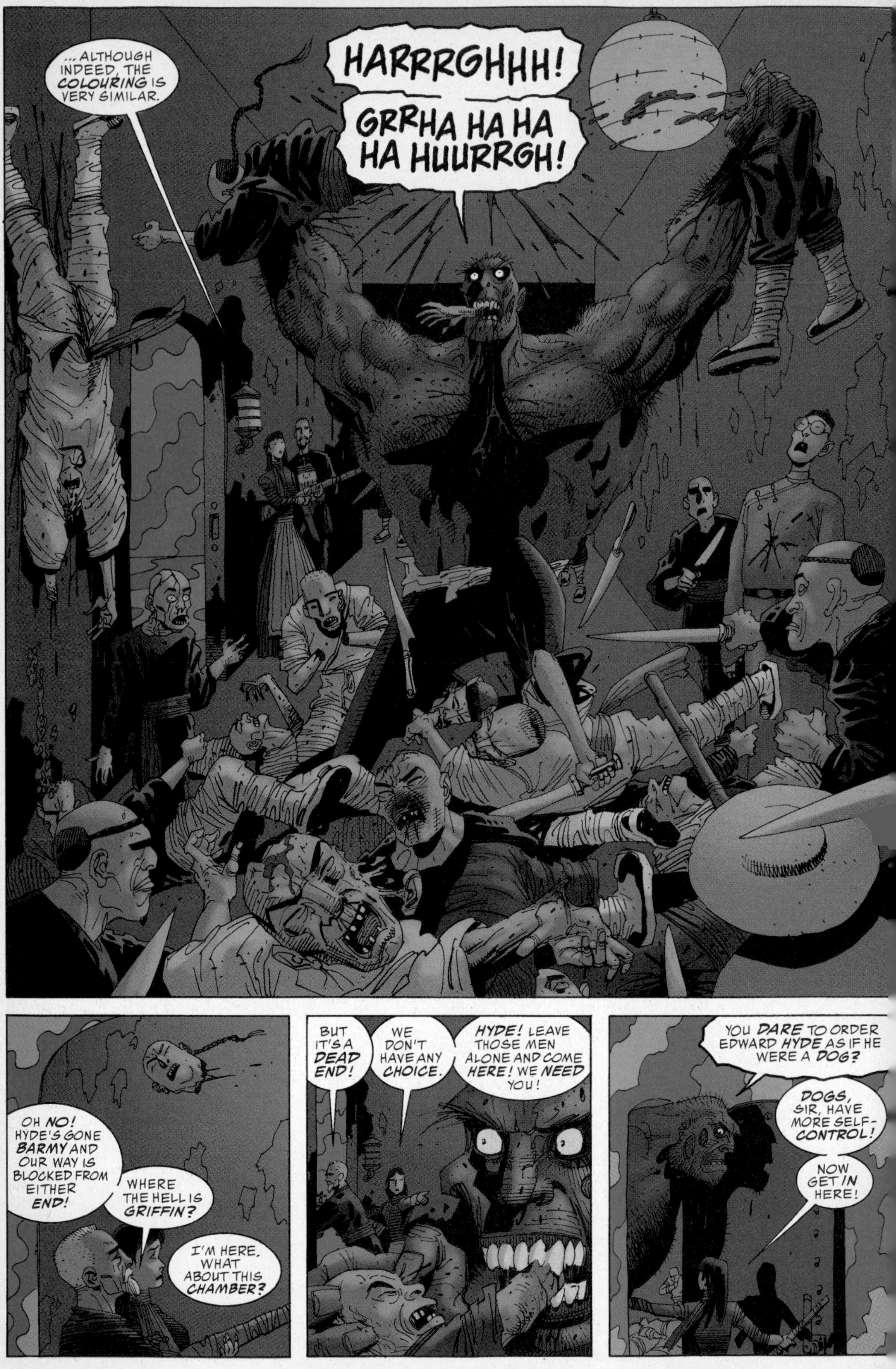
...ALTHOUGH INDEED, THE COLOURING IS VERY SIMILAR.
HARRRGHHH!
GRRHA HA HA HA HUURRGH!
OH NO! HYDE'S GONE BARMY AND OUR WAY IS BLOCKED FROM EITHER END!
WHERE THE HELL IS GRIFFIN?
I'M HERE. WHAT ABOUT THIS CHAMBER?
BUT IT'S A DEAD END!
WE DON'T HAVE ANY CHOICE.
HYDE! LEAVE THOSE MEN ALONE AND COME HERE! WE NEED YOU!
YOU DARE TO ORDER EDWARD HYDE AS IF HE WERE A DOG?
DOGS, SIR, HAVE MORE SELF-CONTROL!
NOW GET IN HERE!

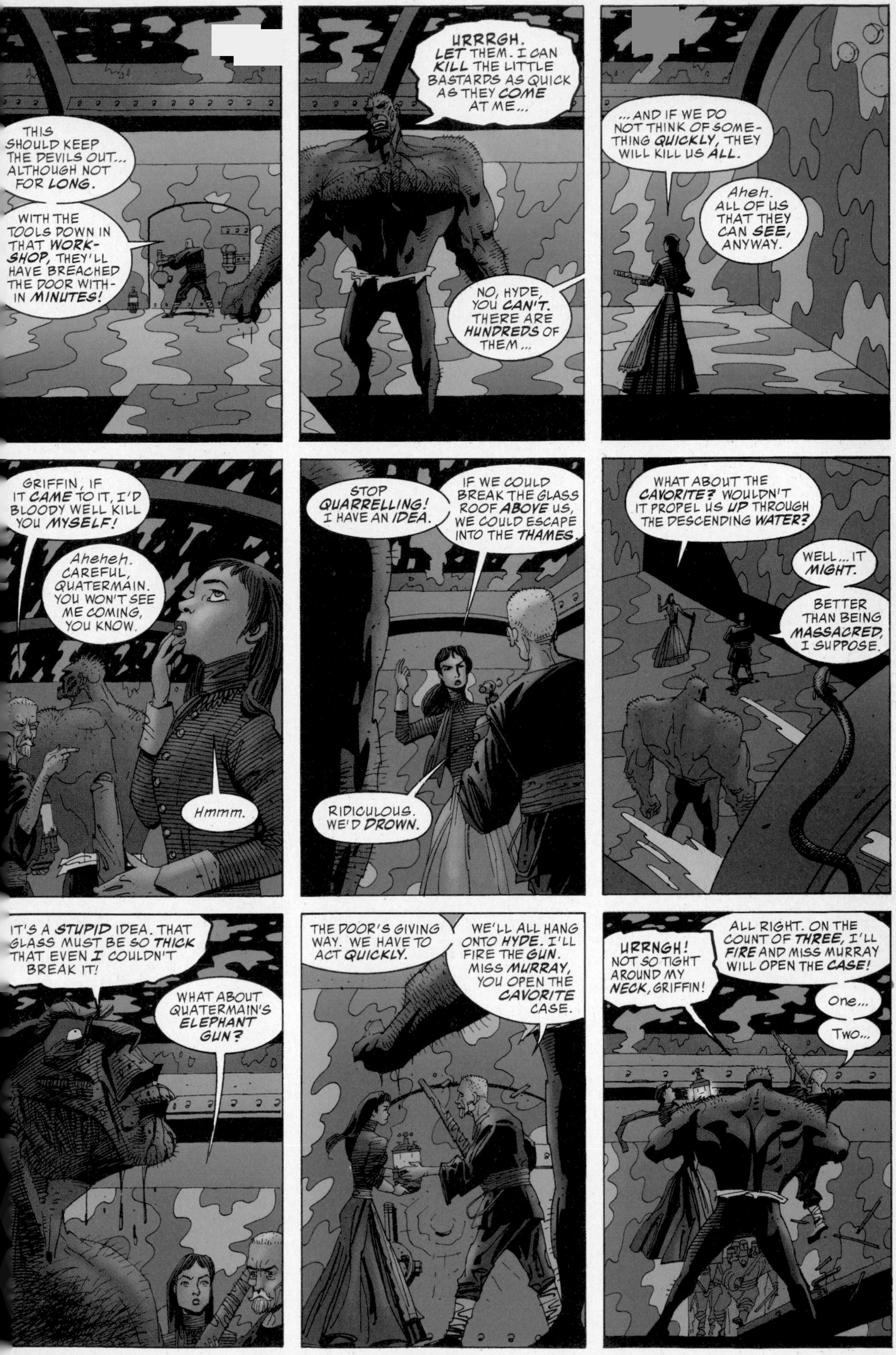
THIS SHOULD KEEP THE DEVILS OUT... ALTHOUGH NOT FOR LONG.
WITH THE TOOLS DOWN IN THAT WORKSHOP, THEY'LL HAVE BREACHED THE DOOR WITHIN MINUTES!
URRRGH. LET THEM. I CAN KILL THE LITTLE BASTARDS AS QUICK AS THEY COME AT ME...
NO, HYDE, YOU CAN'T. THERE ARE HUNDREDS OF THEM...
...AND IF WE DO NOT THINK OF SOMETHING QUICKLY, THEY WILL KILL US ALL.
Aheh. ALL OF US THAT THEY CAN SEE, ANYWAY.
GRIFFIN, IF IT CAME TO IT, I'D BLOODY WELL KILL YOU MYSELF!
Aheheh. CAREFUL, QUATERMAIN. YOU WON'T SEE ME COMING, YOU KNOW.
Hmmm.
STOP QUARRELLING! I HAVE AN IDEA.
IF WE COULD BREAK THE GLASS ROOF ABOVE US, WE COULD ESCAPE INTO THE THAMES.
RIDICULOUS. WE'D DROWN.
WHAT ABOUT THE CAVORITE? WOULDN'T IT PROPEL US UP THROUGH THE DESCENDING WATER?
WELL... IT MIGHT.
BETTER THAN BEING MASSACRED, I SUPPOSE.
IT'S A STUPID IDEA. THAT GLASS MUST BE SO THICK THAT EVEN I COULDN'T BREAK IT!
WHAT ABOUT QUATERMAIN'S ELEPHANT GUN?
THE DOOR'S GIVING WAY. WE HAVE TO ACT QUICKLY.
WE'LL ALL HANG ONTO HYDE. I'LL FIRE THE GUN. MISS MURRAY, YOU OPEN THE CAVORITE CASE.
URRNGH! NOT SO TIGHT AROUND MY NECK, GRIFFIN!
ALL RIGHT. ON THE COUNT OF THREE, I'LL FIRE AND MISS MURRAY WILL OPEN THE CASE!
One...
Two...

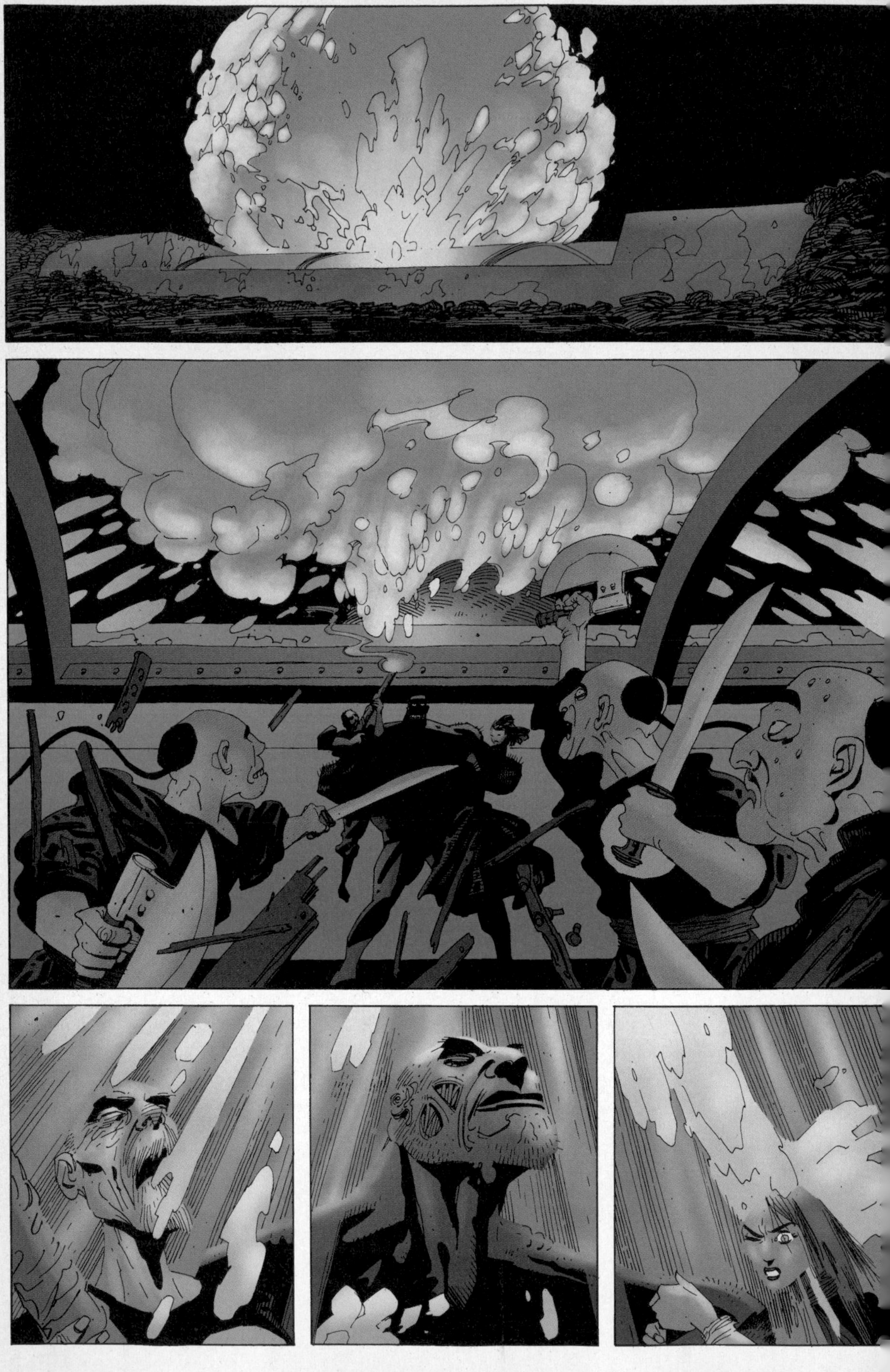

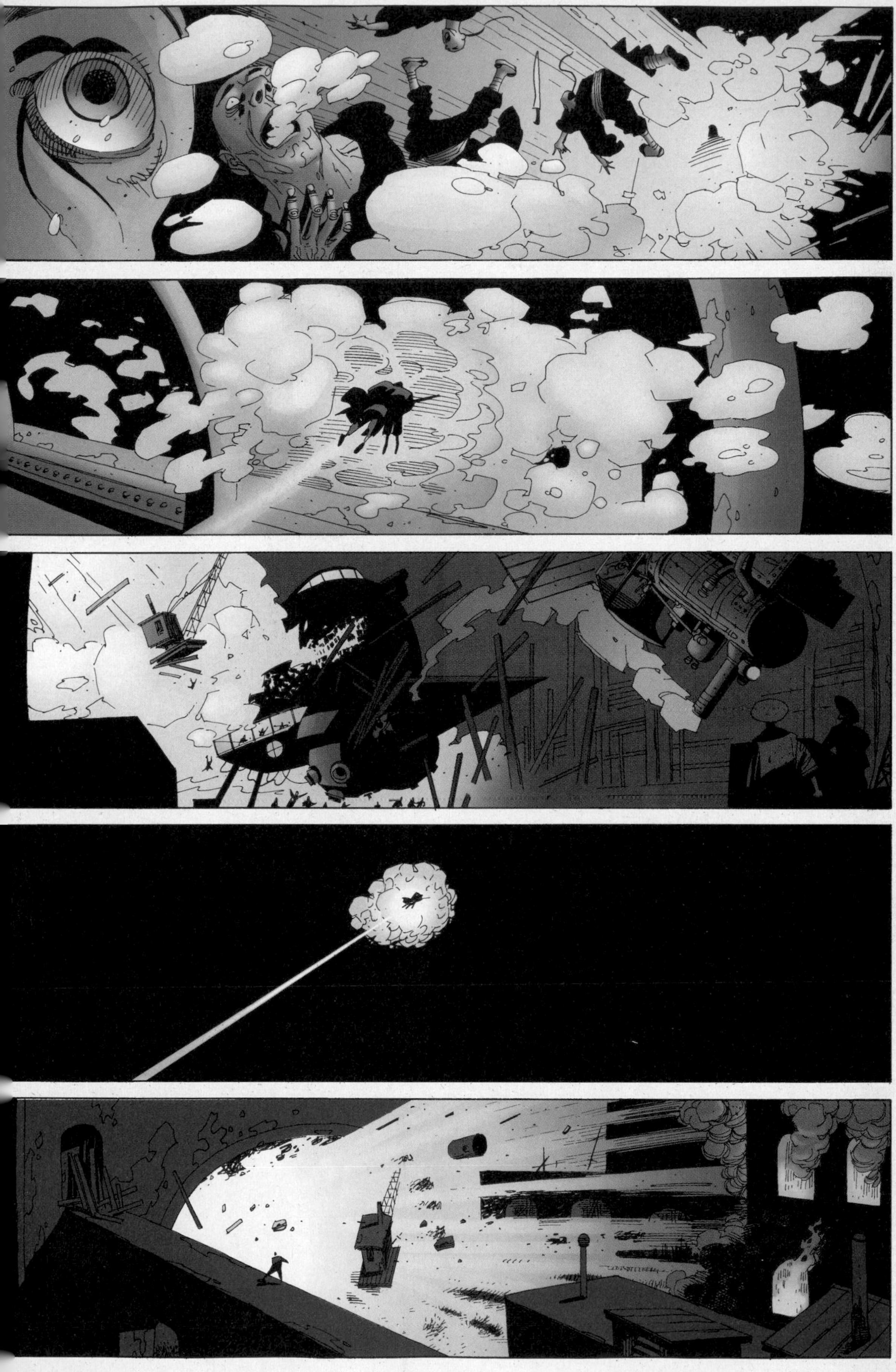

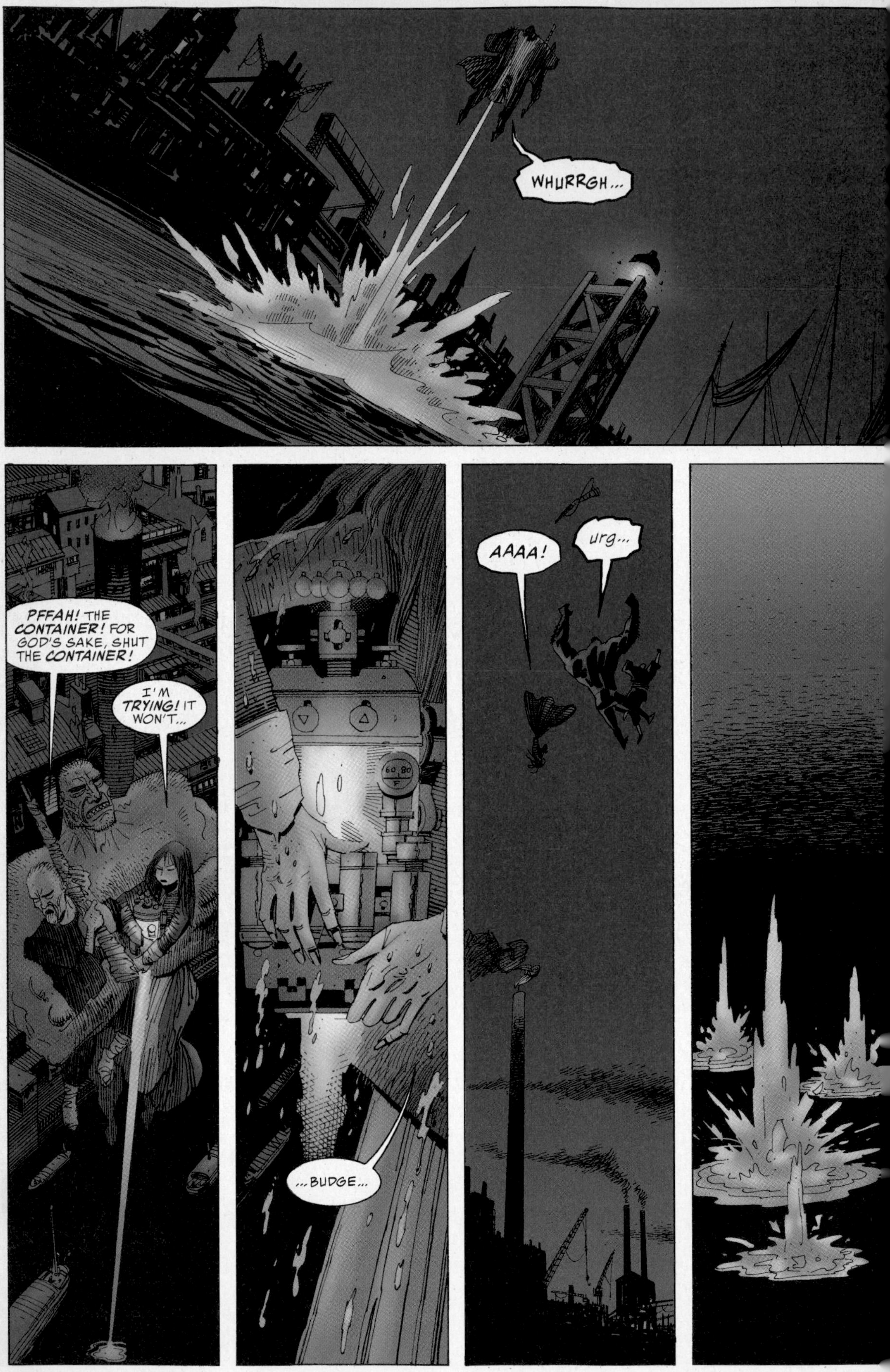

WHURRGH...
PFFAH! THE CONTAINER! FOR GOD'S SAKE, SHUT THE CONTAINER!
I'M TRYING! IT WON'T...
...BUDGE...
AAAA!
urg...

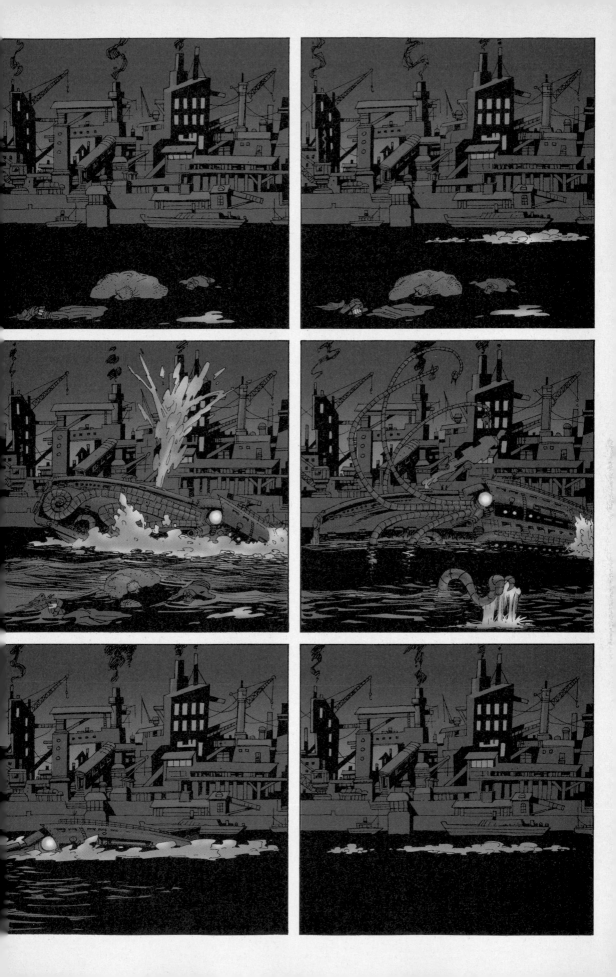

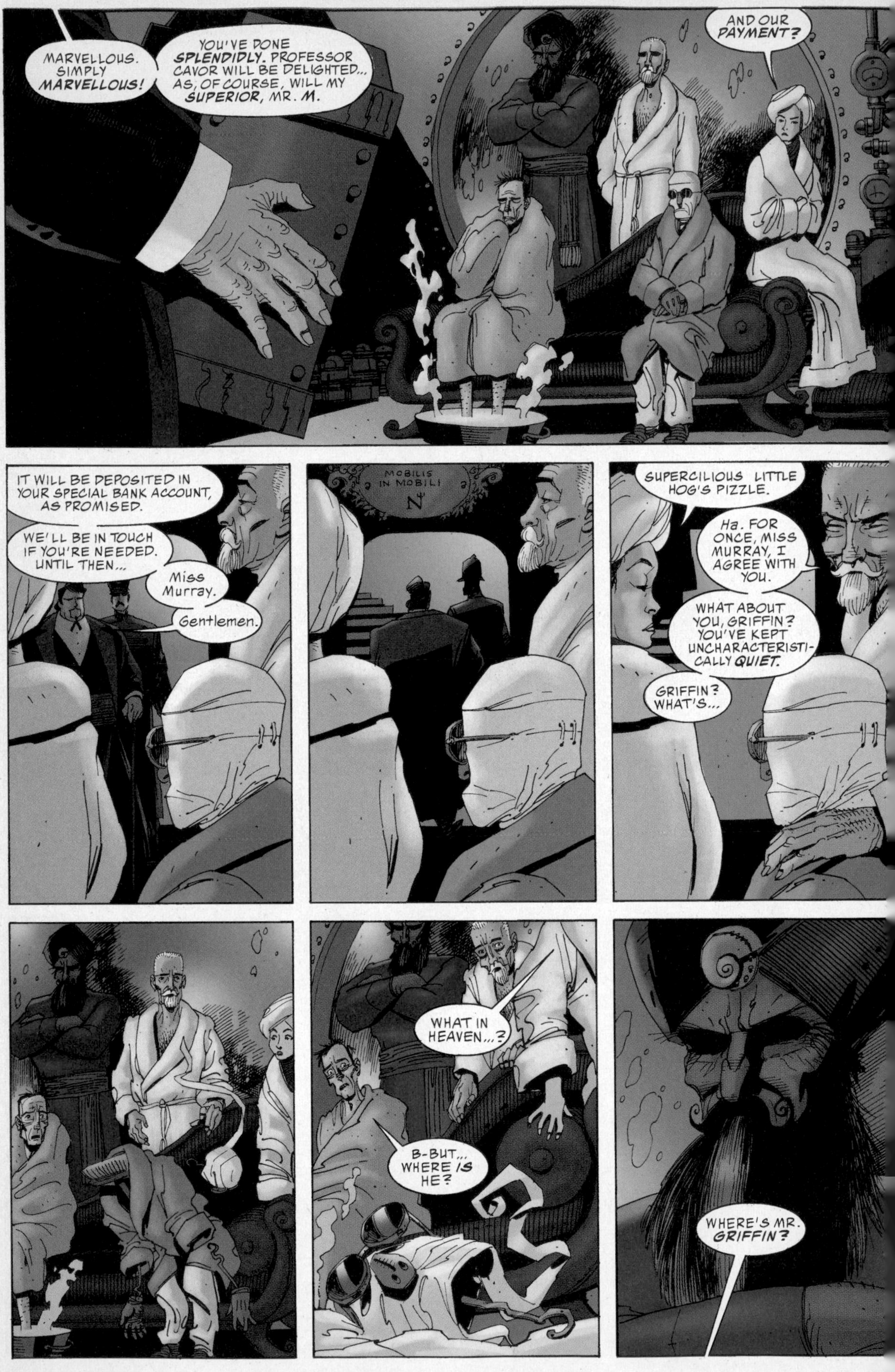
MARVELLOUS. SIMPLY MARVELLOUS!
YOU'VE DONE SPLENDIDLY. PROFESSOR CAVOR WILL BE DELIGHTED... AS, OF COURSE, WILL MY SUPERIOR, MR. M.
AND OUR PAYMENT?
IT WILL BE DEPOSITED IN YOUR SPECIAL BANK ACCOUNT, AS PROMISED.
WE'LL BE IN TOUCH IF YOU'RE NEEDED. UNTIL THEN...
Miss Murray.
Gentlemen.
MOBILIS IN MOBILI
N
SUPERCILIOUS LITTLE HOG'S PIZZLE.
Ha. FOR ONCE, MISS MURRAY, I AGREE WITH YOU.
WHAT ABOUT YOU, GRIFFIN? YOU'VE KEPT UNCHARACTERISTICALLY QUIET.
GRIFFIN? WHAT'S...
WHAT IN HEAVEN...?
B-BUT... WHERE IS HE?
WHERE'S MR. GRIFFIN?

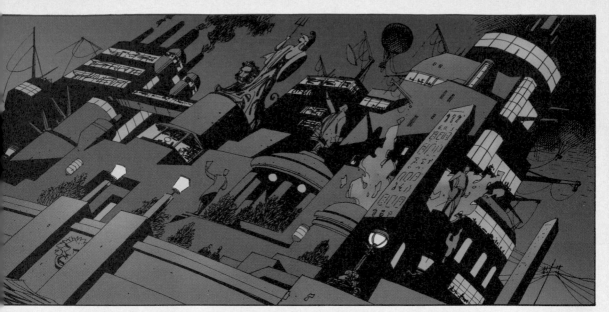

WHAT WAS THAT?

DID YOU HEAR SOMETHING?

Uh....

NO, SIR. CAN'T SAY I DID, SIR.

Hmm.

HER MAJESTY'S MILITARY INTELLIGENCE DIVISION ·5·

Ahh.

MR. BOND. DO COME IN.

I'VE BEEN EXPECTING YOU.

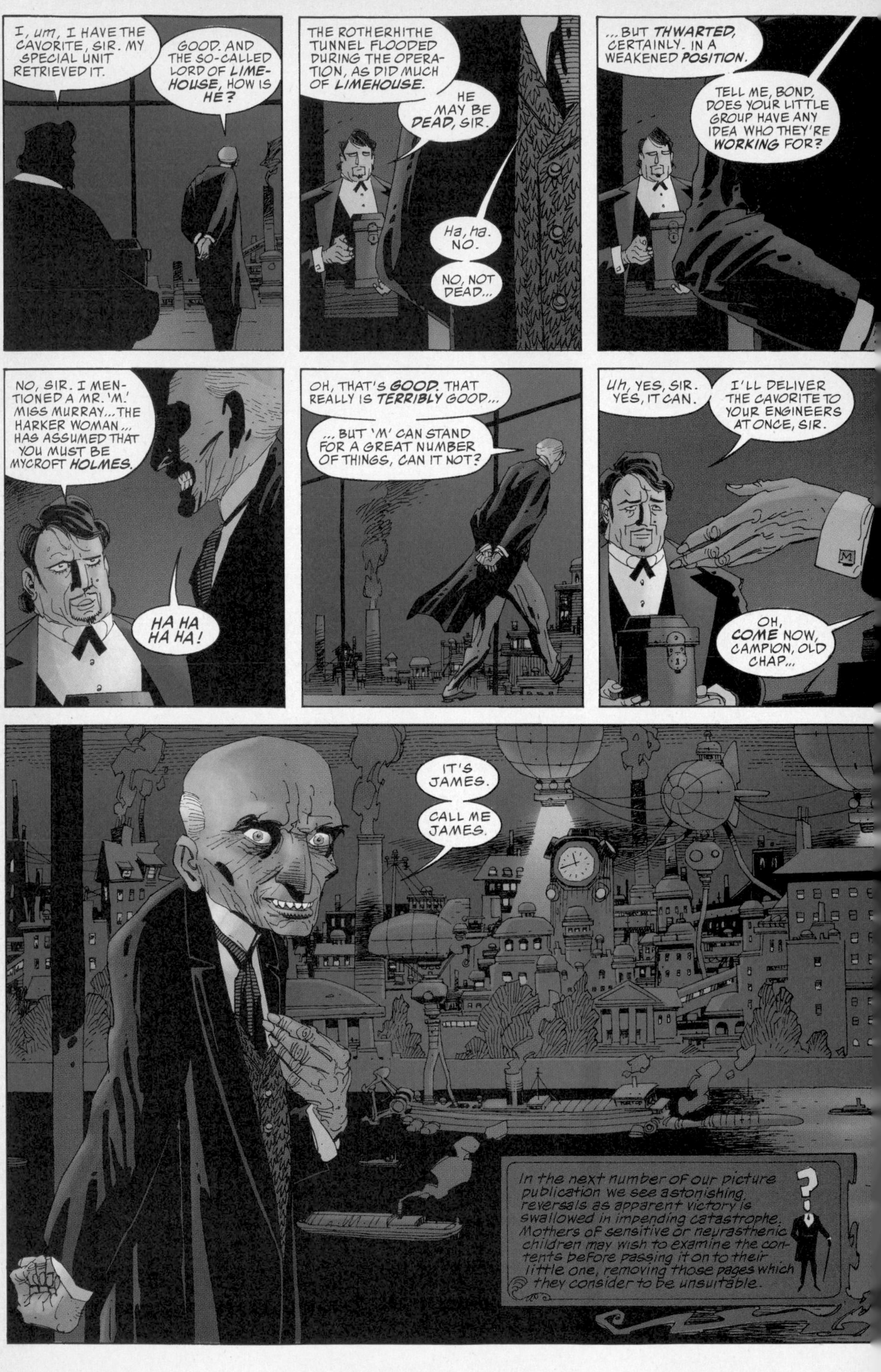
I, um, I HAVE THE CAVORITE, SIR. MY SPECIAL UNIT RETRIEVED IT.
GOOD. AND THE SO-CALLED LORD OF LIMEHOUSE, HOW IS HE?
THE ROTHERHITHE TUNNEL FLOODED DURING THE OPERATION, AS DID MUCH OF LIMEHOUSE.
HE MAY BE DEAD, SIR.
Ha, ha. NO.
NO, NOT DEAD...
...BUT THWARTED, CERTAINLY. IN A WEAKENED POSITION.
TELL ME, BOND, DOES YOUR LITTLE GROUP HAVE ANY IDEA WHO THEY'RE WORKING FOR?
NO, SIR. I MENTIONED A MR. 'M.' MISS MURRAY... THE HARKER WOMAN... HAS ASSUMED THAT YOU MUST BE MYCROFT HOLMES.
HA HA HA HA!
OH, THAT'S GOOD. THAT REALLY IS TERRIBLY GOOD...
...BUT 'M' CAN STAND FOR A GREAT NUMBER OF THINGS, CAN IT NOT?
Uh, YES, SIR. YES, IT CAN.
I'LL DELIVER THE CAVORITE TO YOUR ENGINEERS AT ONCE, SIR.
OH, COME NOW, CAMPION, OLD CHAP...
IT'S JAMES.
CALL ME JAMES.
In the next number of our picture publication we see astonishing reversals as apparent victory is swallowed in impending catastrophe. Mothers of sensitive or neurasthenic children may wish to examine the contents before passing it on to their little one, removing those pages which they consider to be unsuitable.

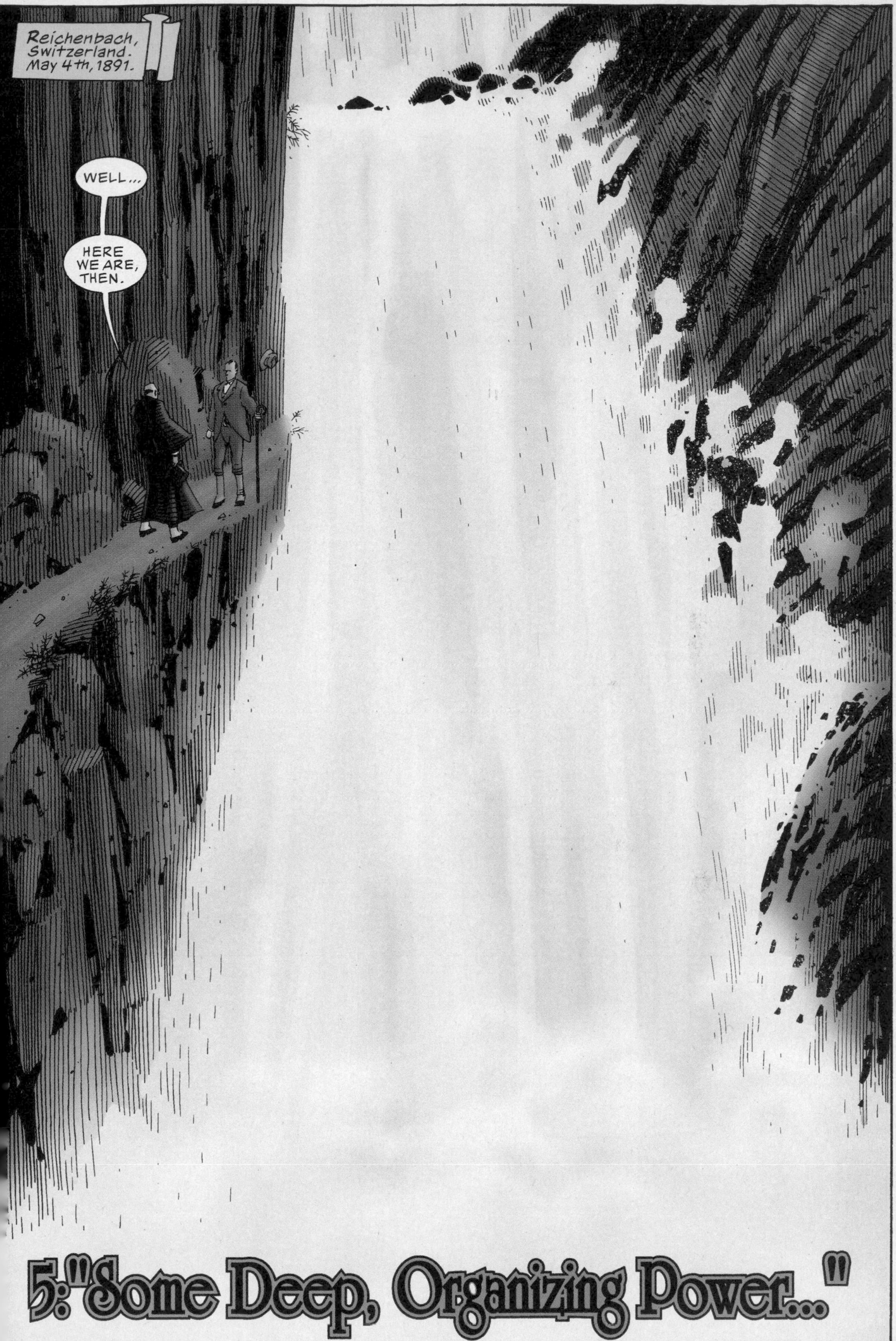
Reichenbach, Switzerland. May 4th, 1891.
WELL...
HERE WE ARE, THEN.
5: "Some Deep, Organizing Power..."

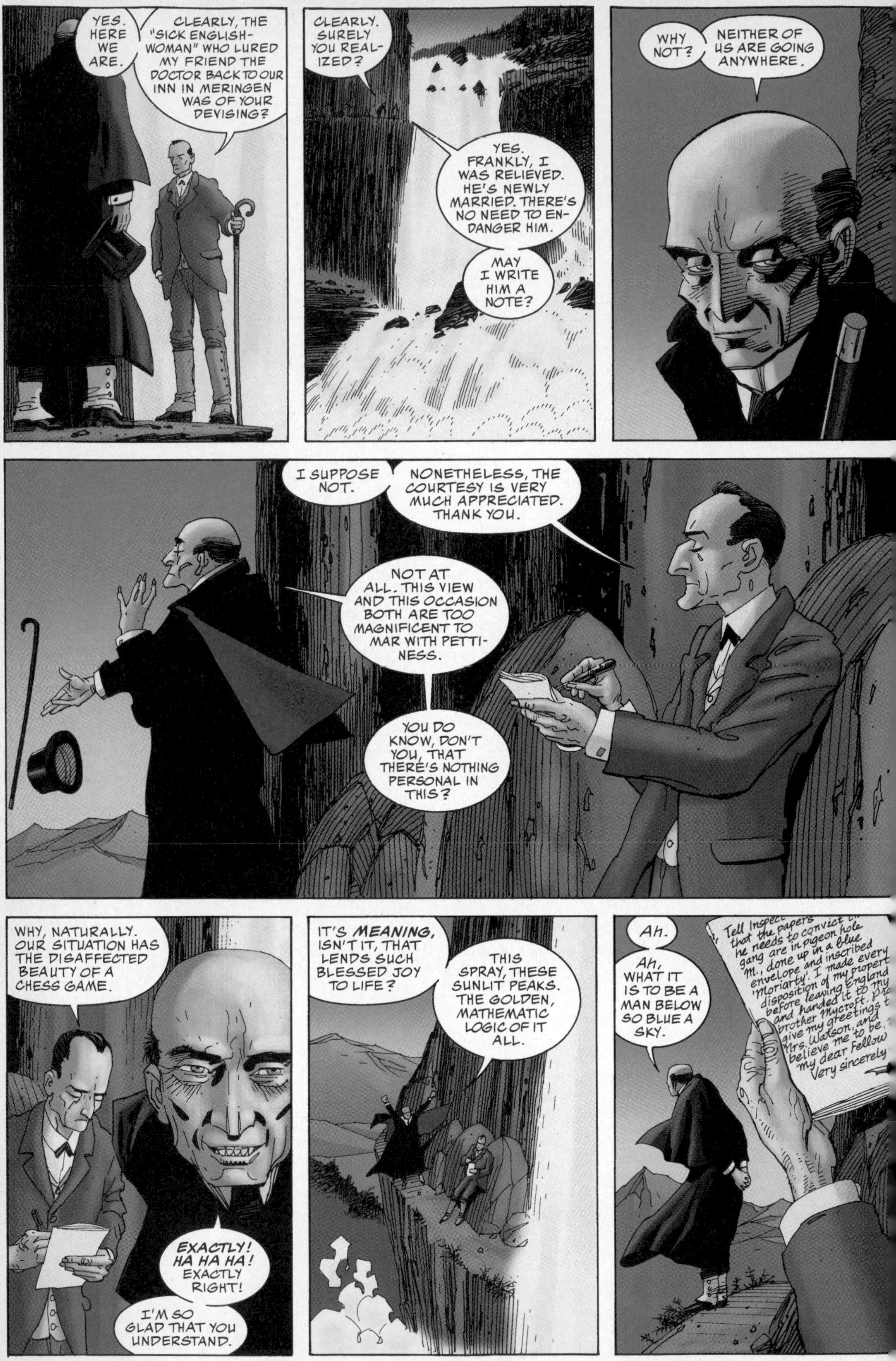
YES. HERE WE ARE.
CLEARLY, THE "SICK ENGLISH-WOMAN" WHO LURED MY FRIEND THE DOCTOR BACK TO OUR INN IN MERINGEN WAS OF YOUR DEVISING?
CLEARLY. SURELY YOU REAL-IZED?
YES. FRANKLY, I WAS RELIEVED. HE'S NEWLY MARRIED. THERE'S NO NEED TO EN-DANGER HIM.
MAY I WRITE HIM A NOTE?
WHY NOT?
NEITHER OF US ARE GOING ANYWHERE.
I SUPPOSE NOT.
NONETHELESS, THE COURTESY IS VERY MUCH APPRECIATED. THANK YOU.
NOT AT ALL. THIS VIEW AND THIS OCCASION BOTH ARE TOO MAGNIFICENT TO MAR WITH PETTI-NESS.
YOU DO KNOW, DON'T YOU, THAT THERE'S NOTHING PERSONAL IN THIS?
WHY, NATURALLY. OUR SITUATION HAS THE DISAFFECTED BEAUTY OF A CHESS GAME.
EXACTLY! HA HA HA! EXACTLY RIGHT!
I'M SO GLAD THAT YOU UNDERSTAND.
IT'S MEANING, ISN'T IT, THAT LENDS SUCH BLESSED JOY TO LIFE?
THIS SPRAY, THESE SUNLIT PEAKS. THE GOLDEN, MATHEMATIC LOGIC OF IT ALL.
Ah.
Ah, WHAT IT IS TO BE A MAN BELOW SO BLUE A SKY.
Tell Inspec
that the papers
he needs to convict
gang are in pigeon hole
M., done up in a blue
envelope and inscribed
'Moriarty'. I made every
disposition of my propert
before leaving England
and handed it to my
brother Mycroft.
give my greetings t
Mrs. Watson, and
believe me to be,
my dear Fellow
Very sincerely

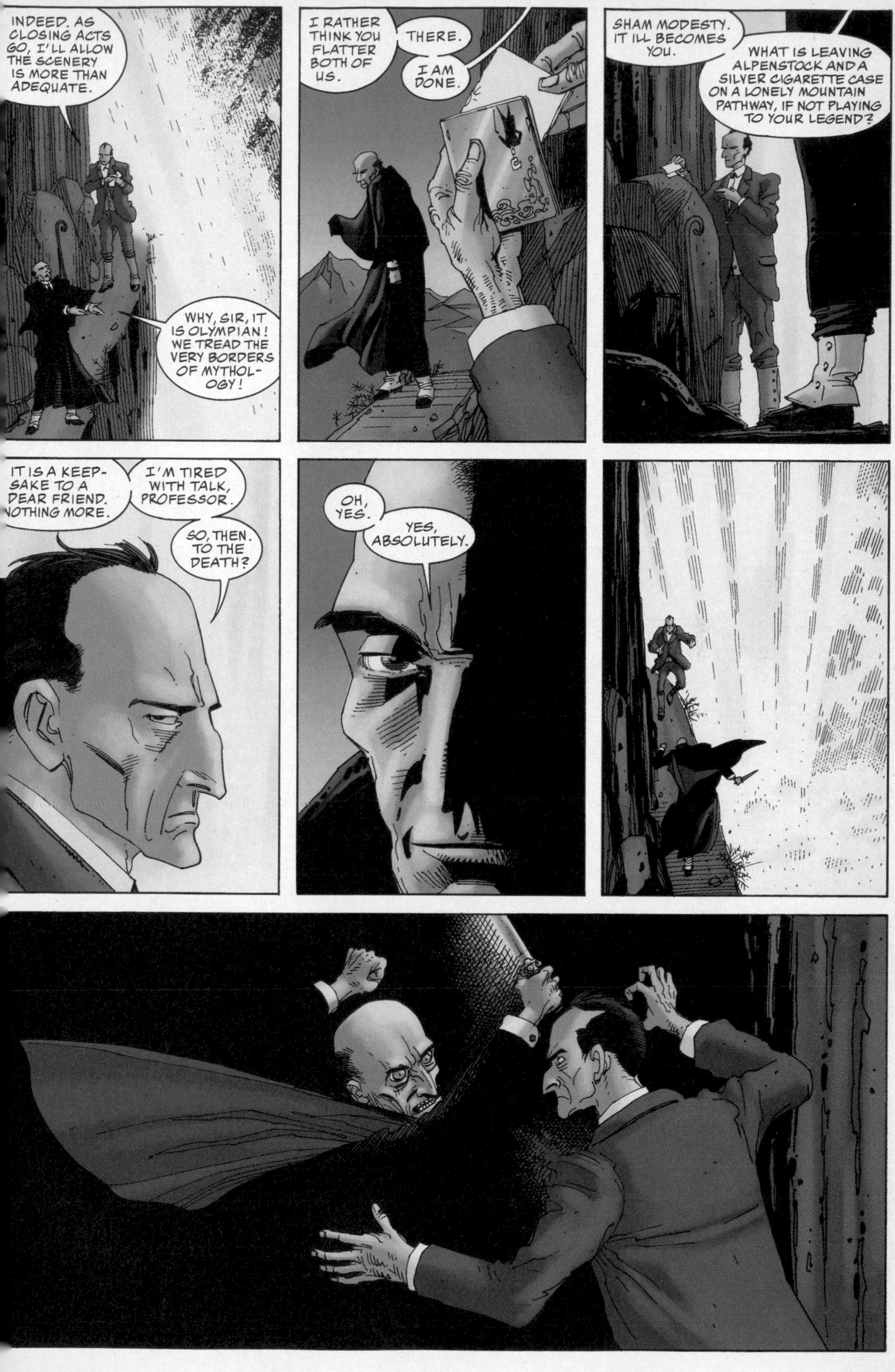

INDEED. AS CLOSING ACTS GO, I'LL ALLOW THE SCENERY IS MORE THAN ADEQUATE.
WHY, SIR, IT IS OLYMPIAN! WE TREAD THE VERY BORDERS OF MYTHOLOGY!
I RATHER THINK YOU FLATTER BOTH OF US.
THERE.
I AM DONE.
SHAM MODESTY. IT ILL BECOMES YOU.
WHAT IS LEAVING ALPENSTOCK AND A SILVER CIGARETTE CASE ON A LONELY MOUNTAIN PATHWAY, IF NOT PLAYING TO YOUR LEGEND?
IT IS A KEEPSAKE TO A DEAR FRIEND. NOTHING MORE.
I'M TIRED WITH TALK, PROFESSOR.
SO, THEN. TO THE DEATH?
OH, YES.
YES, ABSOLUTELY.

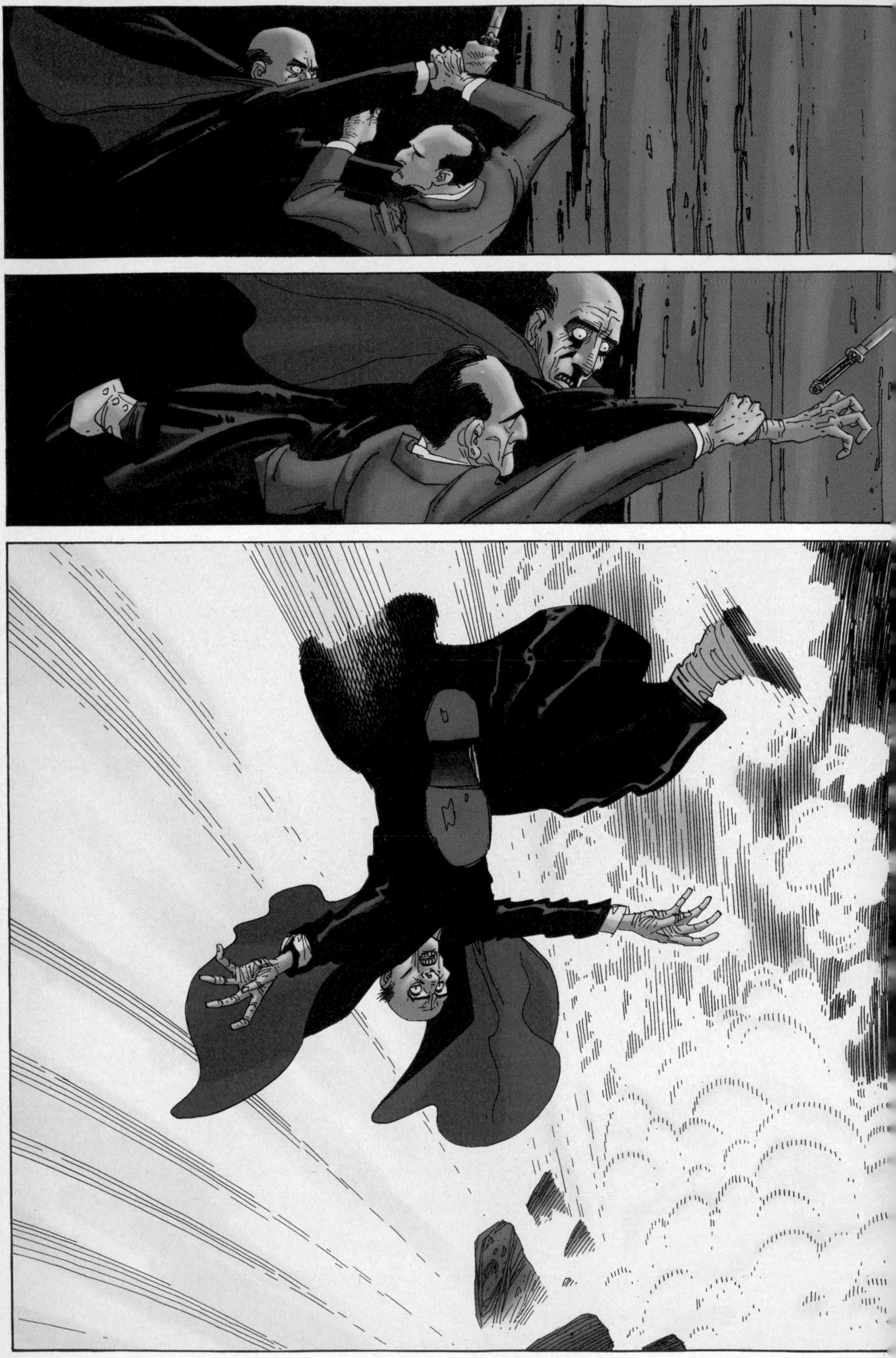

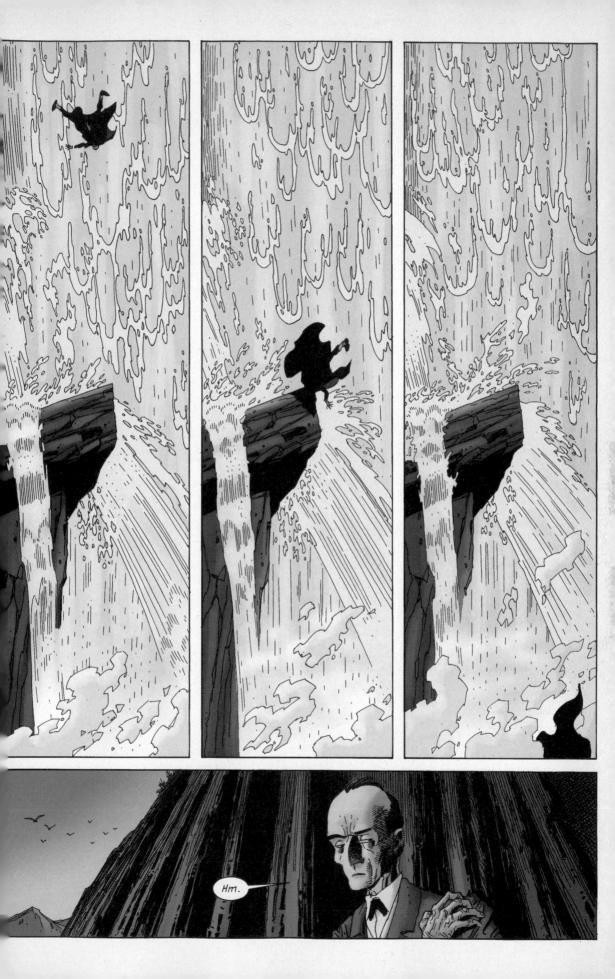

Hm.

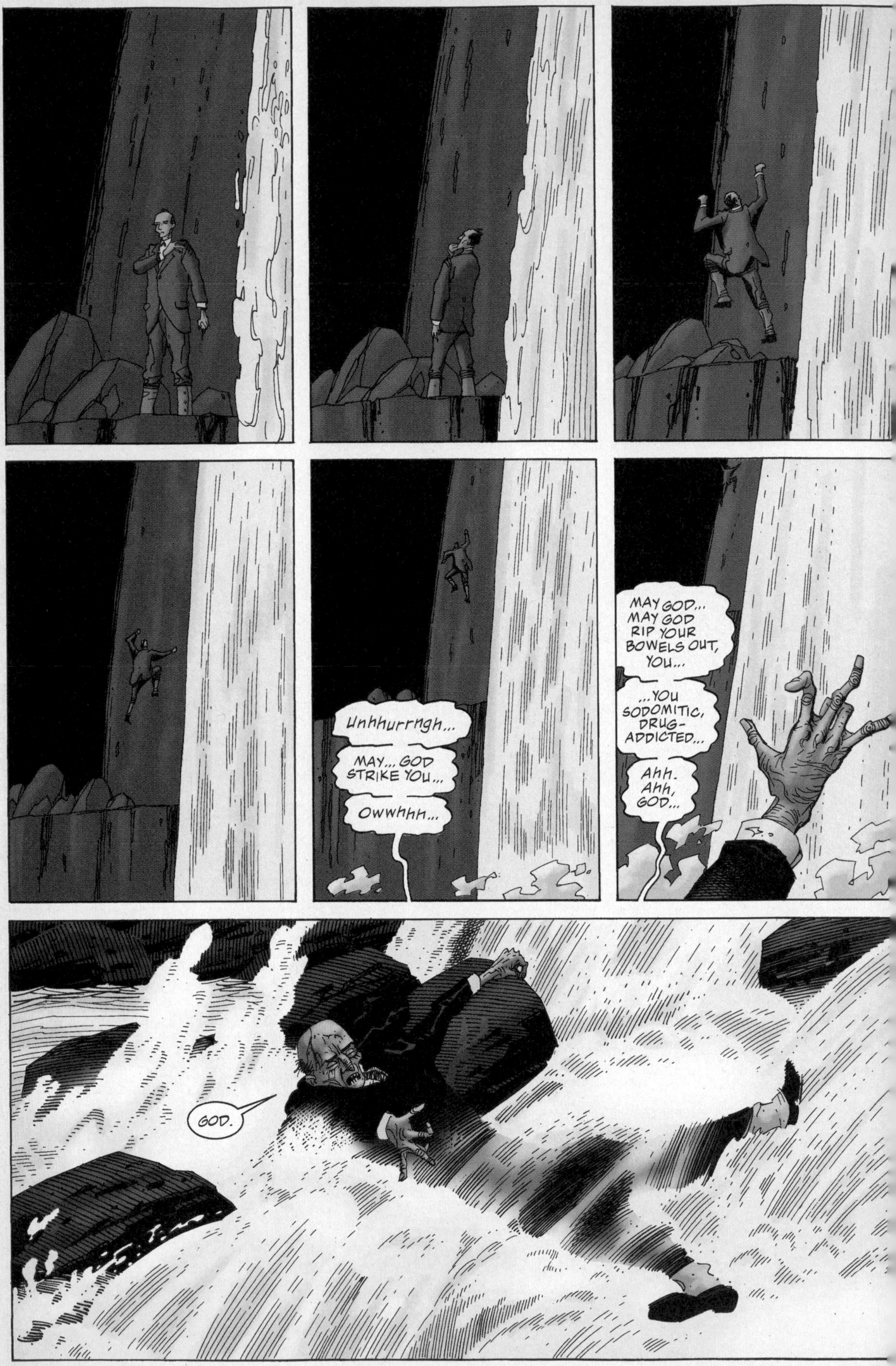
Unhhurrngh...
MAY... GOD STRIKE YOU...
Owwhhh...
MAY GOD... MAY GOD RIP YOUR BOWELS OUT, YOU...
...YOU SODOMITIC, DRUG-ADDICTED...
AHH. AHH, GOD...
GOD.

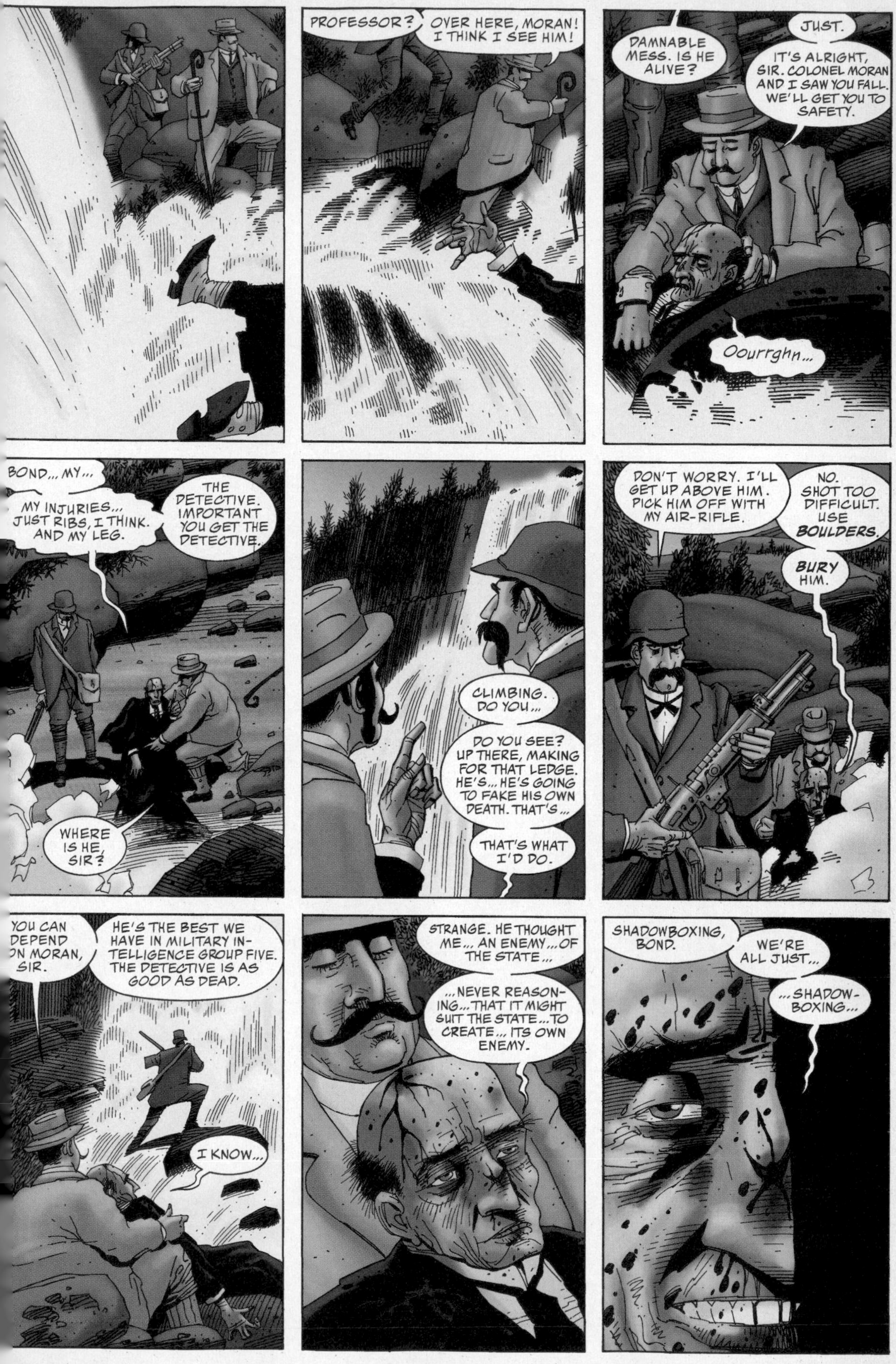
PROFESSOR?
OVER HERE, MORAN! I THINK I SEE HIM!
DAMNABLE MESS. IS HE ALIVE?
JUST.
IT'S ALRIGHT, SIR. COLONEL MORAN AND I SAW YOU FALL. WE'LL GET YOU TO SAFETY.
Oourrghn...
BOND... MY...
MY INJURIES... JUST RIBS, I THINK. AND MY LEG.
THE DETECTIVE. IMPORTANT YOU GET THE DETECTIVE.
WHERE IS HE, SIR?
CLIMBING. DO YOU...
DO YOU SEE? UP THERE, MAKING FOR THAT LEDGE. HE'S... HE'S GOING TO FAKE HIS OWN DEATH. THAT'S...
THAT'S WHAT I'D DO.
DON'T WORRY. I'LL GET UP ABOVE HIM. PICK HIM OFF WITH MY AIR-RIFLE.
NO. SHOT TOO DIFFICULT. USE BOULDERS.
BURY HIM.
YOU CAN DEPEND ON MORAN, SIR.
HE'S THE BEST WE HAVE IN MILITARY INTELLIGENCE GROUP FIVE. THE DETECTIVE IS AS GOOD AS DEAD.
I KNOW...
STRANGE. HE THOUGHT ME... AN ENEMY... OF THE STATE...
...NEVER REASONING... THAT IT MIGHT SUIT THE STATE... TO CREATE... ITS OWN ENEMY.
SHADOWBOXING, BOND.
WE'RE ALL JUST...
...SHADOWBOXING...

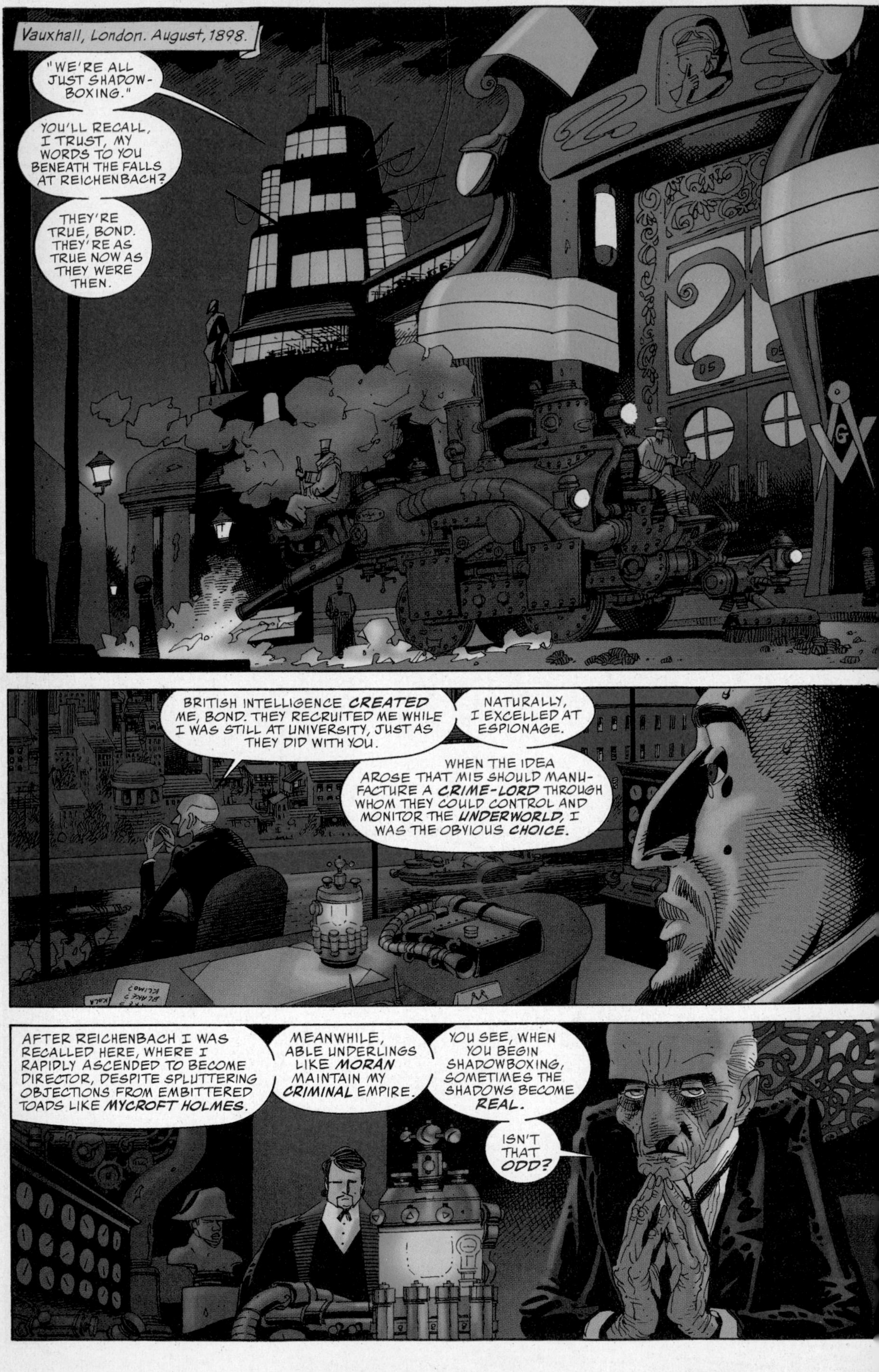

Vauxhall, London. August, 1898.
"WE'RE ALL JUST SHADOW-BOXING."
YOU'LL RECALL, I TRUST, MY WORDS TO YOU BENEATH THE FALLS AT REICHENBACH?
THEY'RE TRUE, BOND. THEY'RE AS TRUE NOW AS THEY WERE THEN.
BRITISH INTELLIGENCE CREATED ME, BOND. THEY RECRUITED ME WHILE I WAS STILL AT UNIVERSITY, JUST AS THEY DID WITH YOU.
NATURALLY, I EXCELLED AT ESPIONAGE.
WHEN THE IDEA AROSE THAT MI5 SHOULD MANUFACTURE A CRIME-LORD THROUGH WHOM THEY COULD CONTROL AND MONITOR THE UNDERWORLD, I WAS THE OBVIOUS CHOICE.
AFTER REICHENBACH I WAS RECALLED HERE, WHERE I RAPIDLY ASCENDED TO BECOME DIRECTOR, DESPITE SPLUTTERING OBJECTIONS FROM EMBITTERED TOADS LIKE MYCROFT HOLMES.
MEANWHILE, ABLE UNDERLINGS LIKE MORAN MAINTAIN MY CRIMINAL EMPIRE.
YOU SEE, WHEN YOU BEGIN SHADOWBOXING, SOMETIMES THE SHADOWS BECOME REAL.
ISN'T THAT ODD?

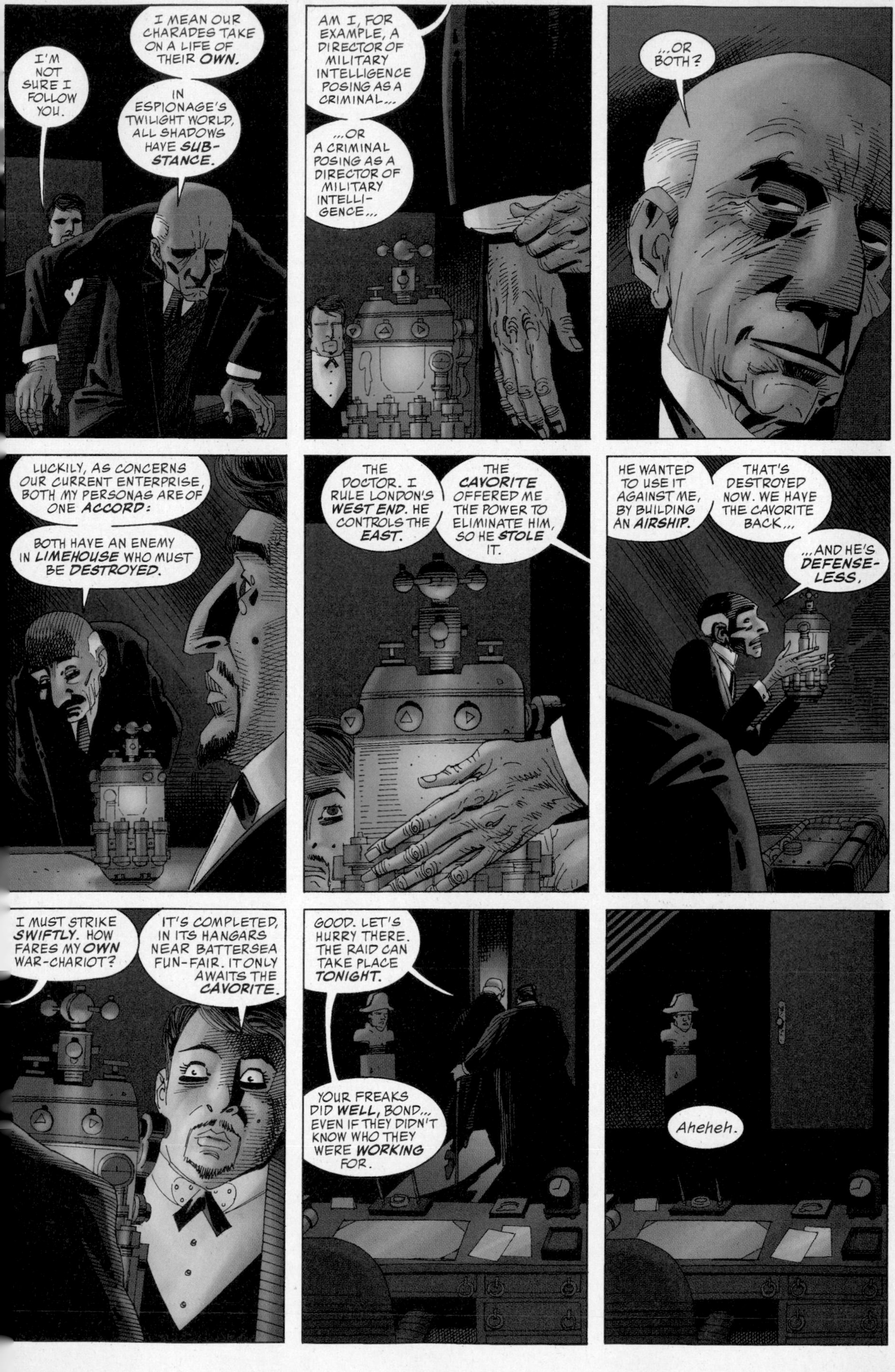
I'M NOT SURE I FOLLOW YOU.
I MEAN OUR CHARADES TAKE ON A LIFE OF THEIR OWN.
IN ESPIONAGE'S TWILIGHT WORLD, ALL SHADOWS HAVE SUB-STANCE.
AM I, FOR EXAMPLE, A DIRECTOR OF MILITARY INTELLIGENCE POSING AS A CRIMINAL...
...OR A CRIMINAL POSING AS A DIRECTOR OF MILITARY INTELLI-GENCE...
...OR BOTH?
LUCKILY, AS CONCERNS OUR CURRENT ENTERPRISE, BOTH MY PERSONAS ARE OF ONE ACCORD:
BOTH HAVE AN ENEMY IN LIMEHOUSE WHO MUST BE DESTROYED.
THE DOCTOR. I RULE LONDON'S WEST END. HE CONTROLS THE EAST.
THE CAVORITE OFFERED ME THE POWER TO ELIMINATE HIM, SO HE STOLE IT.
HE WANTED TO USE IT AGAINST ME, BY BUILDING AN AIRSHIP.
THAT'S DESTROYED NOW. WE HAVE THE CAVORITE BACK...
...AND HE'S DEFENSE-LESS.
I MUST STRIKE SWIFTLY. HOW FARES MY OWN WAR-CHARIOT?
IT'S COMPLETED, IN ITS HANGARS NEAR BATTERSEA FUN-FAIR. IT ONLY AWAITS THE CAVORITE.
GOOD. LET'S HURRY THERE. THE RAID CAN TAKE PLACE TONIGHT.
YOUR FREAKS DID WELL, BOND... EVEN IF THEY DIDN'T KNOW WHO THEY WERE WORKING FOR.
Aheheh.

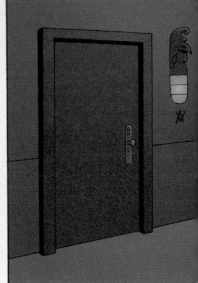

Hm?

BLIMEY.

OO'S
THERE?

COME
ON, I KNOW
I 'EARD
SOMEBODY.

'OO
IS IT?

I'VE GOT A
PISTOL, Y'KNOW.
I'M NOT MUCKIN'
ABOUT.

NOW,
WHERE...

AAA!

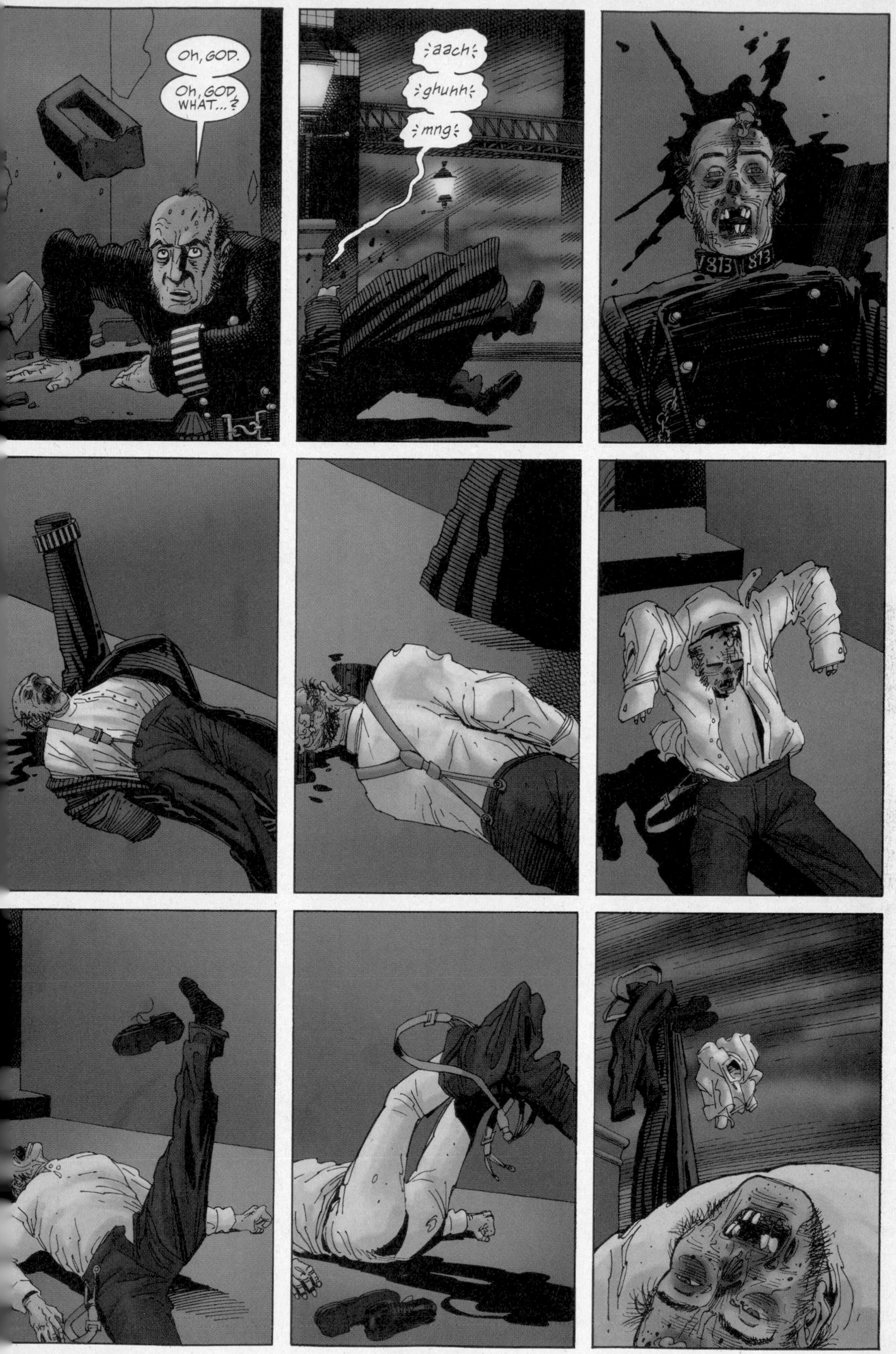
Oh, GOD.
Oh, GOD. WHAT...?
aach
ghunh
mng
1813 1813

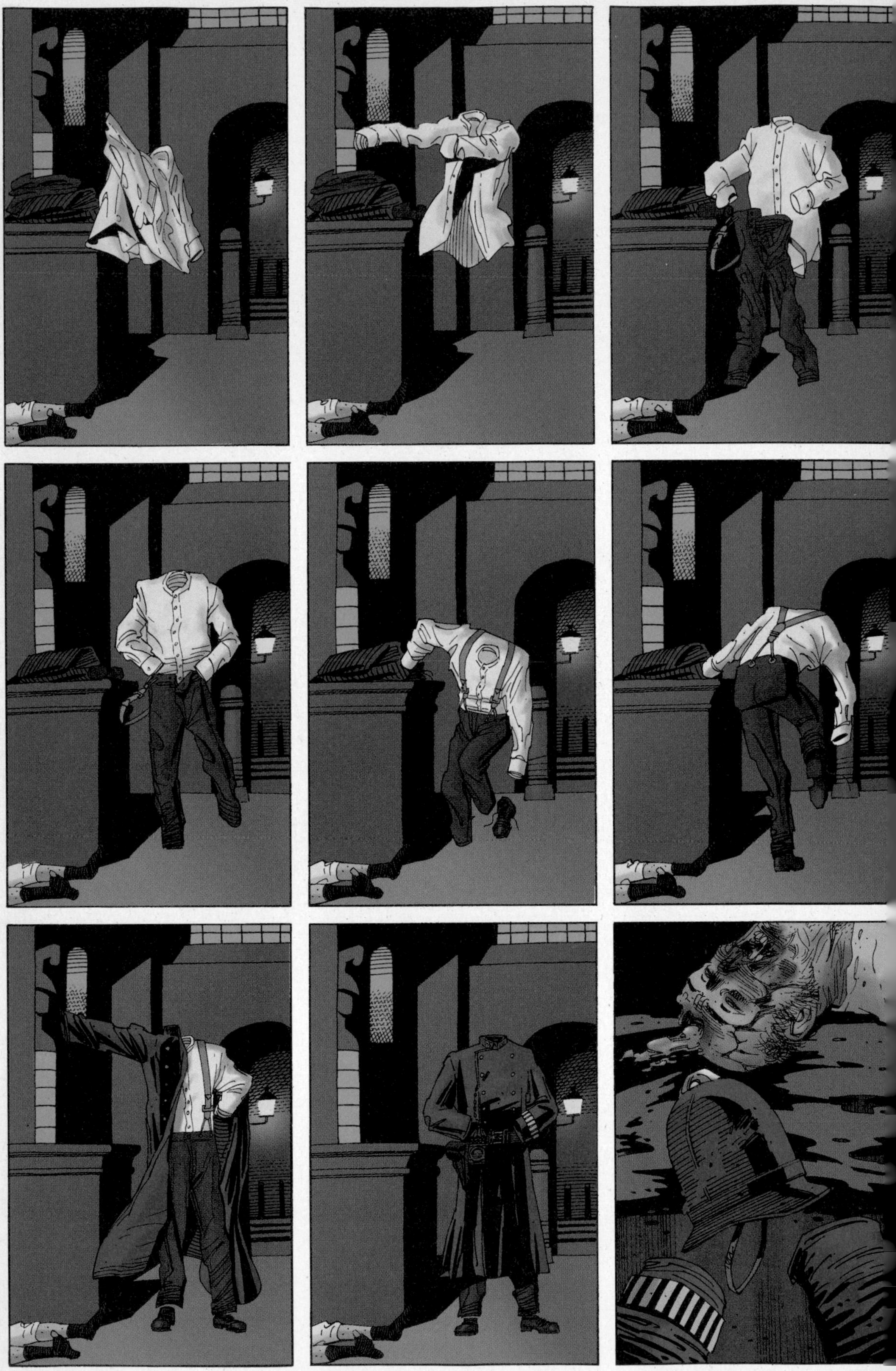

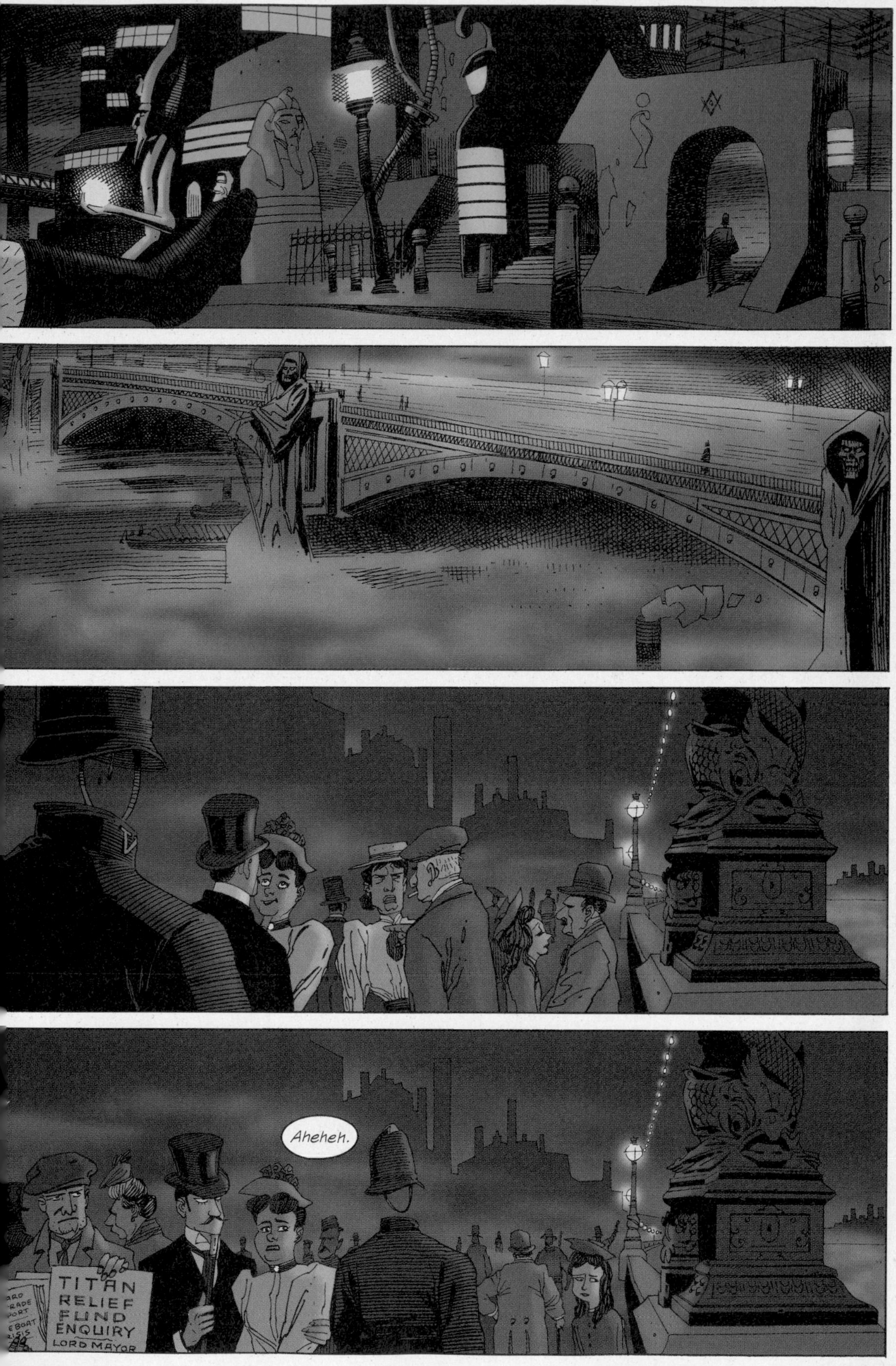
Aheheh.
TITAN
RELIEF
FUND
ENQUIRY
LORD MAYOR

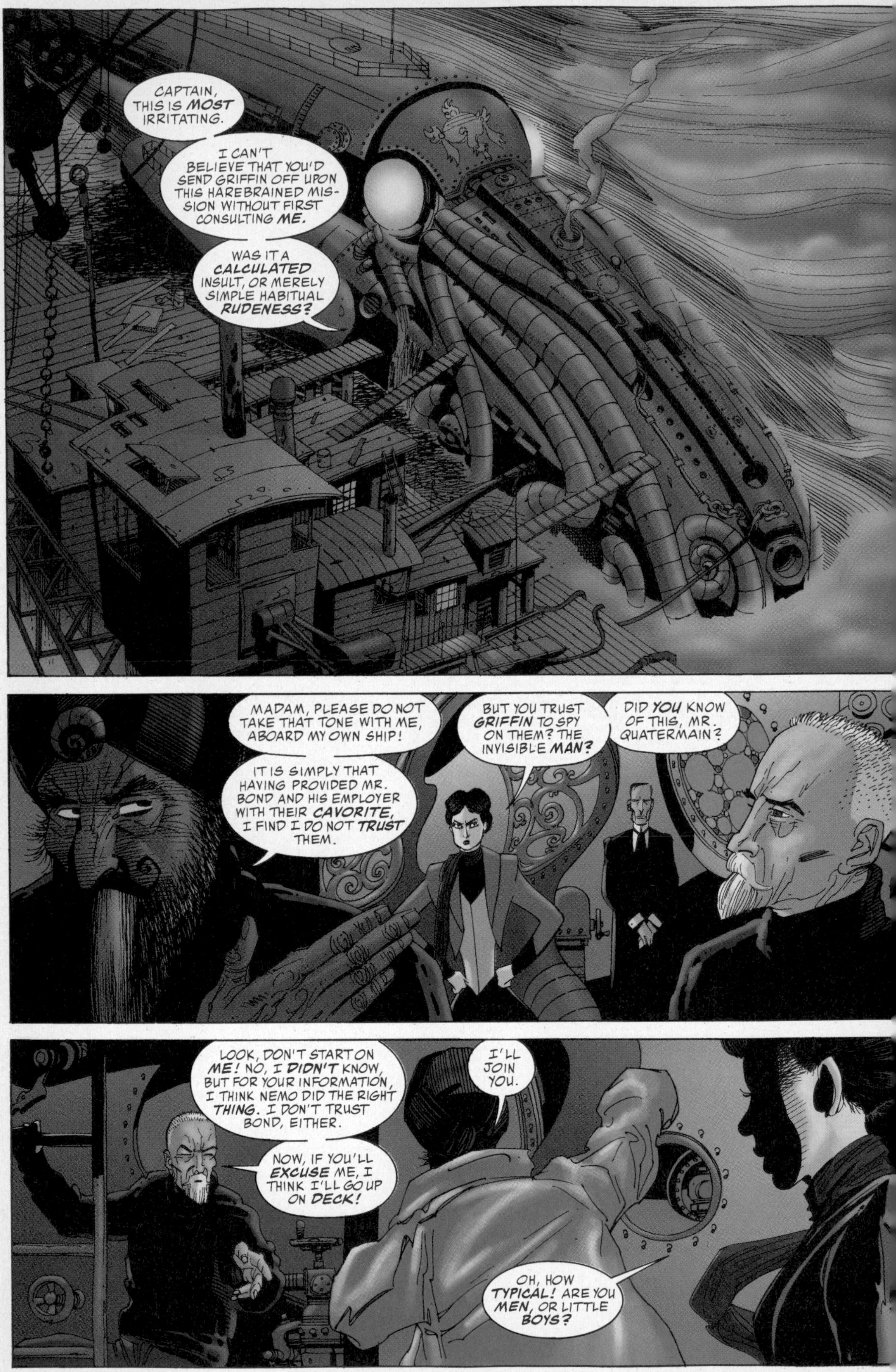
CAPTAIN, THIS IS MOST IRRITATING.
I CAN'T BELIEVE THAT YOU'D SEND GRIFFIN OFF UPON THIS HAREBRAINED MISSION WITHOUT FIRST CONSULTING ME.
WAS IT A CALCULATED INSULT, OR MERELY SIMPLE HABITUAL RUDENESS?
MADAM, PLEASE DO NOT TAKE THAT TONE WITH ME, ABOARD MY OWN SHIP!
IT IS SIMPLY THAT HAVING PROVIDED MR. BOND AND HIS EMPLOYER WITH THEIR CAVORITE, I FIND I DO NOT TRUST THEM.
BUT YOU TRUST GRIFFIN TO SPY ON THEM? THE INVISIBLE MAN?
DID YOU KNOW OF THIS, MR. QUATERMAIN?
LOOK, DON'T START ON ME! NO, I DIDN'T KNOW, BUT FOR YOUR INFORMATION, I THINK NEMO DID THE RIGHT THING. I DON'T TRUST BOND, EITHER.
NOW, IF YOU'LL EXCUSE ME, I THINK I'LL GO UP ON DECK!
I'LL JOIN YOU.
OH, HOW TYPICAL! ARE YOU MEN, OR LITTLE BOYS?

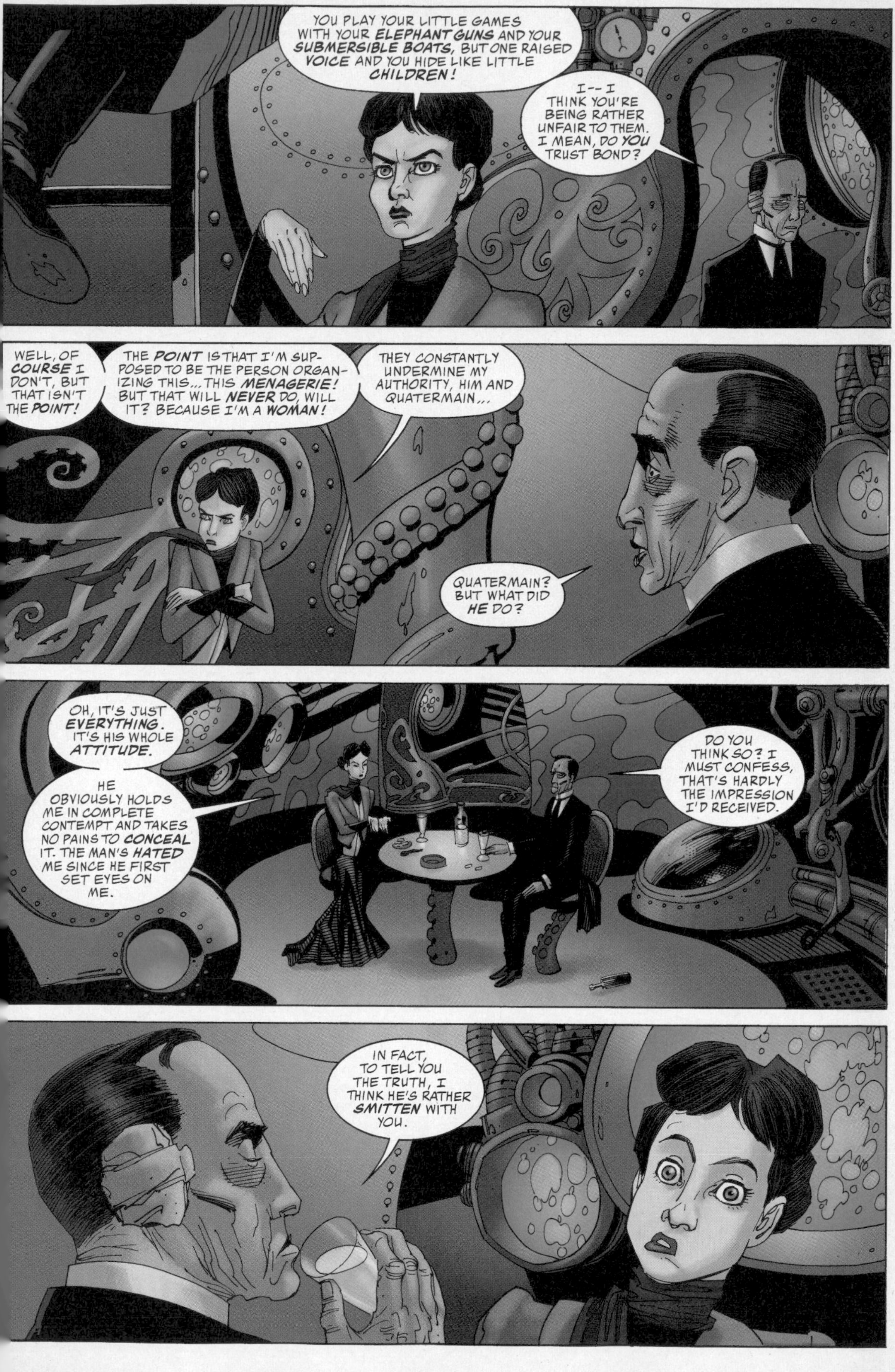
YOU PLAY YOUR LITTLE GAMES WITH YOUR ELEPHANT GUNS AND YOUR SUBMERSIBLE BOATS, BUT ONE RAISED VOICE AND YOU HIDE LIKE LITTLE CHILDREN!
I-- I THINK YOU'RE BEING RATHER UNFAIR TO THEM. I MEAN, DO YOU TRUST BOND?
WELL, OF COURSE I DON'T, BUT THAT ISN'T THE POINT!
THE POINT IS THAT I'M SUPPOSED TO BE THE PERSON ORGANIZING THIS... THIS MENAGERIE! BUT THAT WILL NEVER DO, WILL IT? BECAUSE I'M A WOMAN!
THEY CONSTANTLY UNDERMINE MY AUTHORITY, HIM AND QUATERMAIN...
QUATERMAIN? BUT WHAT DID HE DO?
OH, IT'S JUST EVERYTHING. IT'S HIS WHOLE ATTITUDE.
HE OBVIOUSLY HOLDS ME IN COMPLETE CONTEMPT AND TAKES NO PAINS TO CONCEAL IT. THE MAN'S HATED ME SINCE HE FIRST SET EYES ON ME.
DO YOU THINK SO? I MUST CONFESS, THAT'S HARDLY THE IMPRESSION I'D RECEIVED.
IN FACT, TO TELL YOU THE TRUTH, I THINK HE'S RATHER SMITTEN WITH YOU.

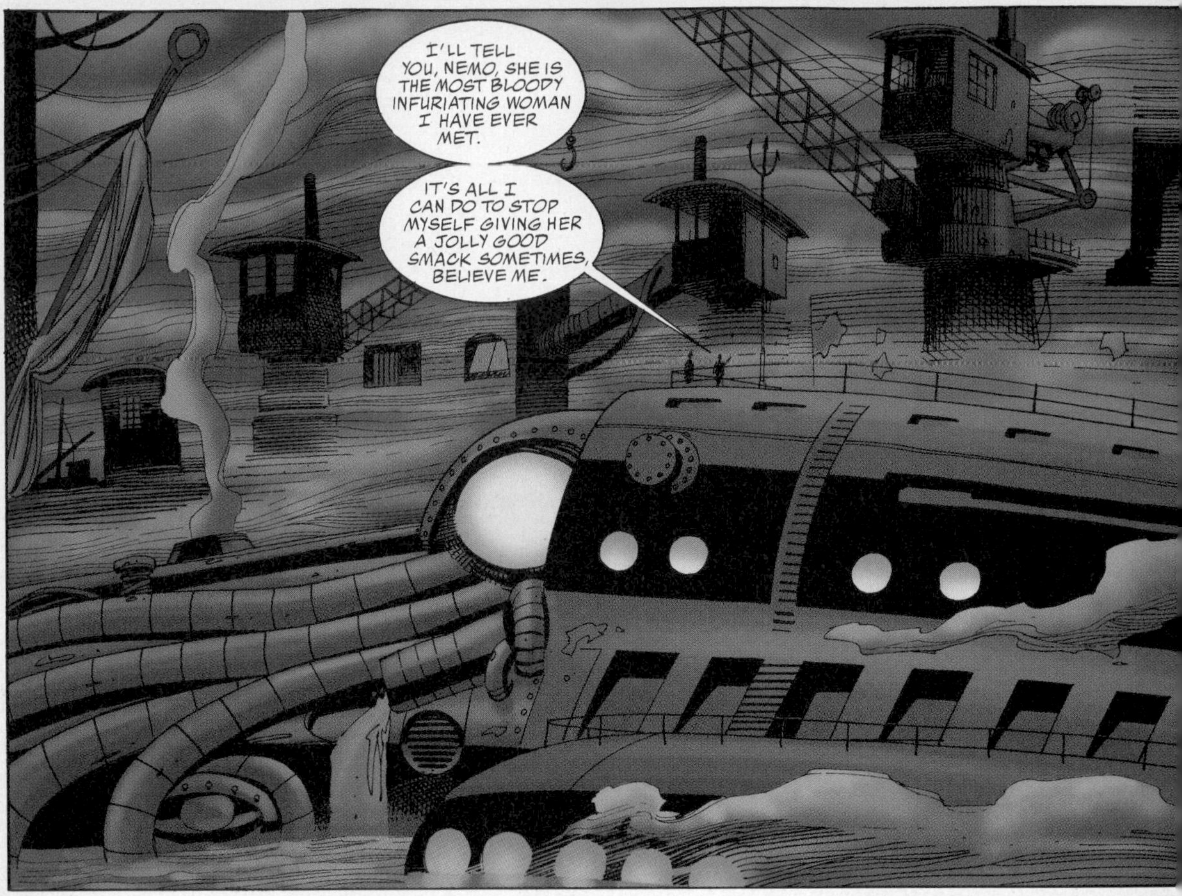
I'LL TELL YOU, NEMO, SHE IS THE MOST BLOODY INFURIATING WOMAN I HAVE EVER MET.
IT'S ALL I CAN DO TO STOP MYSELF GIVING HER A JOLLY GOOD SMACK SOMETIMES, BELIEVE ME.

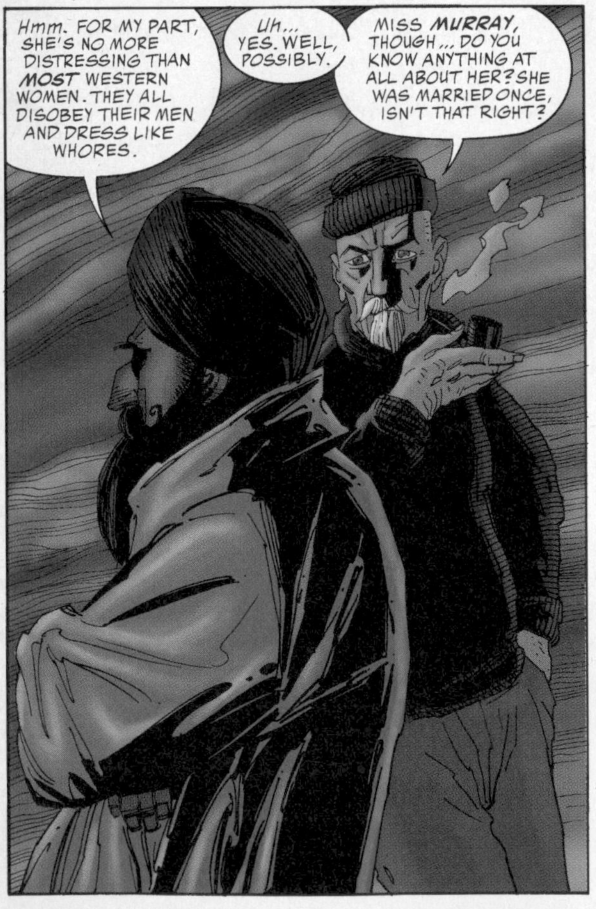
Hmm. FOR MY PART, SHE'S NO MORE DISTRESSING THAN MOST WESTERN WOMEN. THEY ALL DISOBEY THEIR MEN AND DRESS LIKE WHORES.
Uh... YES. WELL, POSSIBLY.
MISS MURRAY, THOUGH... DO YOU KNOW ANYTHING AT ALL ABOUT HER? SHE WAS MARRIED ONCE, ISN'T THAT RIGHT?

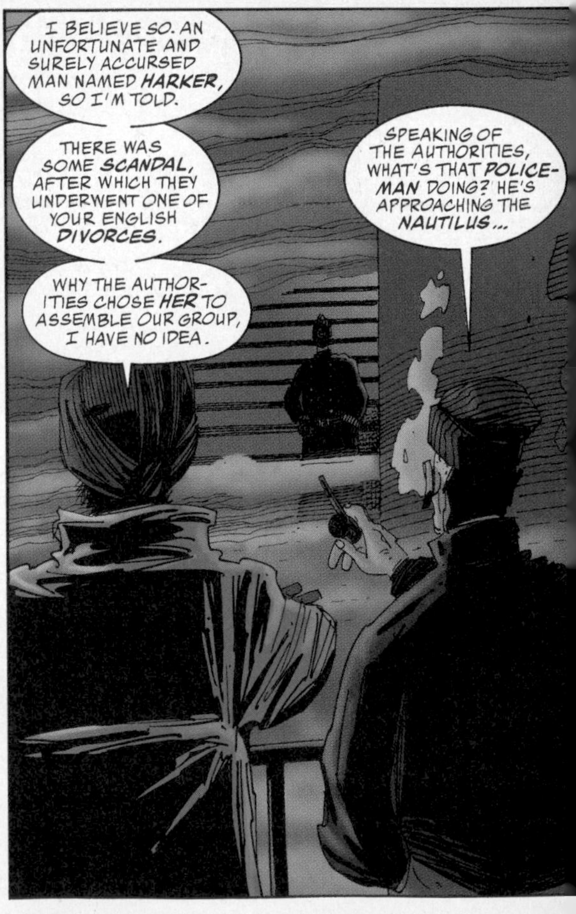
I BELIEVE SO. AN UNFORTUNATE AND SURELY ACCURSED MAN NAMED HARKER, SO I'M TOLD.
THERE WAS SOME SCANDAL, AFTER WHICH THEY UNDERWENT ONE OF YOUR ENGLISH DIVORCES.
WHY THE AUTHOR-ITIES CHOSE HER TO ASSEMBLE OUR GROUP, I HAVE NO IDEA.
SPEAKING OF THE AUTHORITIES, WHAT'S THAT POLICE-MAN DOING? HE'S APPROACHING THE NAUTILUS...

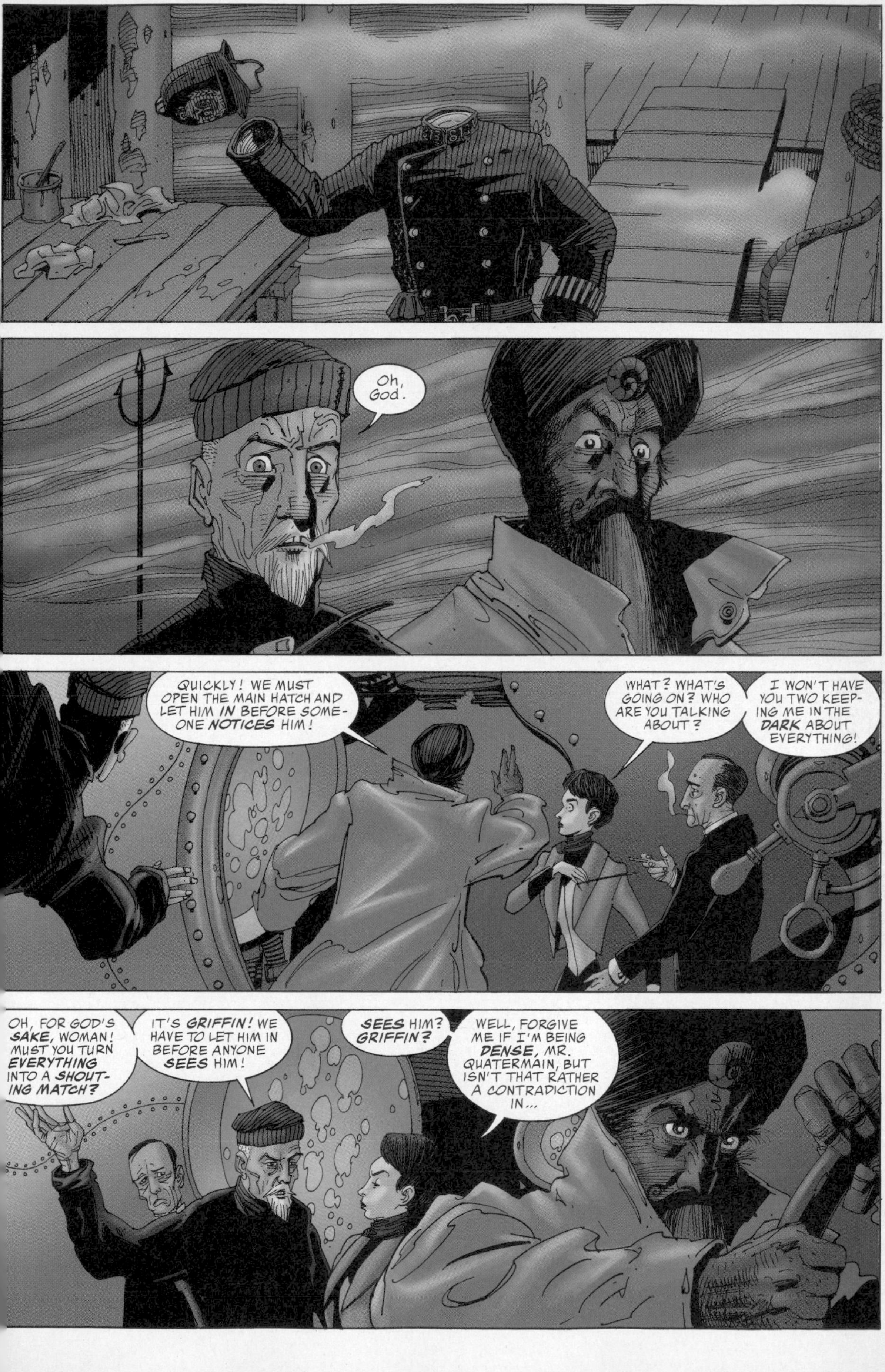
Oh, God.
QUICKLY! WE MUST OPEN THE MAIN HATCH AND LET HIM IN BEFORE SOME-ONE NOTICES HIM!
WHAT? WHAT'S GOING ON? WHO ARE YOU TALKING ABOUT?
I WON'T HAVE YOU TWO KEEP-ING ME IN THE DARK ABOUT EVERYTHING!
OH, FOR GOD'S SAKE, WOMAN! MUST YOU TURN EVERYTHING INTO A SHOUT-ING MATCH?
IT'S GRIFFIN! WE HAVE TO LET HIM IN BEFORE ANYONE SEES HIM!
SEES HIM? GRIFFIN?
WELL, FORGIVE ME IF I'M BEING DENSE, MR. QUATERMAIN, BUT ISN'T THAT RATHER A CONTRADICTION IN...

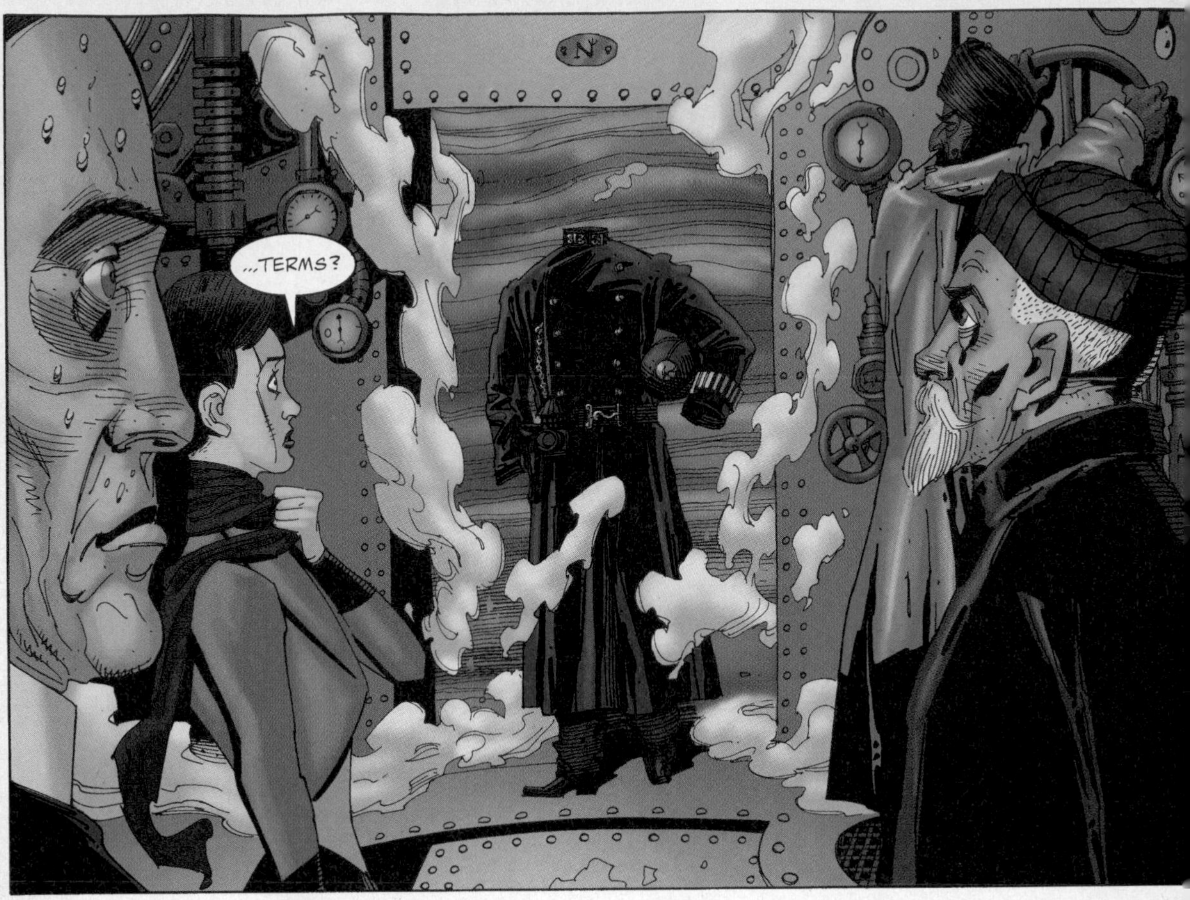
...TERMS?

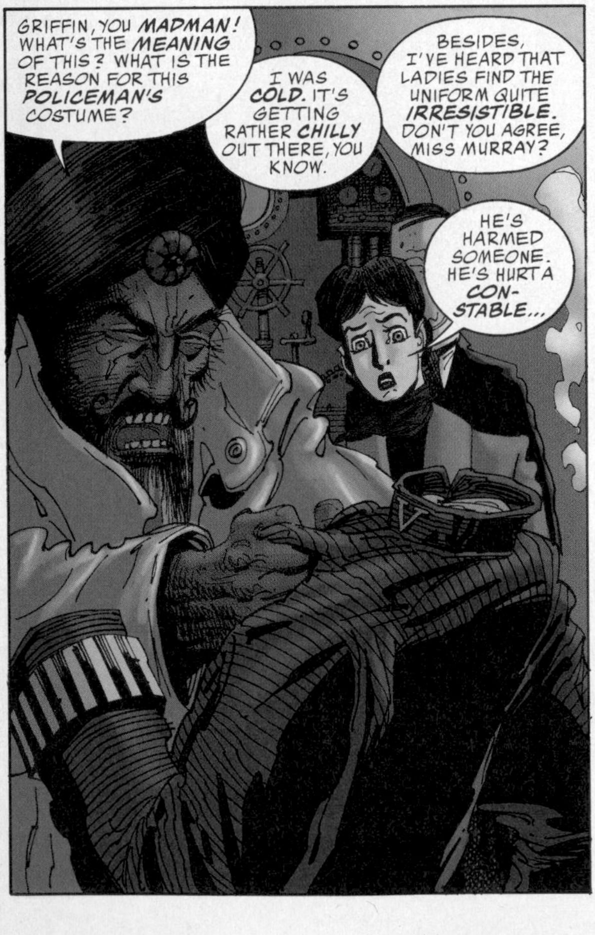
GRIFFIN, YOU MADMAN! WHAT'S THE MEANING OF THIS? WHAT IS THE REASON FOR THIS POLICEMAN'S COSTUME?
I WAS COLD. IT'S GETTING RATHER CHILLY OUT THERE, YOU KNOW.
BESIDES, I'VE HEARD THAT LADIES FIND THE UNIFORM QUITE IRRESISTIBLE. DON'T YOU AGREE, MISS MURRAY?
HE'S HARMED SOMEONE. HE'S HURT A CONSTABLE...

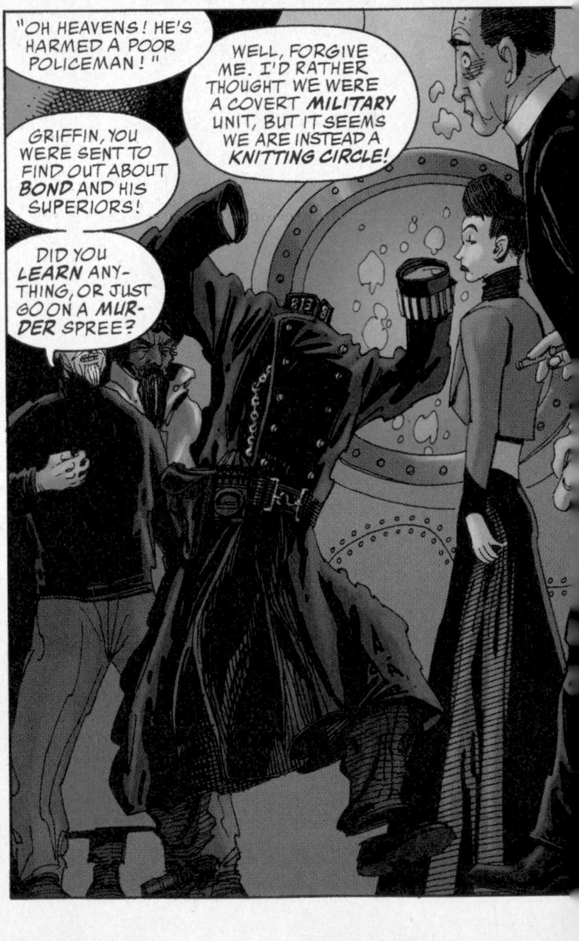
"OH HEAVENS! HE'S HARMED A POOR POLICEMAN!"
WELL, FORGIVE ME. I'D RATHER THOUGHT WE WERE A COVERT MILITARY UNIT, BUT IT SEEMS WE ARE INSTEAD A KNITTING CIRCLE!
GRIFFIN, YOU WERE SENT TO FIND OUT ABOUT BOND AND HIS SUPERIORS!
DID YOU LEARN ANYTHING, OR JUST GO ON A MURDER SPREE?

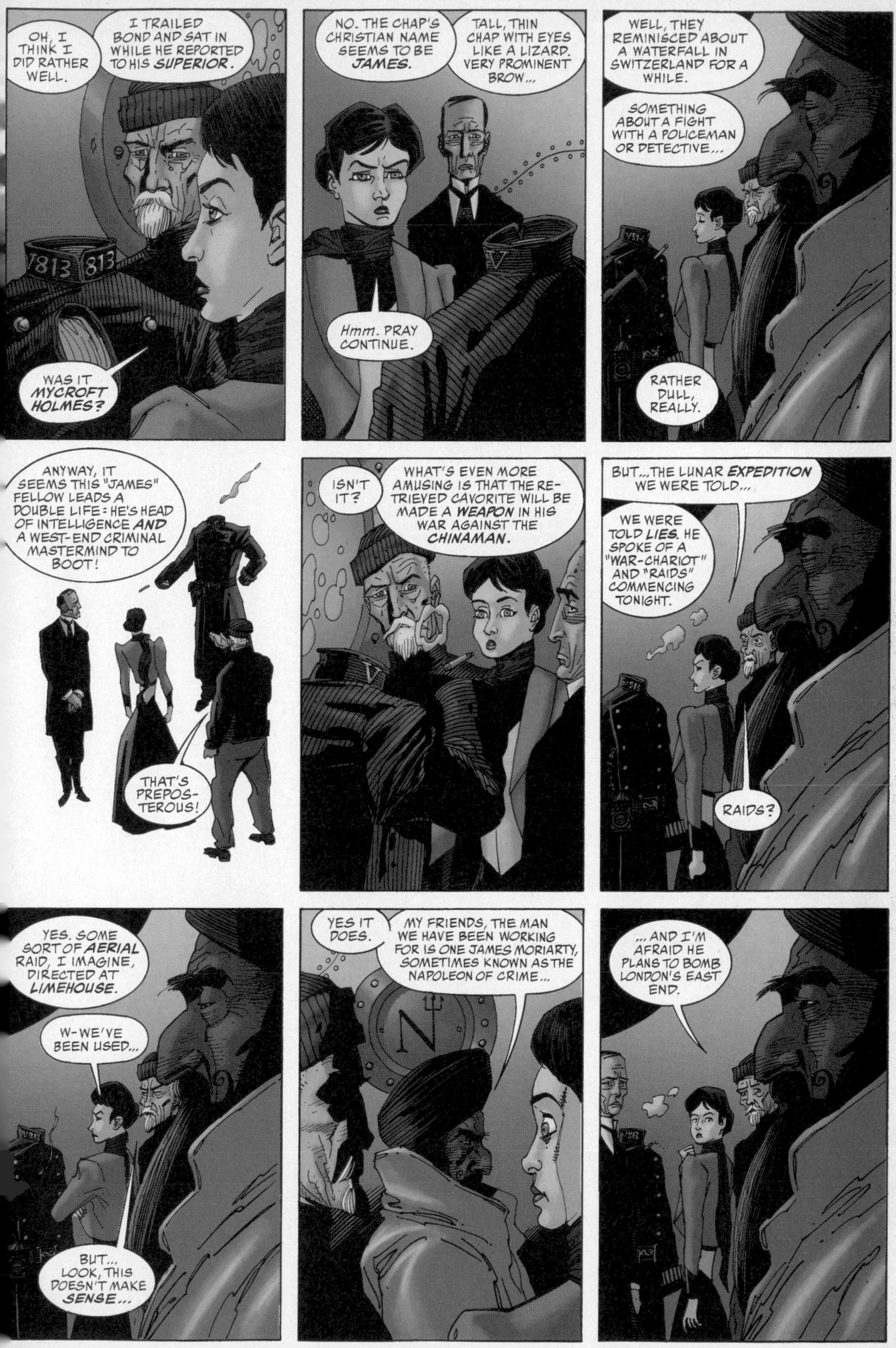

OH, I THINK I DID RATHER WELL.
I TRAILED BOND AND SAT IN WHILE HE REPORTED TO HIS SUPERIOR.
WAS IT MYCROFT HOLMES?
NO. THE CHAP'S CHRISTIAN NAME SEEMS TO BE JAMES.
TALL, THIN CHAP WITH EYES LIKE A LIZARD. VERY PROMINENT BROW...
Hmm. PRAY CONTINUE.
WELL, THEY REMINISCED ABOUT A WATERFALL IN SWITZERLAND FOR A WHILE.
SOMETHING ABOUT A FIGHT WITH A POLICEMAN OR DETECTIVE...
RATHER DULL, REALLY.
ANYWAY, IT SEEMS THIS "JAMES" FELLOW LEADS A DOUBLE LIFE: HE'S HEAD OF INTELLIGENCE AND A WEST-END CRIMINAL MASTERMIND TO BOOT!
THAT'S PREPOSTEROUS!
ISN'T IT?
WHAT'S EVEN MORE AMUSING IS THAT THE RETRIEVED CAVORITE WILL BE MADE A WEAPON IN HIS WAR AGAINST THE CHINAMAN.
BUT...THE LUNAR EXPEDITION WE WERE TOLD...
WE WERE TOLD LIES. HE SPOKE OF A "WAR-CHARIOT" AND "RAIDS" COMMENCING TONIGHT.
RAIDS?
YES. SOME SORT OF AERIAL RAID, I IMAGINE, DIRECTED AT LIMEHOUSE.
W-WE'VE BEEN USED...
BUT... LOOK, THIS DOESN'T MAKE SENSE...
YES IT DOES.
MY FRIENDS, THE MAN WE HAVE BEEN WORKING FOR IS ONE JAMES MORIARTY, SOMETIMES KNOWN AS THE NAPOLEON OF CRIME...
...AND I'M AFRAID HE PLANS TO BOMB LONDON'S EAST END.

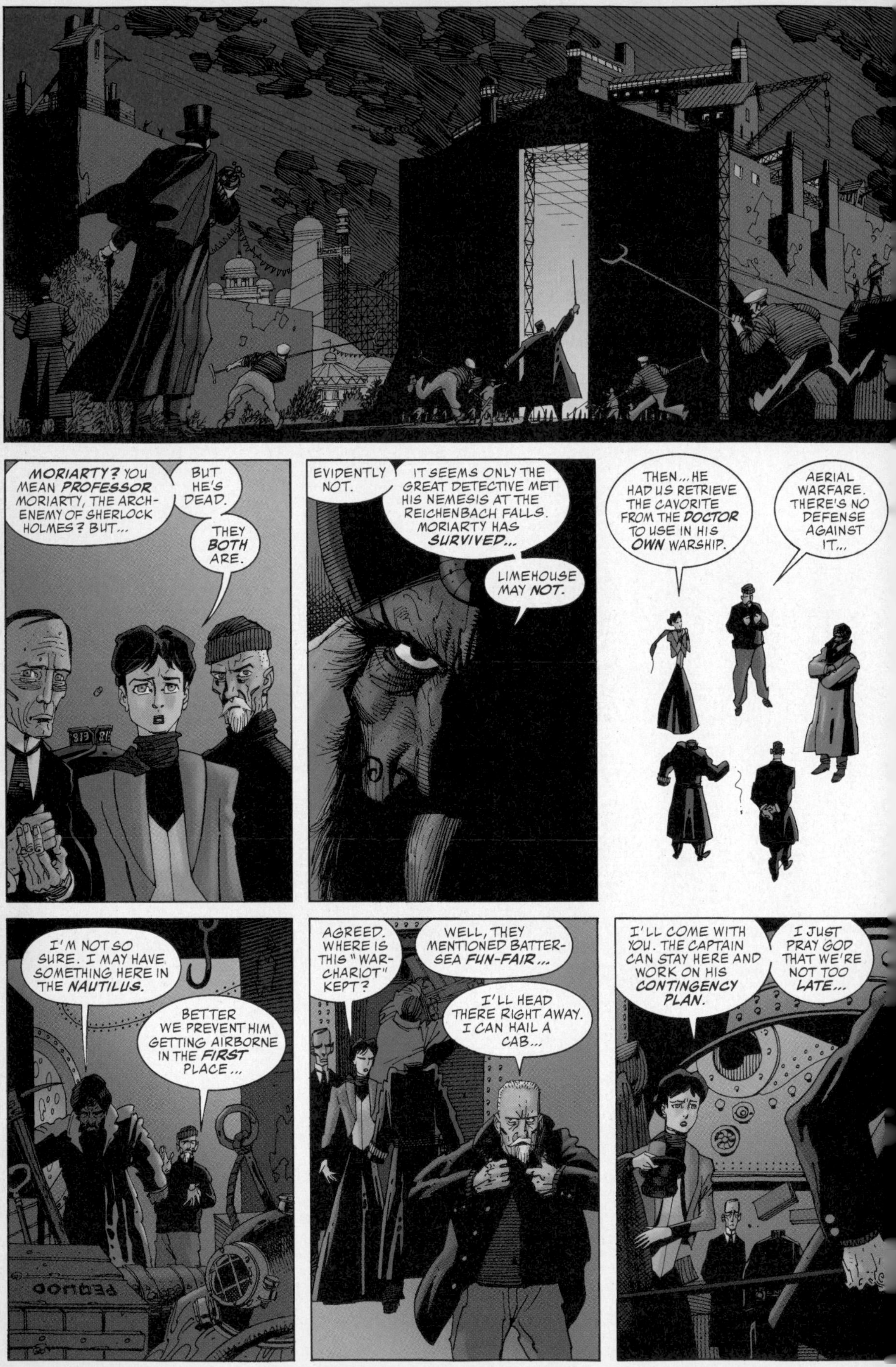
MORIARTY? YOU MEAN PROFESSOR MORIARTY, THE ARCH-ENEMY OF SHERLOCK HOLMES? BUT...
BUT HE'S DEAD.
THEY BOTH ARE.
EVIDENTLY NOT.
IT SEEMS ONLY THE GREAT DETECTIVE MET HIS NEMESIS AT THE REICHENBACH FALLS. MORIARTY HAS SURVIVED...
LIMEHOUSE MAY NOT.
THEN... HE HAD US RETRIEVE THE CAVORITE FROM THE DOCTOR TO USE IN HIS OWN WARSHIP.
AERIAL WARFARE. THERE'S NO DEFENSE AGAINST IT...
I'M NOT SO SURE. I MAY HAVE SOMETHING HERE IN THE NAUTILUS.
BETTER WE PREVENT HIM GETTING AIRBORNE IN THE FIRST PLACE...
AGREED. WHERE IS THIS "WAR-CHARIOT" KEPT?
WELL, THEY MENTIONED BATTER-SEA FUN-FAIR...
I'LL HEAD THERE RIGHT AWAY. I CAN HAIL A CAB...
I'LL COME WITH YOU. THE CAPTAIN CAN STAY HERE AND WORK ON HIS CONTINGENCY PLAN.
I JUST PRAY GOD THAT WE'RE NOT TOO LATE...

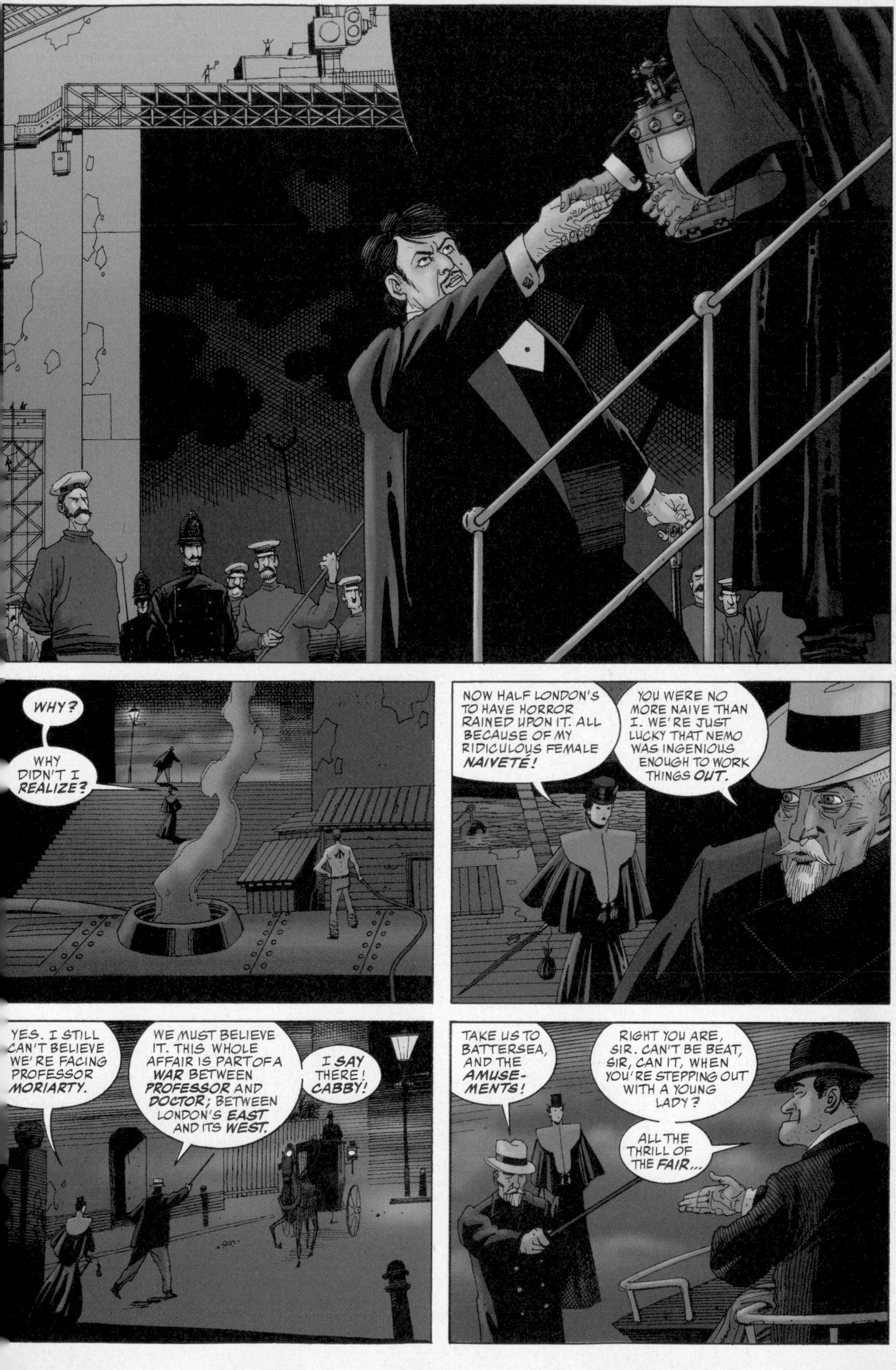
WHY?
WHY DIDN'T I REALIZE?
NOW HALF LONDON'S TO HAVE HORROR RAINED UPON IT. ALL BECAUSE OF MY RIDICULOUS FEMALE NAIVETÉ!
YOU WERE NO MORE NAIVE THAN I. WE'RE JUST LUCKY THAT NEMO WAS INGENIOUS ENOUGH TO WORK THINGS OUT.
YES. I STILL CAN'T BELIEVE WE'RE FACING PROFESSOR MORIARTY.
WE MUST BELIEVE IT. THIS WHOLE AFFAIR IS PART OF A WAR BETWEEN PROFESSOR AND DOCTOR; BETWEEN LONDON'S EAST AND ITS WEST.
I SAY THERE! CABBY!
TAKE US TO BATTERSEA, AND THE AMUSEMENTS!
RIGHT YOU ARE, SIR. CAN'T BE BEAT, SIR, CAN IT, WHEN YOU'RE STEPPING OUT WITH A YOUNG LADY?
ALL THE THRILL OF THE FAIR...

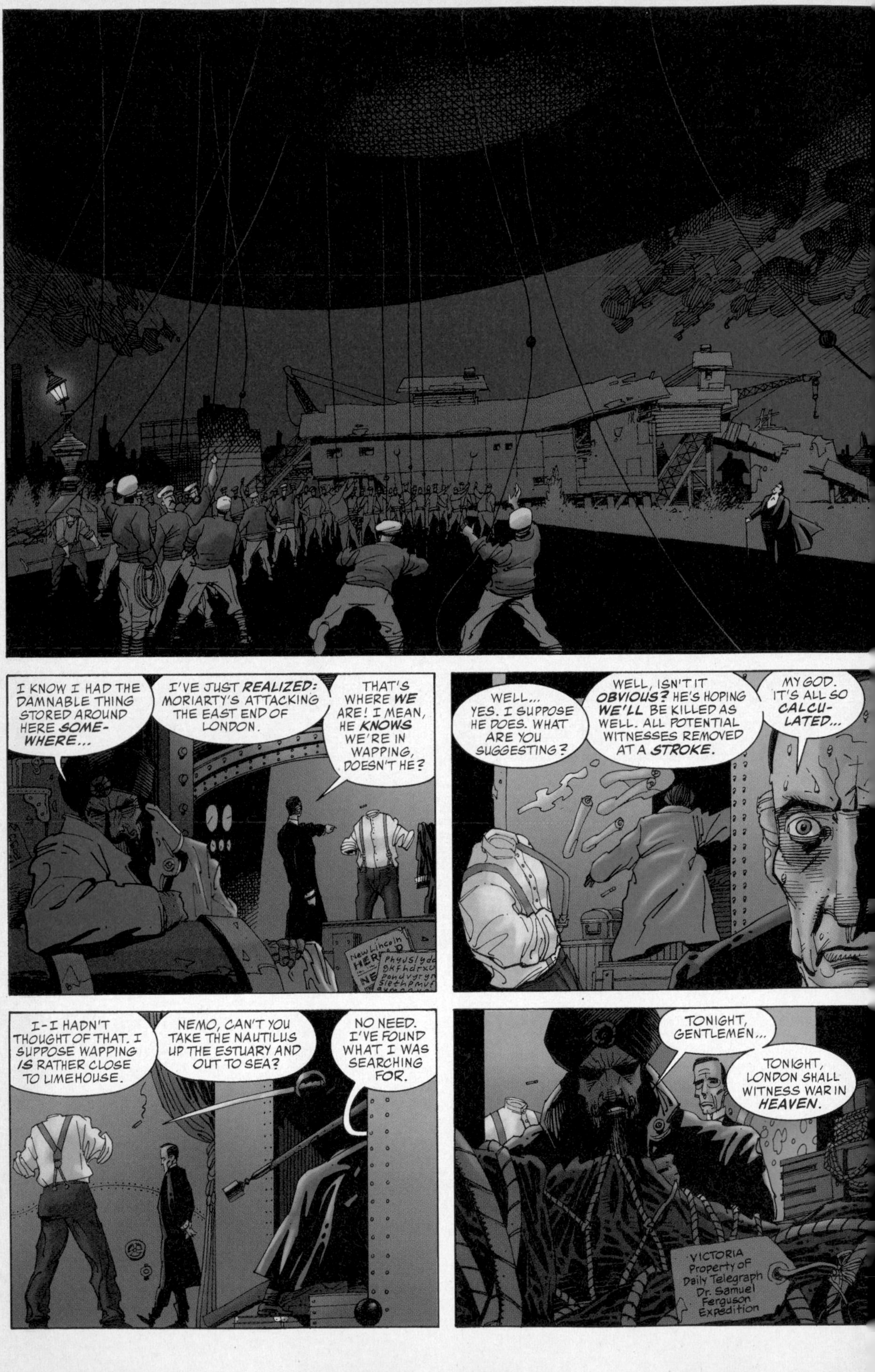
I KNOW I HAD THE DAMNABLE THING STORED AROUND HERE SOME-WHERE...
I'VE JUST REALIZED: MORIARTY'S ATTACKING THE EAST END OF LONDON.
THAT'S WHERE WE ARE! I MEAN, HE KNOWS WE'RE IN WAPPING, DOESN'T HE?
WELL... YES. I SUPPOSE HE DOES. WHAT ARE YOU SUGGESTING?
WELL, ISN'T IT OBVIOUS? HE'S HOPING WE'LL BE KILLED AS WELL. ALL POTENTIAL WITNESSES REMOVED AT A STROKE.
MY GOD. IT'S ALL SO CALCU-LATED...
I-I HADN'T THOUGHT OF THAT. I SUPPOSE WAPPING IS RATHER CLOSE TO LIMEHOUSE.
NEMO, CAN'T YOU TAKE THE NAUTILUS UP THE ESTUARY AND OUT TO SEA?
NO NEED. I'VE FOUND WHAT I WAS SEARCHING FOR.
TONIGHT, GENTLEMEN...
TONIGHT, LONDON SHALL WITNESS WAR IN HEAVEN.
VICTORIA
Property of
Daily Telegraph
Dr. Samuel
Ferguson
Expedition

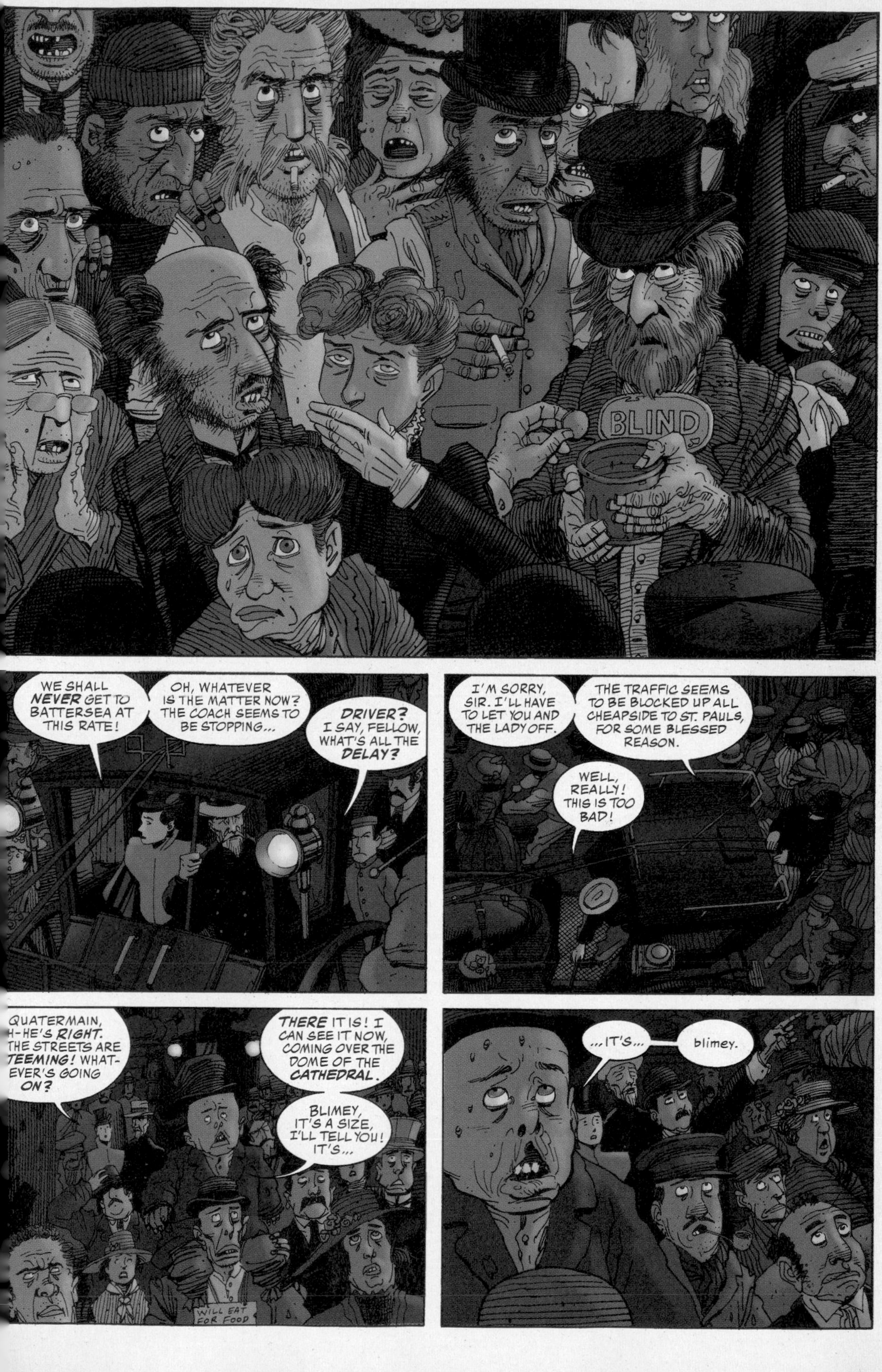
BLIND
WE SHALL NEVER GET TO BATTERSEA AT THIS RATE!
OH, WHATEVER IS THE MATTER NOW? THE COACH SEEMS TO BE STOPPING...
DRIVER? I SAY, FELLOW, WHAT'S ALL THE DELAY?
I'M SORRY, SIR. I'LL HAVE TO LET YOU AND THE LADY OFF.
THE TRAFFIC SEEMS TO BE BLOCKED UP ALL CHEAPSIDE TO ST. PAULS, FOR SOME BLESSED REASON.
WELL, REALLY! THIS IS TOO BAD!
QUATERMAIN, H-HE'S RIGHT. THE STREETS ARE TEEMING! WHAT-EVER'S GOING ON?
THERE IT IS! I CAN SEE IT NOW, COMING OVER THE DOME OF THE CATHEDRAL.
BLIMEY, IT'S A SIZE, I'LL TELL YOU! IT'S...
WILL EAT FOR FOOD
...IT'S...
blimey.

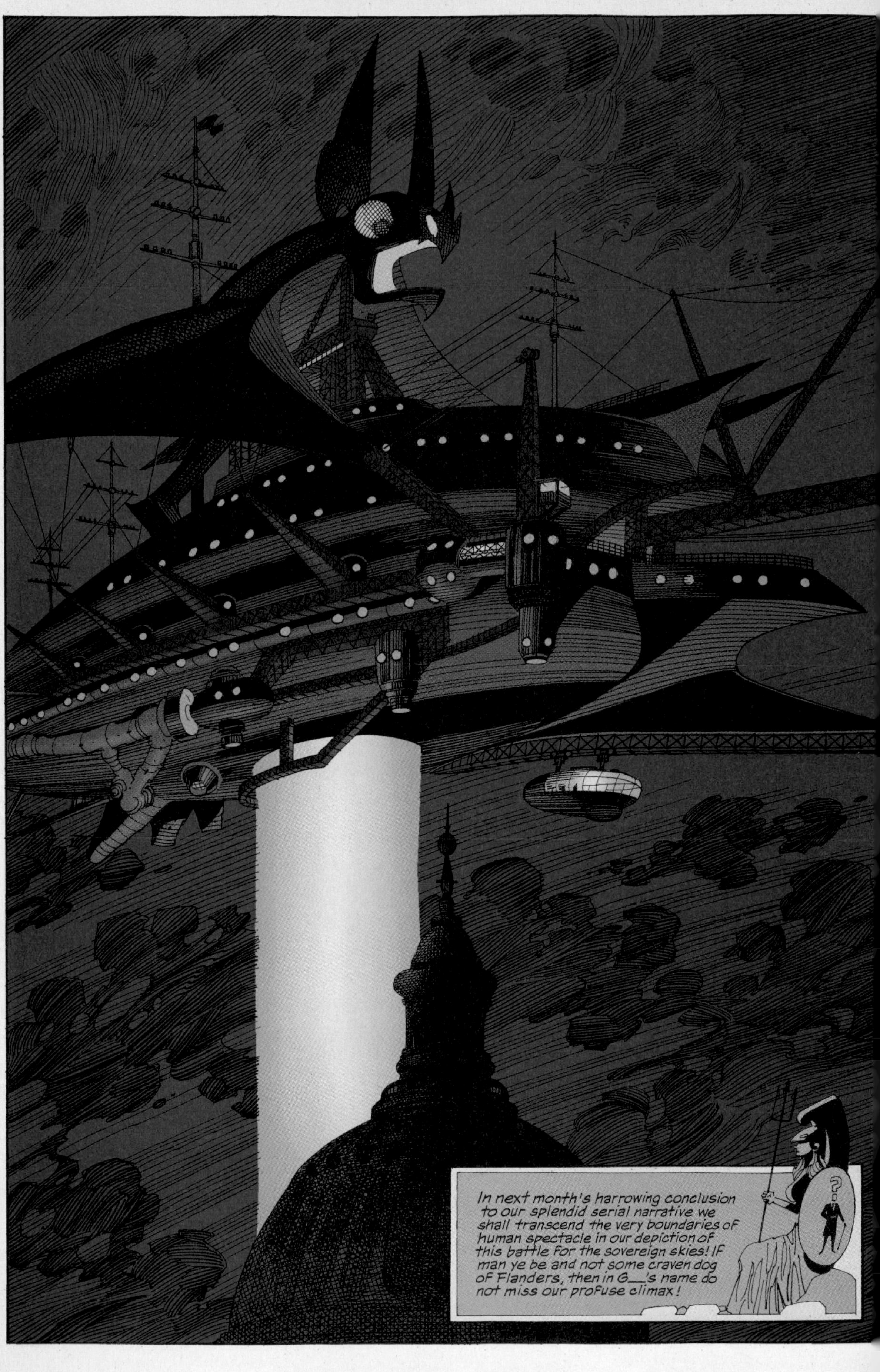
In next month's harrowing conclusion to our splendid serial narrative we shall transcend the very boundaries of human spectacle in our depiction of this battle for the sovereign skies! If man ye be and not some craven dog of Flanders, then in G__'s name do not miss our profuse climax!

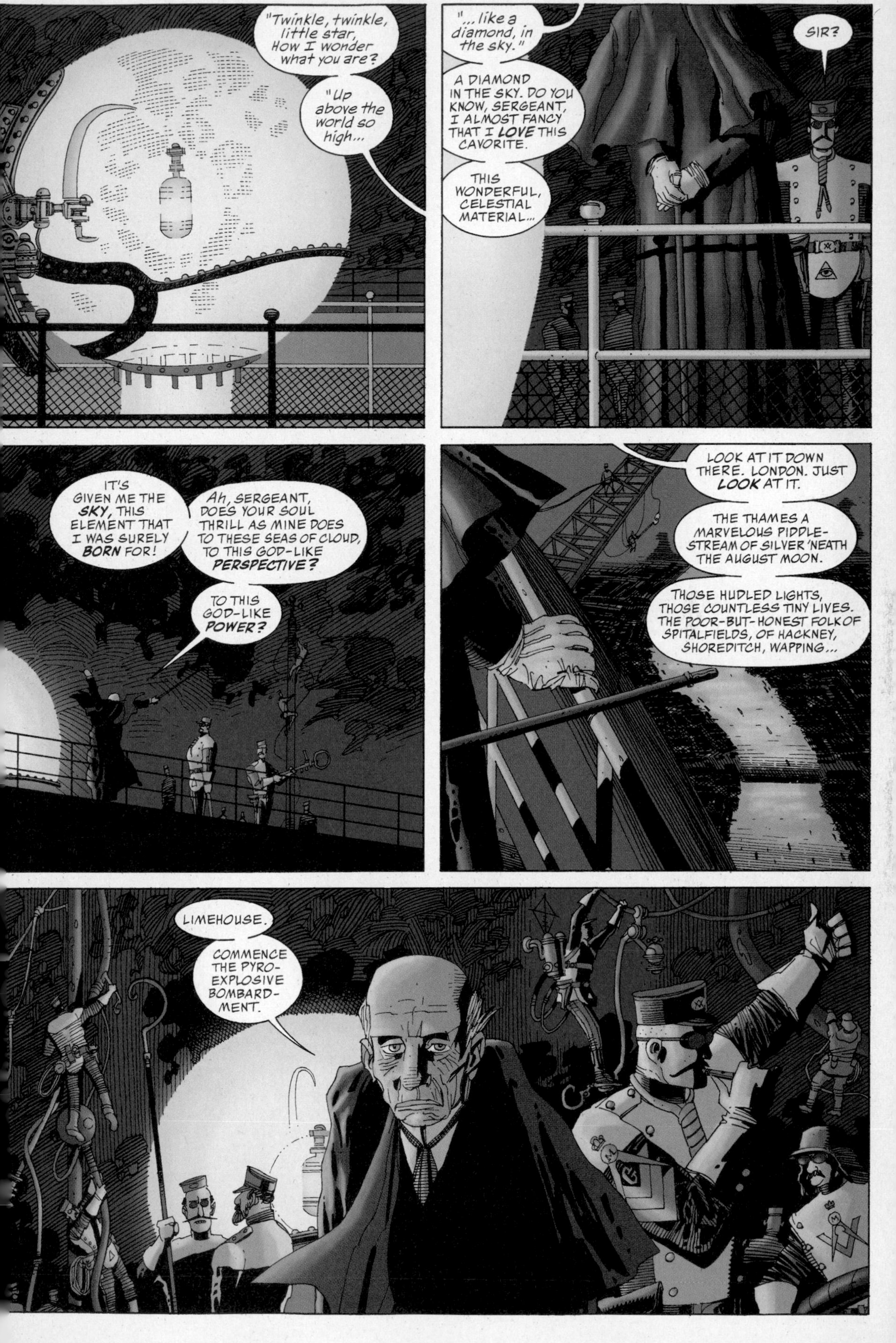
"Twinkle, twinkle, little star, How I wonder what you are?
"Up above the world so high...
"... like a diamond, in the sky."
A DIAMOND IN THE SKY. DO YOU KNOW, SERGEANT, I ALMOST FANCY THAT I LOVE THIS CAVORITE.
THIS WONDERFUL, CELESTIAL MATERIAL...
SIR?
IT'S GIVEN ME THE SKY, THIS ELEMENT THAT I WAS SURELY BORN FOR!
Ah, SERGEANT, DOES YOUR SOUL THRILL AS MINE DOES TO THESE SEAS OF CLOUD, TO THIS GOD-LIKE PERSPECTIVE?
TO THIS GOD-LIKE POWER?
LOOK AT IT DOWN THERE. LONDON. JUST LOOK AT IT.
THE THAMES A MARVELOUS PIDDLE-STREAM OF SILVER 'NEATH THE AUGUST MOON.
THOSE HUDLED LIGHTS, THOSE COUNTLESS TINY LIVES. THE POOR-BUT-HONEST FOLK OF SPITALFIELDS, OF HACKNEY, SHOREDITCH, WAPPING...
LIMEHOUSE.
COMMENCE THE PYRO-EXPLOSIVE BOMBARD-MENT.

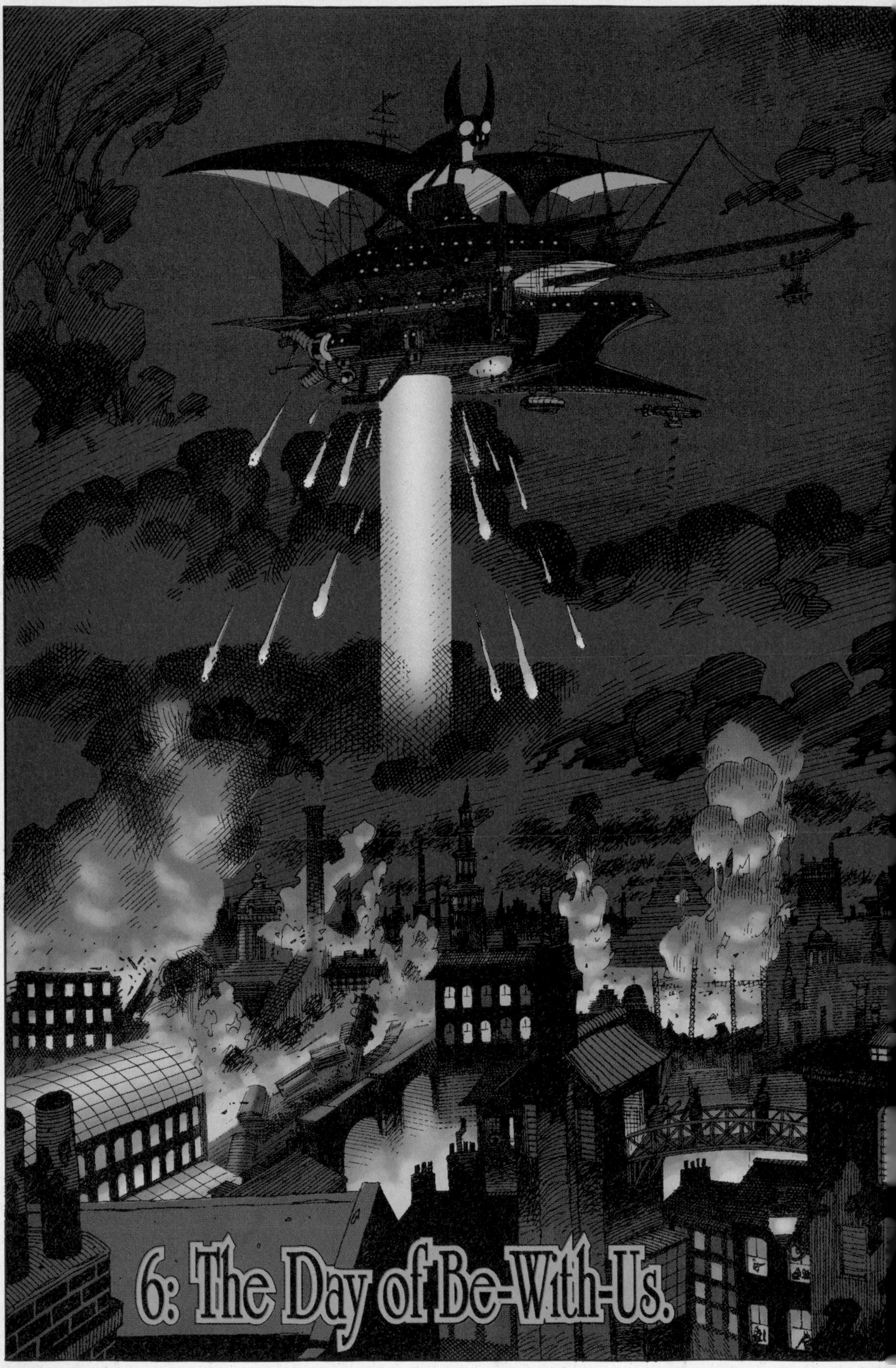
6: The Day of Be-With-Us.

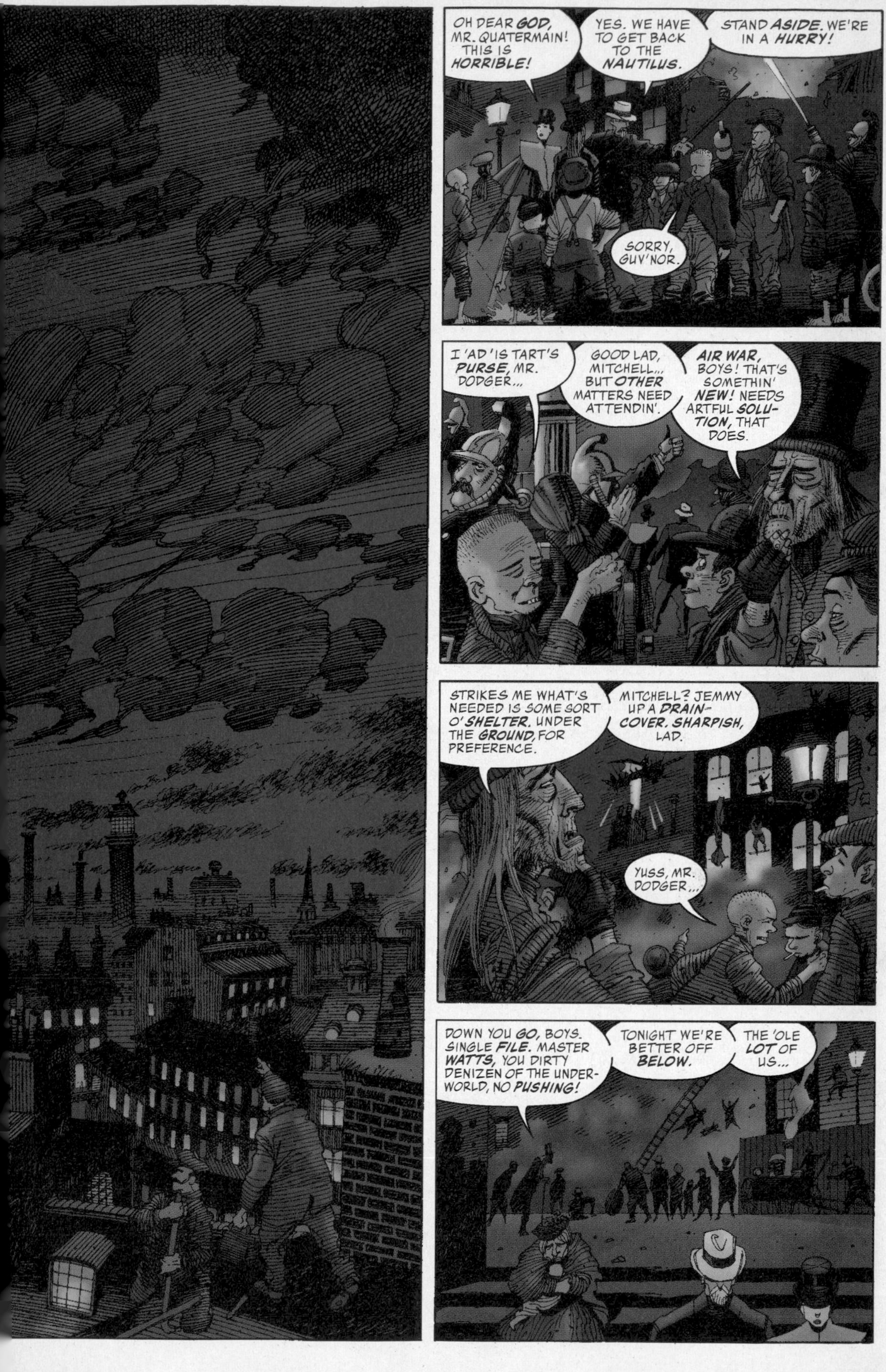

OH DEAR GOD, MR. QUATERMAIN! THIS IS HORRIBLE!
YES. WE HAVE TO GET BACK TO THE NAUTILUS.
STAND ASIDE. WE'RE IN A HURRY!
SORRY, GUV'NOR.
I 'AD 'IS TART'S PURSE, MR. DODGER...
GOOD LAD, MITCHELL... BUT OTHER MATTERS NEED ATTENDIN'.
AIR WAR, BOYS! THAT'S SOMETHIN' NEW! NEEDS ARTFUL SOLUTION, THAT DOES.
STRIKES ME WHAT'S NEEDED IS SOME SORT O' SHELTER. UNDER THE GROUND, FOR PREFERENCE.
MITCHELL? JEMMY UP A DRAIN-COVER. SHARPISH, LAD.
YUSS, MR. DODGER...
DOWN YOU GO, BOYS. SINGLE FILE. MASTER WATTS, YOU DIRTY DENIZEN OF THE UNDERWORLD, NO PUSHING!
TONIGHT WE'RE BETTER OFF BELOW.
THE 'OLE LOT OF US...

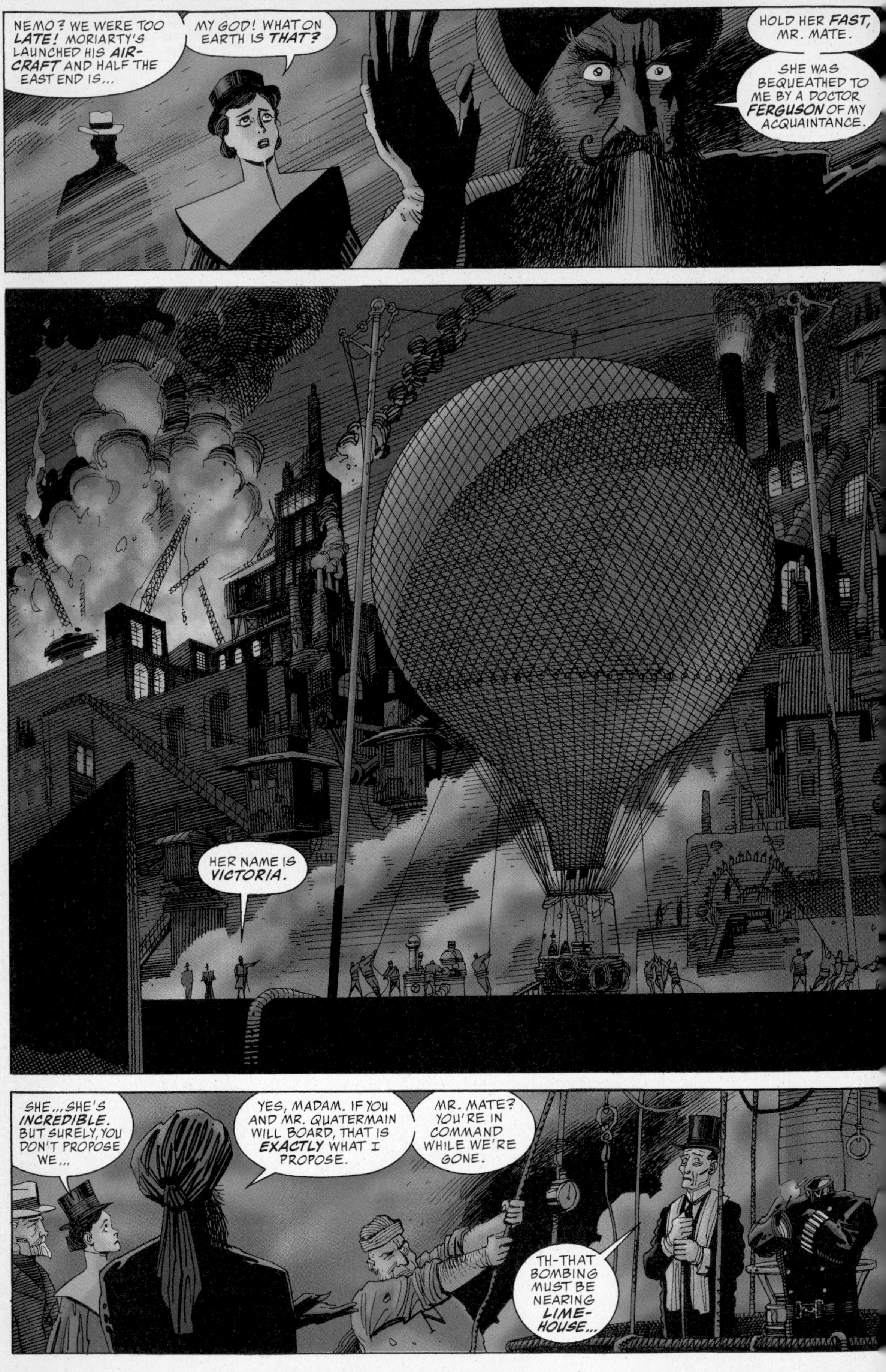
NEMO? WE WERE TOO LATE! MORIARTY'S LAUNCHED HIS AIR-CRAFT AND HALF THE EAST END IS...
MY GOD! WHAT ON EARTH IS THAT?
HOLD HER FAST, MR. MATE.
SHE WAS BEQUEATHED TO ME BY A DOCTOR FERGUSON OF MY ACQUAINTANCE.
HER NAME IS VICTORIA.
SHE... SHE'S INCREDIBLE. BUT SURELY, YOU DON'T PROPOSE WE...
YES, MADAM. IF YOU AND MR. QUATERMAIN WILL BOARD, THAT IS EXACTLY WHAT I PROPOSE.
MR. MATE? YOU'RE IN COMMAND WHILE WE'RE GONE.
TH-THAT BOMBING MUST BE NEARING LIME-HOUSE...

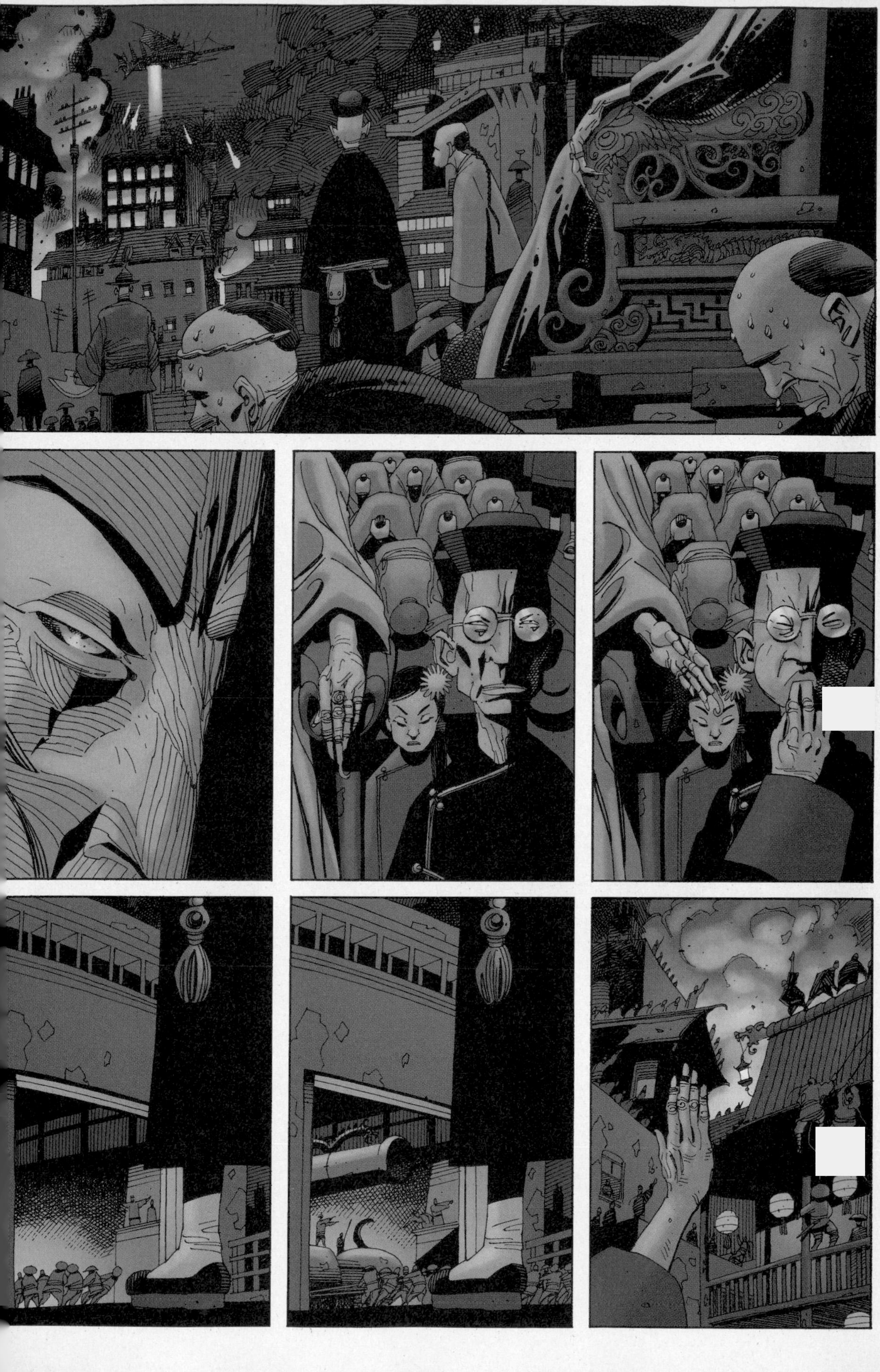

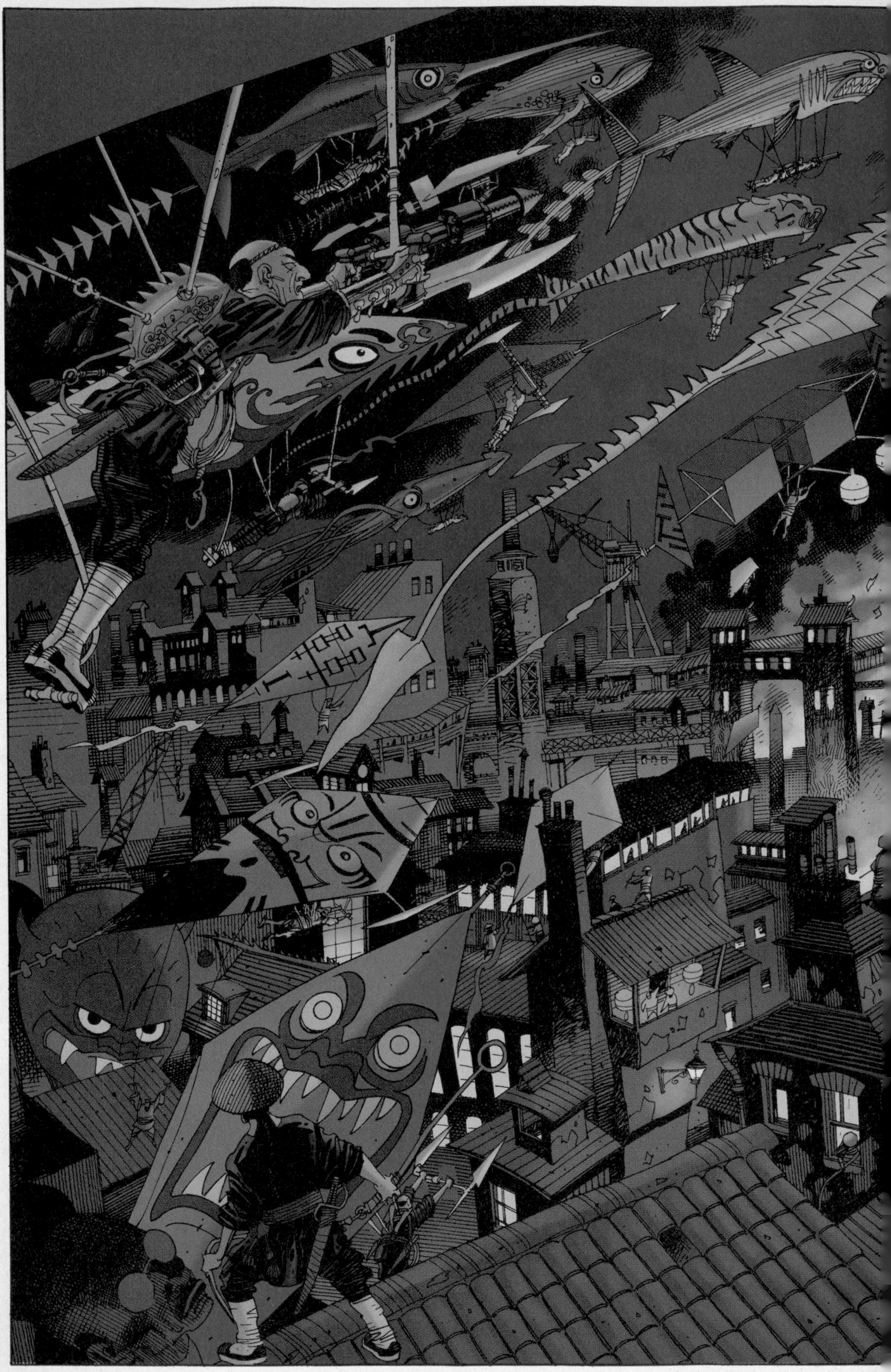

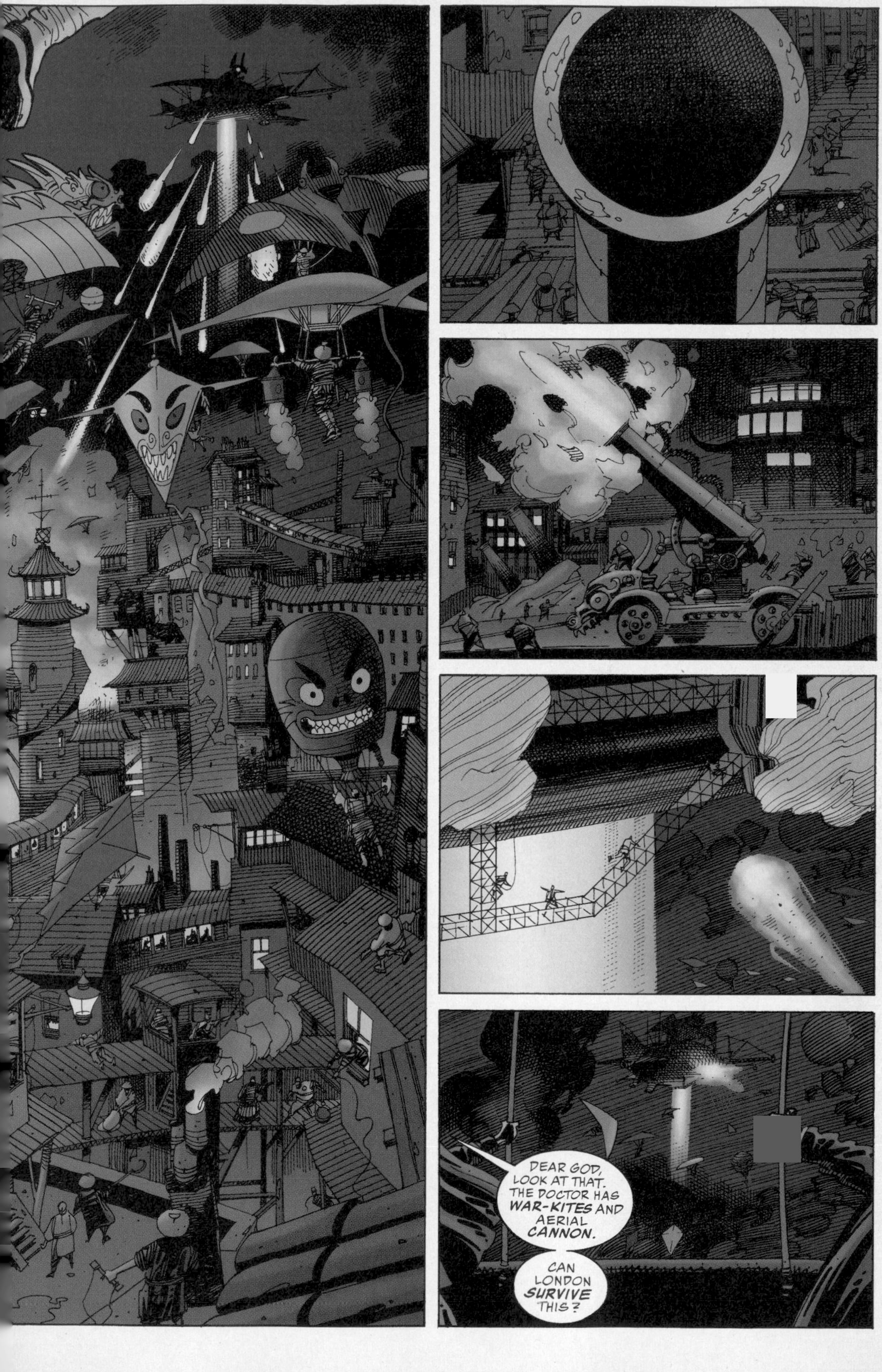
DEAR GOD, LOOK AT THAT. THE DOCTOR HAS WAR-KITES AND AERIAL CANNON.
CAN LONDON SURVIVE THIS?

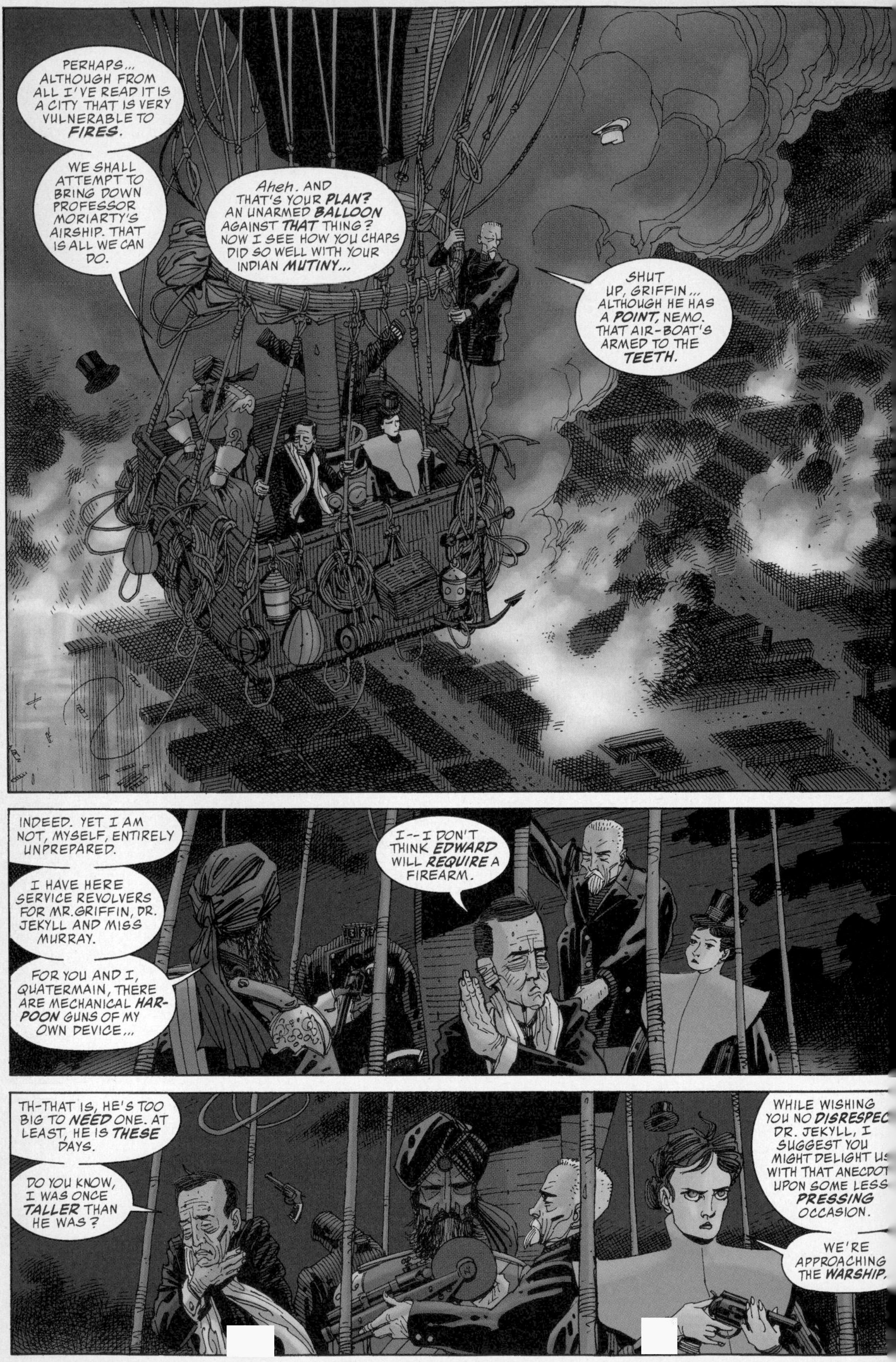
PERHAPS... ALTHOUGH FROM ALL I'VE READ IT IS A CITY THAT IS VERY VULNERABLE TO FIRES.
WE SHALL ATTEMPT TO BRING DOWN PROFESSOR MORIARTY'S AIRSHIP. THAT IS ALL WE CAN DO.
Aheh. AND THAT'S YOUR PLAN? AN UNARMED BALLOON AGAINST THAT THING? NOW I SEE HOW YOU CHAPS DID SO WELL WITH YOUR INDIAN MUTINY...
SHUT UP, GRIFFIN... ALTHOUGH HE HAS A POINT, NEMO. THAT AIR-BOAT'S ARMED TO THE TEETH.
INDEED. YET I AM NOT, MYSELF, ENTIRELY UNPREPARED.
I HAVE HERE SERVICE REVOLVERS FOR MR.GRIFFIN, DR. JEKYLL AND MISS MURRAY.
FOR YOU AND I, QUATERMAIN, THERE ARE MECHANICAL HARPOON GUNS OF MY OWN DEVICE...
I--I DON'T THINK EDWARD WILL REQUIRE A FIREARM.
TH-THAT IS, HE'S TOO BIG TO NEED ONE. AT LEAST, HE IS THESE DAYS.
DO YOU KNOW, I WAS ONCE TALLER THAN HE WAS?
WHILE WISHING YOU NO DISRESPEC DR. JEKYLL, I SUGGEST YOU MIGHT DELIGHT US WITH THAT ANECDOT UPON SOME LESS PRESSING OCCASION.
WE'RE APPROACHING THE WARSHIP.

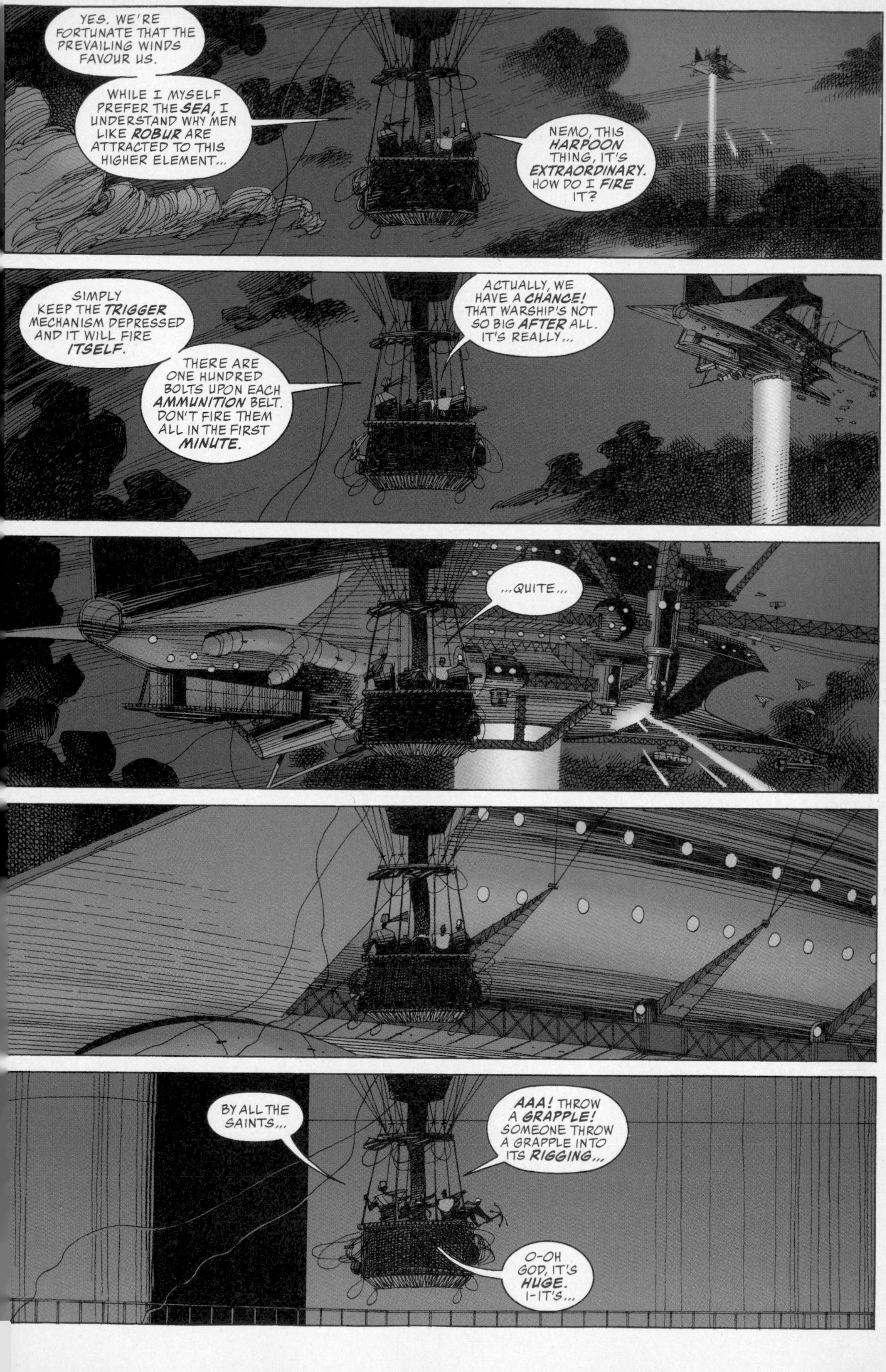
YES. WE'RE FORTUNATE THAT THE PREVAILING WINDS FAVOUR US.
WHILE I MYSELF PREFER THE SEA, I UNDERSTAND WHY MEN LIKE ROBUR ARE ATTRACTED TO THIS HIGHER ELEMENT...
NEMO, THIS HARPOON THING, IT'S EXTRAORDINARY. HOW DO I FIRE IT?
SIMPLY KEEP THE TRIGGER MECHANISM DEPRESSED AND IT WILL FIRE ITSELF.
THERE ARE ONE HUNDRED BOLTS UPON EACH AMMUNITION BELT. DON'T FIRE THEM ALL IN THE FIRST MINUTE.
ACTUALLY, WE HAVE A CHANCE! THAT WARSHIP'S NOT SO BIG AFTER ALL. IT'S REALLY...
...QUITE...
BY ALL THE SAINTS...
AAA! THROW A GRAPPLE! SOMEONE THROW A GRAPPLE INTO ITS RIGGING...
O-OH GOD, IT'S HUGE. I-IT'S...

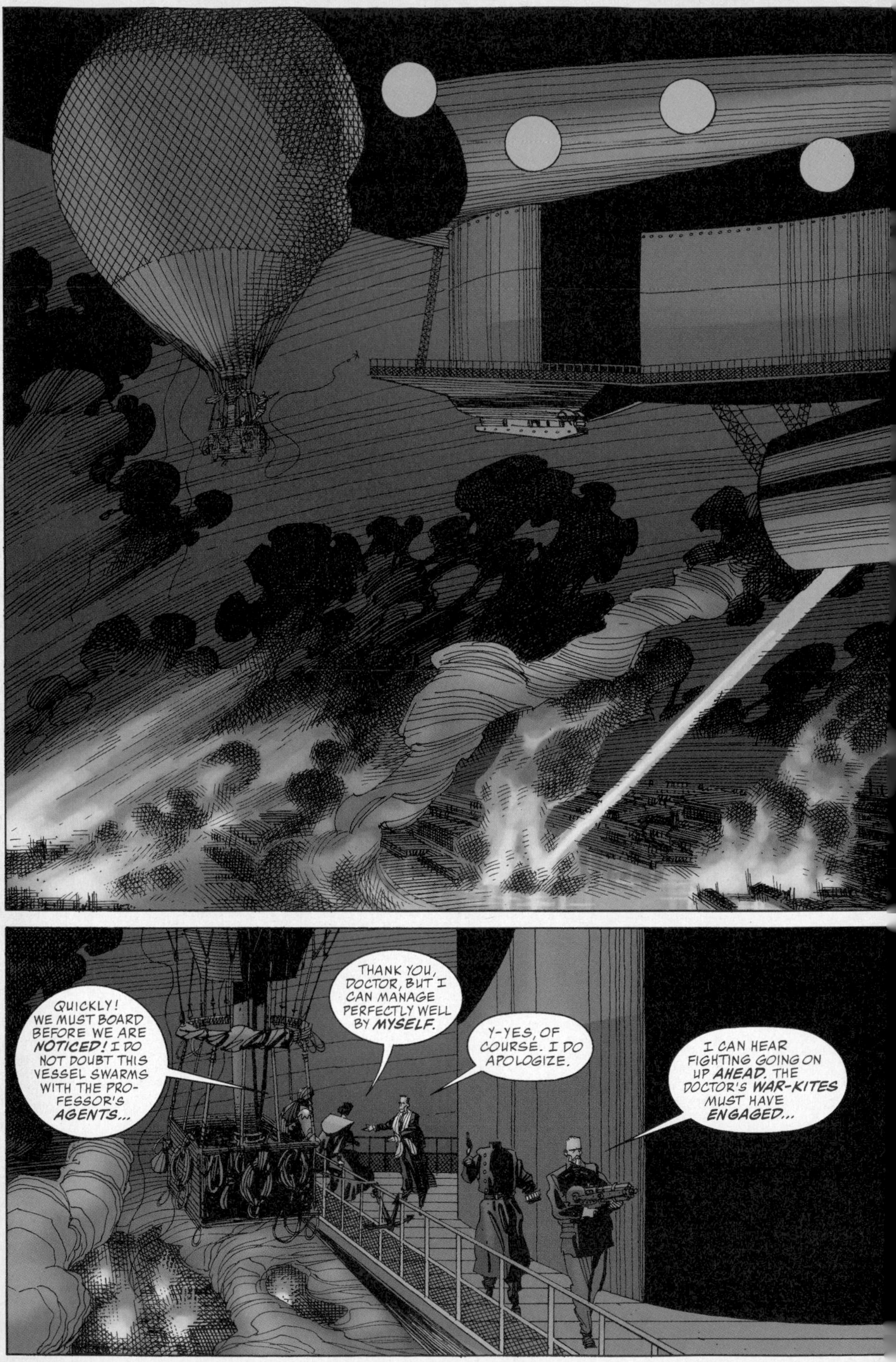
QUICKLY! WE MUST BOARD BEFORE WE ARE NOTICED! I DO NOT DOUBT THIS VESSEL SWARMS WITH THE PROFESSOR'S AGENTS...
THANK YOU, DOCTOR, BUT I CAN MANAGE PERFECTLY WELL BY MYSELF.
Y-YES, OF COURSE. I DO APOLOGIZE.
I CAN HEAR FIGHTING GOING ON UP AHEAD. THE DOCTOR'S WAR-KITES MUST HAVE ENGAGED...

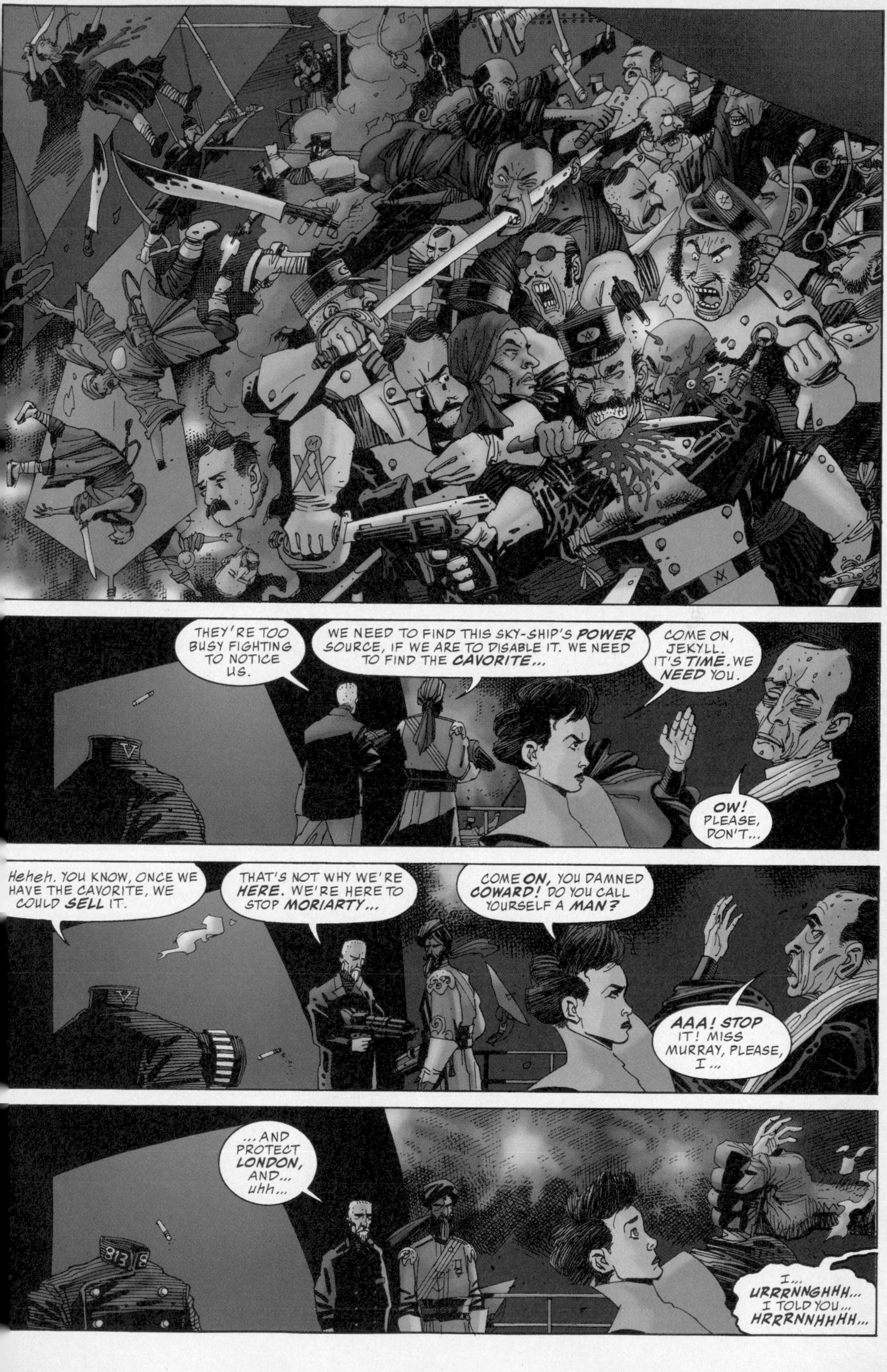
THEY'RE TOO BUSY FIGHTING TO NOTICE US.
WE NEED TO FIND THIS SKY-SHIP'S POWER SOURCE, IF WE ARE TO DISABLE IT. WE NEED TO FIND THE CAVORITE...
COME ON, JEKYLL. IT'S TIME. WE NEED YOU.
OW! PLEASE, DON'T...
Heheh. YOU KNOW, ONCE WE HAVE THE CAVORITE, WE COULD SELL IT.
THAT'S NOT WHY WE'RE HERE. WE'RE HERE TO STOP MORIARTY...
COME ON, YOU DAMNED COWARD! DO YOU CALL YOURSELF A MAN?
AAA! STOP IT! MISS MURRAY, PLEASE, I...
...AND PROTECT LONDON, AND... uhh...
I... URRRNNGHHH... I TOLD YOU... HRRRNNHHHH...

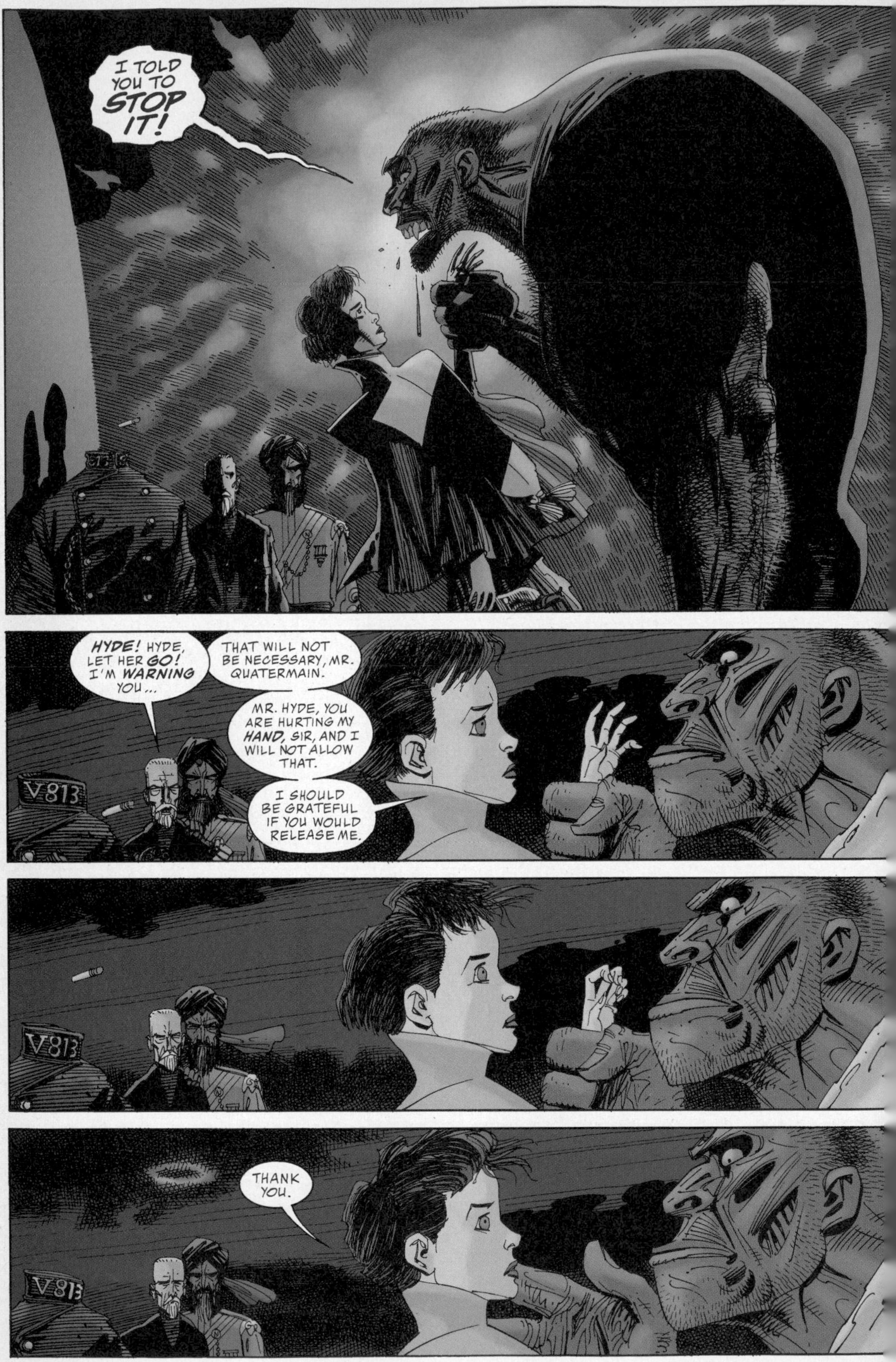

I TOLD YOU TO STOP IT!
HYDE! HYDE, LET HER GO! I'M WARNING YOU...
THAT WILL NOT BE NECESSARY, MR. QUATERMAIN.
MR. HYDE, YOU ARE HURTING MY HAND, SIR, AND I WILL NOT ALLOW THAT.
I SHOULD BE GRATEFUL IF YOU WOULD RELEASE ME.
V813
THANK YOU.

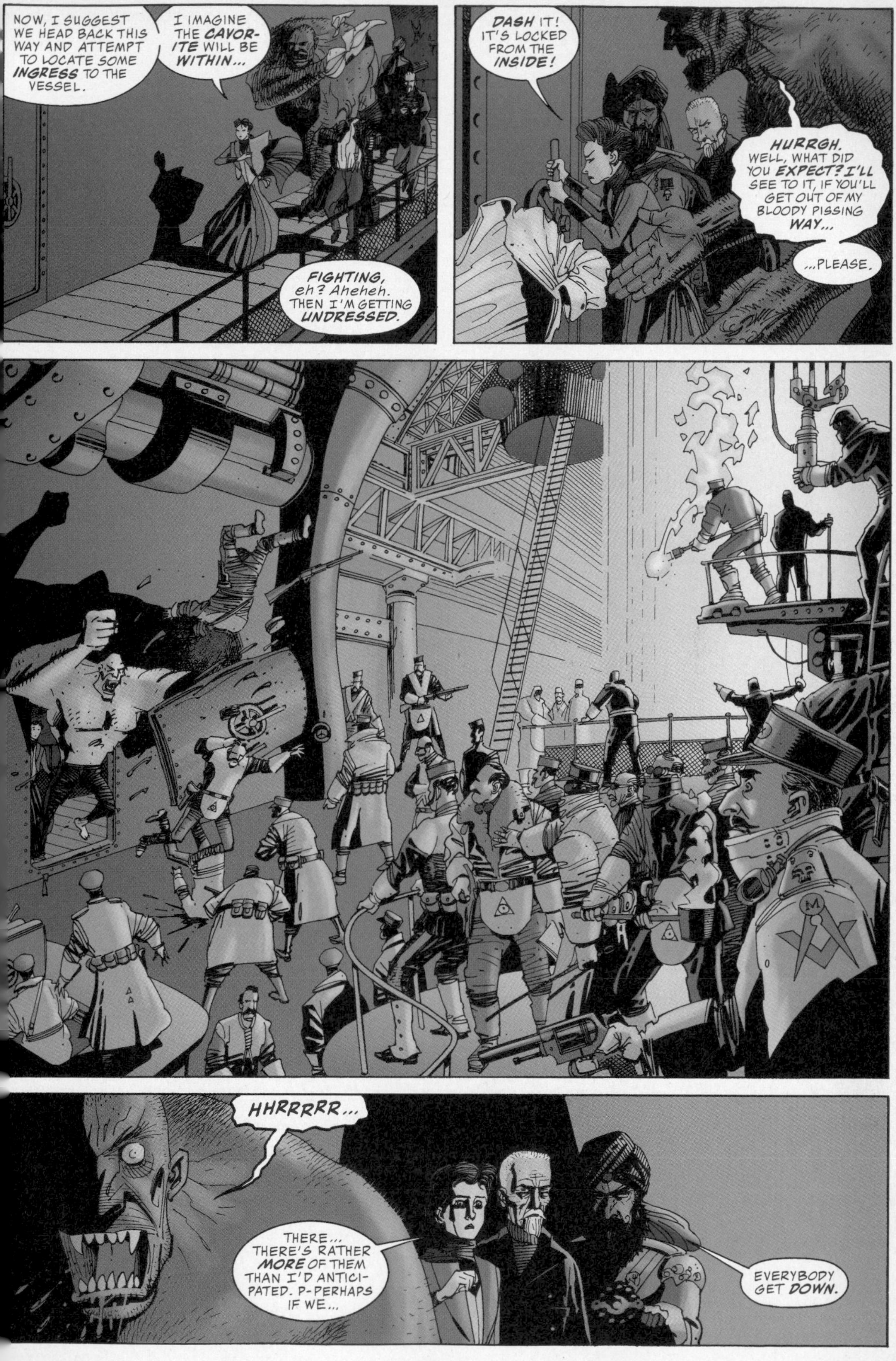
NOW, I SUGGEST WE HEAD BACK THIS WAY AND ATTEMPT TO LOCATE SOME INGRESS TO THE VESSEL.
I IMAGINE THE CAVORITE WILL BE WITHIN...
FIGHTING, eh? Aheheh. THEN I'M GETTING UNDRESSED.
DASH IT! IT'S LOCKED FROM THE INSIDE!
HURRGH. WELL, WHAT DID YOU EXPECT? I'LL SEE TO IT, IF YOU'LL GET OUT OF MY BLOODY PISSING WAY...
...PLEASE.
HHRRRRR...
THERE... THERE'S RATHER MORE OF THEM THAN I'D ANTICIPATED. P-PERHAPS IF WE...
EVERYBODY GET DOWN.

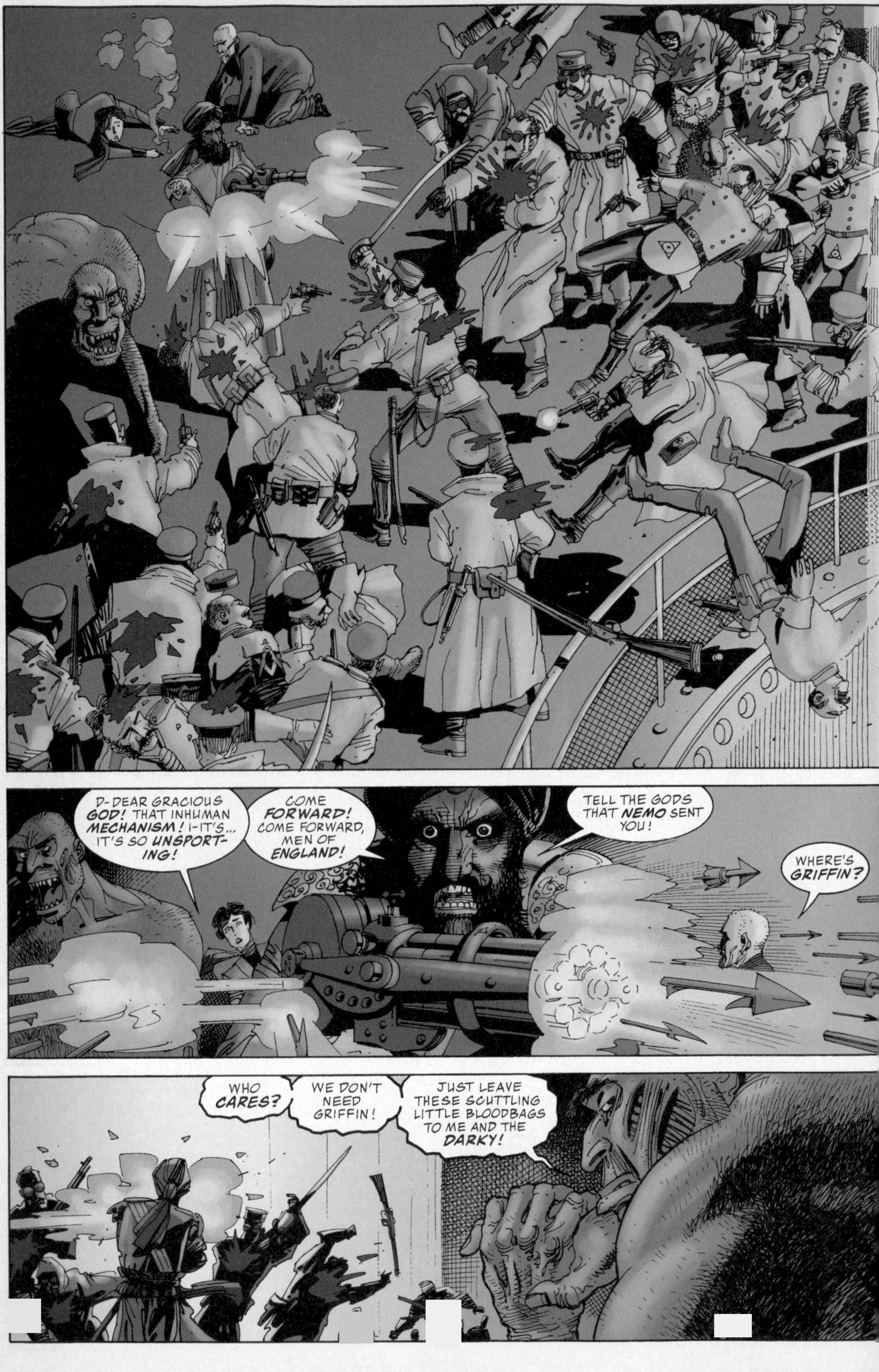
D-DEAR GRACIOUS **GOD!** THAT INHUMAN **MECHANISM!** I-IT'S... IT'S SO **UNSPORTING!**
COME **FORWARD!** COME FORWARD, MEN OF **ENGLAND!**
TELL THE GODS THAT **NEMO** SENT YOU!
WHERE'S **GRIFFIN?**
WHO **CARES?**
WE DON'T NEED GRIFFIN!
JUST LEAVE THESE SCUTTLING LITTLE BLOODBAGS TO ME AND THE **DARKY!**

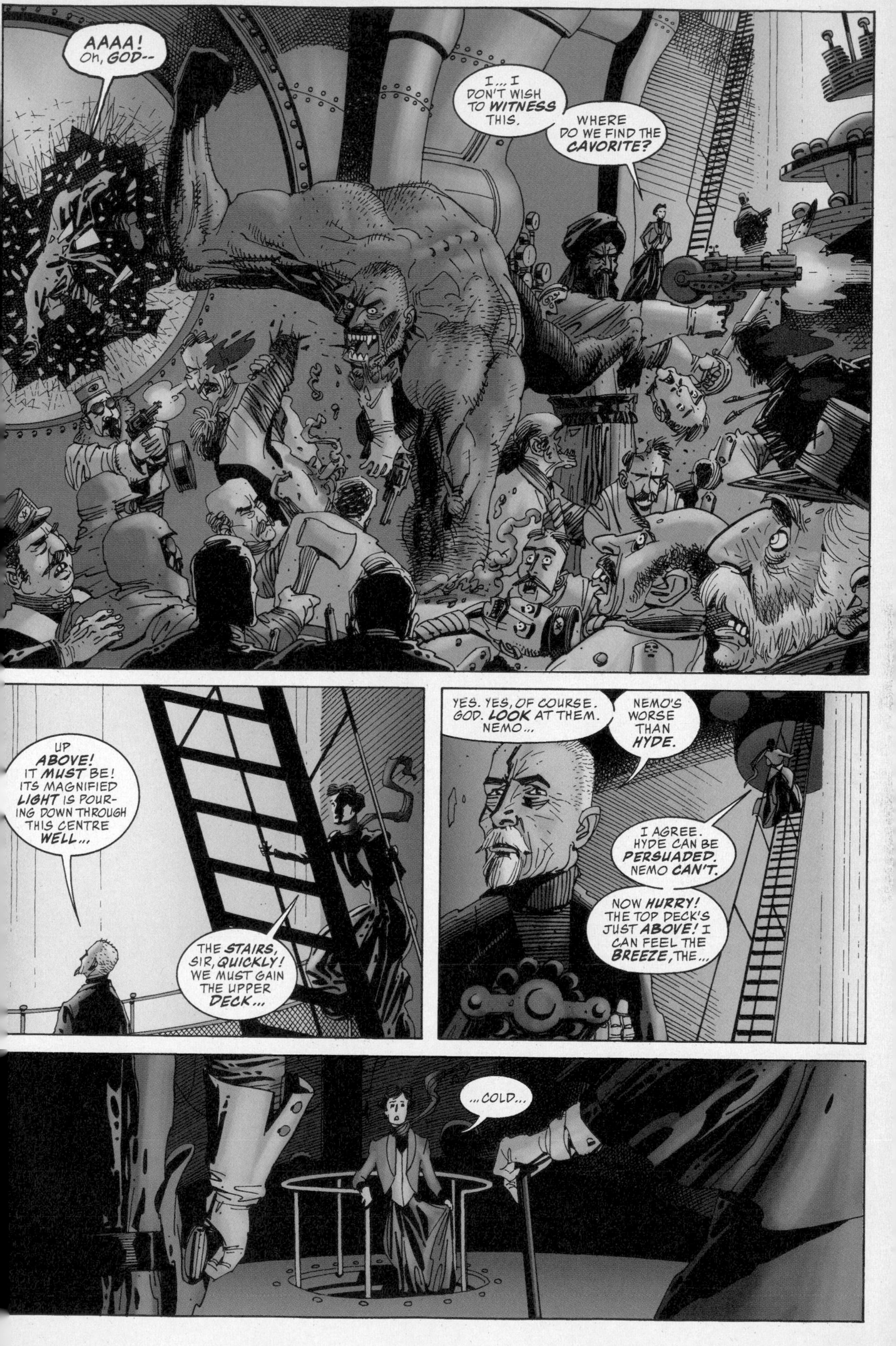

AAAA! Oh, GOD--
I... I DON'T WISH TO WITNESS THIS.
WHERE DO WE FIND THE CAVORITE?
UP ABOVE! IT MUST BE! ITS MAGNIFIED LIGHT IS POURING DOWN THROUGH THIS CENTRE WELL...
THE STAIRS, SIR, QUICKLY! WE MUST GAIN THE UPPER DECK...
YES. YES, OF COURSE. GOD. LOOK AT THEM. NEMO...
NEMO'S WORSE THAN HYDE.
I AGREE. HYDE CAN BE PERSUADED. NEMO CAN'T.
NOW HURRY! THE TOP DECK'S JUST ABOVE! I CAN FEEL THE BREEZE, THE...
...COLD...

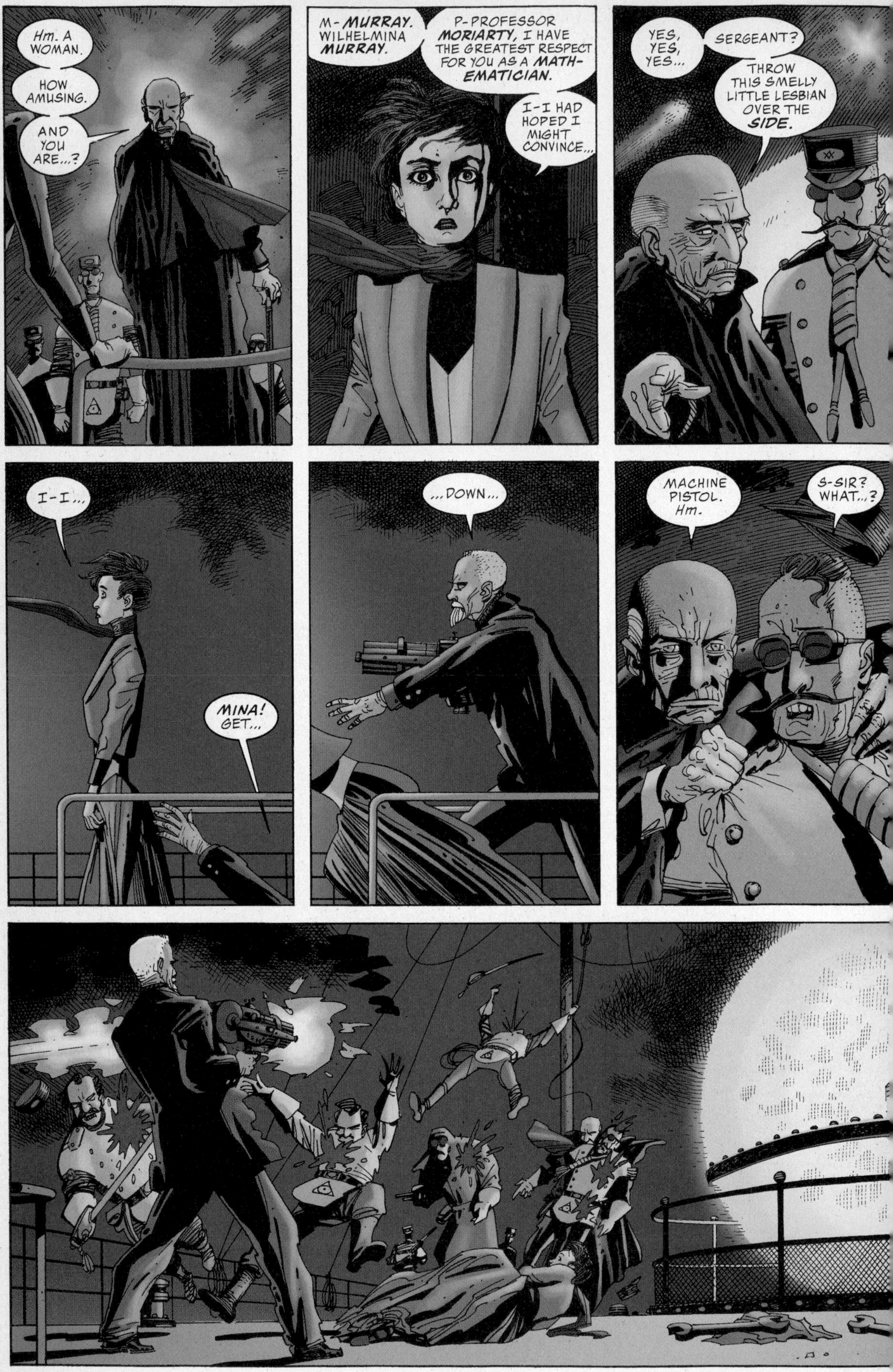
Hm. A WOMAN.
HOW AMUSING.
AND YOU ARE...?
M-MURRAY. WILHELMINA MURRAY.
P-PROFESSOR MORIARTY, I HAVE THE GREATEST RESPECT FOR YOU AS A MATH-EMATICIAN.
I-I HAD HOPED I MIGHT CONVINCE...
YES, YES, YES...
SERGEANT?
THROW THIS SMELLY LITTLE LESBIAN OVER THE SIDE.
I-I...
MINA! GET...
...DOWN...
MACHINE PISTOL. Hm.
S-SIR? WHAT...?

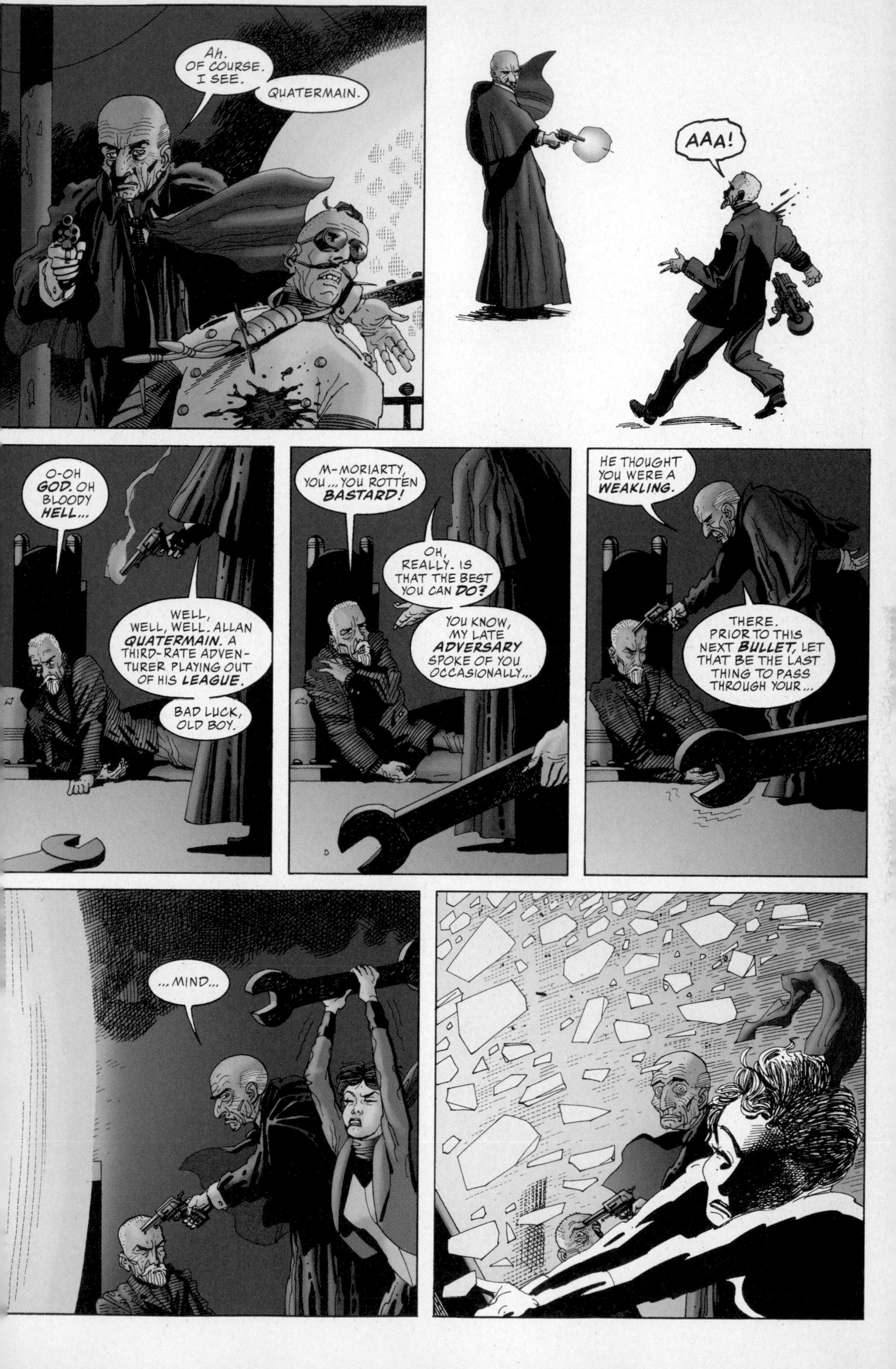
Ah. OF COURSE. I SEE.
QUATERMAIN.
AAA!
O-OH GOD. OH BLOODY HELL...
WELL, WELL, WELL. ALLAN QUATERMAIN. A THIRD-RATE ADVENTURER PLAYING OUT OF HIS LEAGUE.
BAD LUCK, OLD BOY.
M-MORIARTY, YOU... YOU ROTTEN BASTARD!
OH, REALLY. IS THAT THE BEST YOU CAN DO?
YOU KNOW, MY LATE ADVERSARY SPOKE OF YOU OCCASIONALLY...
HE THOUGHT YOU WERE A WEAKLING.
THERE. PRIOR TO THIS NEXT BULLET, LET THAT BE THE LAST THING TO PASS THROUGH YOUR...
...MIND...

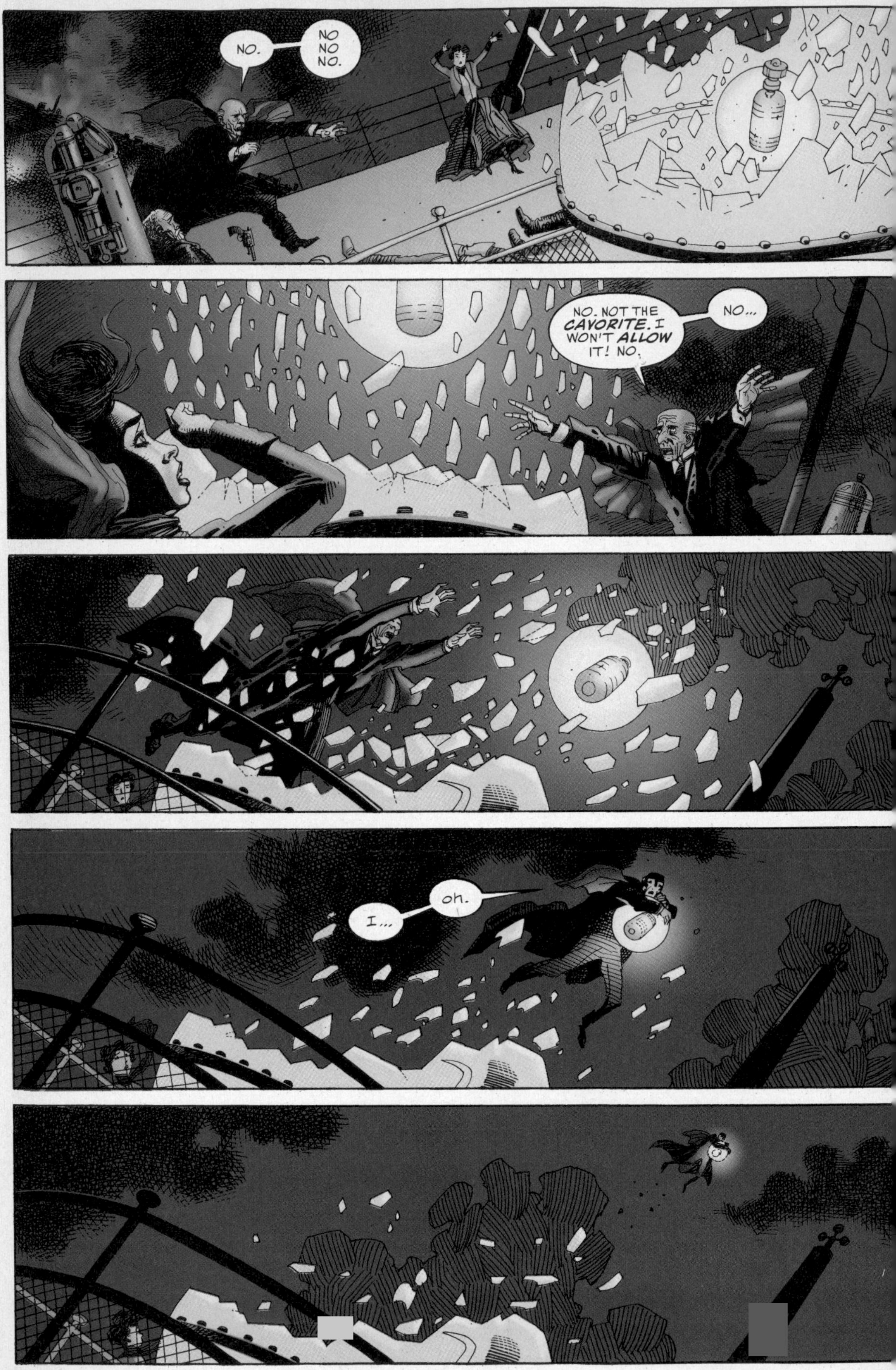
NO.
NO NO NO.
NO. NOT THE CAVORITE. I WON'T ALLOW IT! NO.
NO...
I...
oh.

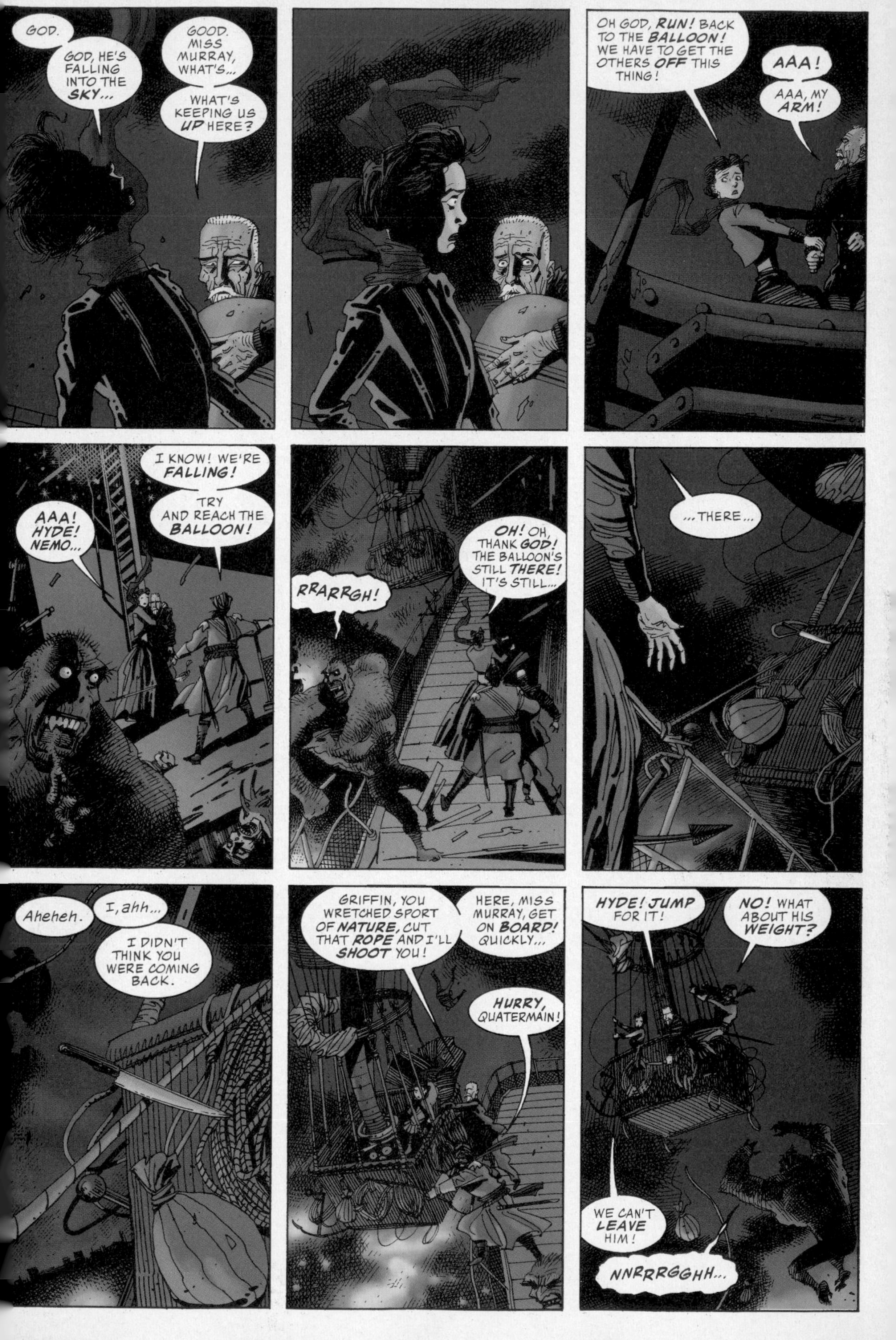
GOD.
GOD, HE'S FALLING INTO THE SKY...
GOOD. MISS MURRAY, WHAT'S...
WHAT'S KEEPING US UP HERE?
OH GOD, RUN! BACK TO THE BALLOON! WE HAVE TO GET THE OTHERS OFF THIS THING!
AAA!
AAA, MY ARM!
I KNOW! WE'RE FALLING!
TRY AND REACH THE BALLOON!
AAA! HYDE! NEMO...
OH! OH, THANK GOD! THE BALLOON'S STILL THERE! IT'S STILL...
RRARRGH!
...THERE...
Aheheh.
I, ahh...
I DIDN'T THINK YOU WERE COMING BACK.
GRIFFIN, YOU WRETCHED SPORT OF NATURE, CUT THAT ROPE AND I'LL SHOOT YOU!
HERE, MISS MURRAY, GET ON BOARD! QUICKLY...
HURRY, QUATERMAIN!
HYDE! JUMP FOR IT!
NO! WHAT ABOUT HIS WEIGHT?
WE CAN'T LEAVE HIM!
NNRRRGGHH...

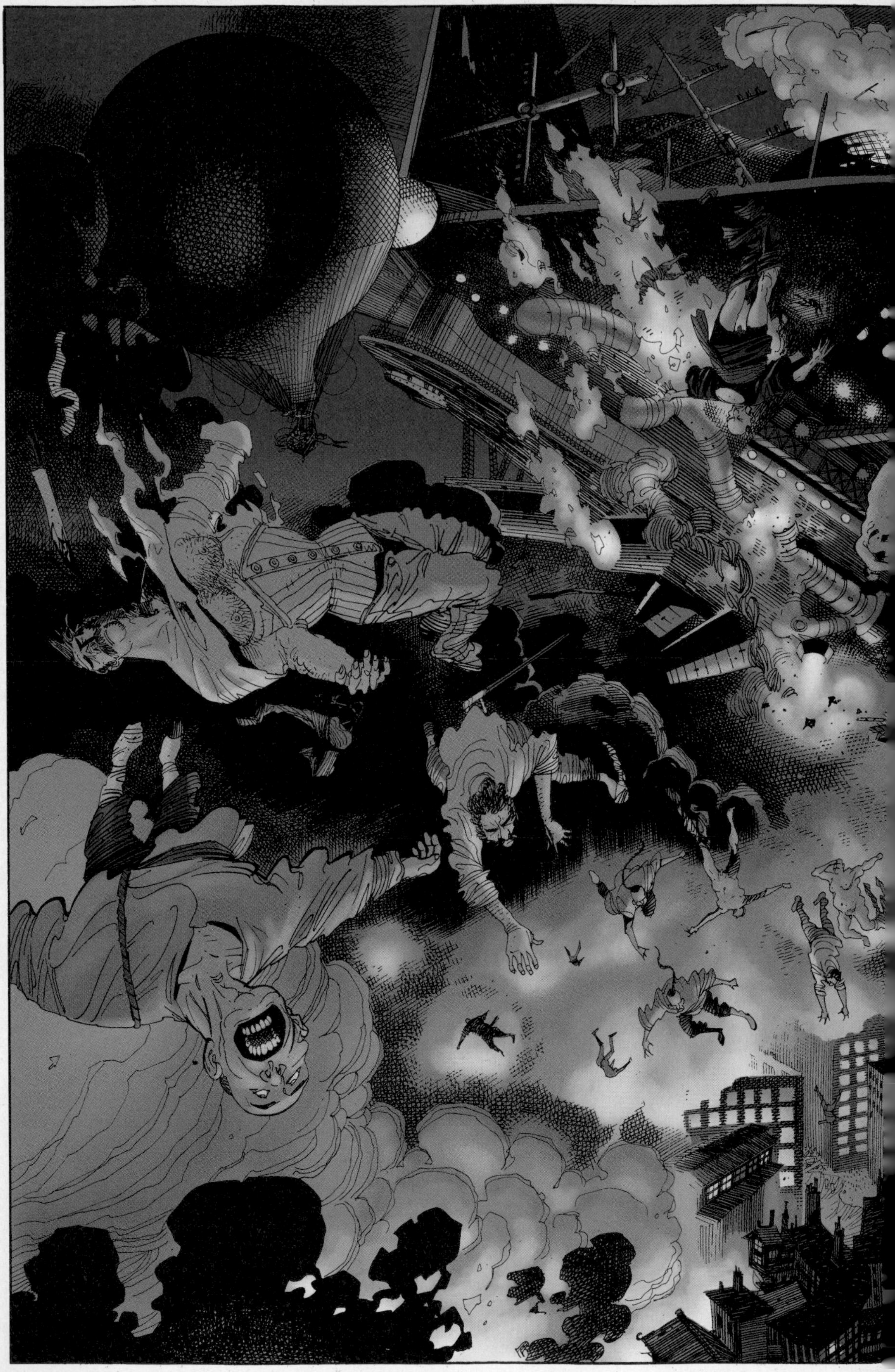

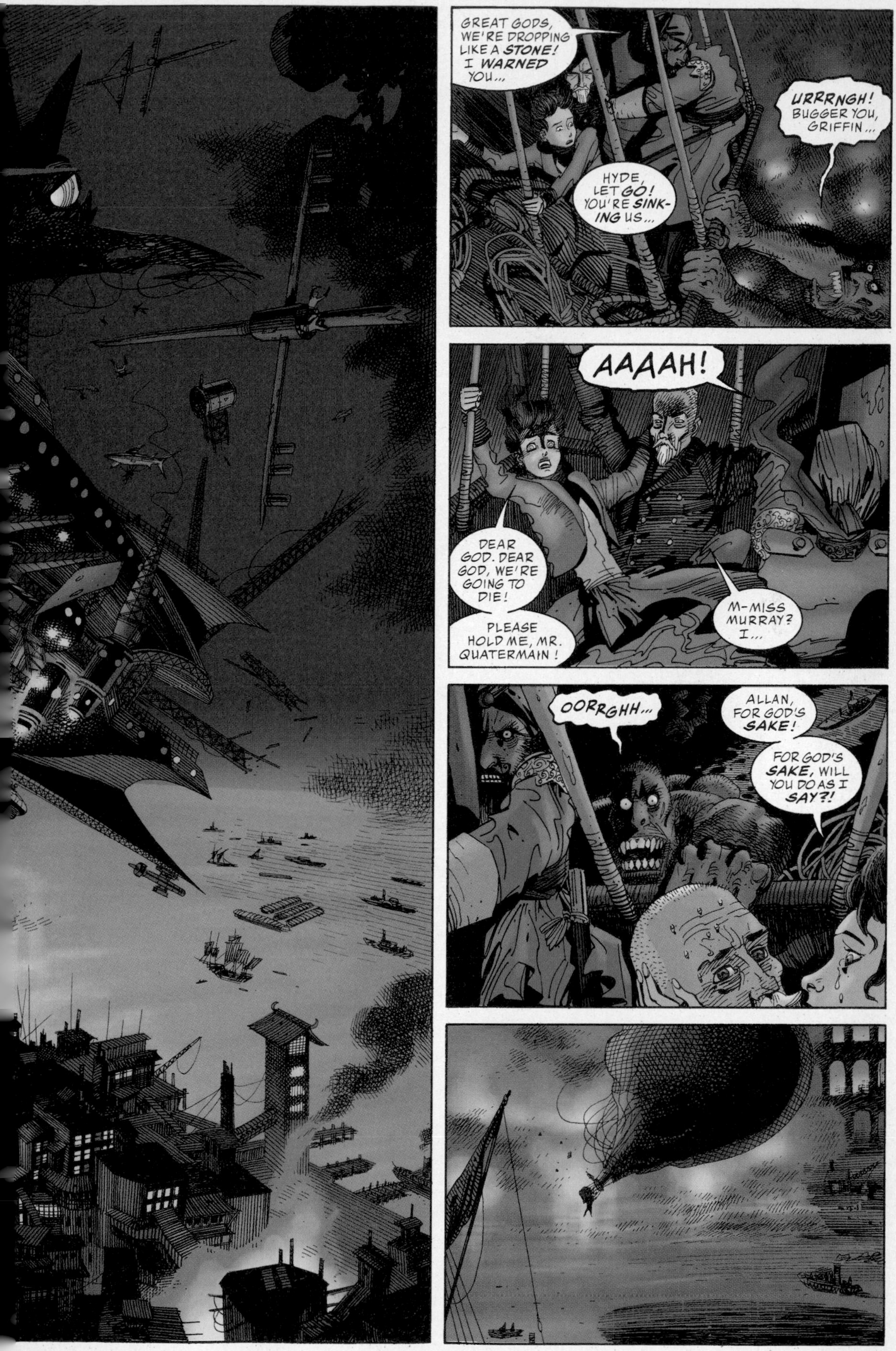
GREAT GODS, WE'RE DROPPING LIKE A STONE! I WARNED YOU...
URRRNGH! BUGGER YOU, GRIFFIN...
HYDE, LET GO! YOU'RE SINKING US...
AAAAH!
DEAR GOD. DEAR GOD, WE'RE GOING TO DIE!
PLEASE HOLD ME, MR. QUATERMAIN!
M-MISS MURRAY? I...
OORRGHH...
ALLAN, FOR GOD'S SAKE!
FOR GOD'S SAKE, WILL YOU DO AS I SAY?!

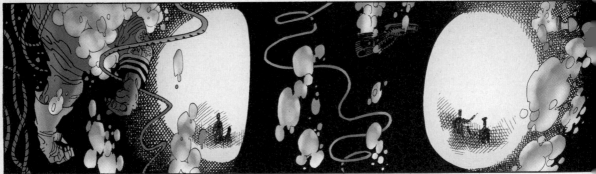

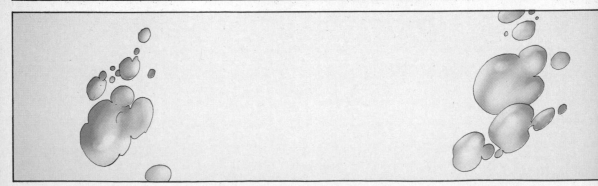

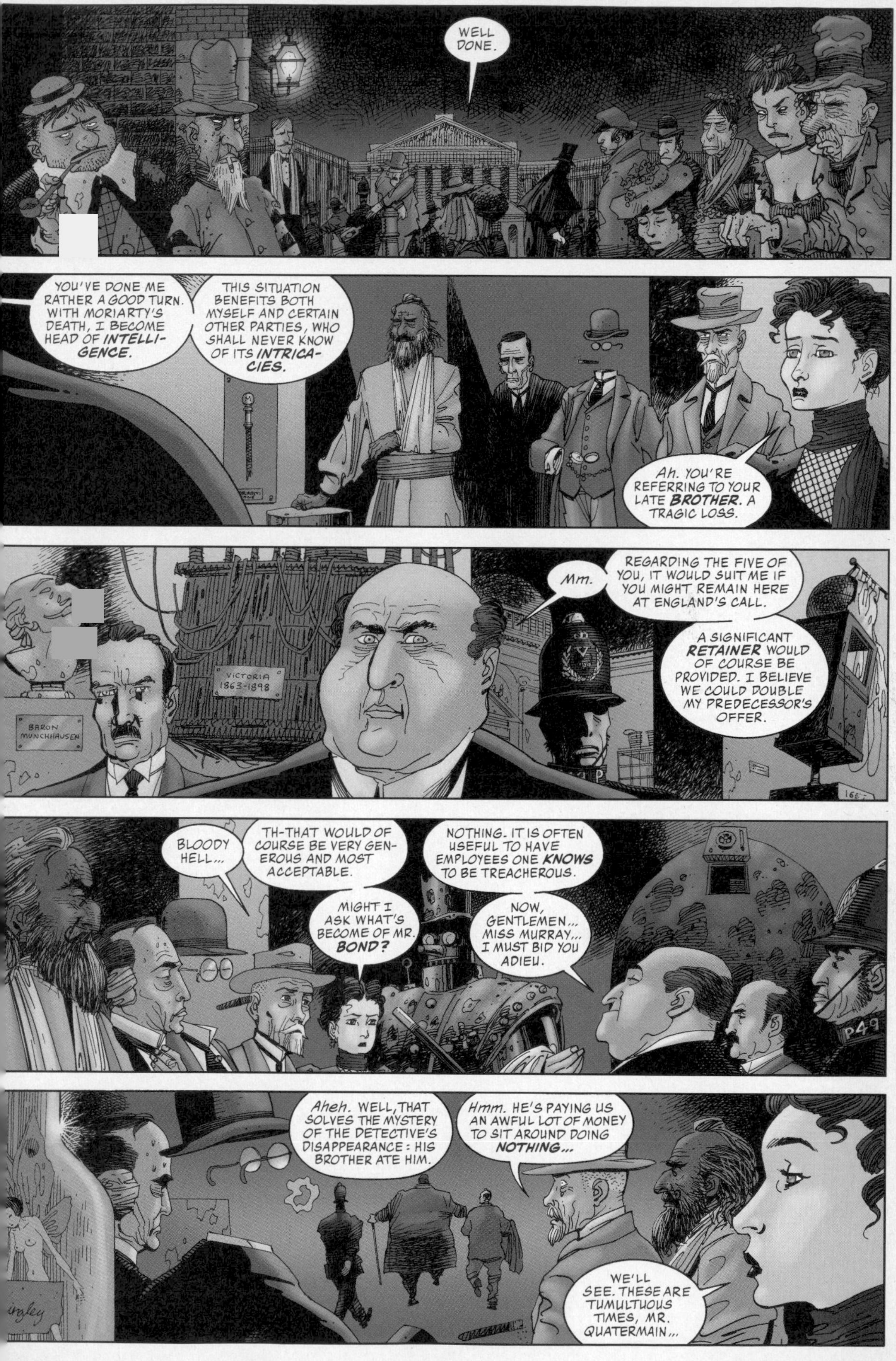
WELL DONE.
YOU'VE DONE ME RATHER A GOOD TURN. WITH MORIARTY'S DEATH, I BECOME HEAD OF INTELLIGENCE.
THIS SITUATION BENEFITS BOTH MYSELF AND CERTAIN OTHER PARTIES, WHO SHALL NEVER KNOW OF ITS INTRICACIES.
Ah. YOU'RE REFERRING TO YOUR LATE BROTHER. A TRAGIC LOSS.
BARON MUNCHKHAUSEN
VICTORIA 1863-1898
Mm.
REGARDING THE FIVE OF YOU, IT WOULD SUIT ME IF YOU MIGHT REMAIN HERE AT ENGLAND'S CALL.
A SIGNIFICANT RETAINER WOULD OF COURSE BE PROVIDED. I BELIEVE WE COULD DOUBLE MY PREDECESSOR'S OFFER.
BLOODY HELL...
TH-THAT WOULD OF COURSE BE VERY GENEROUS AND MOST ACCEPTABLE.
NOTHING. IT IS OFTEN USEFUL TO HAVE EMPLOYEES ONE KNOWS TO BE TREACHEROUS.
MIGHT I ASK WHAT'S BECOME OF MR. BOND?
NOW, GENTLEMEN... MISS MURRAY... I MUST BID YOU ADIEU.
Aheh. WELL, THAT SOLVES THE MYSTERY OF THE DETECTIVE'S DISAPPEARANCE: HIS BROTHER ATE HIM.
Hmm. HE'S PAYING US AN AWFUL LOT OF MONEY TO SIT AROUND DOING NOTHING...
WE'LL SEE. THESE ARE TUMULTUOUS TIMES, MR. QUATERMAIN...

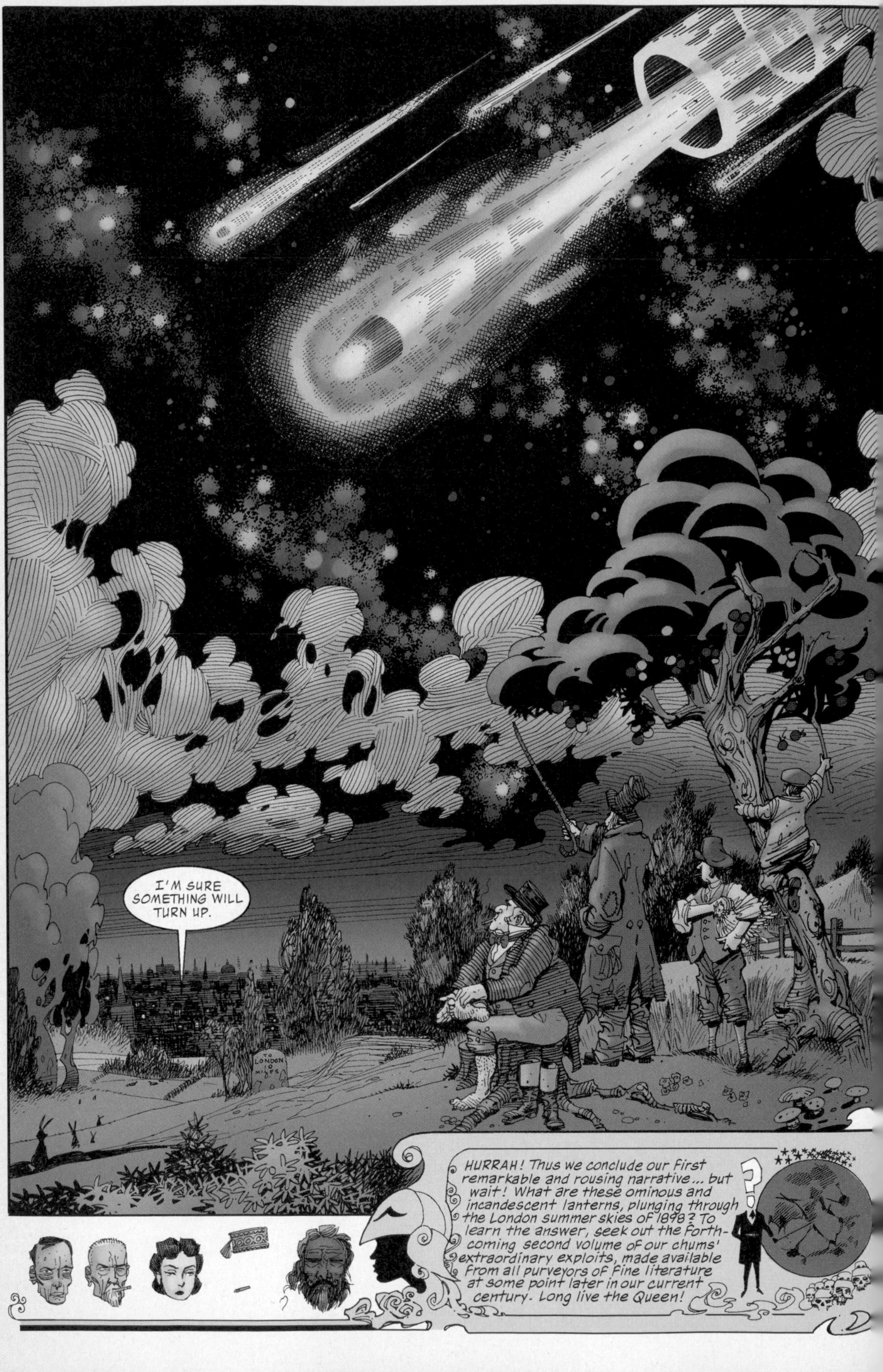
I'M SURE SOMETHING WILL TURN UP.
HURRAH! Thus we conclude our first remarkable and rousing narrative... but wait! What are these ominous and incandescent lanterns, plunging through the London summer skies of 1898? To learn the answer, seek out the forthcoming second volume of our chums' extraordinary exploits, made available from all purveyors of fine literature at some point later in our current century. Long live the Queen!

"We have heard of this device, above London. They say that it was powered by light, but this is surely fantastic. Can it be true? Also, they tell us that the Sikh is still alive and played some part in this affair. I must confess that I do not know what to think. And now these fireballs in the sky! Our element is all in uproar, it would seem. What next? Whatever next?"

Robur, in private correspondence with Luftkapitan Mors, August 12th, 1898

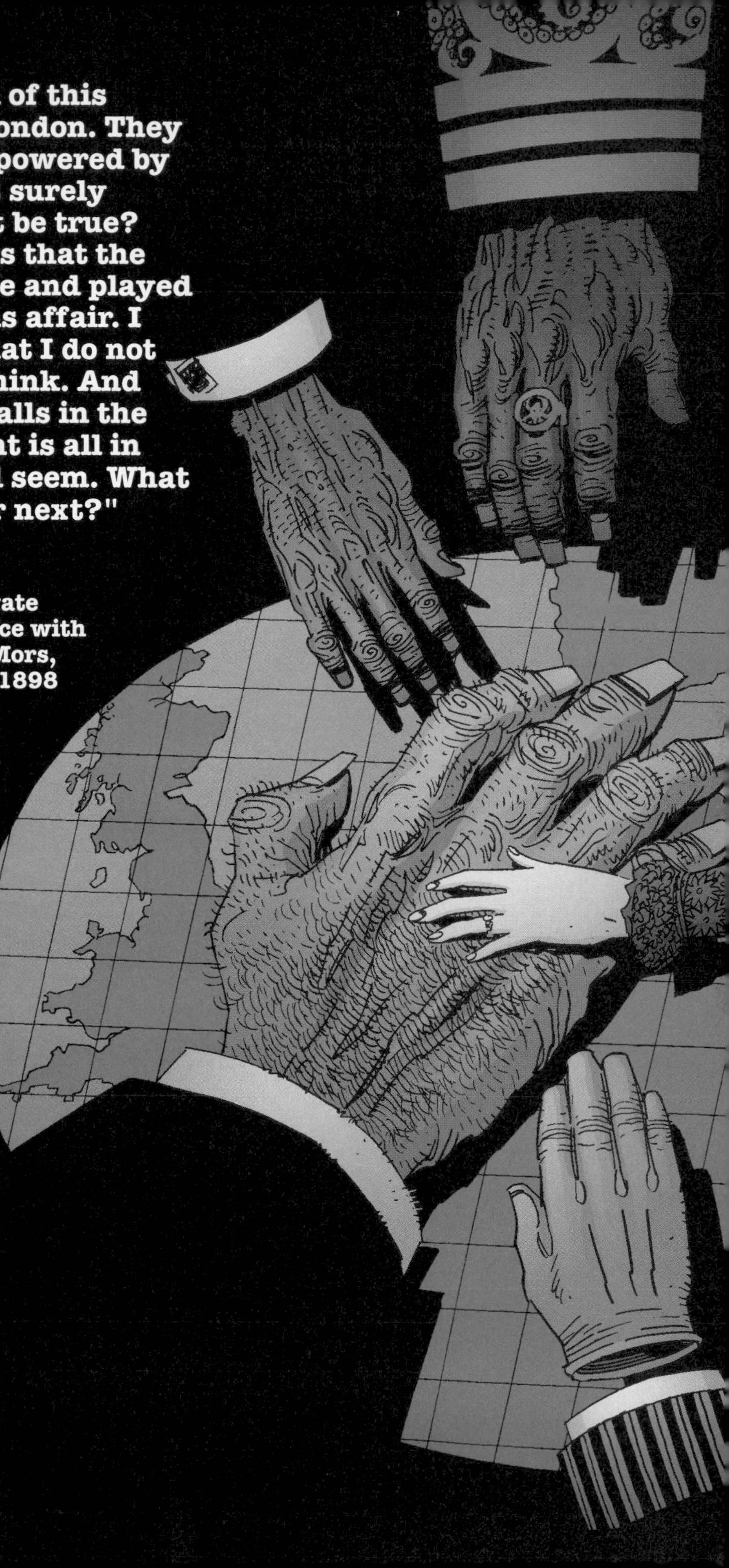

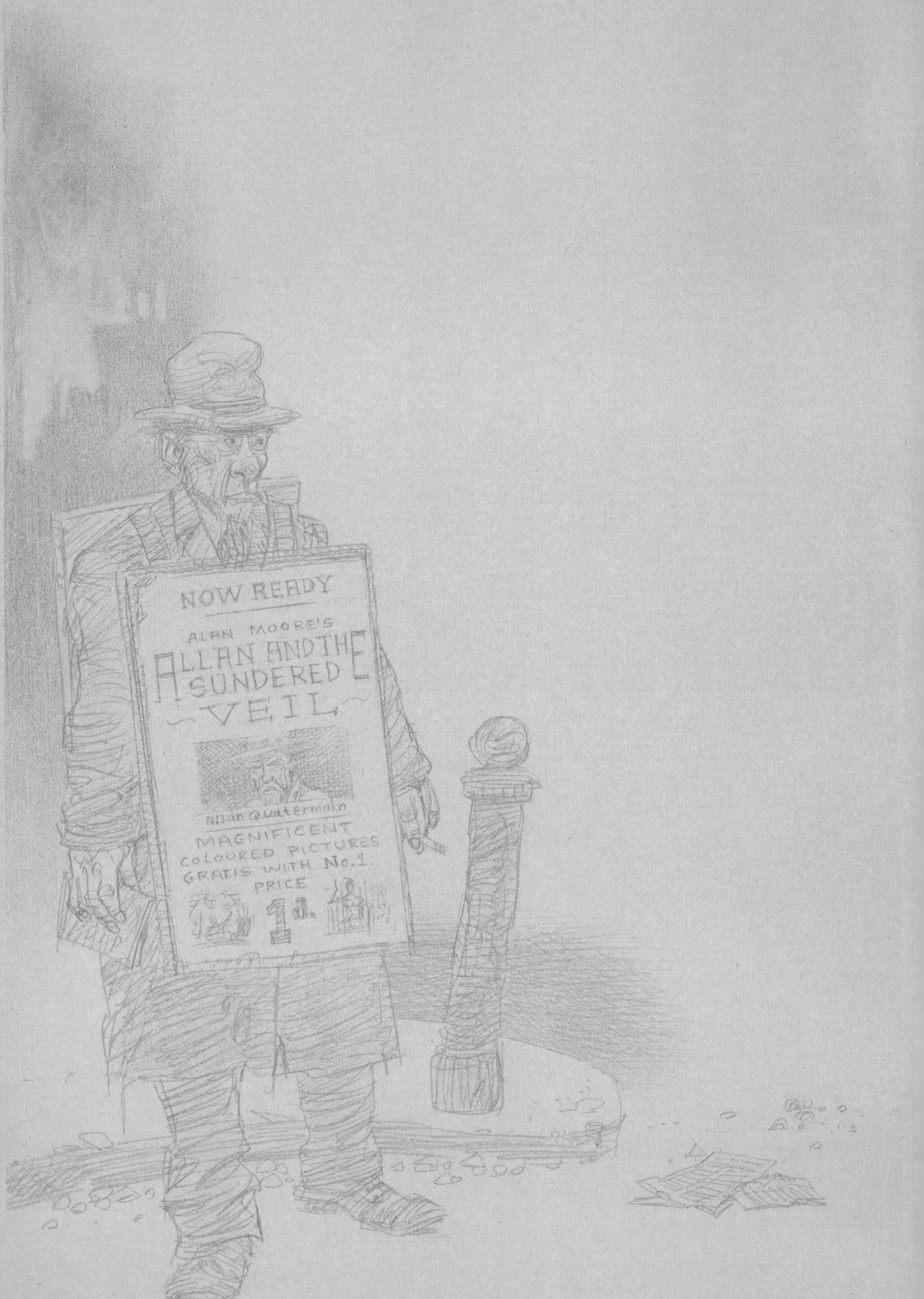

NOW READY
ALAN MOORE'S
ALLAN AND THE SUNDERED VEIL
Allan Quatermain
MAGNIFICENT
COLOURED PICTURES
GRATIS WITH No.1.
PRICE
1d.

THE "BOYS' FIRST-RATE POCKET LIBRARY"
OF COMPLETE TALES.

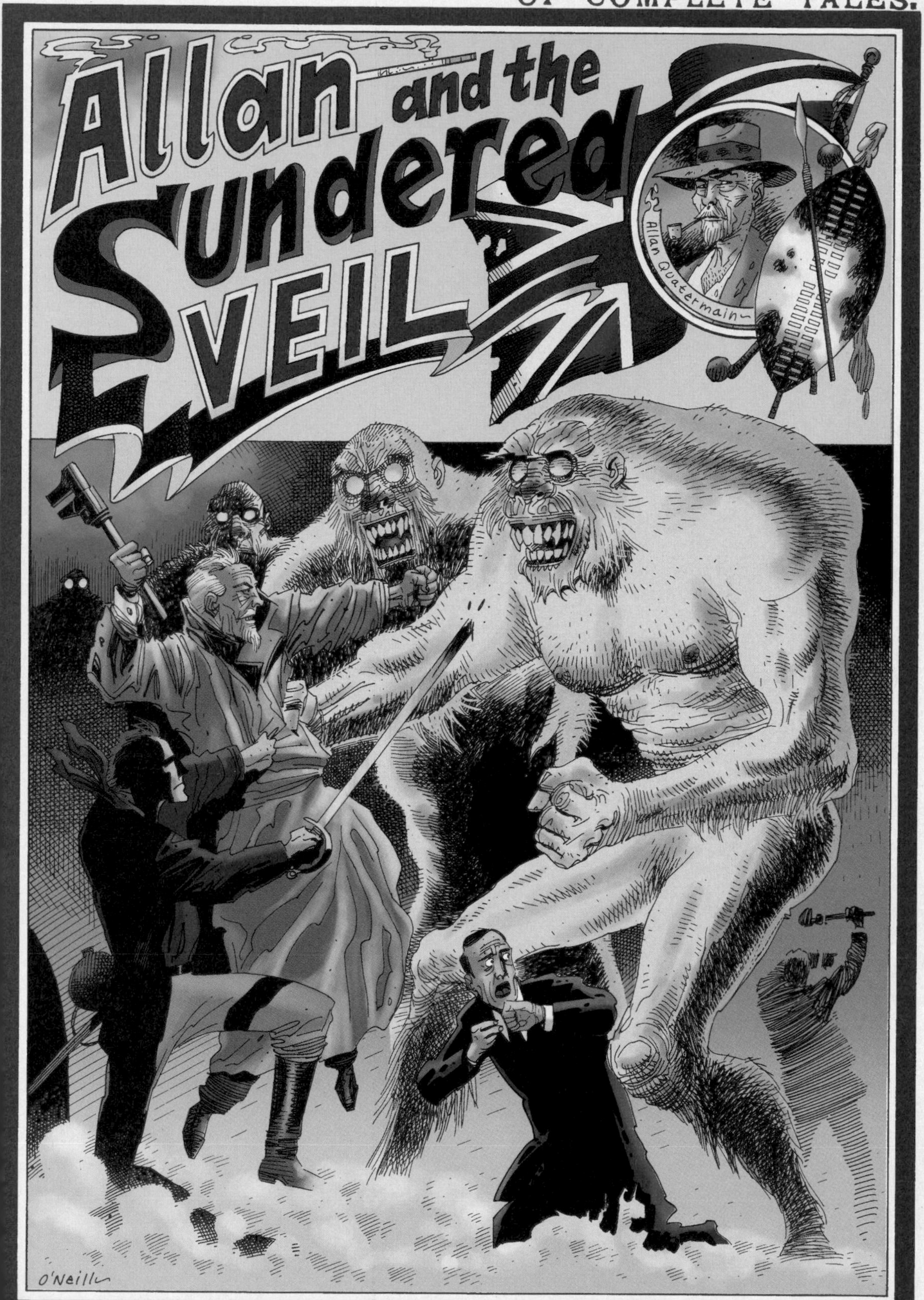
Allan and the Sundered VEIL
Allan Quatermain
O'Neill

He swung his arm out in a great lethal arc.

No.1] London: ALDINE PUBLISHING Co. [1d.

ALLAN AND THE SUNDERED VEIL

Authored by Mr. ALAN MOORE
Accompanying illustrations by
Mr. KEVIN O'NEILL

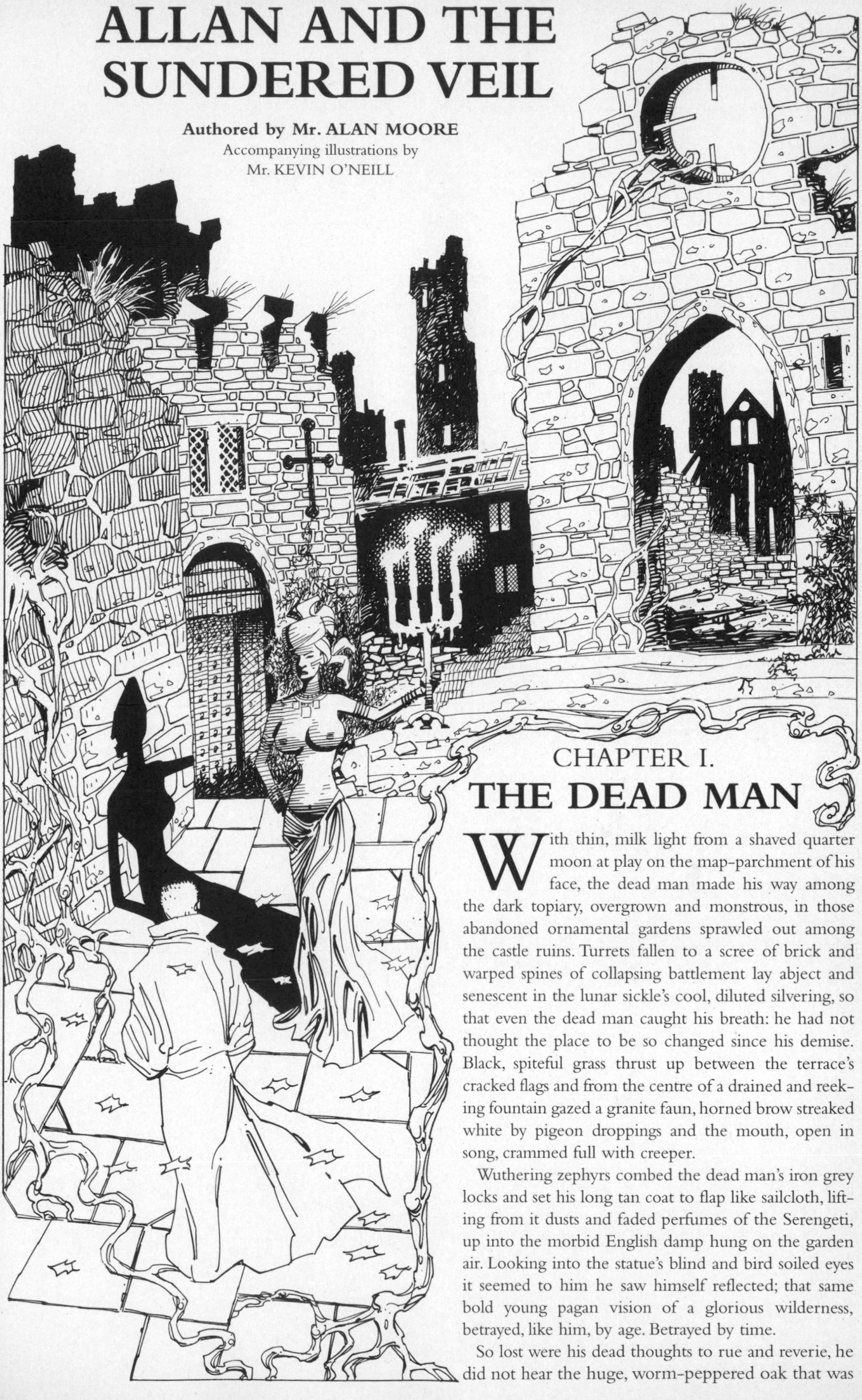

CHAPTER I.

THE DEAD MAN

With thin, milk light from a shaved quarter moon at play on the map-parchment of his face, the dead man made his way among the dark topiary, overgrown and monstrous, in those abandoned ornamental gardens sprawled out among the castle ruins. Turrets fallen to a scree of brick and warped spines of collapsing battlement lay abject and senescent in the lunar sickle's cool, diluted silvering, so that even the dead man caught his breath: he had not thought the place to be so changed since his demise. Black, spiteful grass thrust up between the terrace's cracked flags and from the centre of a drained and reeking fountain gazed a granite faun, horned brow streaked white by pigeon droppings and the mouth, open in song, crammed full with creeper.

Wuthering zephyrs combed the dead man's iron grey locks and set his long tan coat to flap like sailcloth, lifting from it dusts and faded perfumes of the Serengeti, up into the morbid English damp hung on the garden air. Looking into the statue's blind and bird soiled eyes it seemed to him he saw himself reflected; that same bold young pagan vision of a glorious wilderness, betrayed, like him, by age. Betrayed by time.

So lost were his dead thoughts to rue and reverie, he did not hear the huge, worm-peppered oak that was the castle's terrace door swing open at his back. Save for a dull, faint tingle in the thin machete scar that ran across his neck there at the rear, below the hairline, he received no intimation that he was observed until the woman spoke behind him in low, soft-accented tones that whirled the dead man round to face her, wild and startled.

"Lady Ragnall is expecting you. Her Ladyship will be pleased to receive you in the library. Follow me, please."

The speaker was a striking negress, some few inches taller than the dead man was himself, clad in a long skirt of what looked like emerald velvet and hung all about with bracelets, beads and gaudy fetishes, a flickering candelabra held up in one slender hand. Her hair was hidden by the turquoise wrapping of a turban, and before she turned from him to walk away down the decaying castle's silent hall he glimpsed the spiraling raised bumps of ritual disfigurements upon her cheeks, yet could not match the scarring's singular design with those of any similarly-decorated tribe he had encountered while in Africa. It seemed that he had no choice but to follow where she led, down corridors that twisted like intestines, winding ever deeper into the decaying mass of this once-stately building, now a bleak and ghastly carcass.

Walking briskly so that he might match the servant-woman's stride the dead man marveled at the shifting tableau of fantastic despoliation that her candle-halo brought to light about them. Here, garnet-eyed rats nested in the rubble of a great crashed chandelier that all but blocked the passage way before them both. Here, long-obliterated portraits were hung side by side among the roosting bats.

How had the opulent Ragnall estates become reduced to this? More troubling still, how could it be that his dear former friend and patron Lady Ragnall yet resided here, in chambers breached by rain; upon magnificent Axminster carpets annexed long since by the creep of moss and slug and fungus? When first he had glimpsed the moonlit relic of the castle he had known a pang of grief, believing that his wise and learned dowager com

panion must have passed on without issue, leaving her ancestral home and grounds to slide into the great and final disrepair of unreined nature. Grief was now replaced by an insidious and clinging apprehension as he followed the aloof and silent blackamoor between the rotting hanging tapestries, beneath a frescoed ceiling that would suddenly gape open on a patch of glinting and indifferent stars.

At last the ebon beauty paused before a portal of smoke-damaged cedar that the dead man recognized as having been the entrance to the castle library, though now adorned by great and leaping dog-tongues of black soot, the remnants of some earlier catastrophe. Placing one hand upon the door's brass lion-head knob, now streaked with verdigris, the servant woman turned her cool and level stare once more upon the dead man at her heel. Limned by the yellow, stuttering radiance of the candelabra that she held aloft, her high boned face could now be seen more clearly, with the raised dots of her ritual scars uncoiling like two serpents from her cheeks and rearing up along her temples to curl inward at the shaved and hairless browline, meeting at a point between her green and ocean-cryptic eyes. Her alien glamour and her self-possession breathed upon the long-spent ashes of the dead man's passion, nursing embers back to life amongst cold cinders he had thought long since extinguished. If perhaps he were a younger man and bore the marks of fewer wounds upon his body and and his heart...? He grimaced and suppressed a rueful laugh. Perhaps if he were still alive? The bruised and luscious fruits that were her lips moved almost not at all as she pushed wide the ruined library door, and spoke her first words since she had encountered him upon the weed-cracked terrace.

"Lady Ragnall waits on you within."

Dazed by the strangeness of his circumstances, he stepped past her and into the high-roofed room beyond, where for a moment he was dazzled by what seemed a thousand scintilla of light on every side, resolving as his eyes became accustomed to the glitter into dozen upon

dozens of wax candles, fabulous grotesques of spilling tallow set at random on the many mantles, shelves and surfaces contained within the library. There at the center of this glittering firmament, couched deep within the threadbare covers of a great bed made from two divans pushed one against the other was the gaunt and altered form of Lady Ragnall, quite unrecognizable save for the dancing animation in her clever eyes, sunk low within the wrinkled darkness of their sockets. Glancing up, their quick, voracious gaze settled upon the dead man. Parched lips creasing into a painted smile, at last she spoke, voice thin and cracked yet somehow poignant, like a broken harpsichord.

"Dear Mr. Quatermain. How good of you to come. I've been expecting you, though all good sense informed me I should not."

Her smile here seemed to broaden, taking on a somewhat sly and knowing cast before she spoke again.

"They said that you were dead. I had a letter from Sir Henry's brother, George, to that effect. Apparently you died at dawn three years ago in 1886, from injuries bravely received, away in some darker-than-usual corner of the darkest continent. I must say you look very well, considering."

The legendary hunter and adventurer shuffled uncomfortably and seemed to duck his head within the collar of his long and trailing coat. There was the faintest shadow of a wince accompanying his reply.

"I'd had enough. Surely you know me well enough to understand that? All of the fighting, all the glories and triumphs of my youth, it all became too loud for me somehow. Too rowdy and too wearying to someone of my years, but what was I to do? A world enthused by Mr. Haggard's somewhat overblown and generous accounts of my adventures would not suffer me to rest; would never tolerate the thought of Allan Quatermain, now grey and doddering, pruning his roses in some leaden suburb. No, I gave them what they wanted: a heroic death and an untended grave in some unreachably far corner of the world. Having provided my admirers with a suitable conclusion, I am free to live my afterlife, whatever span I have remaining, as my own."

Here Lady Ragnall levered herself up laboriously until she was propped up by one elbow in her nest of coverlet and pillow. Narrowing her eyes, head tilted in a bird-like manner to one side she scrutinized him shrewdly.

"It was all a yarn, then? All that business that George Curtis mentioned in the letter that he sent, concerning a lost kingdom called Zu-Vendis? Why, he told me that Sir Henry Curtis was now king there and would be no more returning to these isles. He said that you were slain and so too was the Zulu friend you spoke of once. Umslopogaas, was that his name? As George reported things, your warrior companion fell heroically in battle against plotters who might otherwise have robbed Sir Henry of his life. Was this all smoke and mirrors to accompany your vanishing act, Mr. Quatermain?"

Allan sighed heavily and sat himself on the broad arm of the divan there at the foot of Lady Ragnall's makeshift bed.

"Would that it were. I saw Umslopogaas myself as he was slain, hurling his enemy Lord Nasta from a parapet before he raised his bloody axe, Inkosikaas, up to his lips and kissed it, crying out "I die, I die, but 'twas a kingly fray." No, that was real enough, as was ZuVendis and my friend Sir Henry's marriage to its Queen, Nyleptha. Only my demise was sham, a ruse to grant me freedom from my suffocating reputation."

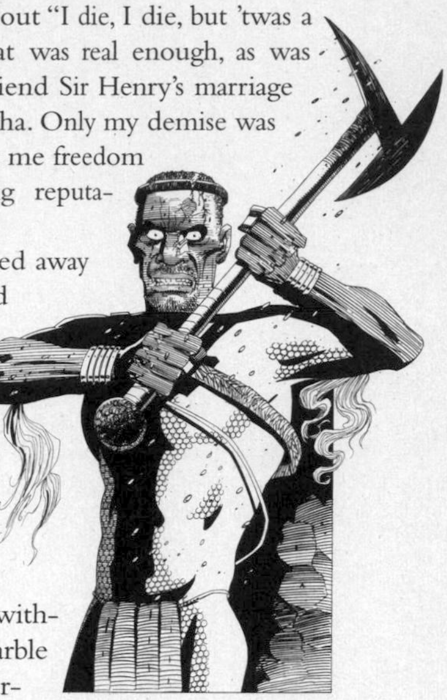

Lady Ragnall looked away from Allan and stared thoughtfully towards the far recesses of the candle-shadowed library, where the explorer noticed that her nubian maidservant was at work building a fire within the room's sole marble hearth. With some surprise he realized that the girl was tearing pages from the folio editions ranked upon the library's many shelves to feed the fledgling blaze. The dowager's chapped voice dragged his attention back to where her frail form nestled in its improvised, untidy cot.

"And yet you came back here. And why was that, I wonder?" Her ancient, knowing eyes were rested now on Quatermain once more, and as he met her gaze he understood that she already knew the answer to her question; would not be deceived by tales of him having returned out of concern for her welfare. His reply was brief and truthful.

"The taduki. I returned for the taduki."

Lady Ragnall smiled. Taduki, strangest of narcotics, to which she alone had access. With taduki, one might rend the veil of Time and be immersed in former lives, as Allan's own adventure with the Ivory Boy would readily attest. With taduki, one might easily escape ones present self and circumstances.

"Ah, taduki. The drug owns us, doesn't it? Addicted to the taste of previous lives we let our current ones go hang. I let my castle fall to ruin while taduki leads me down the byways of eternity. Marisa here prepares it for me, all my other servants fled."

Here Lady Ragnall signaled to the negro woman, who at once began to gather an array of curious paraphernalia from the library's far corner, setting it upon a low, carved table near a weathered armchair by the bed. Allan could see a pipe, a brazier, some powdered leaves.

The serving girl Marisa patiently lit charcoal in the brazier. Looking meaningfully into Allan's eyes, she handed him the pipe. Propped on her pillows, Lady Ragnall watched with vicarious anticipation as the great explorer held the bowl to catch the brazier's fumes, his lips pursing around the pipe's elaborately decorated stem.

Marisa dropped a pinch of powdered leaves onto the brazier and as the vapours hissed up, Quatermain inhaled. The instantly familiar scent coiled tendrils deep within his skull, and even as he felt his present personality beginning to dissolve before the drug's insistant tides he knew that there was something wrong.

The library fell away and he was toppling through a hideous alien abyss where cascaded foreign stars and dreadful gods howled from the Universe's rim. As gibbering blackness swallowed him, the dead man understood that this time the taduki offered not another life. This time it offered him naught but second death, much less heroic than his first, but much more final. Far off, as in another world, he heard the black maidservant start to scream.

Then there was nothing save devouring light.

CHAPTER II.
IN THE RUINS OF TIME

Within the mildewed, umber husk of Lady Ragnall's library, lyrically illuminated by the sonnets blazing in the hearth, an intricately carved taduki pipe fell from the nerveless fingers of the great, reputedly deceased explorer Allan Quatermain. Crouched at his side and tending to the brazier upon which the crumpled leaves of the taduki had been vaporized, the Nubian servant gave vent to a sudden piercing scream.

"Marisa? My dear girl, whatever is the matter?"

Lady Ragnall, frail as some exhumed Egyptian queen, sat up as far as she was able in her makeshift bed, formed by two hulking, worn divans pushed up against each other in the firelit library's centre. Her wet eyes fixed in an anxious, questioning look upon the servant woman who was kneeling now beside the sprawled, convulsing body of the old adventurer. Marisa gaped in horror at the flailing, stringless mannequin that writhed before, knuckles pressed against her tropic lips, face paling visibly so that the ritual whorls of beautiful disfigurement raised on her soft obsidian cheeks stood out in dark relief. Across the palsied shadows of the chamber floor, the thin marsh-heron voice of Lady Ragnall came again, more urgently.

"Tell me what's wrong! Is Mr. Quatermain alive or dead?"

Marisa could not speak. Trained as a priestess of the sacred drug taduki in the furthest eastern reaches of the Congo before coming here to assist in the dowager's experiments with the divine narcotic, she had taken on the drug's mysterious visions as a form of second sight, and did not always see things quite as others did. Now, as Marisa's disbelieving gaze took in the spectacle of the weathered explorer twitching on the parquet flooring, she beheld a spectacle that neither she or any priestess in her long tradition had heard tell of, much less witnessed.

Quatermain was inside out. At least, that was the first impression that Marisa gained on glimpsing the profusion of exposed internal organs; the exploded bones of an exterior skeleton. And yet, the more she watched the slaughterhouse grotesque that shuddered on the wooden tiles in front of her, the more she was not sure. It seemed to her bewildered sight as if something more subtle and peculiar were occurring.

For one thing, it appeared as if the man still had flesh on the outside, but altered somehow, made transparent to reveal the inner body... and yet that too was not the entire truth of things, Marisa realized as she watched in frightened fascination. It wasn't simply that one could see through the body's outer layers. It was that one could see around them to the viscera inside, as from some unimaginable vantage point that looked on things inside and out and saw both vistas simultaneously. Quatermain's face was visible, stunned terror frozen deep into its features, and yet somehow these were lifted out from the main mass of the explorer's head, like an expanded section in a diagram. Peering around these hanging jigsaw fragments, one could see the marble whiteness of the skull, itself somehow cross sectioned to expose the brain, unfolded through an alien plane of space revealing naked cortex, neural marrow at its centre. Every inch of the adventurer's wracked body, both inside and out, was visible to the appalled Marisa in its intimate and hideous finery.

Worse still, if the man's limbs moved in any way, a more terrible phenomenon became apparent: every gesture left there in the air behind itself a stream of solid-seeming after images, so that the movement of one horribly translucent arm would yield a fan of bones, each feathered with a foggy down of veins, like pinions from some phantom swan; some form out of an alien geometry.

The non-Euclidean shape rippled before her in such violent contravention of the normal laws governing space and reason that Marisa felt a heavy wave of nausea welling within her. Closing tight her eyes, she willed her vision to return to normal, free from the grotesque perspectives her taduki-trained perceptions had so suddenly afforded her. When she opened them again, Quatermain's body had become once more a reassuring, opaque solid. Ominously still, he sprawled upon the library's chill parquet in a death like trance. As if from far away, Marisa heard the agitated cries of Lady Ragnall.

"Speak, confound you! What is wrong with Mr. Quatermain?"

Marisa looked up at her Mistress in confusion, jade eyes dazed and blinking like one led from darkness into

light, or woken from some mystifying dream.

"Forgive me, Mistress," the maidservant stammered. "I have been pierced by a vision, strange and terrible. It seems to me as if your friend has not been taken by the drug into a previous life, as has transpired before, but rather torn from past and present altogether, taken to a wasteland that is quite beyond all time, or space, or anything we know."

Here Marisa fell silent, her eyes downcast. It was quite the longest speech that Lady Ragnall had, in all their years together, heard the ebon beauty utter. Cocking her frail, bird-like skull to one side as she paused, considering, the dowager at last pursed her thin lips decisively and offered up her verdict on this new and worrying turn of events.

"Then fetch pillows and blankets so that we at least can make his body comfortable. If Mr. Quatermain's soul has been taken from us, then we must do all we can to bring it back."

Without replying, Marisa stood up and hurried from the flickering library to do as she'd been bidden. In the chamber now was no sound save the reedy, rattling wheeze of the decayed aristocrat herself, still sat bolt upright in a stale and yellowed froth of bedsheets; that, and the much fainter breathing of the man sprawled all but lifeless on the floor. Oh, my dear Mr. Quatermain, thought Lady Ragnall. What dark continent are you exploring now?

Quatermain had felt the consciousness torn from his body, gripped by the drug's phantasmal diamond fist. He'd heard Marisa scream and then awareness was dashed from him by a cold, obliterating light. Now he was lost. As sensibility returned, he found himself afloat, a ghostly form amidst a shimmering violet limbo. What had happened? This was not the breathtaking immersion in past incarnation that the drug had hitherto provided. All about him dream-like forms congealed from viscous twilight, half-materialized before once more dissolving into opalescent nothing. Smoldering ferns and mollusc spirals, scintillating on the brink of substance.

Scarcely had Quatermain formed the conscious wish for some navigable geography by which to find his way, than suddenly the ectoplasmic medium about him seemed to quiver, crystallizing and condensing into landscape. There below his wraith-like feet, lush tufts of pale mauve grass grew from mud of rich indigo. A queasy hybrid vegetation, writhing blossoms neither wholly cuttlefish nor thistle, sprouted from the spectral verges. These surely were marshlands of the mind, a terrible Sargasso of the psyche where souls foundered in an astral mire. Somewhere ahead of him were voices, murmuring, and meagre firelight glistering in the starless gloom.

Advancing, the explorer beheld two incongruous figures, hunched over a dim and heatless fire whereon burned the unpleasant squid flowers, tentacles curling upon themselves, withering in the queer green flames. To one side of this cheerless blaze there sat a stooped young man, lugubrious features weirdly underlit by the wan radiance of the campfire. Cross-legged on the mauve turf opposite this dreamy individual sat a person stranger yet, a strongly built man decked out in the dusty grey apparel of a Southern officer of the American War between the

States. Both men glanced up suspiciously at Quatermain's approach.

"I mean no harm," the adventurer said in haste, noting that the Confederate captain's hand moved cautiously towards the sabre hanging at his side. "My name is Allan Quatermain, and I fear I am lost. Tell me, where are we and how came you here? Are we alive, or dead and in some purgatory unpredicted by religion?" Here a meaningful glance passed between the seated figures before the stooped, younger man made a reply, his voice and manner mild and academic.

"I am Randolph Carter. This is my great-uncle John. I fear we are as lost as you appear to be." The young man went on to describe an improbable New England of the twentieth century, a life spent in reclusive exploration of the world of dreams. During one such excursion through what the young man referred to as "the gates of Deeper Slumber," he had strayed unwittingly into these current psychic wastelands, previously unknown to him. Here he had met the shade or astral double of his distant relative, a man mysteriously lost in battle a century before. At this point the Civil War veteran took up the tale, his low commanding voice almost a whisper.

"I don't know about this twentieth century Randolph talks about. All I know is that I was dying in a cave and staring at the planet Mars just hanging there above me in the grey dawn sky, its strong unblinking light amidst the fading stars. Suddenly, I'm wrenched from my body, just as if the pull of Mars is drawing up my soul towards it... but instead I end up in this dismal, gaseous place, where I run into Randolph, who tells me that he is my great nephew from Providence, Rhode Island. Next thing, you turn up from nowhere."

"Not exactly nowhere," Quatermain responded. "I'm from England in the last half of the nineteenth century. It seems I've been propelled here by a drug I ingested. Normally it causes vision of time past, but in this instance it would seem to have removed me from time altogether. What is more, in my experience as a hunter, I'm not sure that this locale is an entirely friendly one."

He gestured toward the gloom beyond the greenish halo of their fire. Something of bulk dragged itself through the furthest weeds. Elsewhere, a faint, dry sound like rattling lobster claws.

A nervous perspiration dewed the young man's brow, and panic cracked his high pitched voice. "It sounds like we're surrounded. What are we to do? I'm hardly what you'd call a fighting man."

The soldier favored his great nephew with a scornful look. "Seems the spunk has gone out of the Carter clan since my day. You'd best let me handle this." There was a satisfying hiss of steel as the Confederate captain drew his sword. Not one to shrink from combat, Quatermain lifted a blazing branch of the anemone-tipped bracken from the fire, arcing it through the darkness.

The swathe of emerald flame briefly illuminated something very like a monstrous centipede made of translucent gelatine, a frogspawn cluster of a dozen eyes grouped at one end that glittered momentarily in the ghastly viridian light. Worse shapes shifted suggestively in the encroaching murk. Quatermain's voice was low and grim.

"There's dozens of the things. I somehow don't think sticks and swords will rescue us from this. We have to..."

Quatermain broke off in mid speech. Something strange was happening in the gloom before them. A faint luminescent pulse disturbed the stygian blackness, growing stronger and more regular with every moment.

The explorer gasped in disbelief as the peculiar throb of light resolved itself into a ghostly figure, seated in mid-air upon the saddle of a dazzling contraption made from brass, the man's garb not dissimilar to that of Quatermain's own era. The bright light around this new arrival and his craft seemed to alarm the squirming presences beyond the firelight's rim, prompting them to withdraw. At this, the stranger called out to the three men.

"Climb aboard. The novelty of my arrival won't deter these horrors long." Pausing, he thought to introduce himself.

"I'm sometimes called the Time Traveller."

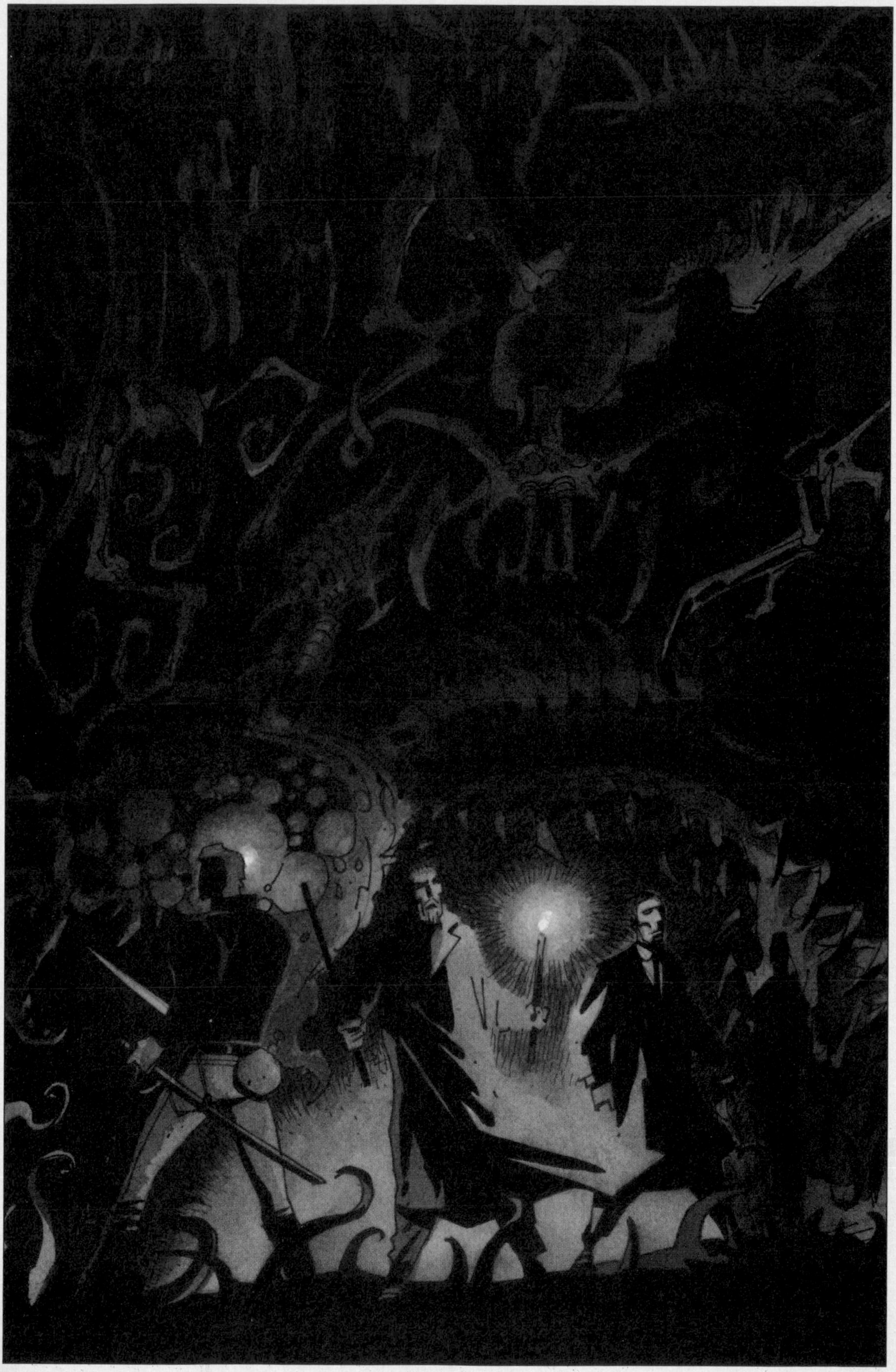

"There's dozens of the things"

CHAPTER III.
IN THE SHADOW OF THE SPHINX

Their knuckles blanched and tight upon the frigid brass rails of the open sphere that carried them, the four men tumbled through the smears of colour and half-realized forms that edged the canvas of Eternity. Outside the regimented centuries, they rode their glimmering and peculiar brazen craft down the etheric, surging waterfall of Time itself amidst the dull boom of the pouring aeons, blinded in the spindrift spray of instants. Allan Quatermain... or, at the least, his astral semblance... clung to the posterior framework of their hurtling time-boat while the rushing storm-breath of cascading ages slapped and stung against his leathered cheek. He struggled to convince himself that this was all some lunatic phantasm conjured by the occult drug *taduki* he'd ingested at the crumbling country seat of Lady Ragnall where his mortal form still lay in a convulsive coma, but he strived in vain. The rushing chrono-chasm and the curious chariot upon which he and his companions shot the rapids of the hours were too immediate and real to be dismissed as mere hallucination. The acclaimed explorer knew within his very soul that were he for an instant to release his grip on the cold tubing of their vessel's rim then he would fall forever, lost and screaming in Infinity. No, this was neither lotus-vision nor mirage. Quatermain hugged the rail and swore beneath his breath.

To Allan's right, clamped white and gasping to the Time-ship's starboard filigree was the dream-body of the young New Englander who claimed to be an astral voyager named Randolph Carter, drawn here from the future reaches of the twentieth century. Clasping their vehicle's intricate pipework opposite the pale and shivering young man, to Allan's left, was the more masculine and sturdy figure of another ectoplasmic traveler, this one originating in the recent past from times not long after America's bloody and tragic Civil War. By some fluke of the timestream it transpired that this grim, battle-weary figure in his flapping coat of dull Confederate grey was a relation, or, more accurately, ancestor to the timid Rhode Island student, being Randolph Carter's lost great-uncle John.

Quatermain had encountered the two men while wandering in the shifting psychic landscape to which the *taduki* had transported him, not long before they were attacked by loathsome alien horrors that seemed native to that twilight realm. Only the intervention of the enigmatic individual whose epoch-spanning engine now transported them had saved the three dream-castaways from a near-unimaginable fate. Quatermain now turned his attention to this last of his co-passengers, who sat astride a saddle at the centre of the skeletal brass shape, expertly readjusting dials and levers sprouted from the chill bronze of his marvelous machine's control assembly. "The Time Traveler," he'd called himself, and judging by his dress he seemed to have his origins not far from Quatermain's own period, which was to say the last half of the nineteenth-century.

"Hold on," their dapper helmsman shouted now, above the howl of the bilennia. "We're almost there!"

The incoherent, glittering continuum that seemed to spiral and rotate about them now appeared to slow, resolving into landscape. Eerie wilderness, though not without a haunted beauty, stretched on every side beneath a canopy of strangely altered constellations, as at last the brass-bound ship came to a halt. Quatermain and the other men stepped down unsteadily onto fine-powdered bonemeal sands that had, at least, the satisfying semblance of solidity.

Rising from the bleached and calceous floor not far from where their craft had come to rest, a towering and flawless statue of pure alabaster stood in sharp relief against the plush, star-sequined velvet of the night. Supine on its massive plinth the white Sphinx sprawled, its weighty feline forepaws resting one atop the other and its smoothly chiseled woman's lips creased faintly in a knowing, almost melancholy smile. It was towards this pristine, overpowering icon of enigma that the strange Time-mariner now strode, bidding his new companions follow in his wake.

Dismissing protests and inquiries from both Quatermain and the two Carters with a brisk shake of his head, the traveler took from his waistcoat pocket a

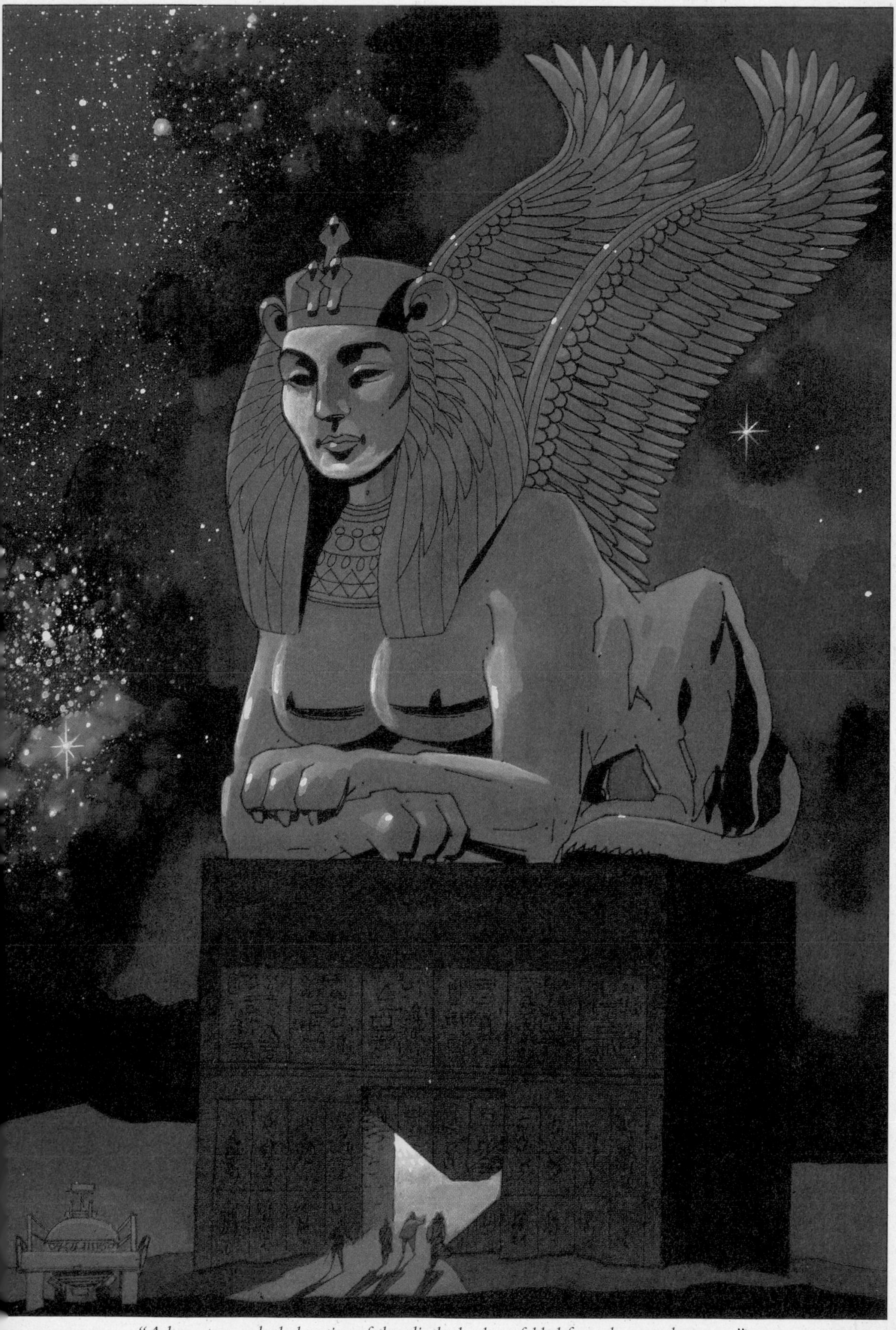

"A large trapezohedral section of the plinth slowly unfolded from the central mass..."

remarkable key-like device made of blue crystal. Pointing this towards the statue's seamless, soaring base appeared to trigger some response within the monolith itself. A large trapezohedral section of the plinth slowly unfolded from the central mass and lifted with the softest purr of mechanism to reveal the entrance of a softly-lit interior concealed within the pallid marble block.

Entering this unexpected hidden room and bidding his three fellows follow him inside, their new friend made once more a gesture with his sapphire key at which the open segment of the sheer white stone descended once more to its previous position, with the trio sealed inside a gold-illuminated chamber, sparsely furnished in an odd quasi-Egyptian style and empty save for reassuringly untidy piles of books and other personal effects presumably belonging to their host.

Seating himself in a hieroglyphic-crowded alcove, Allan noticed a glass oval set into the wall directly opposite his vantage point. As if the framed shape were some magic mirror, images swam lazily across its egg-shaped surface that, after some moments, the explorer recognized as a slowly rotating view of the queer wilderness immediately beyond their chamber. As he watched, the Time-machine itself crawled into view, stood motionless in the skull coloured, starlit wastes. Allan supposed the purpose of this fascinating crystal screen was to allow the Sphinx's occupants to monitor the realm outside, but scarcely had he formed this thought than his attention was called to the traveller who'd brought them here, now standing in the middle of the gently glowing chamber in a posture of address as he surveyed his guests.

"You're wondering, no doubt, whom I might be and, further to this, why I have delivered you to this appalling place."

Their rescuer paused here, as if to gather up his thoughts, before continuing.

"My name is of no consequence. Suffice to say that I am an inventor, formerly residing here in London, who perfected in the last years of the nineteenth century a means of traveling in time. I had adventures in Earth's farthest future after which, following a brief farewell visit to my own day, I have dwelled here in the phantom stream of decades ever since as an explorer, much like your good self."

The traveler here nodded congenially to Quatermain, who frowned in puzzlement by way of a response, unable to contain his curiosity.

"Now wait a minute! Did you just say 'here in London?' Do you mean to tell us that the barren plain beyond these walls is...?" Quatermain trailed off, incredulously, as the traveler completed his inquiry for him, with a rueful smile.

"Is London? I'm afraid so, though it is the London of a period some thousands if not millions of years after the decline of the metropolis that you yourself are more familiar with. London and England both are gone, the names made meaningless by these unending chalky drifts. Only this cryptic Sphinx would seem to have endured the ages, changeless and impregnable. I came across it...or an earlier incarnation of it...during my first jaunt through time, and I have since remodeled it to my own purposes."

"And just what purposes would those be, friend?"

It was the gruff Confederate who spoke, his shrewd and war-wise eyes unblinking as he weighed up their deliverer. The scientist gave a curt nod, as if acknowledging the soldier's question and its obvious validity, before continuing.

"I am afraid my answer will yield little comfort. Briefly, in my explorations of the chronologic flow, I have discovered something dreadfully amiss within the fields of human time. My sojourns in the stream of being have convinced me that our own material Universe, its past, its present and its future, is but one plane of a splendorous and infinitely greater structure that comprises nothing less than the totality of all Existence, manifested in both physical and spiritual dimensions. You will guess my horror, then, when I discovered that there seems to be a vast, near unimaginable *hole* torn in the fabric of Creation, and that certain atmospheres or entities are leaking through this dreadful and apocalyptic pit from *somewhere* else!"

Silencing a frightened exclamation of surprise from Randolph Carter, the Time-traveler continued.

"You yourselves encountered some of the more insignificant spawn of these vile, trans-existential beings shortly prior to my arrival on the astral plane to which your various adventures had transported you. Understand that I was actively seeking you there. All three of you are heroes, each in your own fashion, and I'm desperately in need of some assistance in my efforts to prevent further contamination of our Universe by these unfathomable alien grotesqueries."

Quatermain interrupted. "Would those be the things you speak of?" he said, pointing to the oval screen.

In the glass eye of the monitor-device, the previously trackless hinterlands beyond the safety of the Sphinx were suddenly aswarm with an insidious life. Awful and shambling simian forms whose greatest horror was the faint humanity remaining in their slack albino faces shuffled through the dunes outside, uncomfortably near the undefended Time-machine. Gaze fixed upon the shimmering crystal of his watching-glass, their host's voice burned with stifled anger as he spoke.

"They're Morlocks, known to other eras as *Mi-Go*, or as abominable snowmen. While they're not the entities that I referred to, they appear to serve them. I had not expected to find them so far downriver in the flow of Time. If we'd prevent them wrecking my machine and thus stranding us here upon Eternity's bleak margins, we must be prepared to fight."

At this the timorous Rhode Island student gave a low moan of dismay, though his great-uncle seemed more cheered. The elder Carter drew his army-issue cutlass from its sheath and chuckled. "It's about time" was his sole remark. Producing from the chamber's further recesses a small selection of weighty mechanic's tools that might be used as weapons, the grim chrono-naut armed Quatermain, the younger Carter and himself before training his blue glass key upon the chamber door's interior.

"Be ready to rush out at them as soon as I raise up the door. If we can beat a path to my conveyance then I'll carry us from here towards a date less inhospitable."

At this the key pulsed once with a faint sapphire light

and the trapezohedron that gave entrance to the Sphinx's hollow base swung upwards soundlessly. Then everything happened at once.

Quatermain rushed out over the wan talcum sands, clouds of luminous dust at his heel. With the heavy industrial spanner his host had provided he swung his arm out in a great lethal arc that demolished one side of the blind, ape-like face looming suddenly in at him, out from the shadows. To one side he saw Randolph Carter fall screaming with one of the livid and shaggy monstrosities crouched on his back, but before he could leap to the youngster's assistance the Carter lad's great-uncle stepped from the darkness and took the brute's head off with one cutlass-swipe.

By now the temporal argonaut had reached his precious machine, although not without blood, brains and ghastly white Morlock-fur clotting the carpenter's hammer that he so effectively swung. He was straddling his saddle and sparking the Time-vessel's engine to life as both Quatermain and Captain Carter helped Randolph into position upon the ship's framework. The starry desert sky above them seemed to swirl and turn as the machine began to lift them from their desperate situation.

It was then that Quatermain felt something crash against him from behind. As snowy simian arms wrapped tight about his throat he realized that the grub-pale horrors were aboard the Time-machine.

CHAPTER IV.
THE ABYSS OF THE LIGHTS

Quatermain knew that in reality his mortal body was elsewhere, back in the solid world and no doubt comatose upon the floor of Lady Ragnall's ruined, flame-lit library; victim to an overdose of the time-twisting drug taduki. The form he presently inhabited, though modelled to recall in every way the old explorer's fleshy shell down to the clothing that was draped about it, Allan knew to be some kind of astral construct shaped from dream-stuff, and presumably with no more substance than that of a moment's fancy. Even so, a dreadful apprehension deep within the marrow of his being told him that wherever he might be, whatever numinous state he may have ascended to, there were yet things here that might injure him. Indeed, might even kill him.

One such creature, an albino and Neanderthal monstrosity that Quatermain's newfound companion the Time Traveller referred to as a Morlock, lunged now at the scarred adventurer with jaws agape, revealing what seemed to be nothing but protracted canines, dripping with a ragged lace of milky and opaque saliva.

Everything had happened so quickly. Exiled from normal consciousness by the taduki, Quatermain had found himself within an eerie, metamorphic landscape where he had encountered two more displaced souls, the timorous New England dreamer Randolph Carter and the dour Confederate officer who, it transpired, was Carter's long-presumed dead Uncle John. Attacked by horrors native to those shifting twilight latitudes, they were reprieved by the arrival of the man who styled himself the Time Traveller, astride the brazen vessel upon which he braved the torrent of the aeons. First conveying them along the timestream to his base of operations in the huge plinth of an enigmatic carven sphinx, the Traveller had warned them of a dreadful flaw in space and time itself, a gaping hole torn in the very fabric of existence through which unimaginable horrors from beyond threatened to burst through into gross material existence. Scarcely had the Traveller completed his account before his sanctuary was entirely overrun by brutish servants of the trans-dimensional monstrosities, shambling and pallid ape-things that the Traveller had called Mi-Go, or Morlocks. One of these had leapt aboard the brass-frame vessel of the Chrononaut just as it began to ferry the four men to safety, and now clawed frantically at Quatermain as it hung roaring from the Time-ship's rail with murder in its blind and cataracted eyes.

The creature's next blow raked Quatermain's shoulder, and the sudden stinging wetness told him that his apprehensions were well founded. He was bleeding, though the blood, presumably, was not that of the body but a far more precious spiritual fluid that flowed through the human soul. There were, then, after all, things here with a capacity to harm him. Worse, it seemed that they might harm him upon levels and in

bone, which collapsed beneath the impact. Scrabbling against the rail for purchase, frantic in sightless agony, the Morlock had time for a solitary dog-like yowl of dreadful pain before the force of Allan's backswing slammed into its temple to release a gruel-like spray of brains.

Convulsing, clenching in its mortal spasms, the monstrosity gripped fast upon the pipe-work of the Time-ship's frame even as its grotesque and stunted body began slowly and with an almost majestic air of inevitability to topple back towards the streaming void that shrieked about them. With a sense of helpless and despairing foresight, the explorer understood what was about to happen and attempted vainly to dislodge the creature's death-grip on the railing with his wrench, knowing within himself that he was far too late.

The thin, brass pipe ruptured beneath the creature's morbid weight, finally bursting at a collared joint with an ear-splitting screech and a great gout of what appeared to Quatermain to be prismatic steam, scintillant, almost sequined to the naked eye. Crouched over his controls, the Traveller looked round to view the damage to his vessel, colour draining from his face in fright as he set eyes upon the hissing rend within his Time-car's frame. Its thick, grey fingers finally torn from the damaged pipe by the vast suction of the vessel's slipstream, the dead Morlock was ripped with incredible ferocity into the vehicle's wake, amongst the ravelling plumes of shimmering steam or plasma streaming from the leak the lifeless beast had made.

To Allan's horror, as he watched the bleached corpse fall away from him, he saw that it was undergoing what could only be described as a repellent and unnatural blossoming. What seemed a thousand heads, four thousand limbs and countless fingers sprouted in a solid and organic after-trail behind the tumbling sub-man, so that it became an elongated, almost centipedal shape, twisting grotesquely in upon itself as it retreated to a livid speck in the seething and awful maelstrom of the centuries exploding at their back. It was almost as if every moment, every slice of the Morlock's trajectory were carved in space behind it as it spiralled away through the fourth dimension's awesome and eternal Now, that constant and unending hyper-moment in which all creation and the terrible and fathomless abyss of history were contained.

It was with difficulty that Quatermain wrestled his attention from the spectacle of the receding Morlock, but there were more urgent matters to attend to. The Time-craft seemed to be losing altitude, if there could be said to be such a thing as altitude in this bewildering domain. The queer and spectrumatic steam now twisted upwards from the mangled fitting, and a horrid tingling in the soles of Allan's feet told him that they were falling. Falling slowly, it would seem, as through some thick and viscous medium, but falling nonetheless. Now he could hear the panicked imprecations of the Traveller hunched at the Chronopede's controls above the whistling rush of their descent.

"I'm losing power. We're going down into the inert Time-soup that stagnates below the race of history's

ways that he had not imagined. Could one's spirit bleed to death? A true and final death, beyond all hope of resurrection? He had no time to dwell upon these metaphysical complexities before the screeching ape-thing launched itself at him once more.

The Time-ship lurched, unbalanced by the Morlock's weight, and clinging to the craft's far sides, both the Confederate captain and his frightened nephew yelled with anger and alarm respectively. Wrestling with the craft's controls, the temporal argonaut was shouting something, but above the howling of the time-winds and the bellowing of Quatermain's sub-human adversary, the explorer could not make sense of the helmsman's cry. The blind brute had a grip on Allan's coat, and inexorably pulled the struggling human closer to those awful, snapping teeth. The single hand with which he gripped the vessel's brasswork slithered dangerously for several inches before Quatermain could check himself and take a firmer grip, and the explorer knew that if he did not manage to reverse this situation quickly, he would be flung from the ship into the bottomless and surging chaos through which the craft hurtled.

Remembering the huge mechanic's wrench that he still gripped in his free hand, Quatermain swung his arm in a relentless weighted arc that thudded gratifyingly against the white fur matted on the monster's cheek impulsive current. Best hang on to something tight. I've no idea how far we have to fall."

His forehead bright with nervous perspiration, the young student Randolph Carter from Rhode Island spoke up here, voice high and quivering.

"I-Isn't this time itself we're dropping through? How do you know that we won't fall forever?"

The Traveller's grim silence in response to this was all the answer any of the men required. They did as they were bidden and clung fast against the Time-ship's broken ribs as it continued its unhurried, irreversible descent into the dark and nebulaic swirl of raw and random time below.

Though it was scarcely possible within such straits to take the measurement of passing moments, it did not seem long before the gruff voice of the elder Carter roused the others from their bleak, despairing torpor as they gazed into the depthless, hopeless wastes about them.

"I see something down below us. If these are time's backwaters, like our travelling friend informs us, then I reckon what I'm looking at must be some kind of swamp gas."

Narrowing his slate-flecked eyes, Quatermain peered into the yawning chasm under them. Something approached, although he could not tell if this phenomenon were rising up towards them through the chronic murk, or if they in their turn were sinking towards it.

"He's right. I can see coloured lights, like Chinese lanterns, getting closer to us. What in God's name are they, man?"

This last remark of Allan's was directed at the temporal voyager himself, who frowned and slowly shook his head as the strange luminosities tracked ever nearer.

"I don't know. This is a phenomenon that I've not previously encountered. Why, the shape looks almost geometric. Watch out! Here's one coming at us now!"

The four men held their breath and watched in stupefied amazement as one of the glowing forms ascended slowly past them on their vessel's starboard side. It was, as the Time Traveller had noted, a perfectly realized geometric solid, possibly a dodecahedron, that was easily some fifty times as big as was their craft itself. It was illuminated softly from within by a pale yellow radiance that washed across the faces of the quartet in a xanthic and unearthly glaze as they hung, hushed and gaping, from the Time-ship's pipes and bars. The Traveller whistled softly, underneath his breath.

"A chrono-crystal. A fourth-dimensional mathematic growth within the five-dimensional fluid underlying all existence. I'd always theorized that such things should be possible, but to have my hypothesis proved so spectacularly right…"

He trailed off as two more of the immense incandescent shapes, one blue and one a luscious mauve, floated up past them with an eerie, massive grace. With all other eyes fixed upon the glowing geometric marvels as they drifted by, only the fidgeting and nervous Randolph Carter, glancing down, raised the alarm.

"Dear God! One of those things is coming right underneath us!"

The timid scholar's fears were validated, catastrophically, almost as soon as they were voiced. With a bone-jarring

crash and a great splintering squeal of brass on glass, their craft impacted with the topmost surface of a lucid and colossal jewel, a tesseract of watery, radiant amethyst that Quatermain reckoned to be almost a furlong in diameter as he picked himself up unsteadily from the smooth, hard plain of mollusc-purple silicate where he'd been flung by the collision of their craft with this giant meta-object. Climbing to his feet, he felt the crystal surface singing faintly there beneath his palms and knew that this was matter of a higher order than that which he was accustomed to.

Not far away both Randolph Carter and his uncle similarly hauled themselves erect, while nearby the Time Traveller, seemingly not much worse for wear, was extracting himself from the dented pipework of his fabulous invention. Allan noticed a thin trail of blood crawl slowly from the Traveller's hairline, where it seemed his head had been brought into contact with the ship's controls, but the explorer did not think the injury looked serious. Indeed, the temporal astronaut danced back and forth with great enthusiasm on the surface of the Brobdingnagian gem where they were beached, peering into its depths excitedly.

"Look! It's responding to our presence! I see pictures moving in the inner facets down beneath our feet."

The Traveller's voice rang with the pure thrill of discovery. As Quatermain and the other two men looked down into the scrying-glass on which they stood, they realized that the Time-voyager was correct. Deep down within the crystal, images were shifting and transforming in a slow kaleidoscope.

Allan's attention was seized by one vignette in particular: a wasted, almost skeletal old man sprawled on a pallet on what seemed to be a beige rug in an opium den, a thin pipe clasped there in his nerveless fingers. Crouching by the man, a striking woman in a long, red scarf seemed to be speaking urgently to the near cadaver. There was a sudden start of purest horror as Quatermain realized that the drugged and wretched creature slumped there in bug-haunted squalor was himself.

"An Aleph," the Time Traveller sighed, almost ecstatically. "Behold, my friends, Time's very fulcrum. Gaze, if you dare, into the diamond eyepiece of Infinity!"

CHAPTER V.
THE GLINT IN FORTUNE'S EYE

The high-stoked blaze of manuscripts and folios within the fireplace of Lady Ragnall's derelicted library lapped with a dozen brazen tongues of light across the lifeless, sweat-gemmed cheek of Allan Quatermain, the once-famed, now supposedly deceased explorer sprawled upon the scuffed and dust-cauled parquet of the library floor. The dowager herself, ensconced within the tumuli of bedding on the face-to-face divans and scrutinizing the unconscious form of the adventurer for any flicker of vitality, was not entirely certain that her friend's demise was still the world-deceiving hoax he had intended it to be. Stretched before her, gaunt and still and almost without breath, the death of Allan Quatermain seemed of a sudden all too credible.

Her Ladyship was not without some personal experience in feigning death so as to thwart the gross intrusions of the living, having staged her own end some years earlier to live since then in blissful undisturbed seclusion as the stately pile of Ragnall Hall fell into luscious ruin about her, tended only by the statuesque obsidian beauty named Marisa who was even now crouching beside her coma-stricken guest, dabbing his cheek with dampened rags and murmuring beneath her breath in the strange, sing-song chant of her own tongue. The frail aristocrat supposed Marisa to be weaving, in her native language, charms to draw Quatermain's absent or abducted spirit back from such strange and dangerous realms as those to which his latest dalliance with the drug taduki had transported him.

Marisa, stooping with the radiance of flaming rhetoric and poesy from the hearth-fire casting smears of shuddering light across the sumptuous charcoal-crayon vellum of her skin, was the sole source of the peculiar narcotic which transcended time, the same drug to which Lady Ragnall and now, it would seem, her Ladyship's explorer friend were showing symptoms of addiction. Quatermain, reported dead in some unreachably remote, half-fabled region of the globe had made his way instead to Ragnall Hall where, despite the alleged death of the hall's inhabitant, he still maintained some desperate hope of finding a last trace, a residue of that which he desired: taduki, the mysterious substance by which men and women might escape the confines of their lives, their times and their identities, as Allan had himself experienced upon diverse occasions in the past. Finding Lady Ragnall quite alive and in no short supply of the required plant-extract the adventurer had, perhaps, indulged too deeply and too readily. Now he stretched, rigid and near death, there on the floor beside Marisa while she mopped his brow and whispered queer and foreign incantations over his apparent corpse

She wondered where he was, to which domain of the great spirit-country he had been displaced. Wiping his grizzled chin, where foam had dried, she noticed a faint twitching, almost imperceptible, there at the corners of his eyes, as if some dream-moth struggled in the cobweb of his sleep. When those crusted lids flickered and opened, but an instant later, the dark beauty ceased her sussurus of chants, her own eyes flooding with relief, with gratitude that the immortal spirits had returned her friend to them.

And then with fear.

The time jewel drifted in the backwash of the hurtling present, hung suspended, floating and becalmed there at the frayed surf hem of Time's unbounded swell. The massive violet crystal, in its mute and enigmatic grandeur, rose up slowly, like a bubble in some treacle-thick and viscous medium, some endless spill of glittering amber with its scintillant and fluid reaches yawning to all sides of the ascending bauble. Perched upon the temporal gem's top side like houseflies on one pendant ornament of some vast chandelier were tiny specks, blackened to silhouette against the amethystine glow of their surround. The specks were four men and the cracked remains of the now-foundered engine that had brought them here, all lodged atop this faceted and purple stone and, so to speak, marooned.

Kneeling upon the cold, hard smoothness of an upper face of the enormous chiseled bead, Quatermain stared down incredulously at the scenes and shapes that flowed and shifted, seemingly below the surface of the luminous, translucent plain beneath him. Visions of his past, of moments crystallized within the time-gem's substance, merged with visions of what seemed to be his future, vivid and outlandish episodes such as the old adventurer had not previously witnessed in his mortal span thus far, nor even suffered to imagine.

Stark vignettes of incidents that he recalled from travels with his late, lamented friend Sir Henry Curtis blended seamlessly with horrifying glimpses of a life as yet unknown. He saw himself, an opium addicted skeleton, dragged from a heathen drug den by a small but striking-

ly attractive Englishwoman, the prim, cherry-stained rosebud of her lips pursed in a disapproval that seemed constant. He saw himself fighting for his life, aboard some great and frightful skyboat above a dark, benighted city; struggling in the wind-lashed rigging with a large, impossibly-constructed gun that seemed to fire harpoon after harpoon. The woman from the earlier fragment clung against his side, her body pressing to him in the howling night.

The vision shifted. Now he watched a hideous subhuman beast that was absurdly garbed in the remains of what seemed to be formal evening dress, the creature bellowing and laughing hideously as it attacked some great metallic thing that Quatermain could not make visual sense of. More shapes moved against a fire-lit skyline, glinting metal hulks supported on what seemed the spindly legs of monstrous iron flamingos. The explorer had no sooner grasped that he was witnessing some dire, apocalyptic future war when the picture changed.

Now he saw the familiar small, determined woman clad in nothing but a dirty blanket, shrieking, overcome by horror in what looked to Allan's travelled eye like the interior of a dark and rural building, possibly in the Americas. Arcane symbols were inscribed in noxious, nameless fluids on the bare boards of the floor and on the walls, and there was something thrashing over in a distant corner of the room. Quatermain saw himself, screaming as loudly as the woman while engaged in combat with a tentacled and writhing shape that seemed to reach in some way through the walls of the dilapidated farm-house. To his great surprise, another man seemed to be aiding him in this horrendous conflict, whose demeanor Quatermain believed he recognized.

He glanced up from the fascinating and hypnotic vistas swirling on the surface of the gem and looked towards another of the stranded figures trapped there with him on the time-jewel's upper face, the young New England visionary Randolph Carter. Looking back at the horrific

incident depicted in the gem, Quatermain shook his head in disbelief. The man assisting him against the squirming nightmare in the farmhouse was identical to the pale youth that crouched not far from the explorer, staring down into the crystal depths beneath him and absorbed in his own visions, with his long, underlit face transfixed by terror that was luminous. Could it be Quatermain and Carter would meet at some future point in the material world; fighting alongside one another in some as yet unforeseen, unfathomable combat? Was this drifting diamond atoll truly showing things that were, as yet, to come? Were the strange, flickering images that swam in its depths the genuine, predictive sparks that danced across the glittering eye of fate, of fortune and of destiny?

Randolph Carter, lost within his own cascade of vision, groaned with recognition and with longing as there in the jewel before him he saw the familiar vista of his native Arkham, with its gambrel rooftops gilded by the last, long rays of afternoon. To think that, in his mortal form, he slumbered even now in that beloved place, with nothing save his misdirected spirit-self to keep him here upon this glittering plateau of lost souls, where ghostly images of horrors gone or horrors yet to come slithered across the violet surface that he stood upon. Why couldn't he be gone from here, and wake in his New England bed? If only he were stronger-willed, a fearless fellow like his Uncle John...

The elder Carter crouched nearby and gazed in wonderment at scenes of strange red deserts, almost-naked ruby-clad princesses and green, towering men that had too many arms, all flowing through the hard-glazed ground beneath him. Hearing Randolph's groan he glanced up in annoyance at his spineless nephew, only to recoil with some surprise at the alarming realization that the lad was starting to become transparent, as if fading gradually from sight. Why, staring through the young man's stooping body, Captain Carter could quite clearly see the fourth unwilling member of their entourage, the man who'd brought them here and called himself a traveller in time, who tinkered with the damaged framework of his aeon-leaping craft, away on Randolph Carter's further side. The steely-eyed Confederate officer swore softly underneath his breath and called out to his fellows.

"Look there! My young nephew's disappearing from plain sight!"

Quatermain and the tinkering, distracted chrononaut looked up from their diversions to watch in astonishment as the moonstruck and pale New Englander winked finally from view, leaving but three of them there on the priceless, drifting boulder. The Time Traveller seemed mortified, as if the younger Carter's disappearance should have been foreseen.

"I might have known. Since you three are not physically immersed in this dimension as are my machine and I, then when you wake up from your curious dreams, or astral wanderings, or drugged stupors, you will vanish from this place. It's only I myself who must remain here till my engine is repaired."

The grim Confederate officer absorbed this information, glancing wistfully to where the visions of a life to

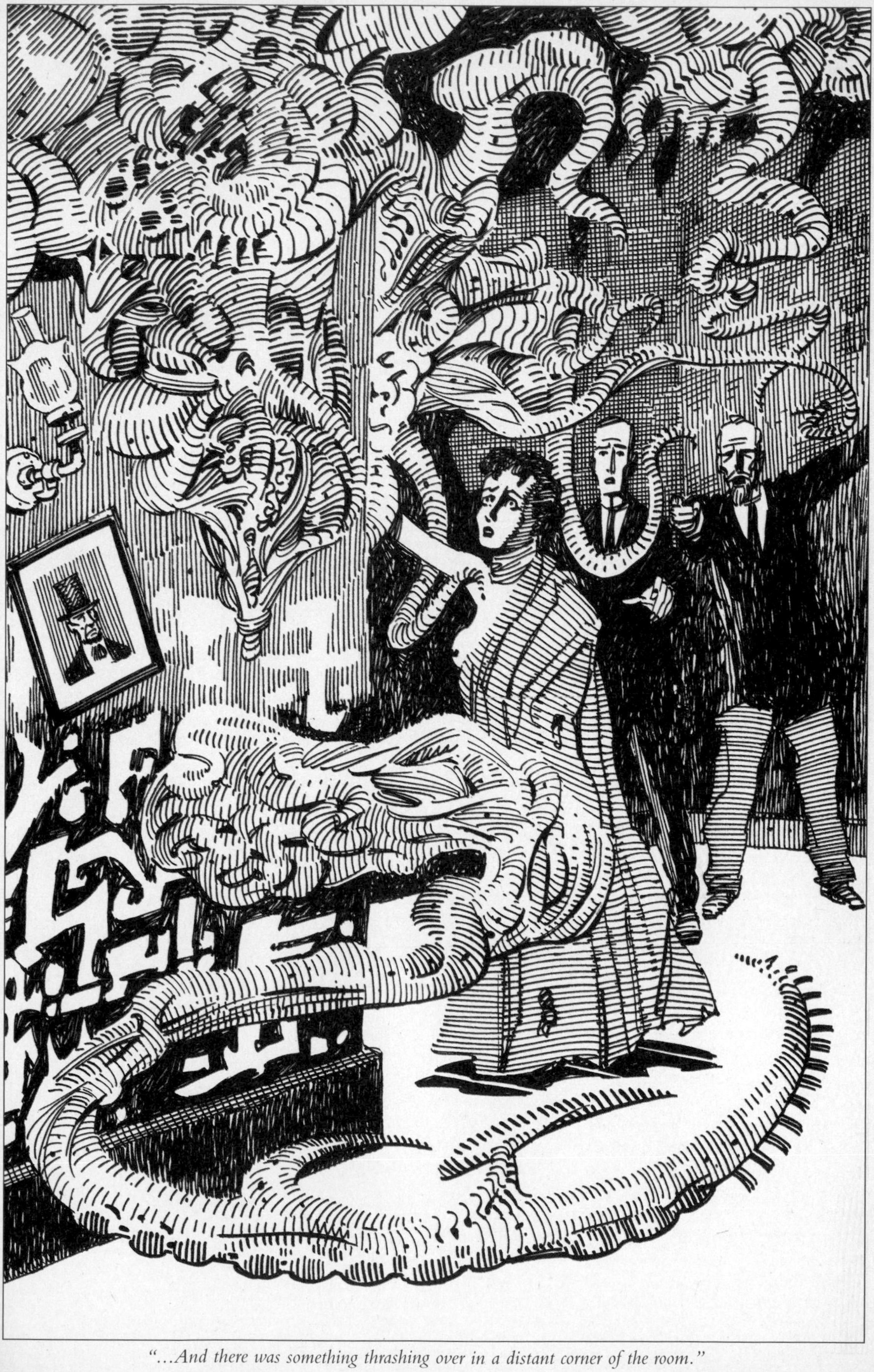

"...And there was something thrashing over in a distant corner of the room."

come still trickled ceaselessly beneath the purpled ice. A dark-eyed woman rode, bare breasted, on a great eight-legged reptile underneath two moons. Somewhere inside him, he made up his mind.

"Look at him! Now the other Carter's going, too!" Quatermain grabbed the traveller's sleeve and pointed to the tall cavalry officer as he became more wraith-like and was, of a sudden, gone from view. The traveller shook his head.

"I wanted to alert you to the threat our cosmos faces from the Universe beyond, where nether-horrors squirm and howl. Now you'll be gone before I can tell you a fraction of the things you'll need to know to aid you when you at last face the adversary."

Quatermain hardly listened, looking back instead to the relentless diorama that unravelled in the violet watch-glass 'neath his heels. The visions there seemed more familiar than they had previously. He saw himself arriving at the ruins of Ragnall Hall, met by the grave Marisa with her candelabra. In another facet of the gem he watched himself inhale the drug then fall into a faint, tended to in his slumber by the servant girl. In still a further surface of the jewel he saw...

"No! God, what monstrosity is this?"

The veteran explorer reeled back from the awful drama that unwound within the crystal here below him. He was filled with the unshakable conviction that he must return to Lady Ragnall's library and his unconscious form. This thought was barely formed before he too began to wax translucent, melting like a fog at dawn from the Time Traveller's disappointed gaze.

The temporal argonaut walked over to the spot upon the surface of the giant precious stone from which his last companion, Quatermain, had lately disappeared. The traveller wondered what had caused that sudden terrified expression in the instants before the adventurer was gone from this reality. He looked down past the gleaming toe-caps of his shoes, into the crystal depths. The image seemed to be of a dilapidated library. Two women, one a Moorish beauty and the other one a wasted crone, were cowering against a wall there at the room of book's far side. Lurching towards them, ghastly in the firelight as it crawled, inverted, like a monstrous crab across the chamber's floor, its lips drawn back to croak strange and unnerving alien syllables was...

The Time Traveller took an involuntary step back from the ghastly image, swallowing hard. This could not be occurring. Why, the elderly explorer had not been gone from his body for more than a moment in the natural world! How could their enemies have struck so quickly? He steeled himself and looked, once more, into the glass.

The hideously contorted body that advanced across the library floor towards the women was clearly the mortal shell of Allan Quatermain. But the grotesque alien intelligence that glared out from the burning, hate-filled eyes...

That wasn't Allan Quatermain at all.

CHAPTER VI.
THE AWAKENING

It had nothing save the dimmest semblance of a self, of an identity. At rest and in its natural state it was one single facet of what might be termed a self-aware idea, a living compound symbol that existed only in the deepest fathoms of the human mind, or in the strange, unbounded immaterial oceans that those depths afforded access to. Those few explorers, be they lunatic or warlock or philosopher, who'd sought to sound these eerie, insubstantial territories and to catalogue the entities they found there, had identified the over-arcing idea-colony and had given it a name. They called it Yuggoth. They perceived it, variously, as a planet, as a god, or as a state of mind.

The myriad lesser notions which comprised this hive-like meta-being were in turn seen as subsidiary deities, who functioned both as avatars and envoys to the central, hideously animate conceptual core. These individual agents were collectively termed Lloigor, with a separate name ascribed to each, a different range of attributes. To each was allocated its own species of subservient elementals, subjugated to its alien will.

The creature that was currently enjoying the sensations of material form there in the fire-lit library of half-ruined Ragnall Hall was then, in a sense, not one but rather several overlapping gels of consciousness, of self. Somewhere within it, it was Yuggoth, the mother-complex of insidious alien ideas that drifted in the dark backwaters of the human mind and soul. Upon a lower, more immediate level it was the Lloigor named Ithaqqa, worshipped in the arctic regions as a demon of the upper air, or of the intellectual faculty in man. Most intimately, in as much as one might say that it was capable of understanding anything, it understood itself to be a nameless elemental of the kind known as wind-walkers, or sometimes as Wendigo.

In its customary habitat, which was a timeless, blissful vortex of deep, curdled indigo, its shape and form were like the astral counterpart of some repulsive gorgeous hybrid between the crustacean and the coelenterate. From its light-beaded upper canopy of jellyfish-frilled skirts depended long and trailing many-jointed legs, cased in an iridescent chitin. While at rest, the thing existed in an infinite continuum of perfect and delirious pleasure, but, at this current place and moment in the fields of space-time, it was not by any means at rest. It was at work, and active in the solid, awkward world of flesh and matter.

The body it inhabited had an unpleasant warmth; a soft, five-pointed star of rind and pulp enclosing a strange, spider-like machinery of brittle bone. An awful heaviness weighed everywhere about it in its new surroundings, and it first failed to comprehend how such a delicate, unwieldy organism might be made to move at all. While tugging randomly at nerves and muscles in the leaden darkness that surrounded it, it chanced to raise what seemed to be twin shutter-mechanisms covering the host-creature's optic sensors. Light and form and colour flooded in, a stunning and incomprehensible deluge.

It seemed to be within an enclosed cube of perfectly transparent gas constrained by flat plane surfaces of solid and material substance, overhead, below, and to all sides. Within this area were other forms, apparently inanimate, and two separate shapes, five pointed in the manner of the elemental creature's current host, that moved, and from which hateful, high-pitched noises issued. Lifting itself up as best it could upon the bone struts radiating from its central body-mass, the Wendigo began to crawl across the cold, hard surface there beneath it, as it made its way towards the chamber's other living beings, to investigate. To see what they were made of.

Allan Quatermain was falling, in a gemmed glissade of sheer and whirling brilliance, tumbling from the weird ethereous latitudes in which he had so lately travelled, back towards the mortal plane where his corporeal form, vacated of its spirit, sprawled insensate on the parquet floor of Lady Ragnall's crumbling library.

In his discorporate wanderings, the explorer had seemed to encounter other displaced souls, encamping with them, ultimately, on the upper surface of a massive and bewildering time-gem in whose depths disturbing glimpses of present and future were made visible. Just such a glimpse, of the horrific circumstances currently back there in the mortal world at Ragnall Hall, had spurred the numinous adventurer to take flight back to the material realm and his abandoned flesh, before it was too late.

Below him now, if there was any such thing as below in the directionless cascade of which he was a part, Quatermain saw an image, small at first, of the familiar, book-lined, hearth-lit room where he had quaffed the bitter and transporting fumes of the exotic drug taduki, it seemed an eternity ago. By concentrating on this scene of relative stability within the furious metaphysic flow about him, Allan found that he was able to propel himself towards it, so that it appeared to swell about him, opening to enfold him in the mundane petals of that human room, that human moment.

The frenetic, howling tumult of the psychic flow about him ceased. Quatermain floated, an invisible and disembodied wraith, at a point just below the reassuringly firm-looking and familiar ceiling of the library. Turning his attentions to the drama being acted out beneath him on that hellishly-illuminated stage, the famous hunter's most phatasmagoric apprehensions were in one stark instant realized.

Crawling through the leaping, page-strewn shadows of the library floor, arched over backwards like a monstrous quadrupedal crab, its head and face inverted so that the familiar features found a new and alien context with the rolling eyes below the grimacing, contorting gash that was its mouth, the recklessly abandoned mortal shell of Allan Quatermain had clearly become host to a new and most decidedly unwelcome tenant.

Sat bolt upright on her makeshift bed there at the chamber's centre Allan saw the frail and bird-like Lady Ragnall screaming, shrill with panic, as the horribly contorted and possessed form of the great explorer moved with an unsettling and arachnid-like deliberation towards the dowager and her imposing maidservant, the statuesque Marisa. This proud beauty of the Africas stood fast between her mistress and the nightmare which advanced upon them both through the deceptive, flickering fire-glow, her hands moving in what Quatermain assumed to be magical gestures, these accompanied by rapid streams of incantation from the woman's full, dark lips. She seemed to be attempting to repel the hostile and invasive spirit that had taken residence within the skin of the adventurer, resorting in extremity to ancient charms and rituals of banishment drawn from the long traditions of her people, who had known the drug taduki since time immemorial.

The spells and imprecations seemed to have no visible effect upon the progress of his stolen body as it lurched and creaked across the floor towards the frightened women. Quatermain feared that whatever strange intelligence was currently residing in his borrowed flesh was one from far outside the witch-woman's experience, or, indeed, her wildest dreams. He feared, further to this, that he himself knew with precision what had commandeered his empty shell.

During his sojourn outside the perimeters of ordinary reality, he had encountered a most enigmatic individual known only as "The Time Traveller." This personage had sought to alert Allan and the astral crew that Quatermain had by then fallen in with to the dangers of a monstrous, alien threat from outside our familiar Universe. It seemed now, to the bodiless and hovering adventurer, as if these otherworldly forces had enjoined in a precautionary attack upon such mortals as might serve to hinder their infernal and unfathomable design.

The crawling travesty had by now reached the desperately incanting servant woman. One of its hands, contorted to a crab-like claw, lashed out to fasten viciously upon the ankle of the ebon beauty, fingernails pressed hard into her skin and drawing blood. Its eyes glared, mad with hatred, in that almost unfamiliar and inverted face. It snapped its teeth together with a dreadful clacking sound that left the floating, disembodied Quatermain with no illusion as to its intentions. If he did not wish to witness his own body as it murdered and attempted to devour two helpless women, then he must act quickly. Working solely from his instincts, as he'd done through his entire career, he mustered such resources as there were in his ethereal form and dived towards his capering and stolen flesh.

To be immersed in mortal form again, the hot breath whistling his lungs, was as profound a shock as to plunge suddenly into an icy pool. More shocking still was the appalling, hideous sensation of a body shared, the sense that he was not completely alone inside his skin. No sooner had his astral self re-entered the familiar contours of his earthly frame than Allan felt himself attacked by something that was with him in that previously inviolate and personal darkness. A brief impression came to him of mollusc-sticky ruffs and rills, of clattering, many jointed legs that scrabbled frantically for purchase on his psychic essence, yet he found that he could not construct a picture of exactly what he wrestled with. It was, perhaps, the very pinnacle of fear, as if one were tied fast inside a lightless sack with some unknown and vicious jungle beast for company. He screamed, and there in his interior blackness, something screamed beside him.

As the suddenly convulsing body of their guest released its painful hold upon her ankle, bloodied fingers clawing at the air, Marisa gasped and took a step back. She gazed down with uncomprehending horror at the old man's body as it thrashed and writhed and twisted at her feet. Quatermain seemed to scratch and slap at his own face, as in a paroxysm of self-disgust. Foam-spattered lips worked, upside down, upon that crazed, contorted face, and yet it seemed as if not one but two unearthly, anguished howls were issued from within.

Remembering her mistress suddenly, Marisa glanced behind her at the shape slumped in the hollow of the face-to-face divans. The thin, emaciated hand was raised across the sunken breast, that neither rose nor fell, to clutch the fabric of the dowager's robe into a crumpled rose above the heart. The eyes stared, empty, into flame-licked emptiness and with a cold, dull pang Marisa understood that Lady Ragnall was no more among the living. Though the dowager had, through the long years of Marisa's service, grown to be more of a companion than employer, the dark beauty could spare no more than an instant in regret for Lady Ragnall's passing. There were more immediate matters that must be attended to, if she and Quatermain were not to follow her late mistress to the land of shades. Steeling herself, she returned her attention to the thrashing and possessed form at her feet.

Quatermain's features and the agonised expression stretched across them seemed to flow and flicker in the hearth-light, so that for an instant it would be the face of the explorer Marisa saw, with human pain and panic shining from his eyes, only to be replaced in the next moment by a grimacing, contorting travesty, in whose gaze only murder and appalling knowledge burned. Marisa thought that, at the last, she understood what had occurred.

Conditions such as this had been described by her own tribesmen in relation to taduki-usage, part of their accumulated lore about the subject, but Marisa noted, only in the very oldest and most sinister of their traditions did they speak of monstrous possessions such as Quatermain seemed to be presently in thrall to. When they spoke of such they would refer to the phenomenon by a variety of names, and all these names, Marisa understood, spoke only of one thing: Great Old Ones. Fruit of Yuggoth. Lloigor. Creatures from beyond the rational boundaries of Being, hoverers upon the edge of space and time that sought for nothing save an entry to the human world, that they might claim it as their own. These many names were never mentioned by Marisa's people without a reflexive movement of the hand, the sketching of a talismanic symbol in the air to ward away malignant influence. Wild-eyed, the tall obsidian beauty looked about her for a scrap of paper and some writing tools with which she might construct this "Elder Sign" herself and in this manner aid the man who writhed and twisted like a landed fish upon the library floor before her.

She ripped out the empty flyleaf from a book of Swinburne's poetry that was nearby, and plucking up a letter knife, attempted to draw blood from her own hand with which she might inscribe the necessary prophylactic hieroglyph. As she did so, Quatermain rolled over in his paroxysm, shuddering and roaring in his hideous battle with himself. One of his flailing legs thrashed out and, in its passing, knocked one of the larger blazing books from its position in the hearth, onto the parquet floor. The spiteful tongues of flame licked up towards the dry and brittle pages of the other tomes that lined the chamber's walls. Marisa cursed, and knew that she had even less time to accomplish that which needed to be done. The paper-knife moved once, decisively, across her palm, and as the blood welled up, Marisa dipped her finger in it, as a stylus, and began to scrawl her scarlet ritual marks upon the torn-out page.

Quatermain was in Hell. He knew, with a despairing certainty, that his was not the stronger of the warring personalities that skirmished in his flesh. The drive and fury of the ectoplasmic foe's attack had the implacable, unreasoning intensity of a typhoon or hurricane. Another moment, Allan knew, would see his very soul torn up and shredded, made to so much spiritual confetti by the dozen clawing, scrabbling arms of his attacker. As the utter essence of him was dragged bloodied to the howling threshold of annihilation, Quatermain was all but unaware that there about him, Lady Ragnall's library had begun to burn as if in an approximation of the purgatory in which he knew himself to be.

Afraid to get too close to the explorer's whirling arms lest she be blinded, stunned, or made by other means incapable, Marisa hoped that she had drawn her hasty

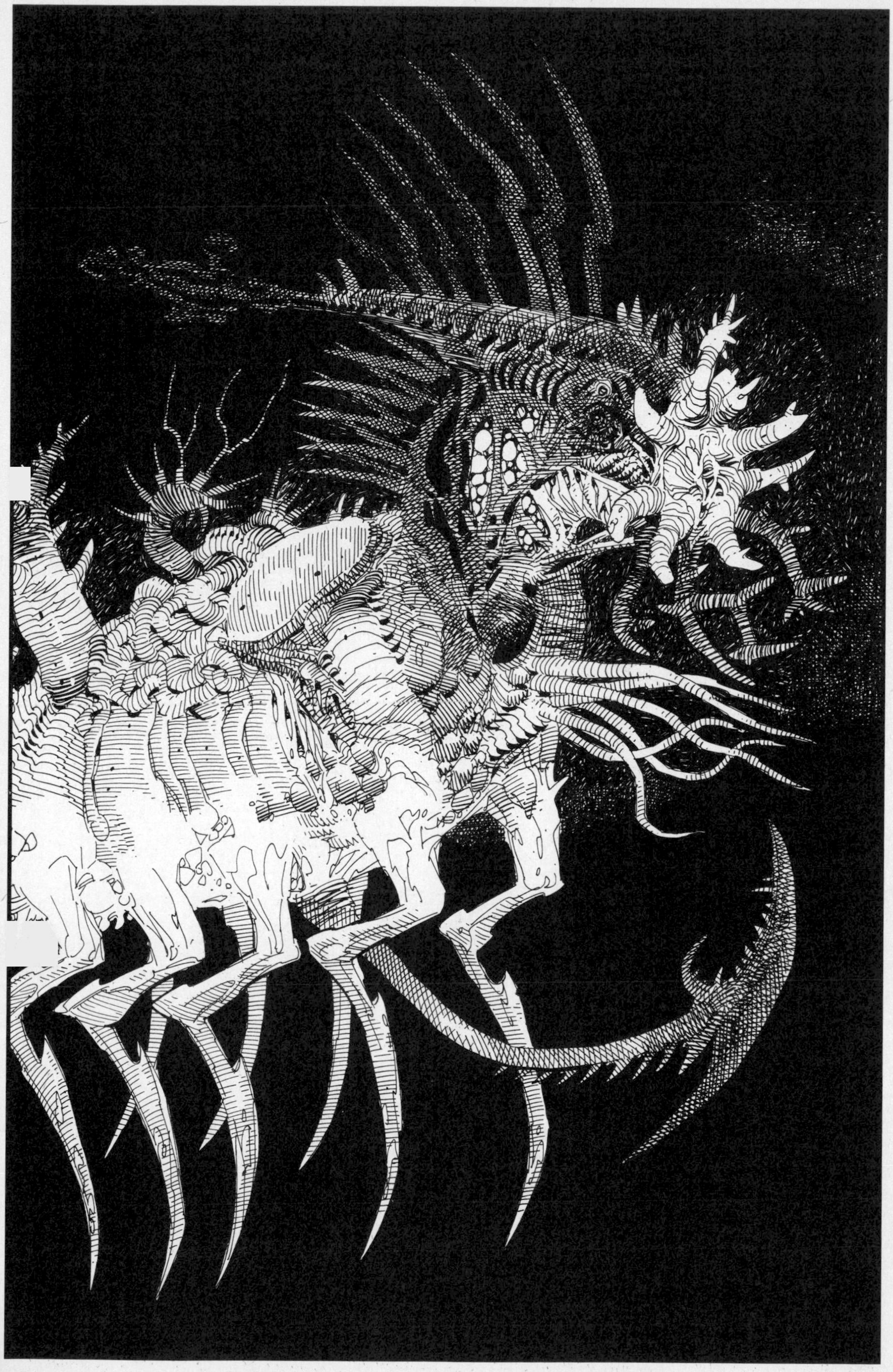

"A brief impression came to him of mollusc-sticky ruffs and rills..."

talisman correctly. Carmine lines described a seven-pointed star, with, at its centre, the hooked sun-wheel sacred to the Vedic faiths. Summoning all her courage, she lunged forward, shouting ancient names of power as she pressed the ensanguined scrap to the explorer's perspiration-beaded brow.

Quatermain screamed, the blackness about him all of a sudden pierced by a strange, esoteric mark, limned in red fire, whose radiance was blasting, devastating, terrible. He screamed, but that which was beside him in the blackness screamed much louder, with an urgency that sounded almost mortal. Boiling up out of his mind, his body, the possessing creature was, for a bare instant visible to human sight. Marisa gasped and took a step back, marveling at the shimmering display of bilious light that hung above the still-convulsing form of the adventurer. It was a thing of undulating veils, grotesquely mobile and articulated pincers, wavering in centipede-like unison. The sparks of brightness next became an after-image of themselves, a rash of coloured blotches spreading on the retina, and then were gone.

Marisa helped the dazed and mumbling explorer to his feet, then did her best to steer the pair of them out from the blazing library to the chill terraces and lawns beyond the confines of the fire-doomed mansion. Quatermain sprawled, resting with his back against a dark and hulking tree-stump in the manor grounds, the leaping flame-light of the burning building dancing in his glazed and staring eyes. Tearing a strip from her long gown to quell the bleeding from her palm, the servant girl considered, at some length, what she should do about the clearly traumatised adventurer.

He was, quite evidently, cursed. Amongst Marisa's tribe it was well known that those who earned the enmity of the Great Old Ones from outside of time and space would, in all likelihood, be plagued continually by these deathless and malicious entities for the remainder of their lives. To be in close proximity to persons so afflicted was to risk calling the dire attentions of the Old Ones down upon one's self. Marisa's safest course of action was, unfortunately, all too plain. Staring, mesmerised and horror-stricken, at the conflagration that devoured both Lady Ragnall's homestead and, somewhere inside, the dowager herself, Quatermain did not notice as Marisa took her leave. He was not destined to encounter her again, nor would he ever more experience the drug which she alone had access to, that terrible and captivating render of reality known in the world's most occult, twilight corners as taduki.

Of course, all this was years ago.

Quatermain barely now remembered that appalling night, or the disorienting morning after when he found himself, ill and amnesiac, stumbling through the grounds surrounding the burned-out remains of Lady Ragnall's manor. The black, enigmatic servant woman and her cache of the drug that Quatermain now hungered for were nowhere to be found.

Allan had drifted, as a tramp, to London, and from there had worked his passage to the Middle East, where opium was plentiful and would to some degree assuage the pain of separation from the old adventurer's preferred

narcotic, the sublime taduki. Now he floated in a carefree, amniotic darkness, possibly in some side street of Cairo, though in truth, he cared not where he was. The only flaw in the explorer's artificial paradise was the persistent female voice that seemed to penetrate his reverie, demanding his attention, begging him to wake. Reluctantly, he let his eyes creak open.

She was beautiful. And yet the pursed, prim rosebud mouth, the carefully bound-up black hair all kindled in the world weary explorer's breast a pang of faint alarm, of recognition. Had he seen this face before, and if so, where? In the insensible, drug fuddled depths of Allan's mind sounded a chime of deep unease, a chill and shiver-bringing wind blown through the veil, the curtains that surround our narrow, mortal premises. He did not know this woman, did not want to face the fraught, precarious future that he sensed she represented.

"Go away," he slurred, then once more closed his eyes.

But she did not go away.

And everything occurred, according to its course.

THE END

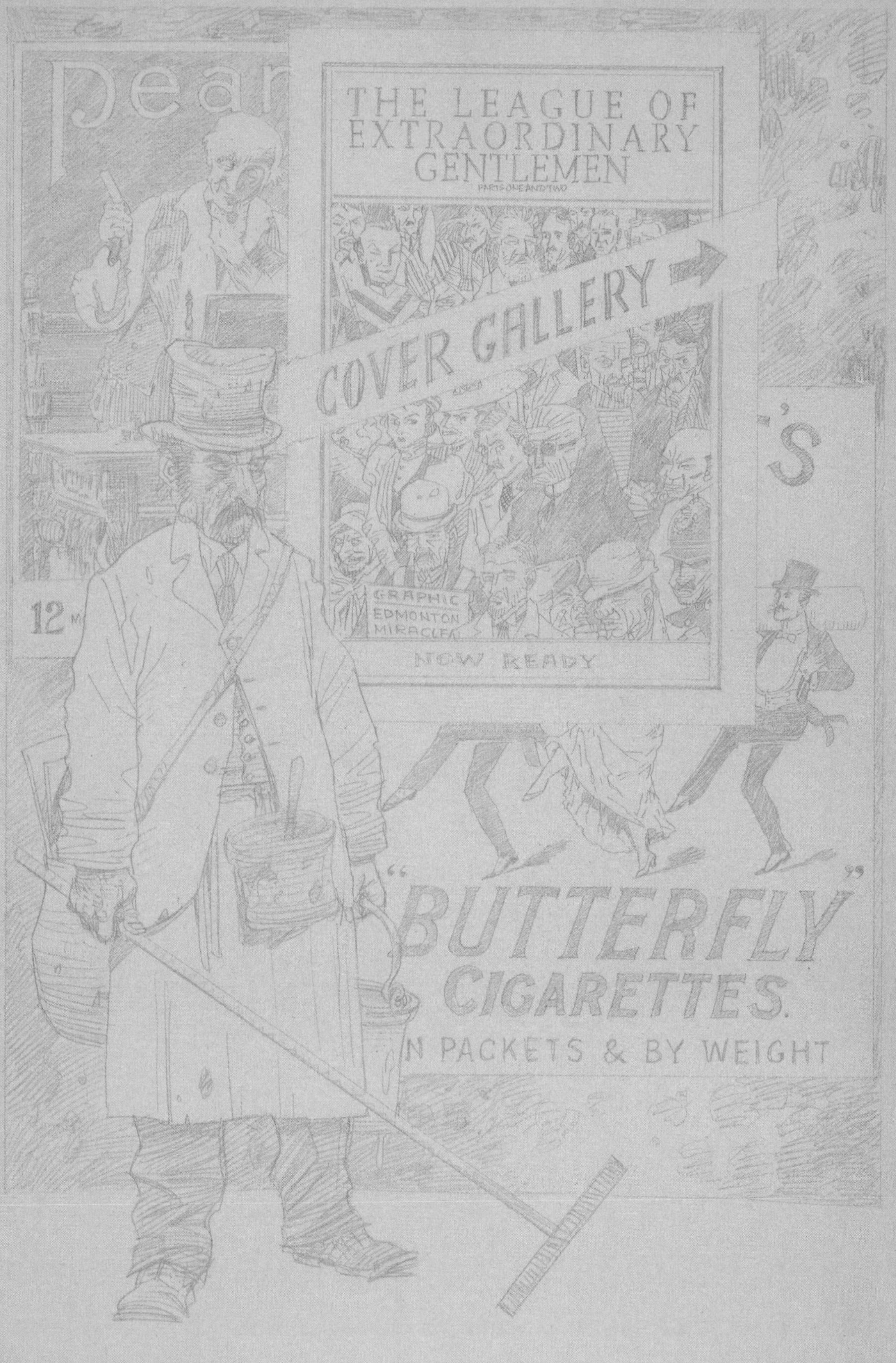
Pear
THE LEAGUE OF
EXTRAORDINARY
GENTLEMEN
PARTS ONE AND TWO
COVER GALLERY
GRAPHIC
EDMONTON
MIRACLE
NOW READY
'S
12
"BUTTERFLY"
CIGARETTES.
N PACKETS & BY WEIGHT

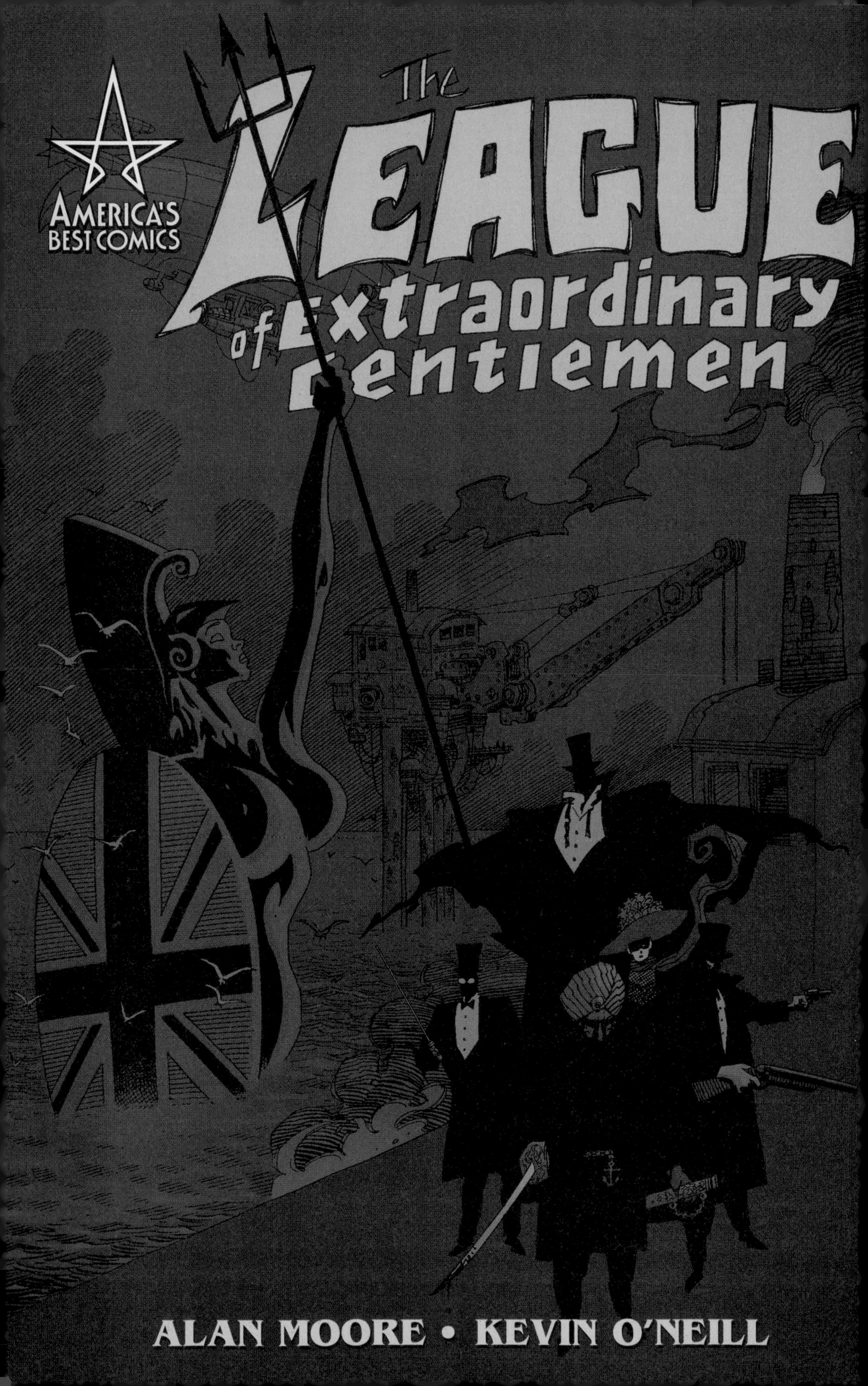
AMERICA'S BEST COMICS
The League of Extraordinary Gentlemen
ALAN MOORE • KEVIN O'NEILL

No. 1 of a GRAND NEW PICTURE PAPER

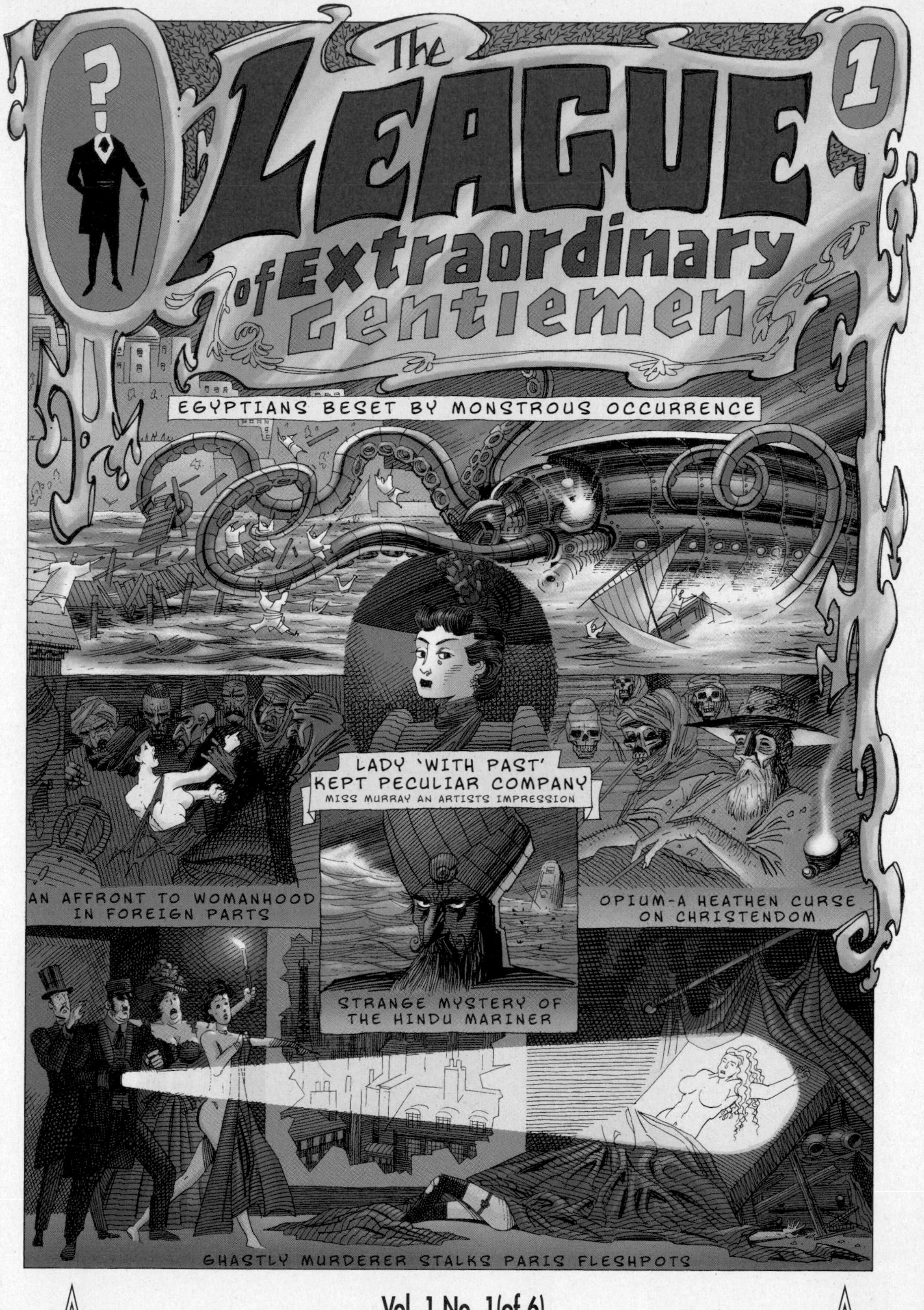
?
1
The LEAGUE of Extraordinary Gentlemen
EGYPTIANS BESET BY MONSTROUS OCCURRENCE
LADY 'WITH PAST' KEPT PECULIAR COMPANY
MISS MURRAY AN ARTISTS IMPRESSION
AN AFFRONT TO WOMANHOOD IN FOREIGN PARTS
OPIUM-A HEATHEN CURSE ON CHRISTENDOM
STRANGE MYSTERY OF THE HINDU MARINER
GHASTLY MURDERER STALKS PARIS FLESHPOTS

Vol. 1 No. 1(of 6)

by ALAN MOORE & KEVIN O'NEILL

AMERICA'S BEST COMICS

Published for the proprietors by America's Best Comics

AMERICA'S BEST COMICS

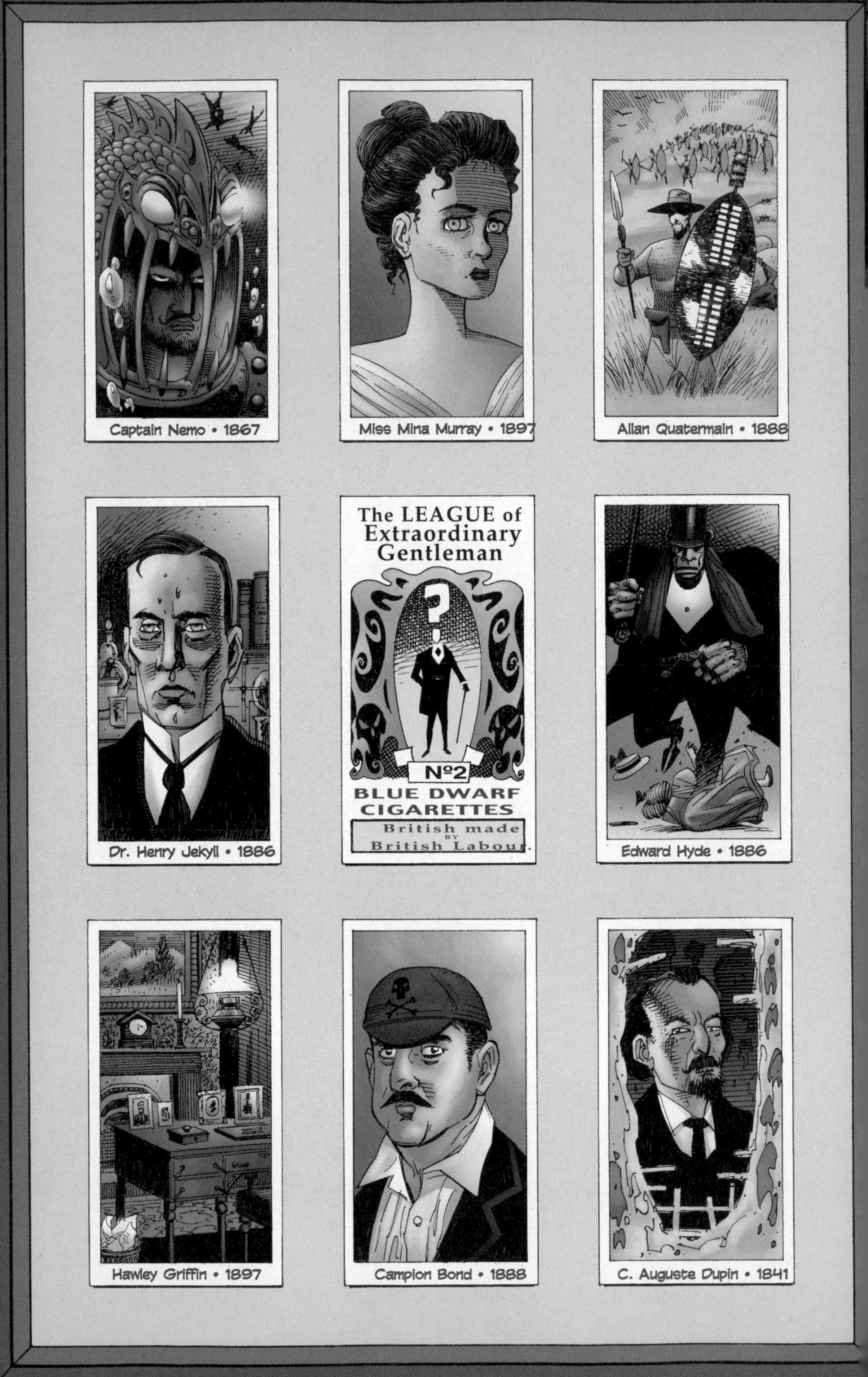
Captain Nemo • 1867
Miss Mina Murray • 1897
Allan Quatermain • 1888
The LEAGUE of Extraordinary Gentleman
?
Nº2
BLUE DWARF CIGARETTES
British made BY British Labour.
Dr. Henry Jekyll • 1886
Edward Hyde • 1886
Hawley Griffin • 1897
Campion Bond • 1888
C. Auguste Dupin • 1841

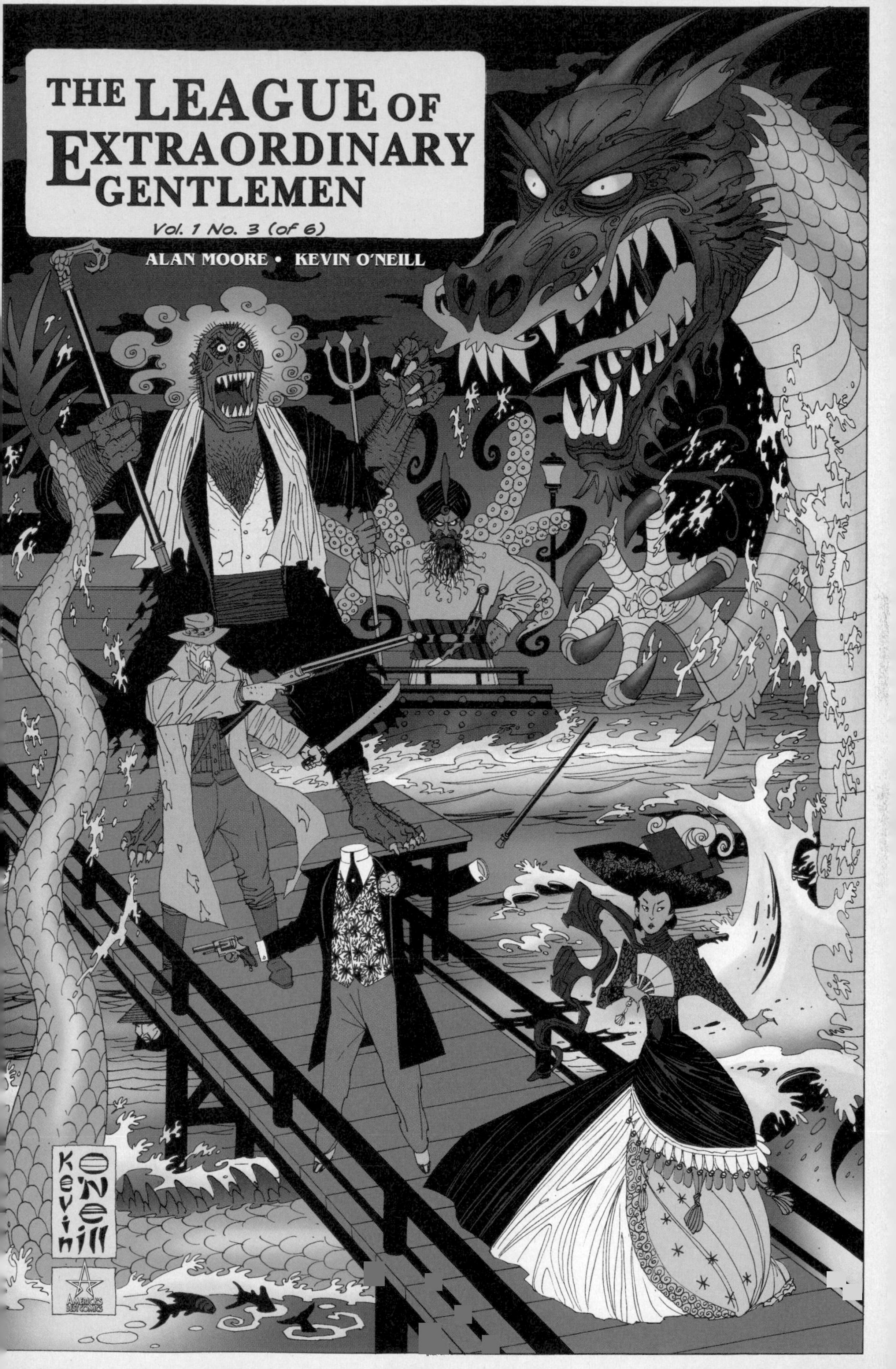
THE LEAGUE OF EXTRAORDINARY GENTLEMEN
Vol. 1 No. 3 (of 6)
ALAN MOORE • KEVIN O'NEILL
kevin o'neill
America's Best Comics

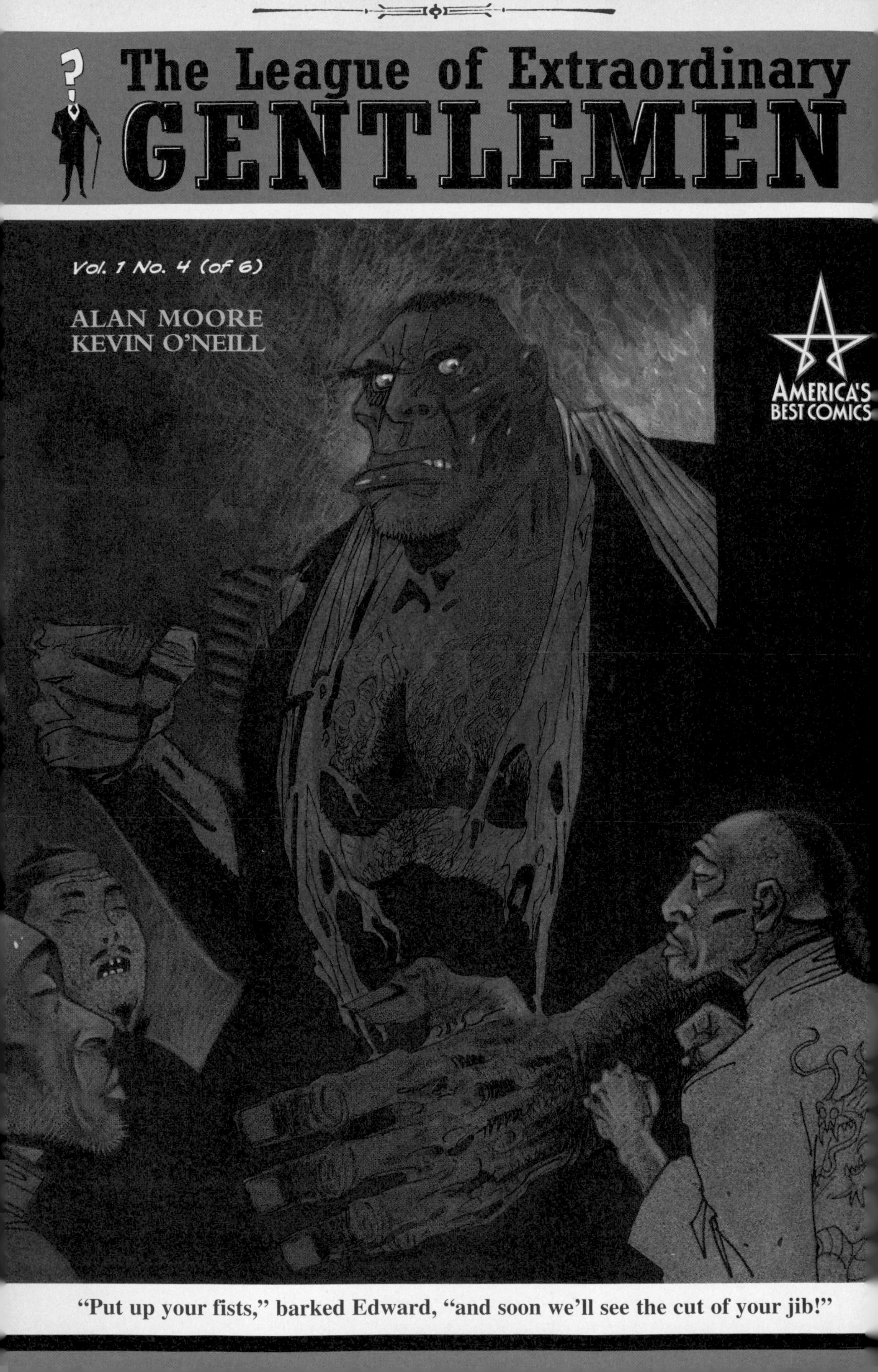
The League of Extraordinary
GENTLEMEN
Vol. 1 No. 4 (of 6)
ALAN MOORE
KEVIN O'NEILL
AMERICA'S
BEST COMICS
"Put up your fists," barked Edward, "and soon we'll see the cut of your jib!"

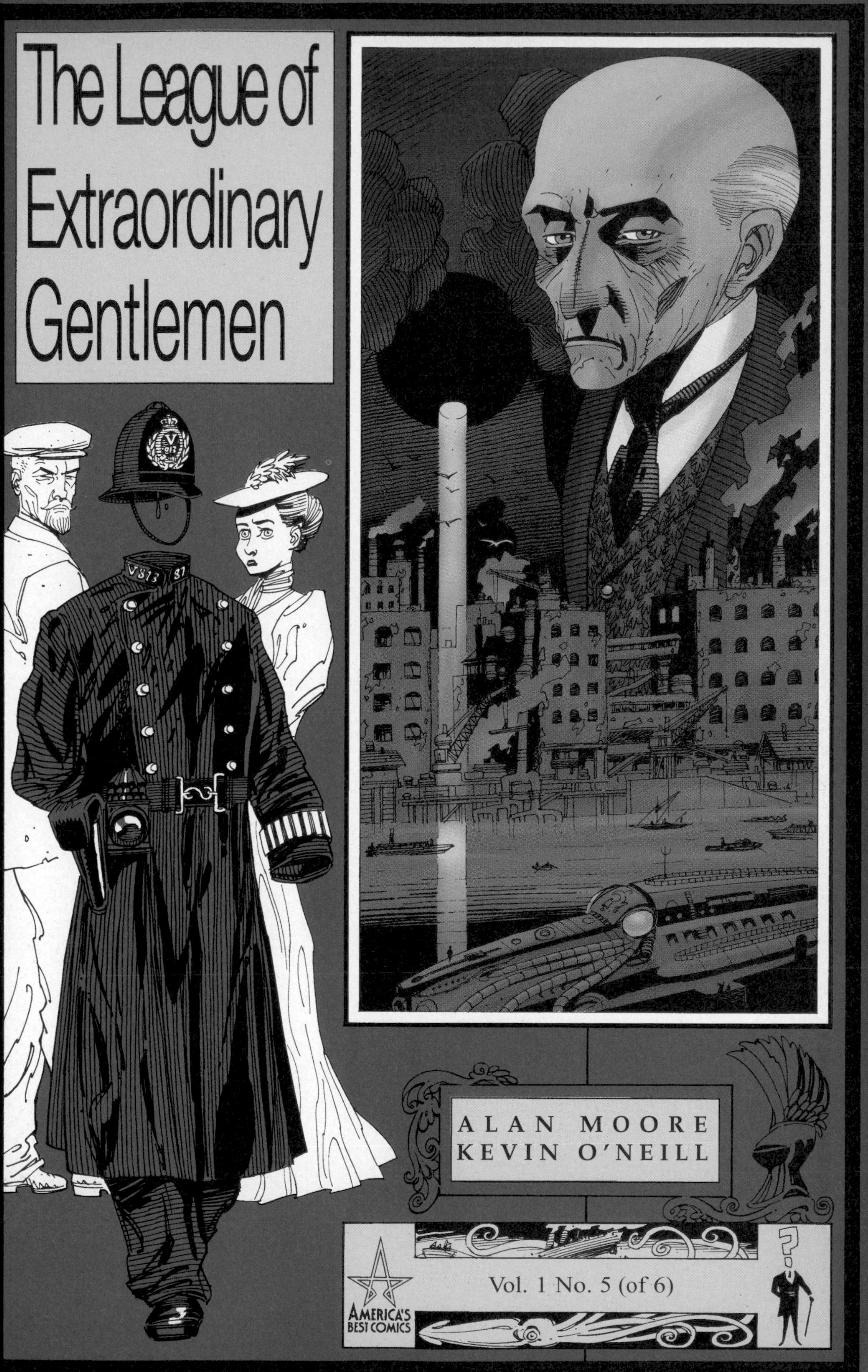
The League of Extraordinary Gentlemen
ALAN MOORE
KEVIN O'NEILL
Vol. 1 No. 5 (of 6)
AMERICA'S BEST COMICS

OGDEN'S "TAB" CIGARETTES IN PENNY PACKETS CONTAINING 5

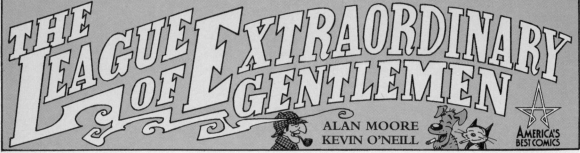

THE LEAGUE OF EXTRAORDINARY GENTLEMEN

ALAN MOORE
KEVIN O'NEILL

AMERICA'S BEST COMICS

VOL. 1 No 6 (OF 6) SEPTEMBER

"THROUGH TRUSTING IN A PORTLY GENT – OUR CHUMS HAVE AN EMBARRASSMENT"

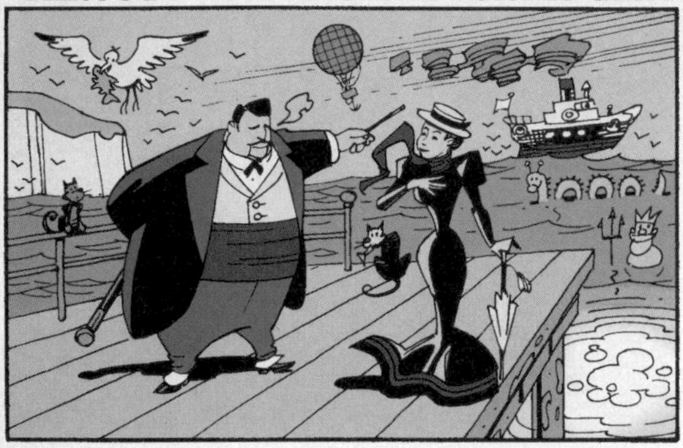

Meeting Miss Murray on the pier, stout Mister Bond cooed in her ear
"You must leave for a foreign land, there to enlist a doughty band
Who'll serve our country and our Queen! To Egypt, now, by Submarine!"
So, aided by a foreign gent (a Naval captain), off she went!

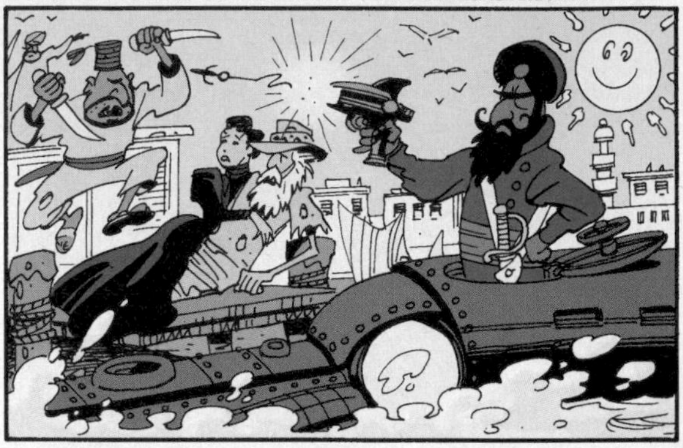

In Egypt, from the addict's pain, they rescued Mr. Quatermain.
Taking him with them 'neath the sea as they embarked for Gay Paree!
In Paris, they were satisfied to nab the beastly Edward Hyde
Then sail him back to Albion fair, awaiting further orders there.

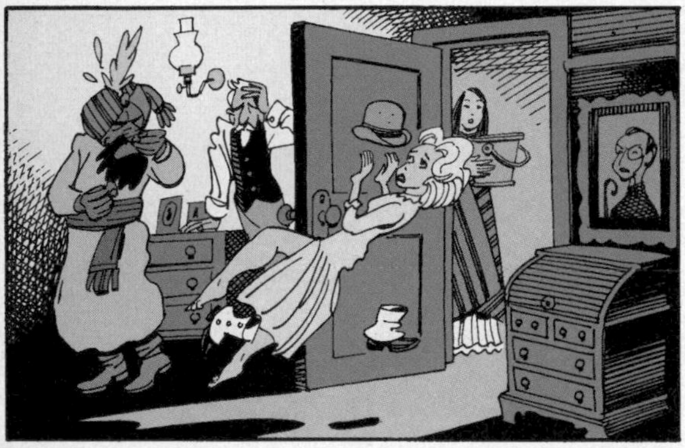

They found their last chum in - what fun! - a girl's school in North Edmonton!
With Griffin taken firm in hand, our extraordinary band
Discover the outrageous plan of crafty Johnny Chinaman
Who's stolen Blighty's Cavorite - a metal with the power of flight!

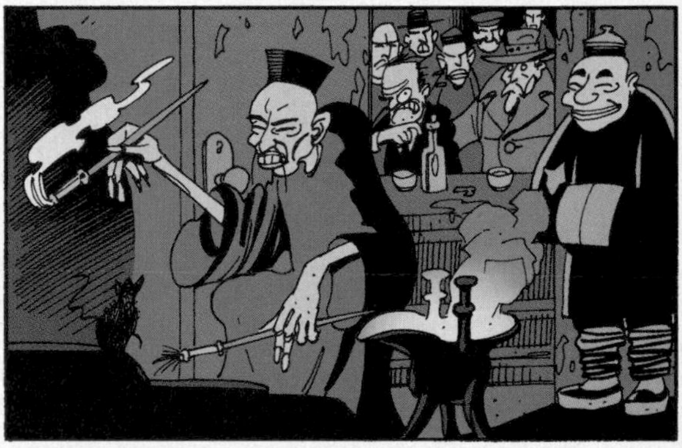

In Limehouse, at the arch-fiends lair, they end his mastery of the air,
And see the mystery element returned to England's Government.
In river-tunnels deep as night, they seek the fearful Cavorite
So that they can at once abscond with it to give to Mr. Bond.

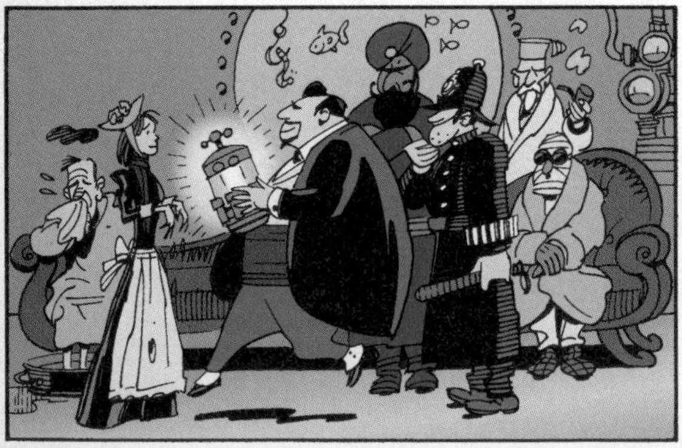

The chubby fellow's filled with glee! "You've all done jolly well!" says he.
"Take this reward and have some nosh, a slap-up meal at *Maison Posh*!
The Cavorite, with great relief, I'll give to Mr. "M", my chief.
He'll be delighted, I just know! Still, simply must dash! Cheerio!"

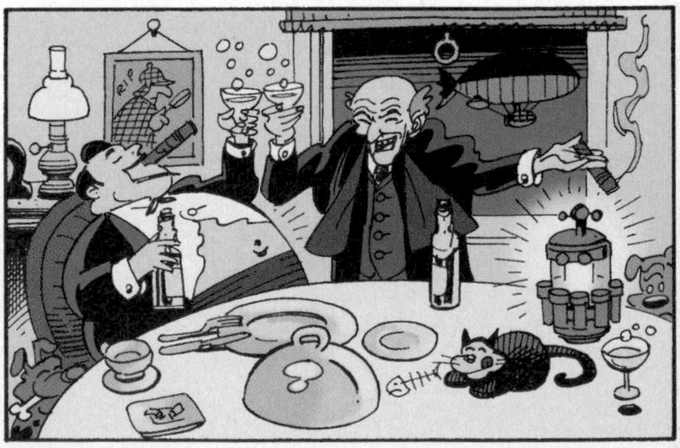

But wait! What's this? "M", all this time, was the Napoleon of Crime!
Professor Moriarty cries "Tonight, my Chinese rival dies!
I'll simply bomb East London flat, see what the blighter makes of that!"
Horrors! How can our comrades win? To learn the answer, seek within...

THE LEAGUE OF EXTRAORDINARY GENTLEMEN

PARTS ONE AND TWO

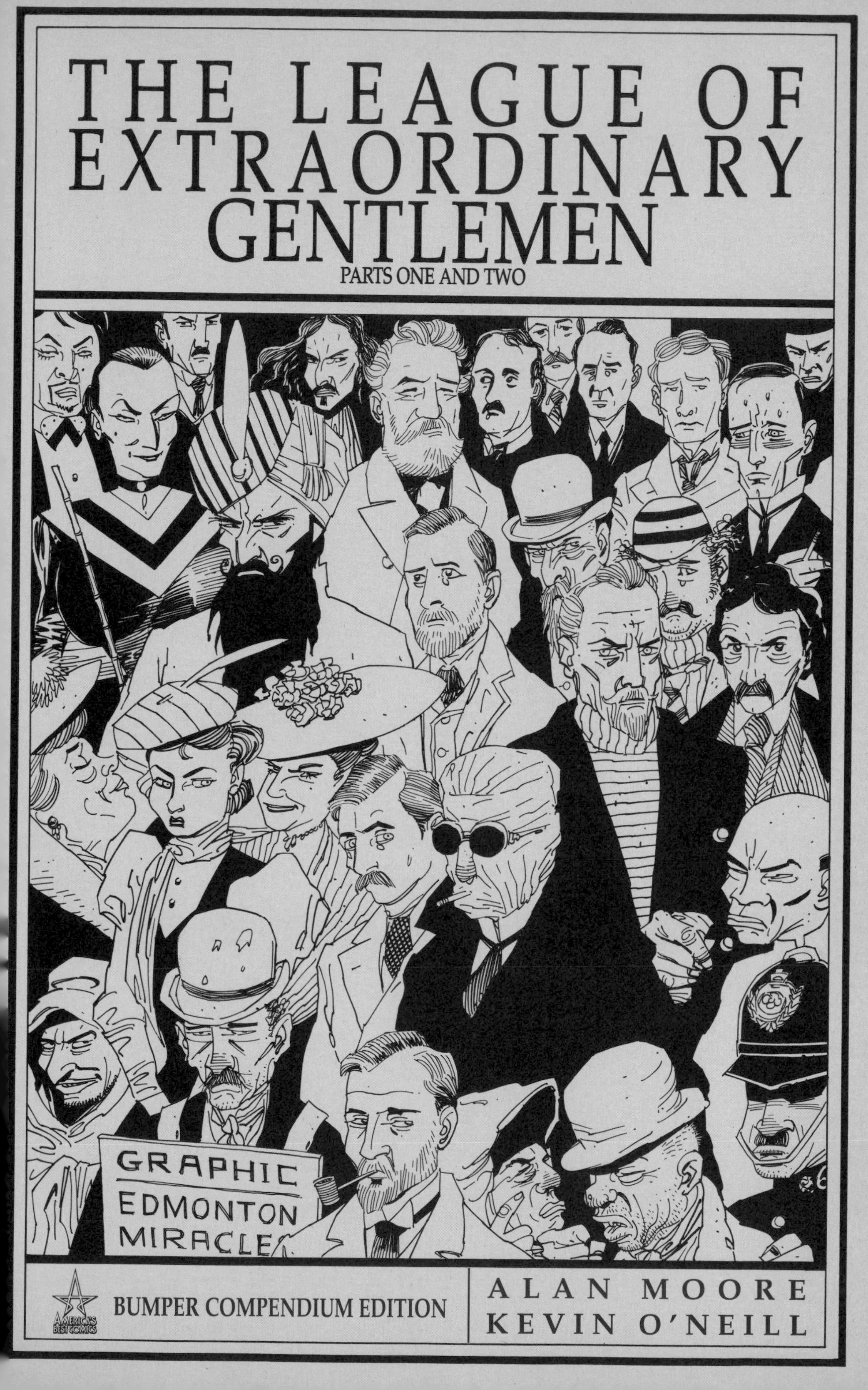

GRAPHIC
EDMONTON MIRACLE

BUMPER COMPENDIUM EDITION

ALAN MOORE
KEVIN O'NEILL

THE LEAGUE OF EXTRAORDINARY GENTLEMEN

BUMPER COMPENDIUM EDITION
PARTS THREE AND FOUR

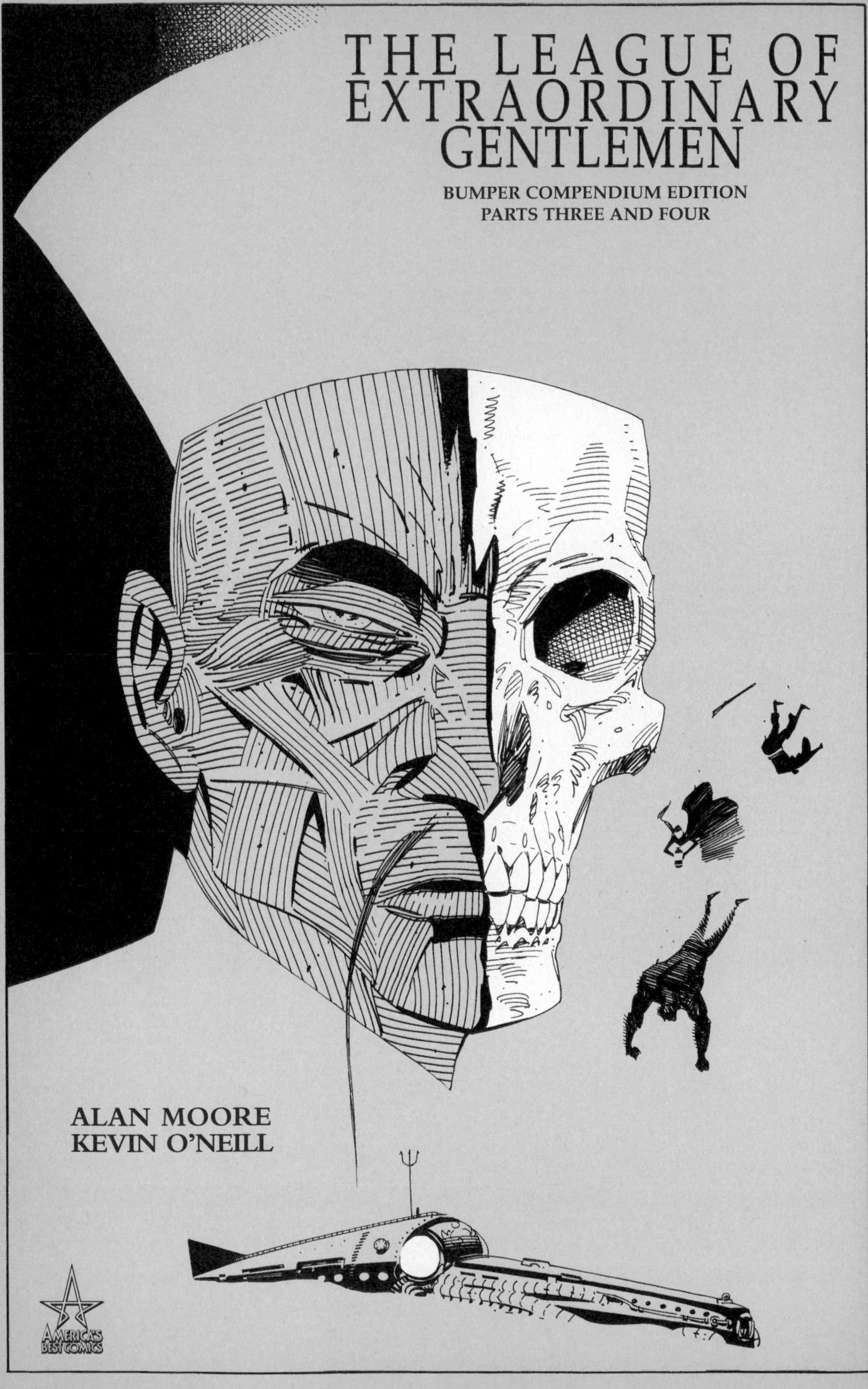

ALAN MOORE
KEVIN O'NEILL

AMERICA'S BEST COMICS

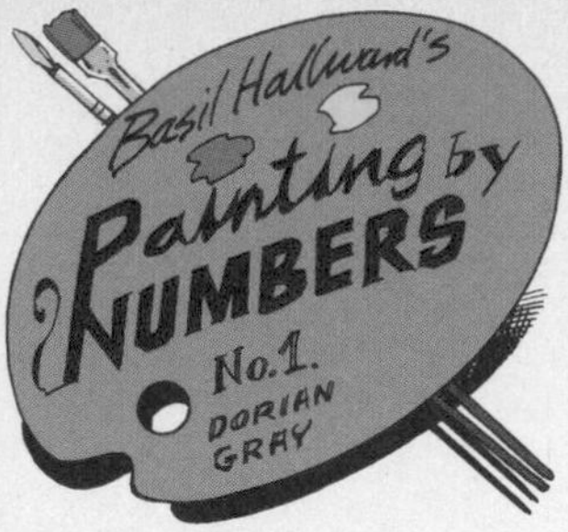
Basil Hallward's
Painting by
NUMBERS
No. 1.
DORIAN
GRAY

This innovative painting-made-simple concept is that of the noted artist Basil Hallward, who had intended, prior to his unfortunate disappearance, that this should be the first in a line of portraits-by-numbers, produced with children or the amateur painter in mind.

Simply paint in the colours, as numbered, then leave the resultant work in an attic for some years while you pursue a life of insobriety, petty crime and whoring. To see if your efforts measure up to those of the artist himself, we refer you to Mr. Hallward's finished portrait on the second page following.

1. light anemia
2. human flesh (smoked)
3. pustule yellow
4. gingivitic pink
5. duodenal green
6. pale verdigris
7. gravemoss
8. moral grey
9. charnel ash grey
10. light hypothermia
11. dysentery green
12. monoxide blue
13. fetter-rust
14. old dialysis gold
15. butcher's slab pink
16. child-molester's eyes cerulean
17. miasma
18. medium headstone
19. spoiled fruit sienna
20. fingernail grey

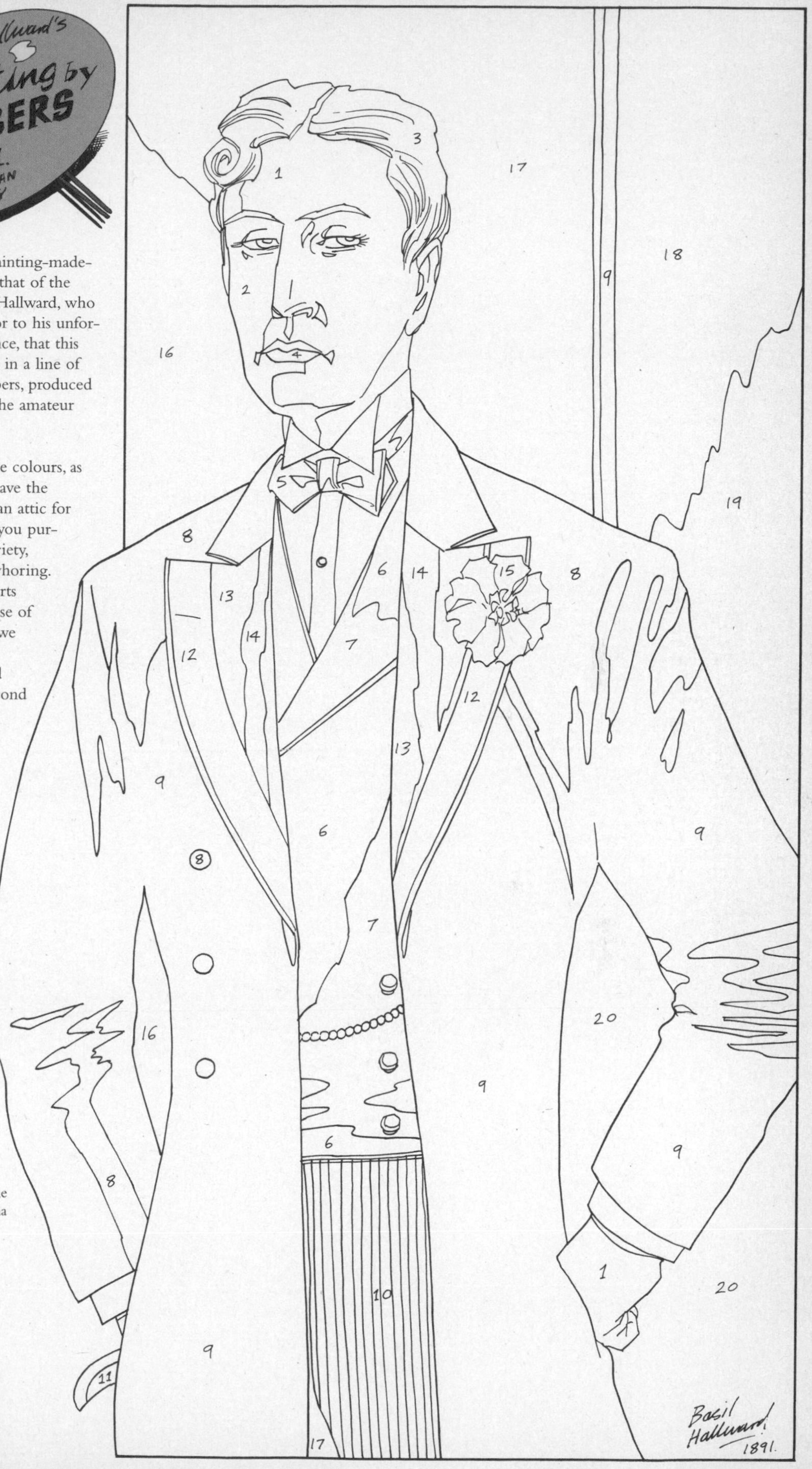
Basil Hallward!
1891.

THE VELOCI-MIDDEN

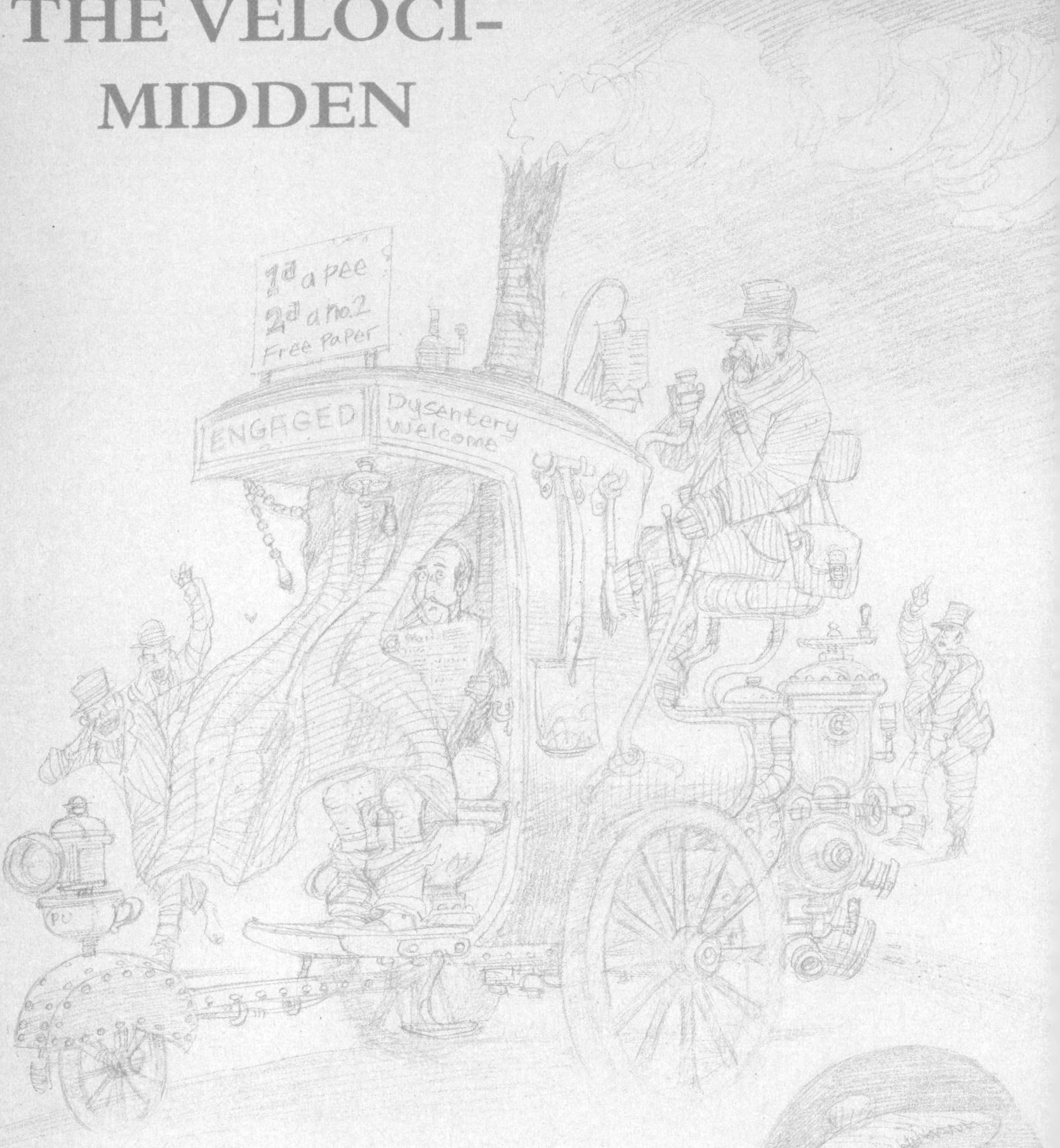
1d a pee
2d a no.2
Free Paper
ENGAGED
Dysentery Welcome
PU

This Commode/Runabout, ingeniously self-powered by a methane-burning engine, was a brainchild of THE FERGUS OF FERGUS, an eccentric Highland laird plagued since childhood both by chronic alcoholism and a related stomach disorder that had on numerous occasions rendered the laird incontinent whilst travelling on public transport. It was on such an occasion that the Fergus of Fergus first uttered his famous remark, "What A' wouldnae gi' for a gret beg mobile lavvy!" His subsequent invention, the patented VELOCI-MIDDEN, saw limited use in Glasgow and Dundee during the late 1870s, but was abandoned when some undetermined dietary change amongst its customers caused the vehicular water-closet to suddenly and unpredictably accelerate, often to speeds in excess of one hundred and thirty miles per hour. Accidents were both horrific and socially distressing, and on October 15th, 1879, "Auld Reekie" took a last emotional ride back to its Sauchiehall Street depot, cheered by the handful of spectators who had turned out, in heavy rain, for the occasion.

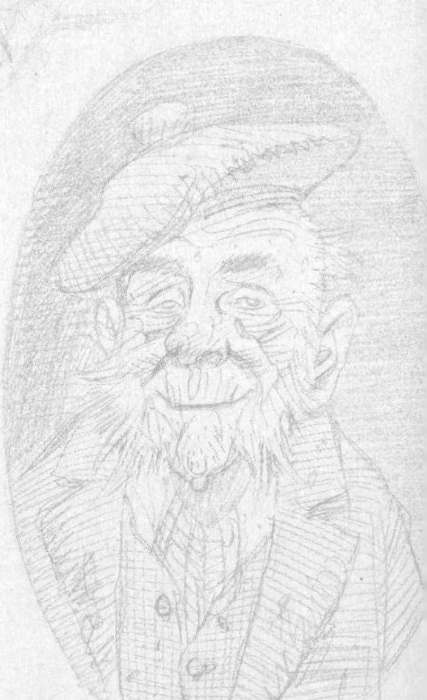

THE FERGUS OF FERGUS

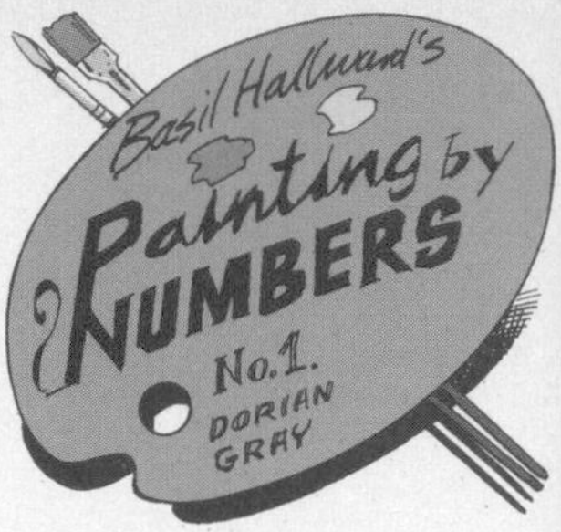
Basil Hallward's
Painting by
NUMBERS
No.1.
DORIAN
GRAY

The popular painting-by-number series that Hallward had envisioned was curtailed by his disappearance. A further painting-by-numbers piece was commissioned from another artist, the American Mr. Richard Pickman, but unfortunately neither lithographic copies of his submission "Unorthodox Churchyard Picnic Scene-by-numbers," nor the artist himself, have survived. Thus, Hallward's painting-by-numbers scheme joins such other failed adventures as the Caligari Self-Assembly Cabinet and the Holmes "Play in a Day" violin course.

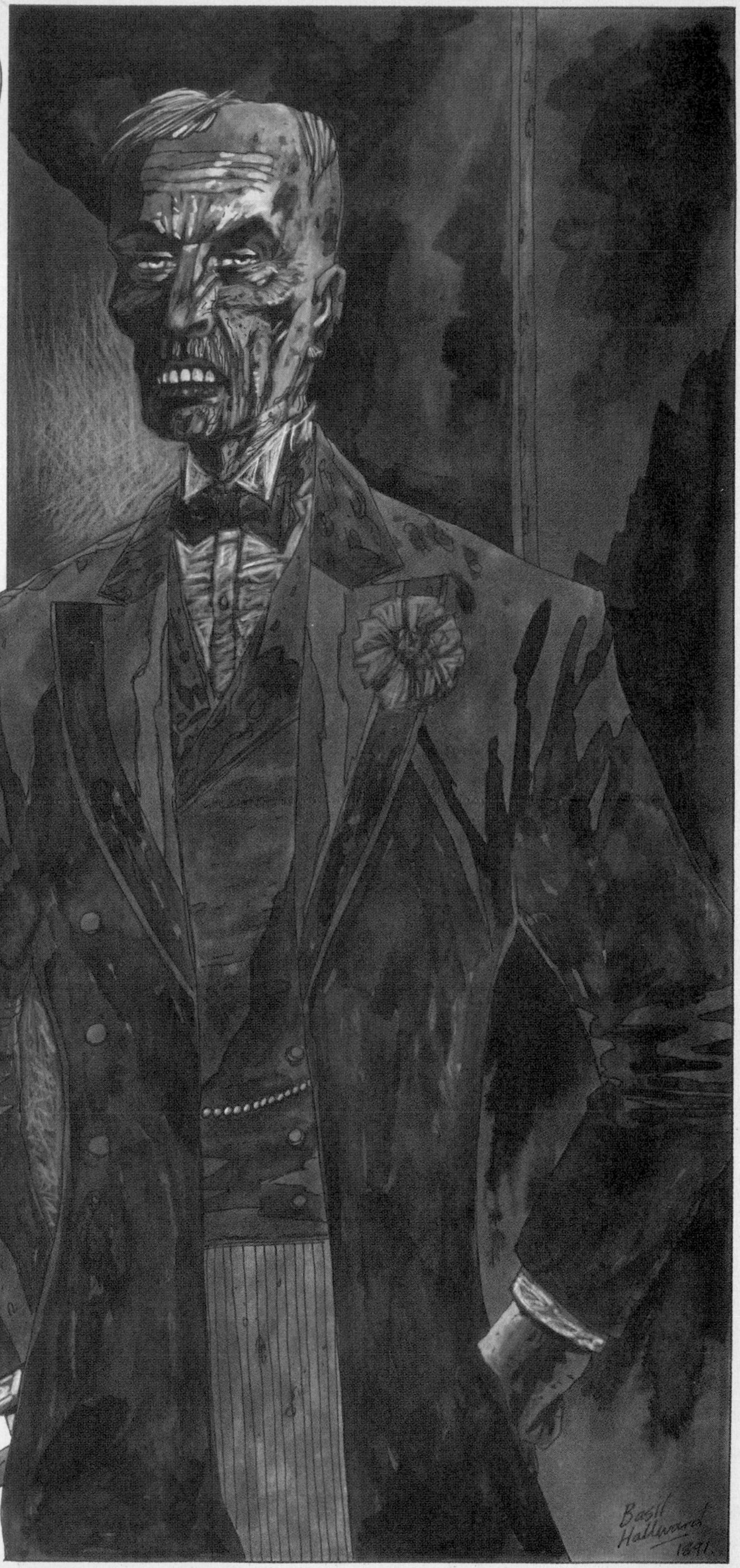
Basil Hallward 1891.

"DASHED GOOD TRY, SIR!"

Our tribute to those who, but for poor foresight and timing, might have been hailed as the scientific colossi of their epoch, but instead are largely forgotten, even amongst their immediate families.

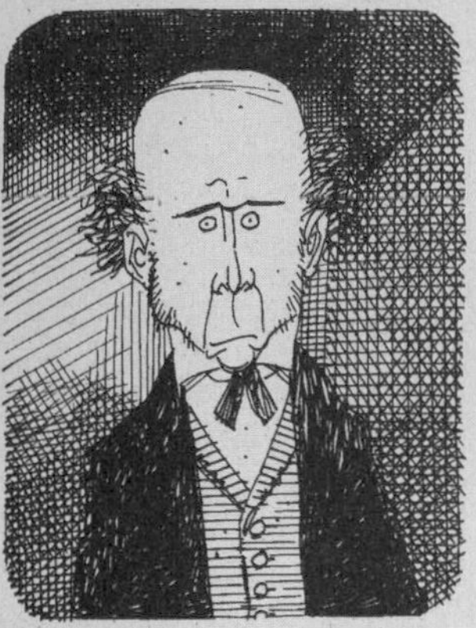

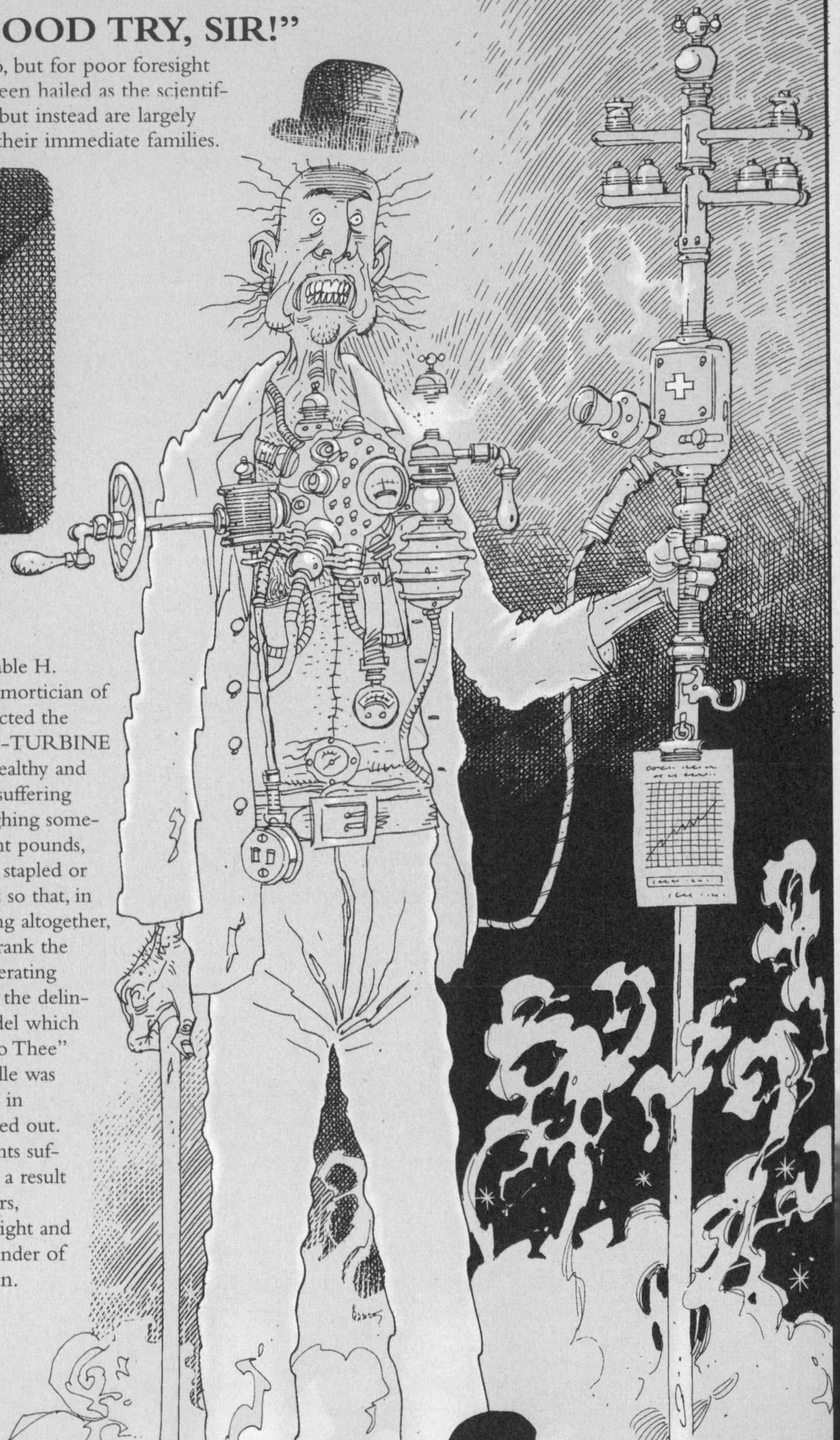

DR. BARNSTABLE HERZEGOVINA BARNSTABLE

It was in 1862 that Barnstable H. Barnstable, a bachelor and mortician of Great Yarmouth, first perfected the ELECTRICAL CARDIO-TURBINE as a means of ensuring a healthy and regular heartbeat in those suffering from cardiac distress. Weighing somewhat in excess of fifty-eight pounds, the device could either be stapled or glued to the patient's chest so that, in the event of his heart failing altogether, the patient could swiftly crank the side-handle, hopefully generating enough current to re-start the delinquent organ. An early model which played "Nearer My God To Thee" when the emergency handle was turned was found wanting in solemnity and swiftly phased out. After various elderly patients suffered fatal electrocution as a result of poorly-attached catheters, Barnstable dropped from sight and reportedly spent the remainder of his life posing as a woman.

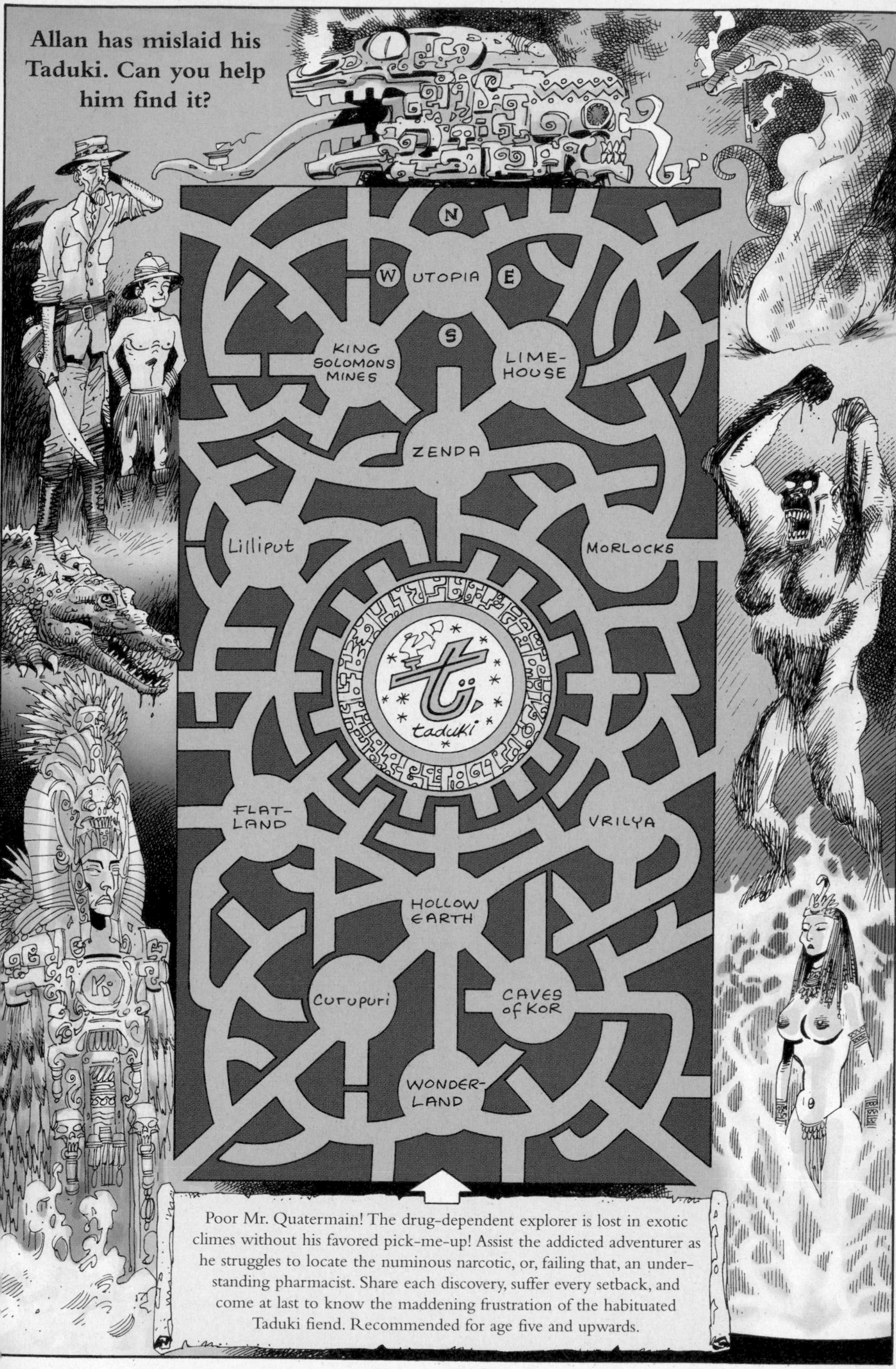
Allan has mislaid his Taduki. Can you help him find it?
N
W
E
S
UTOPIA
KING SOLOMONS MINES
LIME-HOUSE
ZENDA
Lilliput
MORLOCKS
taduki
FLAT-LAND
VRILYA
HOLLOW EARTH
Curupuri
CAVES of KOR
WONDER-LAND
Poor Mr. Quatermain! The drug-dependent explorer is lost in exotic climes without his favored pick-me-up! Assist the addicted adventurer as he struggles to locate the numinous narcotic, or, failing that, an understanding pharmacist. Share each discovery, suffer every setback, and come at last to know the maddening frustration of the habituated Taduki fiend. Recommended for age five and upwards.

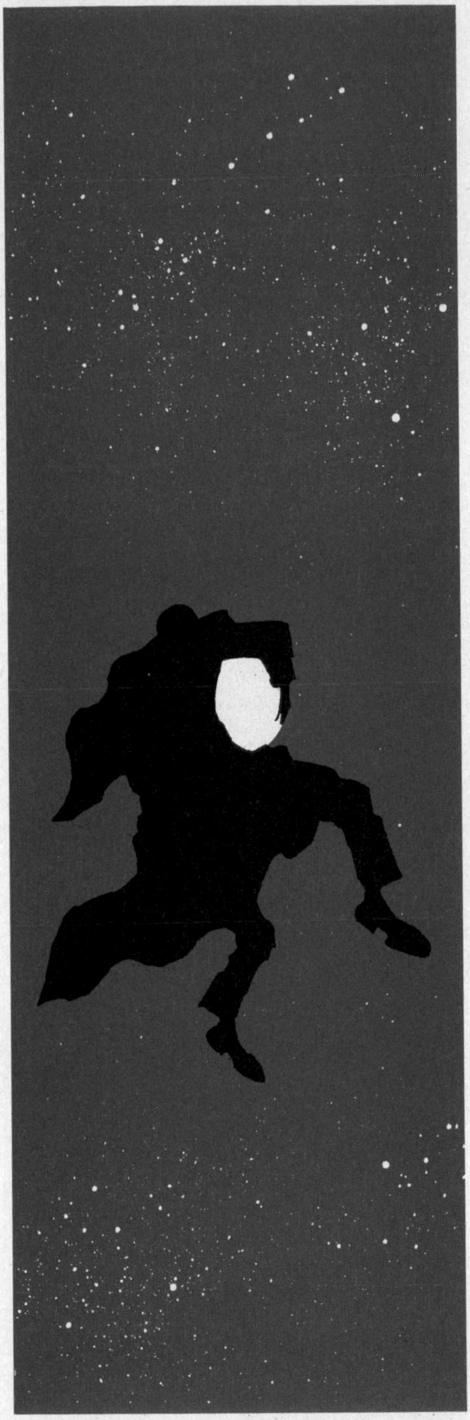